BIRTH OF A CEMETERY

Forest Lawn Memorial-Park

John F. Llewellyn

TROPICO PRESS®

GLENDALE, CALIFORNIA

Printed in the United States of America

Forest Lawn® is a registered trademark of Forest Lawn Memorial-Park Association.

Front Cover: *Family Guidance* by Enzo Pasquini, Italian (1922-1996) in Garden of Contemplation, Forest Lawn-Glendale.

All photographs and illustrations are by the author unless credited otherwise.

Tropico Press®
TropicoPress.com

Library of Congress Control Number 2018902228

Publisher's Cataloging-In-Publication Data
(Prepared by The Donohue Group, Inc.)

Names: Llewellyn, John F.
Title: Birth of a cemetery : Forest Lawn Memorial-Park / John F. Llewellyn.
Description: Glendale, California : Tropico Press, [2018] | Includes
    bibliographical references and index.
Identifiers: ISBN 9780966580167 (hardcover) | ISBN 9780966580174
    (trade paperback) | ISBN 9780966580181 (ePub)
Subjects: LCSH: Forest Lawn--Glendale (Cemetery : Glendale, Calif.)--
    History. | Cemeteries--California--Glendale--History. | Cemeteries--
    Social aspects--California--Glendale. | Los Angeles County (Calif.)--
    History.
Classification: LCC F869.G5 L54 2018 (print) | LCC F869.G5 (ebook) |
    DDC 979.493--dc23

For Carol

Also by John F. Llewellyn:

A Cemetery Should Be Forever
The challenge to managers and directors

Saying Goodbye Your Way
Planning or buying a funeral or cremation for your-
self of someone you love

Contents

Preface . . . . **xvii**

Introduction . . . . **xxi**

Abbreviations . . . . **xxiv**

Principal People and Organizations . . . . **xxv**

1. **Beginnings** **1**
   Los Angeles in the Early 1900s ◆ The Evolution of
   Cemeteries ◆ Early Cemeteries in Los Angeles ◆ The
   Men with a Plan ◆ Land Purchase ◆ Depot
   Street ◆ Ready to Start

2. **Setting Up the Cemetery** **19**
   Forming Forest Lawn Cemetery Association ◆ Rules
   and Regulations ◆ Forest Avenue Right-of-
   Way ◆ Refinancing the Mortgage ◆ Preparing for
   Burials ◆ Cemetery Lot Sales Begin

3. **Financial Challenges** **33**
   Sluggish Sales ◆ Undertaker Referrals ◆ Cash
   Shortage ◆ Demise of a Salesman ◆ Accounting
   Concerns ◆ Lockwood Resigns ◆ Charles Morgan
   Arrives ◆ Perpetual Care Fund and Cash Flow
   Problems ◆ Collections on Accounts ◆ New
   Salesman ◆ Auto Expenses ◆ Heath and Blain ◆ The
   Llewellyn Family ◆ Recruiting John Llewellyn

4. **Trouble for Treadwell** **57**
The Wheeler-Dealer ◆ Stock Ownership
Dispute ◆ Concerns about Blain ◆ Concerns
about Finances ◆ A Future Successor ◆ Chattel
Mortgage ◆ Compensation for Wells ◆ Wells Replaces
Treadwell

5. **Billy Takes the Cure** **73**
A Possible Replacement ◆ Farewell to Billy ◆ Mrs.
Blain's Requests ◆ Court Petition ◆ Resolution

6. **Attempted Coup** **79**
TL&I Appoints Morgan ◆ Morgan Wants
More ◆ Making His Move ◆ Reversing the
Coup ◆ Heath's Overpayments

7. **The Partition Suit** **87**
Background ◆ Suits and Countersuits ◆ Thornton
Joins the Legal Team ◆ Deed Discovery ◆ Pursuing
Settlements ◆ The Foreign Corporation
Argument ◆ Anticipating a Loss ◆ Court
Ruling ◆ Dividing the Property ◆ TL&I Files
Appeal ◆ The Aftermath

8. **Wells Makes His Mark** **105**
Gaining Visibility ◆ Protests Over Expansion ◆ The
Hillside Sign Controversy ◆ A Rival Sign ◆ The Price of
Newspaper Ads ◆ Designing Letterhead ◆ Moving the
Llewellyn Monument ◆ Calling on Undertakers ◆ Auto
Expenses ◆ Avoiding Annexation ◆ Tropico Becomes
Independent Municipality (1911) ◆ Relations with
Other Cemeteries

9. **Settlement with Treadwell** **125**
Back Pay ◆ Promissory Notes ◆ Allegations of Illegal
Loans ◆ Settlement Negotiations

Contents

10. Eaton and Sims Arrive 131
Charles Sims ◆ Correspondence with Wells ◆ Hubert
Eaton ◆ Getting to California ◆ The Selling
Contract ◆ American Securities Company ◆ Preparing
to Sell ◆ Other Cemetery Opportunities

11. Property Management Challenges 153
Street Improvements ◆ Moving the Arch ◆ Other
Property Issues ◆ The End of Burt Richardson

12. Startup Tensions 167
Settling Accounts ◆ Handling Installment
Payments ◆ Monthly Letters ◆ More Contract
Disputes ◆ Strained Relationships ◆ Pop's
Compromise ◆ Eaton Contemplates Parting
Ways ◆ Proposed Contract Changes ◆ The End of a
Partnership ◆ Sims Moves On

13. Trying to Cooperate 185
Continuing Conflicts ◆ Eaton Wants to Buy
TL&I ◆ 1914 Finances ◆ Perpetual Care Funds
Bill ◆ More Division Disputes ◆ Commission
Negotiations ◆ Cancellations and Trade-Ins ◆ Another
Extension ◆ 1915 Audit Report ◆ Slow Progress

14. Expanding Sales Efforts 203
Spreading the Word ◆ Lot Repurchase
Offer ◆ Insurance Ideas ◆ Mausoleum Pros and
Cons ◆ Getzendanner Resigns ◆ Possible New
Selling Agent ◆ Eaton's Sales System ◆ Recruiting
and Training Salesmen ◆ Sales Letters ◆ Managing
Ineffective Salesmen ◆ Contacts with Other
Cemeteries

15. Eaton the Entrepreneur 223
Selling Residential Lots ◆ Scouting for a New
Cemetery ◆ Planning a New Company ◆ Taking the
Next Steps ◆ Encountering a Roadblock ◆ Tension

with Glora ◆ Proposed Stock Deals ◆ Eva
Blain's Shares ◆ Protecting Eaton's Selling
System ◆ AS&F Formed ◆ Proposal from Frank
Hamilton ◆ Preparations for Merging ◆ Merritt
Llewellyn's Stock

16. **Building for the Future** 241
The Builder's Creed ◆ Sharing His Vision ◆ Time
to Build ◆ Pratt's Report on Plans ◆ Choosing
a Crematory Manufacturer ◆ Mausoleum Sales
Manager ◆ Design Decisions ◆ The Grand
Tour ◆ Construction Decisions ◆ Operating
Practices ◆ Annexation and Building
Codes ◆ Church Nears Completion ◆ Crematory
Publicity ◆ Mausoleum Construction ◆ Church
Dedication

17. **Consolidation and New Roles** 273
Consolidation into AS&F ◆ Dissolution
Procedures ◆ Pratt's Plan for New Roles ◆ Borrowing
from the Perpetual Care Fund ◆ Where's the
Auto? ◆ Purchase of Bedford Property ◆ New
Agreements ◆ TL&I Dissolution ◆ A Boom in Burials

18. **Eaton Versus Wells** 291
Illusion and Reality ◆ Eaton's Proxy Votes ◆ Lot
Owners Meeting ◆ Special Meeting ◆ Salvos and
Volleys ◆ Farewell to Wells

19. **Problem Solved** 307
Turmoil and Tension ◆ Resolving the Issues ◆ Forming
Forest Lawn Memorial-Park Association ◆ Looking
Ahead ◆ A New FLMPA ◆ Solution Found

Epilogue 321

Appendix A. Major Events Timeline 327

Appendix B. FLCA Certificate of Incorporation 332

Appendix C. 1906 FLCA Rules 334

Appendix D. "The Reasons Why" 341

Appendix E. Little Church Dedication Speech. 351

Appendix F. Directors & Officers 1905-1926 354

Notes 365

Bibliography 405

Index 420

About the Author 444

Figures

Figure 1. Los Angeles Cemeteries, c. 1906. 6

Figure 2. T. Paterson Ross. 10

Figure 3. Noble Chapel 11

Figure 4. Andrew Glassell Descendents. 14

Figure 5. TL&I Stock Certificate 15

Figure 6. Susan Glassell Mitchell Land Sale 17

Figure 7. TL&I Land Sale to FLCA 21

Figure 8. 1906 TL&I Co and FLCA Contract 23

Figure 9. Forest Lawn Location. 24

Figure 10. Park Leading to Cemetery 25

Figure 11. Forest Lawn Entry Arch, c. 1906 26

Figure 12. Forest Lawn Letterhead, c. 1907 27

Figure 13. Forest Lawn Receiving Vault. 28

Figure 14. Cemetery Plan January 10, 1906 29

Figure 15. J. B. Treadwell's "Car Landing" Improvements. 30

Figure 16. Southern Pacific Funeral Cars, 1905 31

Figure 17. Charles O. Morgan 42

Figure 18. Llewellyn Iron Works Building 51

Figure 19. John Llewellyn 53

Figure 20. Treadwell's Oil Well Wharf 59

Figure 21. Land Partition Map 101

Figure 22. 1912 Advertisement. 110

Figure 23. Llewellyn Monument 112

Figure 24. Evergreen Cemetery 113

Figure 25. Tropico Annexation 117

Figure 26. Forest Lawn Cemetery Plan, c.1911. 119

Figure 27. Sketch of Depot Street Realignment 120

Figure 28. Area Quitclaimed to J. B. Treadwell 129

Figure 29. Charles B. Sims 133

Figure 30. Hubert Eaton, c. 1913 136

Figure 31. Organization Structure 1912 139

Figure 32. FLCA Letterhead, c. 1912. 140

Figure 33. Contract Assignment 142

Figure 34. Wells's Sketch of Entry Arch Location. 155

Figure 35. Engineer's Entrance Drawing 156

Figure 36. Arch and Wing-Wall Move 157

Figure 37. Shoring and Support for Arch Move 157

Figure 38. Moving the Arch on 20" X 20" Beams 158

Figure 39. Burt W. Richardson 163

Figure 40. Thomas Mizar 164

Figure 41. Differing Cash Distribution Methods. 168

Figure 42. Cemetery Plan c. 1914 207

Figure 43. Valhalla Mausoleum 208

Figure 44. Vault or Outer Burial Container 212

Figure 45. Prospect card c. 1916.. 214

Figure 46. Hubert Eaton c. 1917 218

Figure 47. American Security & Fidelity Co.. 236

Figure 48. The Builder's Creed 242

Figure 49. Little Church Toilet Location. 253

Figure 50. Mausoleum Crypt Rosette 254

Figure 51. Cypress Lawn Receiving Vault Detail 261

Figure 52. Azalea Terrace in Great Mausoleum 263

Figure 53. Azalea Terrace Entrance 264

Figure 54. Forest Lawn Mausoleum Rendering c. 1918 265

Figure 55. Forest Lawn Cemetery Plan c. 1918 266

Figure 56. Little Church of the Flowers 2017 267

Figure 57. Little Church Dedication Announcement 269

Figure 58. Little Church Dedication Plaque Sketch 270

Figure 59. Little Church Bronze Dedication Plaque 271

Figure 60. FLCA Takes Over Selling 279

Figure 61. Eaton's "Legal View" of TI&I Valuation. 280

Figure 62. Eaton's "Businessman's" Valuation 280

Figure 63. New Revenue Split 285

Figure 64. "Vote Yes" for Cemetery Exemption 290

Figure 65. Forest Lawn Phone Book Ad, 1918 293

Figure 66. FLCA Notice About Hubert Eaton 300

Figure 67. Annual Interments 1906–1926 303

Figure 68. Forest Lawn Memorial-Park Association 315

Figure 69. FLCA Merged into FLMPA 1996 324

Figure 70. Last One Standing 1999 324

Figure 71. Cover of "The Reasons Why" 350

Preface

Although I have been formally involved with Forest Lawn Memorial-Park in Glendale, California, for forty-five years, it has always been a part of my life. My father was working for Forest Lawn when I was born and he became CEO upon Hubert Eaton's death in 1966. I followed my father as the chief executive and am now board chair. I grew up listening to my parents talk about Forest Lawn and Hubert Eaton—they referred to him as "Hubie." Eaton died before I came to work at Forest Lawn, and I had little contact with him before that. Evidently, when my brother and I were young, we got into a spat at the Eatons' house. Hubert's wife, Ann, said she never wanted to see us again—and she didn't. It was only after Ann's death that we started to see Uncle Hubert at holidays. And that was only for a few years, because he passed away the year I graduated from high school.

The impetus for this book was Forest Lawn's centennial in 2006. When I became aware that boxes of documents from the early 1900s were still in our vaults, I was intrigued. Although I had been raised on the stories of Hubert Eaton saving the small, struggling cemetery, these documents suggested that there was an untold story of Forest Lawn's early years.

Previous writings about Forest Lawn's history have centered on Hubert Eaton starting a sales program in a struggling cemetery in 1913, parting the proverbial waters, and leading it to the land of success, innovation, and acclaim in 1917. The Eaton years at Forest Lawn have been covered in Adela Rogers St. Johns's *First Step Up*

Toward Heaven and Ralph Hancock's *Forest Lawn Story*. Both were written during Hubert Eaton's life, and both were heavily influenced by him. Although Eaton is an important character in this book, Hancock's and St. Johns's books give much more detail of Eaton's history and work at Forest Lawn over many decades.

The books by St. Johns and Hancock are not entirely objective, since both were written under terms of contracts with Forest Lawn. Eaton and other people at Forest Lawn reviewed drafts of St. Johns's book as it was being written. When Eaton did not like what was written, he dispatched my father to get it changed to something acceptable. I suspect that Hancock's book may have had a similar treatment.

Writing this book has been a long, intriguing, and educational journey for me. The process has given me some insight into life in Southern California in the early 1900s. I have a renewed appreciation and understanding of Forest Lawn's roots, what Hubert Eaton created, why the institution evolved the way it did, and the struggles of those who preceded him. The organization has an amazing commitment to service and the community, much of which has roots in philosophies espoused by Eaton. I am proud to be a part of this organization and to be able to tell the tale of Forest Lawn Cemetery's early years and its evolution to become Forest Lawn Memorial-Park.

While in the final stages of writing this, I had occasion to help my wife's family make funeral arrangements at a small stand-alone funeral home. Having been exposed to Forest Lawn all my life, I sometimes forget how special it is. As we scrambled to hire a florist, print personalized prayer cards, find a suitable urn, and a multitude of other details, I realized that Eaton's concept of "everything in one place" was truly consumer friendly.

I have had the support of many people through the years I have worked on this. My thanks to Wendy Martin of Claremont Graduate University for her encouragement after reading a very early and very rough draft of initial chapters.

Many people at Forest Lawn have been helpful and supportive of this project. Suzanne Davidson of Forest Lawn's legal department assisted with research, found published cases, and helped me comprehend the legal issues. Doug Gooch, keeper of Forest Lawn's corporate archives, was a great and eager help with research and was most patient as I pawed through old records. He additionally found some wonderful documents that have worked their way into this tale. Clint Granath helped with survey data leading to the creation of the maps showing the land transactions. Kim Pawlik showed her amazing capacity to absorb details, finding inconsistencies needing clarification. My wife, Carol, has been supportive of this project and my preoccupation with it over many years. She has challenged me to make this "understandable to people without law or finance degrees." Her keen eye helped smooth out a number of kinks in the narrative.

I was most fortunate to work with Kathy Carter for editing. Kathy has an amazing ability to keep details in sync while not letting the details interrupt the story. Her insights helped put a sense of order into what was initially a very rough manuscript. Thank you, Kathy, for your valuable help on this project! The final proofreading was done by ProofreadingServices.com and Sandi Schroeder built the index. I'm indebted to all these people for their help, but in the end, I take responsibility for any issues that exist.

Introduction

When Forest Lawn started in 1906, it was an ordinary cemetery of the time—a small tract of land with tombstones, located away from major development. The businessmen who started the cemetery struggled to make it a success. The story of that struggle has remained largely untold. The story is interesting not only in terms of the birth of Forest Lawn Cemetery and its evolution to become Forest Lawn Memorial-Park, but also as a reflection of California at the beginning of the twentieth century.

Birth of a Cemetery is about Forest Lawn from its very beginning until it achieved a stable corporate structure and became financially viable in the 1920s. It is an unvarnished account of the struggles before Hubert Eaton, as well as how he gained control. This is the first time that this part of the Forest Lawn story has been told. Nothing written here is meant to denigrate what Eaton accomplished. Rather, this tale makes it clear that it was hard work, in addition to talent and inspiration, that made the Forest Lawn Memorial-Park of today possible.

As this book has progressed, I have learned about many interesting people in Forest Lawn's early years. The years before Eaton had their own cast of characters. Architect Tom Ross and his father brought their distinct personalities—the former creative, the latter administrative—to the very beginning. The Rosses' dealings with the less than ethical behavior of J. B. Treadwell, as well as the attempted coup to take over Forest Lawn by Charles Morgan, are all part of the history. And despite what Shakespeare said about lawyers, attorneys are key players in Forest Lawn's history. Claims and litigation abounded—one case even made it to the California Supreme Court. The drunkenness of first superintendent Billy Blain added conflict to the early struggles. In addition to business issues, there was intrigue and manipulation. Eileen Bedford's suicide and the murder of Burt Richardson are all part of the story. Forest Lawn had been operating for seven years before Hubert Eaton arrived on the scene, and his actions during his early involvement with Forest Lawn reveal a side of his character missing from other books.

There are a few misconceptions that need to be clarified about Eaton and Forest Lawn.

Many people have believed that Hubert Eaton started the cemetery. This results from confusion over him being labeled the "founder" of Forest Lawn Memorial-Park. Eaton did not claim to have started Forest Lawn Cemetery. What he did claim to have founded was the "memorial-park" plan for cemeteries. Thus, when Forest Lawn Cemetery became Forest Lawn Memorial-Park, he was the founder of the latter.

Eaton was not the first to use the term "memorial park." However, previously the term was used without a consensus regarding what it meant. When Hubert Eaton adopted the term and added a hyphen—"memorial-park"—he wanted his new term to signify something entirely different from a traditional cemetery. Although Eaton's memorial-park provided a sacred resting place for the departed, he believed it should be much more. He wanted it to be a place of comforting beauty and inspiration, so he coined the term "memorial-park" to encompass his vision. Gone would be the "stoneyards" of tombstones, replaced by statuary and other art for all to enjoy. Eaton would create his memorial-park as a place for the living, and one that "educates and uplifts the community."

He had the audacity to open the first funeral home (mortuary) on dedicated cemetery grounds for the convenience of families.[1] Today much of this seems ordinary. But at the time, it was revolutionary.

The fact that over the last one hundred years Eaton's ideas have been mimicked so many times is testament to how well they have resonated with the public as well as the industry.

Over the years, Forest Lawn has been praised and parodied. One of the best perspectives of Forest Lawn was from California historian Kevin Starr, who described Eaton's vision as something that "would fulfill each promise of the Southern California dream: beauty, serenity, redemption, and peace."[1]

This is the story of Forest Lawn's early years and the role Hubert Eaton played in its transformation.

Abbreviations

AS&F	American Security & Fidelity Co.
FLCA	Forest Lawn Cemetery Association
FLInc	Forest Lawn Memorial Park Association, Inc.
FLMPA	Forest Lawn Memorial-Park Association
Pop Ross	Thomas Ross
TL&I	Tropico Land & Improvement Co.
Tom Ross	T. Paterson Ross

Principal People and Organizations

American Securities Co.
(1912–1917)

Formed by Hubert Eaton and Charles Sims to sell cemetery property in Forest Lawn before need.

American Security & Fidelity Co. (AS&F)
(1916–1999)[1]

The result of a merger of Tropico Land & Improvement Company (TL&I) and American Securities.

Bedford, Eileen Glassell
(1882–1907)

Susan Mitchell's younger daughter.

Bedford, Lucile R.
(1904–2001)

Only child of Eileen Bedford and granddaughter of Susan Mitchell.

Blain, William J. (Billy)
(1870–1910)

First superintendent of Forest Lawn Cemetery Association (FLCA).

Boynton, C. C.
(1874–1960)

Attorney who initially represented J. B. Treadwell and Tropico Land & Improvement Co. (TL&I) in the partition suit. Later represented only Treadwell. Son-in-law of Treadwell.

Eaton, Hubert (1881–1966)

Charles Sims's partner in American Securities; founded American Security & Fidelity Co. (AS&F). Created "memorial-park" concept. First general manager of Forest Lawn Memorial-Park Association (FLMPA).

Ely, Glenn M. (1886–1931)

Trustee of Forest Lawn Cemetery Association (FLCA).

Flint, Motley (1864–1930)

Prominent banker and trustee of Forest Lawn Cemetery Association (FLCA).

Forest Lawn Cemetery, a.k.a. Forest Lawn Memorial-Park

These names refer to the place itself, as opposed to the corporations that managed it—Forest Lawn Cemetery Association (FLCA) and Forest Lawn Memorial-Park Association (FLMPA).

Forest Lawn Cemetery Association (FLCA) (1906–1996)

The original cemetery operator and developer; holder of the perpetual care fund. Merged into FLMPA in 1996.

Forest Lawn Memorial-Park Association (FLMPA) (1917–)[2]

Took over operation of cemetery from Forest Lawn Cemetery Association (FLCA).

Gates, Carroll W. (1860–1920)

Early director of American Security & Fidelity Co. (AS&F) who provided personal guarantee for loans for construction of the Little Church of the Flowers and the crematory.

Getzendanner, E. D.

Sales manager for American Securities Co.

Glassell, Hugh
(1859–1938)

Susan Glassell Mitchell's brother.

Goudge, Herbert
(1863–1929)

Attorney who represented American Securities Co. on question of division of sales dollars and American Security & Fidelity Co. (AS&F) on various corporate matters.

Hamilton, Frank D.
(1879–1956)

Financier for acquisition of Tropico Land & Improvement Co. (TL&I) and founding of American Security & Fidelity Co. (AS&F).

Hawkins, Prince A.
(1871–1939)

Reno attorney consulted by Eaton about interpretation of contract between American Securities, Tropico Land & Improvement (TL&I), and Forest Lawn Cemetery Association (FLCA).

Hazlett, William
(1869–1952)

Attorney who at various times represented American Securities Co., Tropico Land & Improvement Co. (TL&I), and Forest Lawn Cemetery Association (FLCA).

Heath, Dr. George

Second sales manager of Forest Lawn Cemetery Association (FLCA); part of an attempted takeover of FLCA management.

Hollingsworth, William I.
(1862–1937)

Early director of American Security & Fidelity Co. (AS&F) who provided personal guarantee for loans for construction of the Little Church of the Flowers and the crematory.

Lambourn, Lucie Mitchell
(1880–1930)

Susan Mitchell's older daughter.

Llewellyn, John
(1871–1919)

Prominent Los Angeles citizen part of Llewellyn Iron Works family. Early trustee of Forest Lawn Cemetery Association (FLCA). (Not related to author John F. Llewellyn.)

Lockwood, J. J.

First secretary of Forest Lawn Cemetery Association (FLCA).

Loewenthal, Max
(1858–1927)

Attorney who represented Tropico Land & Improvement Co. (TL&I) in land litigation. Represented TL&I and Forest Lawn Cemetery Association (FLCA) in dispute with American Securities Co. over division of cash receipts.

Mitchell, Susan Glassell
(1856–1907)

Sold land for cemetery to J. B. Treadwell.

Morgan, Charles O.
(1854–?)

Second secretary of Forest Lawn Cemetery Association (FLCA). Successor to J. J. Lockwood after attempted takeover of FLCA.

Pratt, George E.
(1881–1973)

Secretary of American Security & Fidelity Co. (AS&F).

Richardson, Burt W.
(1859–1915)

Son of W. C. B. Richardson. Owned land adjacent to Forest Lawn Cemetery. Killed by Charles Mizer on Glendale Avenue in dispute over establishing tombstone sales business.

Richardson, William Carr Belding (W. C. B.)
(1815–1908)

Owner of Santa Eulalia Rancho, adjacent to land acquired for Forest Lawn Cemetery. Donated land to Southern Pacific Railroad.

Ross, T. Paterson (Tom)
(1873–1957)

Architect. Director, officer, and largest investor in Tropico Land & Improvement Co. (TL&I). First wife, Lillian, was J. B. Treadwell's daughter.

Ross, Thomas A. ("Pop")
(1852–1930)

Secretary of Tropico Land & Improvement Co. (TL&I) and handler of administrative details. Father of T. Paterson Ross.

Sims, Charles B.
(1868–1945)

Early before-need cemetery sales promoter. Eaton's partner in first selling contract for Forest Lawn Cemetery.

Thomas, William B.

Attorney. Represented American Security & Fidelity Co. (AS&F).

Thornton, Tom C.

Attorney who represented Eva Blain regarding salary owed her late husband, Billy Blain, and stock he owned in Tropico Land & Improvement Co. (TL&I). Later represented TL&I in land litigation all the way to the California Supreme Court.

Treadwell, John B. (J. B.) (1846–1931)	One of the initial organizers of Tropico Land & Improvement Co. (TL&I). Involved in oil, mining deals, and other real estate deals. First president of Forest Lawn Cemetery Association (FLCA).
Tropico Land & Improvement Co. (TL&I) (1905–1921)	Bought the land for the cemetery. Committed to sell land to Forest Lawn Cemetery Association (FLCA) as it was paid for.
Wells, Norton C. (1874–1958)	Second president of Forest Lawn Cemetery Association (FLCA). Replaced J. B. Treadwell as president and trustee of FLCA in 1910.

CHAPTER 1.

BEGINNINGS

WHEN THE GROUP OF men gathered in San Francisco in the fall of 1905, they may have been thinking about different things. Perhaps architect Tom Ross was thinking about the money he would need to invest in the new cemetery. His father, often called Pop Ross, may have been pondering the way the venture would be structured. Albert Burgren, an engineer and Tom's business partner, might have wondered when the meeting would be over. J. B. Treadwell was likely thinking only about making money. One of the men may have even quipped that they were going to buy land by the acre and sell it by the square foot.

The only certainty was that they had assembled to start a cemetery in Los Angeles, and with their lack of experience, they naively believed it would be easy.

Los Angeles in the Early 1900s

Today, Los Angeles conjures up images of palm trees, great weather, suntanned blondes in convertibles, and the entertainment industry. At the start of the twentieth century, palm trees were just beginning to be popular for landscaping. The weather was great, but any blondes in convertibles would have been in horse-drawn buggies.

1

The first movie in Hollywood was made in 1910 by D. W. Griffith. Ten years would pass before Hollywood became glamourous. Los Angeles was developing economically and culturally. Oil had been discovered in 1892. The first automobile hit the streets in 1897, but the city did not get its first gas station until fifteen years later. The fifth symphony orchestra in the country was started in Los Angeles in 1898. The first Rose Bowl game was played in 1902. William Randolph Hearst founded the *Los Angeles Examiner* in 1903.[1]

In the early 1900s, Los Angeles was in some ways still the Wild West. The discovery of oil during the previous decade had created a population boom beyond the attraction of great weather and opportunity. The city grew from a population of 33,381 in 1880 to 102,479 in 1900, making it the thirty-sixth largest city in the country. San Francisco was the leading city of the West Coast, with a population almost twice the size of the City of Los Angeles. By 1910, LA had grown to become the seventeenth largest city in the nation.[2]

The Evolution of Cemeteries

Cemeteries have been around since before recorded history, and burial has played a central role in virtually every culture, helping societies grapple with the cycle of life and death. Religions seek the meaning of life, and this search includes pondering the end of life. Thus, cemeteries are important for religious and philosophical reasons as well as for practical purposes.

In the Western world, we often think of cemeteries and their evolution in terms of their relationship with Christianity. The word "cemetery," derived from the Greek *koimeterion,* for "a sleeping place," was used by the early Christians for the places set apart for the burial of their dead.[3] At first these cemeteries were outside city walls and were not adjacent to churches. In the third century, burial for Christians moved to catacombs beneath cities. In medieval times, interment in church crypts or churchyards became prevalent.

In *The Last Great Necessity: Cemeteries in American History,* David Charles Sloane, a professor at the University of Southern California, identified eight types of cemetery development in the United States: frontier, domestic, churchyard, potters' fields, town or city cemeteries, rural cemeteries, lawn-park cemeteries, and memorial parks. The first five types originated in the early settlement of the country and, like the other three, continue to exist today.[4]

Frontier graves were practical burials that took place at the site of death. The graves either were unmarked or had only a simple memorial of wood or stone that indicated the deceased's name and date of death.

Domestic or homestead graveyards were designed for more than one burial and generally would be in a farm field. They were small, family owned, and functional.

Churchyard cemeteries, patterned after those of England, were generally the first ones to have any care; the church would often appoint at least a part-time sexton to manage them. Two examples are Trinity in New York and St. Philip's in Charleston, South Carolina.

Potters' fields, exemplified by New York City burial grounds, arose from practical need. They were publicly owned cemeteries for burial of indigents. They were designed in geometric functional patterns and had only plain monuments, if any.

Town or city cemeteries were designed more like formal gardens and had three-dimensional markers, monuments, and sculptures to mark interment sites. Although Potters' fields were publicly owned, these town or city cemeteries could be owned either by a family or by the government.

The rural cemeteries of the mid-1800s marked the beginning of changes in cemeteries. Suburban in location, these were picturesque, natural gardens designed with aesthetics in mind. They were managed by a trustee or superintendent and were privately owned. Memorialization was broadened from granite and marble headstones to sculpture-topped monuments and private mausoleums designed for a single family. Père Lachaise in Paris and Mount Auburn in Cambridge, Massachusetts, were influenced by their designs.

Lawn-park cemeteries came next. These pastoral, park-like cemeteries were an evolutionary step up from the rural cemeteries. They had either entrepreneurial or trustee management. Sloane lists Spring Grove Cemetery and Arboretum in Cincinnati as the archetype for this type of cemetery. According to Sloane, the idea of the lawn-park cemetery actually had its origins in the 1800s, combining "the beauty of the lawn with the artistry of the monument." These cemeteries continued to have large monuments and sculptures but also had close-to-the-ground markers. Sloane also notes that by the late 1870s, many cemeteries had begun using income from perpetual care fund investments to improve their financial positions.

The memorial-park concept would not emerge until 1917. According to Sloane, Forest Lawn Memorial-Park in Glendale, California, is the paradigm for all memorial-park style cemeteries. Hubert Eaton, credited as the founder of Forest Lawn Memorial-Park, was not the first to use the term "memorial park" in reference to a cemetery, but he was the one to create a clear definition of the term, adding a hyphen to identify it as a cemetery with specific attributes. Eaton's memorial-park did away with tombstones; he called cemeteries with them "unsightly stoneyards." He envisioned sweeping lawns with great art, splashing fountains, and singing birds. But that would not happen until later.

Early Cemeteries in Los Angeles

By 1905 the Los Angeles area already had many cemeteries to serve its explosive growth. These were predominantly churchyard and lawn-park style cemeteries—all very traditional, with a multitude of upright stone monuments. The San Fernando Mission Cemetery was over a hundred years old, and a number of other cemeteries had opened in the middle of the nineteenth century. Because of the sprawl of the population, the region's cemeteries were also spread out, not concentrated like they were in Colma, just outside of San Francisco.[5]

The Los Angeles City Cemetery was the first non-Catholic cemetery. It was known by many names, including Protestant Cemetery, Fort Moore Hill Cemetery, and "the cemetery on the hill." The former cemetery site is now occupied by Ramon C. Cortines School (near the corner of N. Grand Avenue and W. Cesar E. Chavez Avenue) and a stretch of the Hollywood Freeway. By 1947 all remains had been moved to other cemeteries. Although there might have been some interments as early as 1847, the earliest documented burial was in 1853 for Andrew Sublette, who was killed fighting a grizzly bear in the Santa Monica Mountains. There was little or no control of the cemetery.[6] An editorial in the *Los Angeles Star* criticized its mismanagement:

> We have frequently alluded to the condition of the place where the departed from amongst us are laid—their final home . . . known as the city burying ground. . . . The term "cemetery" cannot be applied to it with propriety. It is only the bare ground on a barren hill top, where the dead are buried out of sight of the living. . . . The graveyard is, in most communities, considered a hallowed spot—sacred to the best feelings of humanity. . . . No such feelings can ever be evoked by a visit to this burying ground. The sadness, the loneliness, the coldness, the utter neglect, suggested by a sight of the city of the dead, is a deep reproach to the people of this community. . . . With an indifference unaccountable, no steps are taken to guard the sacred soil from intrusion or desecration. The cattle on the hills roam over it; the wild animals prowl over it, seeking their prey—and it is even said that other destroyers than time deface and mutilate the tombs of the departed. . . . There is surely interest enough for the departed remaining among us . . . to induce city authorities . . . [for] the fencing of the city's burial ground, and for the protection of the tombs. . . . We hope steps will be taken immediately to atone for this long neglect.[7]

Despite the newspaper's editorial plea, it was too late to make up for the neglect of the city cemetery. Newer properties—like the Evergreen Cemetery, established in 1877—only emphasized its sad condition. Yielding to pressure, the Los Angeles City Council

Figure 1. Los Angeles Cemeteries, c. 1906.

At the start of the twentieth century, the Los Angeles area had close to fifty cemeteries (partial listing).

Map	Cemetery[9]
A	Calvary Cemetery, est. 1896 (new site)
B	El Monte Cemetery (a.k.a. Savannah Cemetery), est. 1850
C	Evergreen Cemetery, est. 1877
D	Forest Lawn Cemetery, est. 1906
E	Harbor View Cemetery (a.k.a. San Pedro Cemetery), deeded to city in 1883; first burial 1879
F	Hollywood Cemetery, est. 1899
G	Home of Peace Cemetery, est. 1902.[10]
H	Inglewood Cemetery, est. 1905
I	Morningside Cemetery (a.k.a. Sylmar Cemetery and Founders Memorial Cemetery), est. mid-1800s
J	Olive Grove Cemetery, est. 1896
K	Pacific Crest Cemetery, est. 1902
L	Rosedale Cemetery, est. 1884
M	San Fernando Mission Cemetery, first burial 1800
N	San Gabriel Cemetery, est. 1872
O	Wilmington Cemetery, est. 1857
P	Workman Cemetery (a.k.a. El Campo Santo and Little Acre of God Cemetery), est. 1858

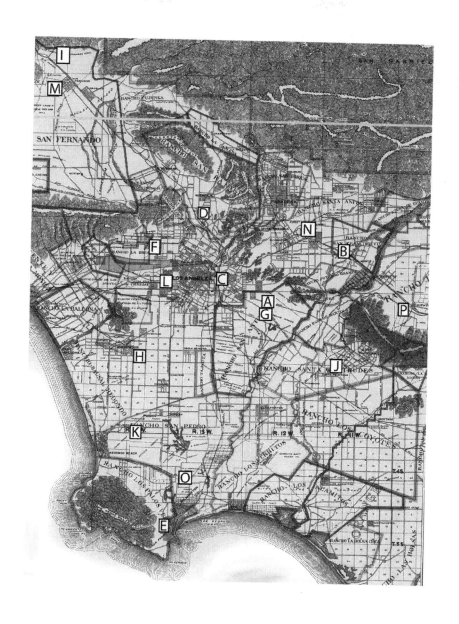

moved to stop further burials in 1879, making exceptions only for "individuals or societies already owning a plot." Over the years, multiple attempts to move bodies to other cemeteries were part of the effort to close the Los Angeles City Cemetery completely. As recently as 2006, more remains were uncovered at the construction site of the Grand Avenue School.[8]

Los Angeles was not alone in having issues with cemeteries, so it was inevitable that the state would regulate them. Having achieved statehood in 1850, California passed its first cemetery statute in 1854, titled "An Act to protect the bodies of Deceased Persons and Public Grave Yards." In addition to prohibitions on entering or molesting public graveyards for "agricultural, mining, or any other purpose," the law provided protection for existing burial places by declaring that the burial of six bodies in any place made it a "public grave-yard."[11]

Passed in 1859, the Act to authorize the Incorporation of Rural Cemetery Associations was the earliest California statute to regulate cemeteries. Cemetery associations were required to have six to twelve trustees with staggered terms. No cemetery could be larger than 320 acres. Voting members had to be "persons of full age" who owned not less than 200 square feet of land—approximately eight burial spaces or plots. Officers were to be elected from among the trustees. The statute further provided that after establishment of the corporation, it should proceed "to purchase suitable grounds for the proposed cemetery, and to the vendor thereof, they are authorized to issue the bonds of the Corporation for the amount of the purchase-money." Proceeds from the sale of lots, plats, or graves were to be used to repay the bonds.[12] A "plat" is a plan of subdivision to divide land into smaller parcels.

The language used to describe cemetery lots can be ambiguous as well as confusing. In the early 1900s it was common for families to buy a family lot composed of twenty or so plots or burial spaces. Confusion between the words arises because the words "lot" and "plot" are often used interchangeably. Often, but not always, the context helps clarify what was intended. Most of the time, a reference to a space or a plot means a single interment (burial) space.

Although the 1859 law did not use the term "nonprofit," it did specify that the income from any property owned by the cemetery association should be used for the "improvement or embellishment" of the cemetery. Furthermore, the "cemetery lands and property of any association formed pursuant to the act, shall be exempt from all public taxes, rates, and assessments."[13]

In a 1912 book about cemeteries, Howard Weed, a landscape architect, observed, "A mistake in the location of a cemetery can never be remedied." He believed a cemetery site should not be too close to a center of population, as it might require "the removal of the dead a few years later in order to make room for the living." At the same time, he opined, being too far from the population was inconvenient, but being adjacent to a streetcar line would be ideal. Weed counseled, "Too much care cannot be taken in the selection of a proper site and in such selection some one [sic] with cemetery experience should be consulted."[14]

It would take time, but Los Angeles would prove to be the incubator for a cemetery that would change the cemetery industry and the public's perception of cemeteries.

The Men with a Plan

It is not clear who had the idea to start the cemetery that became Forest Lawn. However, it is clear that the group was led by San Francisco architect Tom Ross. Others in the group included Tom's father, Thomas Ross, often called "Pop" to differentiate him from his son; Albert Burgren, an engineer and Tom's business partner; and Tom's father-in-law, John B. Treadwell, who went by "J. B." None of the men had operated or developed a cemetery before. Indeed, none had even invested in a cemetery. Only Tom Ross had any experience with cemeteries, and that was only architectural—he had designed the Noble Chapel for Cypress Lawn Cemetery in Colma, California, in 1898.

For this new venture, Tom Ross would be the prime decision maker. His father, Pop Ross, would take care of administrative details. Real estate experience was to come from J. B. Treadwell, who had promoted oil and mining ventures.

Born in Edinburgh, Scotland, in 1873, Tom Ross—professionally referred to as T. Paterson Ross—came to San Francisco in 1890. He was employed by several architectural firms before opening his own office in 1896. He often worked with engineer Albert W.

Architect & Engineer of California, May 1908

Figure 2. T. Paterson Ross

Burgren. Following the 1906 San Francisco earthquake and fire, the two opened an office as Ross & Burgren. Tom Ross also had a prior connection to J. B. Treadwell—he was married to Treadwell's daughter Lillian.[15]

Over his career, Ross designed single-family and multifamily residential buildings, hotels, churches, and many commercial buildings—over 250 structures in all. One anecdote suggests he was not shy about getting credit for his accomplishments. When Ross requested that his name be put on a cornerstone of the Shrine Temple in 1919, he was turned down. Sometime after completion of the building, a visiting scholar translated the phrase chiseled in Arabic script in the marble above the entry door: "Great is Allah and Great is Ross the Architect."[16]

John B. Treadwell (J. B.) came from a well-known family in the mining industry. Born in Garland, Maine, in 1846, Treadwell arrived in California in 1873 after serving as a drummer boy in the first battle of the Civil War. He was influential in persuading Southern Pacific Railroad to switch from coal to oil to fuel its steam engines and was the first man to drill for oil in the ocean. Treadwell was something of a "wheeler-dealer" and, even when involved in the management of Forest Lawn, often explored new deals in oil, mining, or other ventures. Treadwell was no stranger to controversy, whether in his own oil and mining escapades or working for others and was frequently on one side or another of legal matters.[17]

Not long after moving to California, he was involved with "Lucky" Baldwin in several very productive mines. The Comstock Mine in Virginia City, Nevada, was under Treadwell's direction in 1874.[18]

Land Purchase

The group of men realized that if they were to have a cemetery, they would need land. Although the statute authorized cemeteries to issue bonds to raise funds, few cemeteries did so. The typical

Figure 3. Noble Chapel

Designed by T. Paterson Ross, Noble Chapel in Cypress Lawn Cemetery was named after the cemetery's founder, Hamden Noble.

Architect & Engineer of California, November 1912

pattern for cemeteries in the early 1900s in California was that a for-profit company would buy land and sell it over time to a separate company that would develop and operate the cemetery. The group of men intended to do just that. However, they realized that finding suitable land that could be used for a cemetery would be a challenge.

The group left the hunt for property entirely in J. B. Treadwell's hands. They believed his real estate experience in mining and oil exploration would transfer to the task of searching Southern California for land for a cemetery.[19]

Treadwell's search led him to the outskirts of Los Angeles to an area known as Tropico. Alfred B. Chapman had subdivided land along the Los Angeles River in the futile hope that Southern Pacific Railroad would build a depot there, causing a new city to sprout and enhance the value of his land. Instead, the railroad decided to build its depot on land donated by W. C. B. Richardson from his Santa Eulalia Ranch. Southern Pacific called the depot Tropico. Richardson recorded land around the Tropico Depot in 1877 as a town site, planting the moniker of Tropico on the area after considering "Ethelden" and then "Mason."

Tropico was not yet incorporated. Nor was neighboring Glendale, the area north of what is now the intersection of Broadway Avenue and Glendale Avenue. The usual story is that the name Glendale was suggested by a group of women from Chicago who painted the landscape of the valley against the mountains.[20]

After looking at several sites as potential cemeteries, the one that Treadwell liked best was only a few blocks from the intersection of Brand Boulevard and San Fernando Road, Tropico's commercial center. One of the attractive features of this land was that the Pacific Electric "Red Car" line ran down Brand Boulevard with a stop one block away from the proposed cemetery entrance.

The owner of the property that Treadwell wanted to buy was Susan Glassell Mitchell, the heir and daughter of Andrew Glassell. The process of purchasing the land turned out to be more complicated than one might expect, since Treadwell had to deal with an issue of property rights.

Land purchases in Southern California in the early 1900s were often connected to Spanish land grants. After California became the thirty-first state in 1850, the Public Land Commission sorted out the grants and confirmed ownership of various parcels. It was a difficult time for California's economy. By the late 1860s several parcels related to ranchos in Southern California had been sold or lost to foreclosures, resulting in confusion about ownership of land. Andrew Glassell and his law partner, Alfred B. Chapman, filed a lawsuit known as the Great Partition, resulting in Rancho San Rafael being divided into thirty-one parcels distributed between twenty-eight different people. Glassell and Chapman were awarded 5,745 acres, which they further divided and sold over time. Andrew Glassell gave a portion of his land to his daughter, Susan Glassell Mitchell.[21]

Andrew Glassell had given Susan two adjacent parcels of land. Each of them carried a deed provision specifying how the land would be passed on. It was a life estate—Susan had the use of the property only during her lifetime. Upon her death, the property would be passed on to her natural children. They in turn would pass it on to their children, and so on through subsequent generations until there were no heirs.[22]

Treadwell was apparently aware of the deed provision. But when he paid $500 to purchase an option on Susan Mitchell's 151 acres in Tropico, he was unaware that she had two adult daughters. Before exercising the option, Treadwell learned from Susan's brother, Hugh Glassell, that the land bequest from Andrew Glassell passed ownership to those daughters, Lucie M. Lambourn and Eileen G. Bedford. After that revelation, Treadwell declined "to take the land and demanded [his] money back, and went to San Francisco." But Hugh Glassell, acting as agent for Susan, sent him a telegram asking him to come back so they could address the issue of the rights of the two daughters.[23]

The two daughters were very different and had different stakes in what happened to the land. The older daughter, Lucie Lambourn, was a widow and had no children. She was the stable one. On the other hand, Eileen had a reputation for being somewhat wild. A newspaper article described her as "mismarried to a Whiskey Row gambler and saloon keeper named Bedford." The article added that he had operated a gambling establishment in Arizona, which he had given up because there was "nothing in it."[24]

Susan Mitchell disapproved of Eileen's marriage to Charles Bedford. She dealt with that disapproval by specifying in her will that Lucie Lambourn would receive her entire estate, except for five dollars left to Eileen.[25] The pittance to Eileen was to ensure that no one could claim that the omission of Eileen in the will was a mistake. Susan's goal was to make sure that Bedford never put his hands on any family money.

Figure 4. Andrew Glassell Descendents

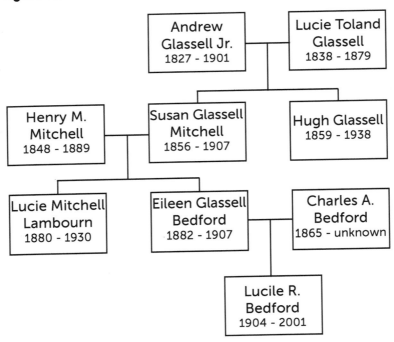

J. B. Treadwell contacted Leslie Brand, namesake of Brand Boulevard and senior officer of the Title Guarantee & Trust Company, for advice on dealing with the issue of rights to the property automatically passing from Susan Mitchell to her two children. Brand proposed that the problem could be solved if Susan Mitchell gave Treadwell a warranty deed.[26] A warranty deed offers the buyer the additional protection that the seller will defend title against the claims of all persons.

With the inheritance issue seemingly settled, Treadwell paid Susan Mitchell $52,300 on September 15, 1905, and received a warranty deed conveying two parcels totaling approximately 151 acres.[27]

While Treadwell purchased land, Pop Ross arranged for the formation of a for-profit corporation to own the land. He named it the Tropico Land & Improvement Company (TL&I). It was incorporated in the Arizona Territory in August 1905 (Arizona became

Figure 5. TL&I Stock Certificate

Forest Lawn Archives

the forty-eighth state in 1912). Arizona was chosen over California because its corporate law was less restrictive. As an Arizona corporation, TL&I would need to hold all its shareholder meetings in that territory, but the board of directors meetings could be held anywhere. Treadwell would later claim that he had "actually attended to the organization" of TL&I, giving no credit to Pop or others.[28]

The first meeting of the board of directors of TL&I convened on September 18, 1905. Tom Ross, Pop Ross, John J. McLaughlin, Albert Burgren, and J. B. Treadwell—the entire membership of TL&I's board of directors—elected Burgren as president. Tom Ross was elected as treasurer, and his father, Pop Ross, as secretary.

J. B. Treadwell told the directors that he had a proposition to sell the company a tract of land, but that he could not make the proposition if he was a director. So he resigned his directorship on the spot.

After a pause, Treadwell made a proposal to sell approximately 131 acres of land to TL&I for $60,000. The directors of TL&I believed Treadwell was offering to sell them all the land he had bought from Mrs. Mitchell at the price he had paid her. They did not know that Treadwell had actually purchased 151 acres from Mitchell and was keeping the remainder for himself. And they also didn't know that Treadwell had paid Mitchell $52,300 for all the land, including the acreage he kept. These facts would not come to light until years later.

Not knowing they were getting the bad end of a deal, the directors of TL&I accepted the offer under the terms requested by Treadwell. They agreed to buy 131 acres for $60,000. The balance of the property price was to be paid to Susan Mitchell in the form of a $32,000 mortgage, so Treadwell would receive $28,000 in cash. In addition, he would be given 100,000 shares of TL&I stock. The stock had a par value of one dollar per share—the company would receive one dollar in cash or the equivalent for each share issued. The 100,000 shares of stock plus the $60,000 land purchase price effectively valued the property at $160,000, three times what Treadwell had paid Mitchell.[29]

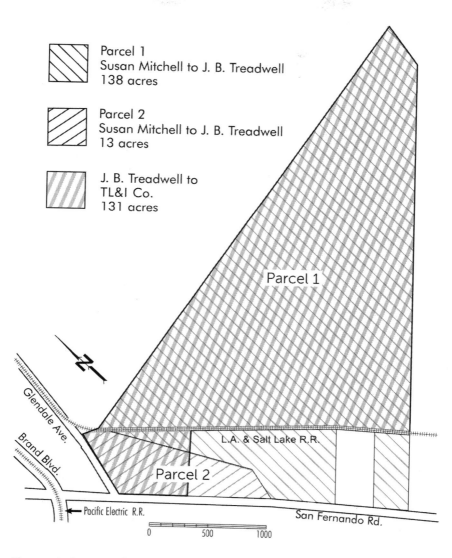

Figure 6. Susan Glassell Mitchell Land Sale

Property acquired from Susan Glassell Mitchell by J. B. Treadwell and portion subsequently sold to TL&I by Treadwell.

After the directors agreed to the land purchase, the meeting adjourned for twenty minutes. When it resumed, Treadwell was reelected as a director. Burgren, who had been elected as a convenience, resigned as president, and Treadwell was elected to fill that post. The meeting adjourned after the directors passed a resolution to sell 50,000 shares of stock for one dollar per share to raise capital.[30]

Two weeks later, Treadwell resigned as president and director of TL&I, and Tom Ross was elected president.[31]

Depot Street

Once TL&I committed to purchase the property from Treadwell, access needed to be improved. To make a better path to the cemetery, Treadwell negotiated with adjacent landowner W. C. B. Richardson—the man who had helped create the town of Tropico—for a strip of land to be used as a road between Glendale Avenue and Brand Boulevard. Richardson was a vice president of the First National Bank, a prominent citizen, and, reportedly, a millionaire.

The $900 Treadwell paid Richardson provided that until Los Angeles County accepted it for "use as a public highway," the land would be a private right-of-way for the benefit of Richardson and of Treadwell's "lands recently purchased from Susan G. Mitchell." Treadwell turned around a week later and for ten dollars granted right-of-way access to TL&I, agreeing to name it Depot Street. (Figure 6, page 17, shows the area before this purchase, and Figure 7, page 22, shows the addition of Depot Street.)[32]

Ready to Start

The men of TL&I were now ready to start Forest Lawn Cemetery. Though there is no record of why they chose the name Forest Lawn, it may have been inspired by Tom's experience with Cypress Lawn in Colma. Or it could have come from some other cemetery they knew of or had visited. Possibly, they just liked the name.[33]

CHAPTER 2

Setting Up the Cemetery

Having acquired the land in Tropico, the directors of TL&I were now ready to turn it into a cemetery. First they would need to form a separate association to develop and operate the cemetery. Then the land would need to be readied for burials.

Forming Forest Lawn Cemetery Association

At the time Forest Lawn* was started, cemeteries were operated by cemetery associations or religious organizations. The not-for-profit cemetery associations usually had contracts with for-profit companies to provide the land. In the case of Forest Lawn, TL&I was the for-profit land company. The next step was to incorporate a cemetery association. Once cemetery lots were sold, the lot owners would become members of the association and would elect the trustees responsible for managing the cemetery and its perpetual care fund. Today, these associations would be classified as mutual benefit corporations.

---

* References to Forest Lawn's location refer to what is now known as Forest Lawn-Glendale. Forest Lawn Memorial-Park did not begin to expand to multiple locations until the late 1940s.

The Forest Lawn Cemetery Association (FLCA) was incorporated on January 11, 1906, a month before Glendale was incorporated as a city. The certificate of incorporation defined FLCA's purpose as establishment of a cemetery in Los Angeles County, not exceeding 330 acres, which would be used exclusively for the burial of the human dead and have one or more crematories. It also acknowledged that a cemetery needed water rights and land for subdivision into "lots, avenues, and walks." Additional provisions were financial: selling lots to purchasers, making "reasonable charges for cremations," and the application of any surplus from the operation to pay for the land, improvements, embellishments, and preservation of the cemetery. The ultimate objective of the new corporation was to establish a cemetery association to conduct a cemetery "as fully and effectually as such things can be done by a cemetery corporation" and for the "maintenance of first class crematories."[1]

Soon after the incorporation of FLCA, an office was opened in the Chamber of Commerce Building in downtown Los Angeles. The following men were then elected by the incorporators to serve as the first board of trustees: C. B. Barnes, William J. "Billy" Blain, J. H. Dewey, J. J. Lockwood, J. Schoder, W. B. Scott, and J. B. Treadwell. None of the men had a management role in TL&I, but all were shareholders—either by direct ownership or by having shares held for them for issue at a future date. Accordingly, all the new FLCA trustees were supportive of the plan for the relationship between TL&I as the land company and FLCA as the cemetery operator.

At the first meeting of the board, the trustees elected corporate officers: Treadwell as president and general manager, J. J. Lockwood as secretary, and Billy Blain as superintendent. The custom of the time was for the corporate secretary to also oversee administrative functions, such as supervising records and bookkeeping. Blain was employed for one year at a salary of $175 per month.[2]

In the same meeting, the FLCA trustees agreed to a contract with TL&I that specified how land would change hands. TL&I initially owned all the land but was committed to selling burial plots

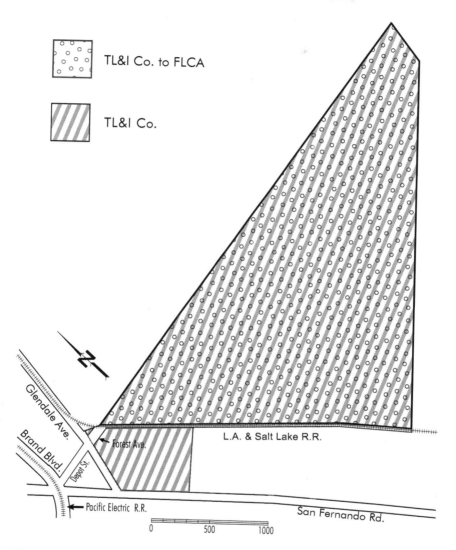

Figure 7. TL&I Land Sale to FLCA

TL&I "sold" FLCA a portion of the land it had purchased from J. B. Treadwell. The land was committed to be sold to FLCA, but clear title was transferred only as land was paid for.

to FLCA, which would then sell them to consumers. FLCA could request that any lot be made available for sale, but could not sell any lot for less than seventy-five cents per square foot. As FLCA sold burial spaces to consumers, it was to send TL&I its share of the proceeds. Only then would TL&I convey title—just of the sold burial space—to FLCA. Thus, deeds to purchasers required signatures from both FLCA and TL&I to convey burial rights. TL&I retained title to all unsold land.

The rather short, three-page, double-spaced contract agreement also gave TL&I control over crucial aspects of FLCA. TL&I had the right to approve the person employed as superintendent. This person had to have cemetery experience as well as skills in landscape design and gardening. The agreement prohibited FLCA from purchasing additional land without the consent of TL&I until 80 percent of the cemetery lots had been sold.[3]

The trustees passed a resolution under which the FLCA "president and Secretary [were] authorized to negotiate and borrow from the [TL&I] such sums . . . as will be necessary to carry out such improvement as to make it a first class cemetery." These loans were to be made at an interest rate not to exceed 6 percent. FLCA was to repay its debt when it became "self-sustaining."[4]

Rules and Regulations

Also at that first meeting, the trustees of FLCA adopted rules and regulations to govern the conduct of the cemetery. The rules limited burials to human remains. Trustees could reject any monument that they believed would hurt the general appearance of the cemetery. All plantings had to be approved by the superintendent. Copings—stone curbs around graves—were prohibited. Vehicles were not allowed to be driven faster than a walk. Horses were required to be tied up when left without a driver. People with firearms or dogs were not to be admitted to the cemetery.[5]

An 1899 California statute required that funds received in excess of current expenses would be held for the perpetual care of the

Figure 8. 1906 TL&I Co and FLCA Contract

The agreement provided that TL&I Co. would provide land and FLCA would develop and operate the cemetery. Both companies had to sign deeds for consumers to get interment (burial) rights.

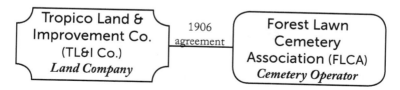

cemetery grounds, lots, and buildings but did not specify a specific amount to go into such a fund.[6] The rules and regulations adopted by FLCA went beyond this general provision. The price quoted to the buyer of a cemetery plot would include both the price of the plot itself and an additional one-third of that amount for the perpetual care fund. For example, if the plot was priced at $75, the buyer would pay that amount plus an additional $25 for perpetual care—$100 in total. The $75 would be split evenly between FLCA and TL&I, and the additional $25 would go into the perpetual care fund. The rules and regulations declared that this perpetual care fund would stand

> as a guardian and care-taker in perpetuity . . . [relieving] the lot owner of any further care or expense, and guarantees not only that his plot shall always be in good repair, but also that nothing it its surroundings shall be unpleasant or incongruous. When in the fullness of time the Cemetery is entirely occupied, it will form an extensive park, rich in foliage, flowers, mausoleums, statuary, and monuments, with funds ample for its perpetual care—a handsome memorial gift to posterity without corresponding burden of tax.[7]

The principal of the perpetual care fund was to be invested to generate income for the upkeep and development of the cemetery.

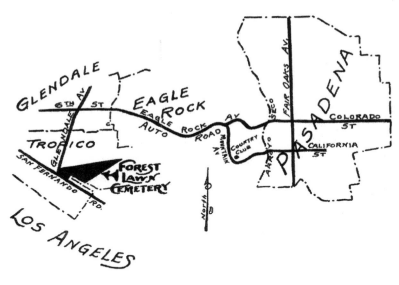

Figure 9. Forest Lawn Location

Under the investment standards of the time, it was common to invest the fund in mortgages secured by real estate. This would generate income while protecting the principal, since it would be possible to foreclose on the property if the property owner did not pay back the mortgage loan. The principal was to be treated as a trust fund to be held for the perpetual care of the property.[8]

Forest Avenue Right-of-Way

The land described in the contract between TL&I and FLCA was land-locked—it did not give access to Glendale Avenue or any other street. The solution was for TL&I to sell FLCA a sixty-six-foot right-of-way from Glendale Avenue to the cemetery land for the sum of $900, and to call that strip Forest Avenue.[9] (See "Figure 7. TL&I Land Sale to FLCA," page 21.)

Forest Lawn Archives

Figure 10. Park Leading to Cemetery

Because the actual cemetery did not begin until beyond tracks of the Los Angeles and Salt Lake Railroad, Forest Lawn's entrance between Glendale Avenue and the railroad tracks was park-like.

Forest Lawn Archives

Figure 11. Forest Lawn Entry Arch, c. 1906

Refinancing the Mortgage

TL&I had acquired the property from Treadwell subject to a mortgage for the balance of the sale price due Susan Mitchell. In November 1906, TL&I replaced Mitchell's mortgage with one from Oscar M. Souden, vice president of US National Bank, with the principal amount of $32,000 being due in three years. The mortgage document called for interest at 8 percent, but Souden executed another document on the same day reducing the interest rate by 2 percent, provided TL&I paid taxes and assessments on the mortgaged property.[10] Over the coming years, Souden would play a key role in TL&I's use of the land.

As part of the refinancing, TL&I received an "unlimited certificate" of title from the Title Guarantee & Trust Company based upon the legal description of the TL&I property. The only exceptions were the right-of-way for the Los Angeles and Glendale Railway Company (referred to in some other documents as the Los Angeles and Salt Lake Railroad) and the mortgage to Souden.[11]

TROPICO, CALIFORNIA

Forest Lawn Archives

Figure 12. Forest Lawn Letterhead, c. 1907

The early FLCA letterheads featured the entrance arch on Glendale Avenue and identified the cemetery as being in Tropico.

Preparing for Burials

When William J. "Billy" Blain became the first superintendent of the cemetery, he was the only one involved with Forest Lawn, other than Tom Ross, who had any cemetery experience. Before coming to California, Billy Blain had been assistant superintendent of a large cemetery in Detroit and had worked at Cypress Lawn Cemetery in Colma. Blain's efforts the first year focused on the design of the cemetery and construction of the supporting infrastructure.[12]

Hired for his landscaping expertise, Blain designed roadways and plantings of shrubs and trees. Because of Los Angeles's dry climate, an irrigation system was also a necessity. The system included sprinklers for the first cemetery sections to be developed as well as infrastructure piping for expansion.

Blain also supervised the construction of the only prominent feature of the new cemetery: a large stone arch at Glendale Avenue, with "Forest Lawn Cemetery" in large metal letters attached to the front.

The second highly visible construction project in Forest Lawn was a receiving vault—a place where remains could be kept before interment. This idea was patterned after the custom in northeastern states, where frozen ground often made it impossible to open graves during cold winters. Remains would be placed in a receiving vault

Forest Lawn Archives

Figure 13. Forest Lawn Receiving Vault

Cemeteries in the west mimicked their eastern counterparts by building receiving vaults.

to await interment when the spring thaw softened the ground. Just as homes in Southern California often had basements mimicking those in colder areas (where foundations had to be below frost depth), cemeteries imitated their eastern counterparts by building receiving vaults. Forest Lawn followed the custom.

Construction of a receiving vault was expected to be finished in 1908 at a cost of less than $2,500 (approximately $152,000 in 2017). Treadwell believed that after construction of the receiving vault, expenses could be cut so that FLCA would "only have to leave enough men to sprinkle and weed the grounds and they can do the grave digging." However, he also acknowledged that he did not know how many men Blain actually needed.[13]

Despite money worries, the receiving vault was finished. In addition, Treadwell made improvements at the entrance to the "car landing"—the point where streetcars stopped on Brand Boulevard and from which

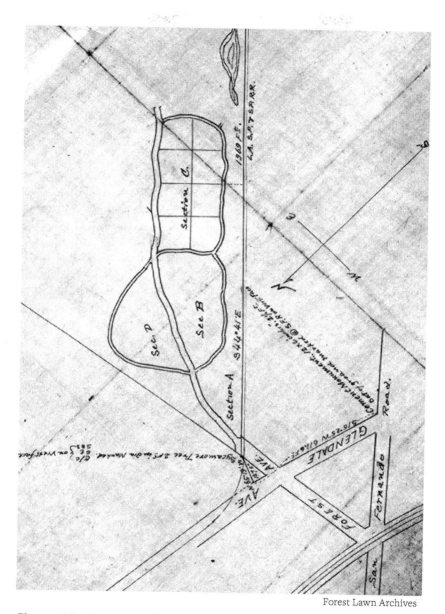

Forest Lawn Archives

Figure 14. Cemetery Plan January 10, 1906

passengers could easily walk to
Forest Lawn—by planting grass
on either side of Depot Street. In
addition to following the receiving vault tradition, Forest Lawn,
like other cemeteries, promoted
transportation of the deceased
to the cemetery via railroad car.
Rates quoted for "car service . . .
for 40 persons and body" went

Forest Lawn Archives

Figure 15. J. B. Treadwell's "Car Landing" Improvements.

from a low of fifteen dollars from Los Angeles on the Glendale and
Tropico car line to a high of seventy-six dollars for transportation
from Newport Beach. Alternatives were available "via [the] Salt Lake
train, daily except Sundays, leaving First Street Viaduct at 2,15 [*sic*]
P.M.; returning arrive at 3,45 [*sic*] P.M. Body $1.50, passengers 25
[cents] Round trip." For those wanting more flexibility, a "Special train
for 40 passengers and body" was available for twenty-one dollars.[14]

Cemetery Lot Sales Begin

The first cemetery lot was sold on August 26, 1906, when W. I. Foley
"went out to the Cemetery while it was nothing but plowed ground
and selected a lot, [with the] price cut nearly in two."[15]

In late 1906, near the end of TL&I's first fiscal year, its certified
public accountant, C. V. Rowe, issued a report showing corporate
assets of $182,000, most of which was land value. The only liability
was a $32,000 real estate mortgage. At the same time, financial
records of FLCA show cash received as $8,916, most of which came
from TL&I; a small amount came from selling crops on cemetery
land. FLCA had cash on hand of only $116—almost enough to pay
its bills, but not the salaries of superintendent Blain or secretary J.
J. Lockwood.[16]

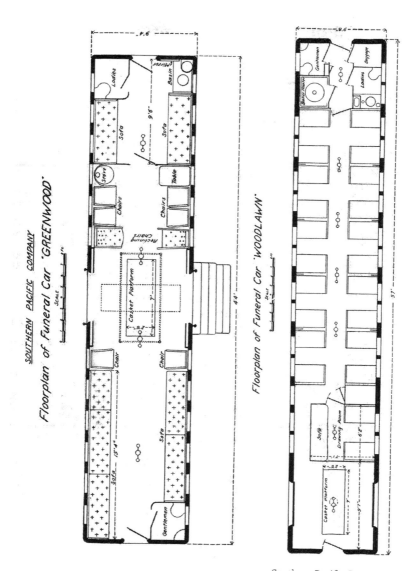

Southern Pacific Company 1905

Figure 16. Southern Pacific Funeral Cars, 1905

Special railroad cars could transport mourners and the casket to cemeteries. The cars "Greenwood" and "Woodlawn" were used between San Francisco and cemeteries in Colma.: Cypress Lawn, Emanuel, Eternal Home, Holy Cross, Mt. Olivet, Odd Fellows, and Shalom.

CHAPTER 3

FINANCIAL CHALLENGES

THE SAN FRANCISCO MEN may not have chosen an ideal time to start a new venture. In 1907, the year after their cemetery opened, the stock market dropped by one-half after an investor tried to manipulate the copper market and the Knickerbocker Trust Company failed. The country entered a recession.[1] It's no surprise that business at Forest Lawn Cemetery got off to a slow start.

Sluggish Sales

At first, lots were sold by cemetery superintendent Billy Blain. But as the cemetery developed, a salesman named J. J. Lanigan was hired to try to improve revenue. Most sales were from people who came to the cemetery, usually because a death was pending or had occurred. Lanigan's job was not only to serve those people but to seek other buyers. Blain continued to help make sales, although this was not his primary responsibility.

Few sales were being made, so cash was tight. In early January 1908, Treadwell could pay all the bills, including payroll, except for the salary due Blain. He wrote Tom Ross that Billy "will kick because he wants some money."[2]

Although prices had been established for various locations within the cemetery, Lockwood cut deals, offering discounts to close sales. For example, Lockwood related to Tom that although the list price for the sale of a two-hundred-square-foot plot was $200, he had discounted the price by fifty dollars to close the sale. This brought the price down to the minimum of seventy-five cents per square foot called for in the TL&I–FLCA contract. However, the amount collected for the perpetual care fund was based on one-third of the $200 list price, not the discounted price.[3]

In 1908, between the first of the year and late March, Forest Lawn had made ninety-five interments. However, there were only ten burials in the first three weeks of March. Treadwell was concerned with the apparent downturn. Blain, the experienced cemetery person, offered encouragement by saying that they "must expect some months to drop down." Lockwood was convinced that part of the problem was "strong competition" from Inglewood Cemetery, but he thought they would "get tired of the game they are playing in a short time."[4] The "game" was lower prices.

Researching records in the county clerk's office, Treadwell found that Inglewood Cemetery had been incorporated with $525,000 in capital stock—21,000 shares with a par value of twenty-five dollars—and its owners had borrowed $75,000 through issuing bonds. A note from Treadwell to Tom Ross estimated Inglewood needed approximately $120,000 in improvements, but the owners were short of funds. He also estimated their expenses were close to $2,500 a month, almost two times Forest Lawn's April 1908 expenses, which explained Lockwood's comment about competition from Inglewood.[5]

Forest Lawn sales had not improved much by mid-1908; "even the undertakers [were] complaining" of slow months. With FLCA having more bills than cash on hand, Treadwell believed that payment on some of the bills would have to be deferred. He also noted that Forest Lawn and Inglewood had the same number of interments (eight) from the City of Los Angeles in April 1908, despite Inglewood's advertising and price cutting.[6]

The slow economic times did not just hurt the undertakers and Forest Lawn. Many of the cemeteries were feeling that cash was tight. Forest Lawn joined other cemeteries—Calvary, Evergreen, Hollywood, Inglewood, and Rosedale, as well as the Cremation Society of Southern California—in agreeing to discontinue burials and cremations on Sundays so that money could be saved by not bringing in extra men on that day.[7]

Saying that payroll was staring him in the face and declaring he was "not leaving a stone unturned to get in money," Lockwood told Pop Ross that unless he could "force collections," FLCA would be short and need help from TL&I.[8]

Treadwell, also concerned with the lack of sales, explained to Tom that he thought the only way to raise the money needed to keep going was to sell additional stock in TL&I. Treadwell thought he could keep things going if he had positive cash flow, but opined that if things did not get better, he would be willing to give up some of his stock so that it could be sold to raise cash. Apparently concerned with his own reputation, Treadwell told Ross he did not want Forest Lawn to fail to pay its bills.[9]

Although he tried to manage expenses, Treadwell found that payroll for the month of June would be $761.55, not including money for Blain, Lockwood, or Lanigan. When Treadwell pressed Blain to cut expenses, Blain replied that one gardener could be eliminated, since all the heavy planting had been completed. However, Treadwell realized the cut would save only $2.50 a day, putting a small dent in the cash flow problem.[10]

In July, collections and sales continued to be slow, since many people were out of town in summer. Lockwood again told Pop Ross that although he was leaving no stone unturned, "it is very hard to get in money."[11]

Though Forest Lawn was still quite new, J. J. Lockwood received an inquiry from Paige & Thorburn Investments of New York asking for information about the cemetery's finances. They wanted to know the number and prices of lots sold, whether dividends had been paid, and where FLCA was incorporated. Although the letter was addressed to Lockwood, Treadwell, as president of FLCA, replied. He explained that FLCA was incorporated but had no capital stock and that its objective was to improve and sell burial lots, although TL&I owned the land. Treadwell told them California laws required that 50 percent of the cemetery sale proceeds, net of amounts due the perpetual care fund, be spent to develop cemetery lots and the remaining 50 percent sent to the "holding company," TL&I. Furthermore, he pointed out that FLCA was contractually limited to selling lots in property owned by TL&I and explained TL&I's capital structure. The letter also noted that Forest Lawn had made 120 burials.[12]

Treadwell painted a more positive picture than the reality. Forest Lawn Cemetery was not yet viable financially.

As FLCA secretary, J. J. Lockwood was responsible for administration, including keeping the financial records. When he looked at the cemetery's finances at the end of August 1908, he was concerned about cash. There was only $175 in the bank, a payroll of $589 was due in days, and office rent also was due. Lockwood wrote Treadwell, who was in San Francisco, that there was "nothing special requiring your presence here but money." Pop Ross responded with a check for $500 as an additional loan from TL&I to FLCA, and a note that Tom Ross would be coming to Los Angeles from San Francisco in a few days. Lockwood was pleased that Tom would be coming to Los Angeles and hoped he would be able to spend more time in the city than he had in the past. He hoped that if Tom spent more time at the cemetery he would better understand the challenges they faced.[13]

Undertaker Referrals

Lockwood believed that Forest Lawn was getting a "cold shoulder" from the undertakers, resulting in little business from referrals. He wanted to "go over this thoroughly" with Tom Ross and Treadwell.

But since neither of these men had any cemetery experience, their thoughts on improving sales were unlikely to help much.[14]

At that time, it was common for cemeteries to rely on referrals from undertakers as a source of business. To curry favor with local undertakers and encourage them to refer families to Forest Lawn, Treadwell met with some of them and gave them stock in TL&I.[15]

Even with the stock gifts, Forest Lawn was getting few referrals from the undertakers. Competition continued to put pressure on Forest Lawn's sales. Treadwell and Lockwood decided they needed to match Inglewood's promise to sell undertakers twenty-five dollar graves for eighteen dollars. Lockwood explained to Pop Ross that Pierce Brothers Undertaking "gave [Forest Lawn] the work" by buying four lots at the discounted price.[16]

Cash Shortage

In September 1908, Lockwood continued to be concerned about funds. He fretted that he was "now placed in a very embarrassing position, not only personally but for the interests of the Cemetery." The cause of his consternation was a payroll due of $654. The workmen were getting uneasy, and Blain was calling him "two to four times a day" to ask if Lockwood had "heard anything" from the Rosses or Treadwell. Lockwood assured Pop Ross that he was doing his best to keep things going and added, almost parenthetically, that once again the payroll did not include any money for Blain. Lockwood again expressed a hope that Tom would come to Los Angeles so that he could talk with him about the cash situation and what needed to be done for the future. Finally, in a comment undoubtedly meant to undermine Treadwell, Lockwood told Tom, "I do not know when our Mr. Treadwell will return, but matters of interest for the cemetery should be attended to at once."[17]

While in San Francisco, Treadwell reviewed the cash situation with Pop Ross. Treadwell wrote Lockwood that he did not know when he would return because he was working on another oil deal. Treadwell added a postscript to the letter, perhaps foretelling a problem to come: "In talking over the perpetual care fund with Ross he says we should pay into the fund all amounts when they become due[,] not hold money out for anything else."[18]

When Lockwood sent Pop Ross the financial reports for October 1908, he noted that he had "placed all money received to the account of Perpetual Care and not used it to meet [operating] expenses, as we have done in the past; and out of the [money] which I hope to get on or before the 10th, there will be about $150.00 or more that will be deposited to the credit of the Fund." Lockwood was acknowledging that more money was due the perpetual care fund than had been deposited in it. The $150 would be a partial reduction in the deficit.[19]

The following month, Lockwood's letter to Pop Ross was much more upbeat than in previous months. He reported that giving streetcar tickets to people had resulted in some thirty groups of prospective buyers coming to the cemetery on a Sunday afternoon. Feeling that things were looking better, Lockwood believed people were now looking at buying cemetery property much the same as investing in other real estate. Salesman Lanigan had shifted his selling strategy as well as his target market. Lockwood credited William Howard Taft's election as president for the change in mood and again assured Pop that Lanigan was doing good work.[20]

Despite the optimistic tone at the beginning of the letter, Lockwood went on to report that money was still tight.

> Now friend Ross, I wish I could make as favorable reports as regards collections. . . . I need from $100 to $200 to make things easy here: while the men are paid Mr. Blain has not had anything, and only a few dollars to Lanigan, and I am placed in a very embarrassing position today.[21]

In Lockwood's next letter to Pop Ross, only two days later, he continued to be positive concerning sales. He reported that sales through November 11 were nearly equal to the entire month of

October. Lockwood believed that "Mr. Lanigan has been working in the past at a great disadvantage on account of the hard times when people did not have the money to invest." Lanigan was promoting purchases of cemetery property with investment as the rationale for the purchase.

Although the sales report sounded wonderful, Lockwood's next sentence disclosed that to meet payroll, office rent, and telephone expenses, he was "obliged to use money that should have gone to the Perpetual Care fund." Even with that, he believed they would still be short of funds to pay all the bills that were due. This was his second allusion to using perpetual care funds to pay operating expenses rather than putting the money in trust.[22]

The gratuitous comments with respect to Lanigan seemed to be a setup for Lockwood's inquiry concerning a suit of clothes "that son of yours [Tom Ross] . . . was to have ordered for me to wear with brass buttons on the coat, same on cap." Lockwood wanted TL&I to pay for the suit because his "company, the Forest Lawn Cemetery, refuses to pay for it." He asked Pop, "Now is this not a little tough when I have presented to me to-day a bill for $99.00 for suits of the other fellows at the Cemetery?"[23]

Not replying to Lockwood's request directly, Pop Ross closed a letter to Treadwell saying, "Tell Mr. Lockwood not to worry about that suit." He added that "we will have a particularly nice style for him and that a design of the [Forest Lawn entrance] Gate would do well for the Cap, and when it is to be paid will give him the pleasure of settling the bill."[24]

Demise of a Salesman

Although Lockwood and Blain were both concerned about the cemetery's finances, they had quite different views of Lanigan. Lockwood thought Lanigan was doing as well as could be done, but Blain did not agree.

Blain wrote directly to Tom Ross in July 1908 to express his concern with Forest Lawn's finances. He suggested a change in sales staff because he thought Lanigan was incompetent—indeed, he claimed Lanigan had made only one sale on his own in eleven months. He thought if Forest Lawn had a "man that is acquainted with the wealthy people, or a couple of women we would see an improvement immediately with less expense. . . . What we ought to have is a middle aged man with a good address, someone . . . that has failed in business but still has the confidence of the business and wealthy people and not afraid to approach anyone." According to Blain, Inglewood was now offering a higher commission to local undertakers, and he thought Forest Lawn should match it. Giving stock to undertakers had helped in the beginning, but more needed to be done. He grumbled there was no reason to delay doing something, as they knew what the problem was with the sales program.[25]

Blain believed that Lanigan would never be able to produce enough sales to make the cemetery successful. To maneuver Lanigan out of the sales position, Blain helped Lanigan find another job.[26] The cemetery would be without a salesman for several months.

Accounting Concerns

In early 1909, Pop Ross wrote Lockwood that he thought the perpetual care fund was much larger than had been reported to him, so "there must be some misunderstanding." Lockwood's reply did not satisfy Pop. Lockwood said, "Now as regards the perpetual care fund, I understood from the little slip you sent me, you only wished to know the amount of money in the Bank." He went on to explain that the fund's balance was $7,034, but that only $1,603 was in the bank. The difference, $5,431, was largely attributed to what was still due and unpaid on accounts. Pop immediately wondered why anything other than uncollected receivables would be due the perpetual care fund, as money due the fund should have been paid over as soon as it was received.[27]

Pop Ross had other questions about the accounting. Trying to understand what FLCA owed creditors, Pop questioned Lockwood about the amounts due to Treadwell, Blain, and Tom. He thought the amounts shown were "beyond what you have mentioned in your monthly reports." Questioning the amount in the perpetual care fund, he asked whether money owed to the fund had been used for operations. Pop concluded, "We cannot understand the report otherwise, but are unwilling to think this is the case as it is quite serious to use a fund of this nature, it being a trust fund."[28]

When Lockwood confirmed that the report was correct, he admitted that for some time, all money that came in was used to pay bills. He believed Pop Ross and J. B. Treadwell had understood that method of operation, but indicated that he was now putting all money due the fund into the fund as soon as it was received. Business had been slow, he reported, but if it improved they could "soon wipe out the amount due the Perpetual Care Fund."[29]

Pop Ross clearly wanted to distance TL&I from Lockwood's actions. He ignored the fact that the misuse of money due to the perpetual care fund had been disclosed by Lockwood the prior November. He wrote Lockwood that he certainly had not understood the improper use of the trust funds, except that Treadwell had mentioned that a small amount had been used by error but was returned to the fund. Pop told Lockwood he was in an uncomfortable position, given that these were trust funds that could not be commingled with operations funds.[30]

Lockwood Resigns

Given Pop Ross's assessment of the seriousness of the improper handling of the perpetual care fund, it was inevitable that this issue would lead to Lockwood's downfall. Apparently, however, Lockwood was surprised that it would be his undoing. On the same day he received Pop's letter, he wrote a letter addressed to the FLCA president and trustees revealing he had learned that his resignation was wanted because of a desire to hire a younger man who would be paid less. Since he had not been asked to reduce his salary, he thought there was no alternative but to resign, but he did ask for two months' pay in lieu of notice. He told them he expected to be out of his office by the first of May.[31]

Upon Lockwood's departure, Pop Ross wrote to Treadwell, on Ross & Burgren letterhead, that "it would appear necessary for an expert to go over the books in the interest of . . . all concerned." He suggested that "the same expert who does Tropico L. & I. Co.'s books be employed," noting that this man, C. V. Rowe, was also the expert accountant for the Mount Olivet Cemetery in Colma. Treadwell telegraphed back a simple "Send Mr. Rowe anytime."[32]

Charles Morgan Arrives

With J. J. Lockwood's resignation effective on May 1, 1909, Treadwell selected Charles O. Morgan as the new secretary. At next meeting of the FLCA trustees, on June 14, Morgan's appointment was ratified and he was officially elected as secretary.[33]

Charles O. Morgan was born on a farm in Madison County, New York, in 1854. He was first admitted to the bar in New York. In 1883 he moved to South Dakota, where he was elected county auditor in 1888. In 1892 Morgan moved to Los Angeles, where he was elected city justice and ex officio police judge in 1898. The *Los Angeles Times* and *Los Angeles Herald* endorsed Morgan's candidacy. The *Herald* proclaimed, "All who want a judge of high personal integrity and purity cannot err in casting their ballots for Charles O. Morgan." When his term expired in 1903, Morgan resumed his private law practice. After working at Forest

Los Angeles Herald, Oct. 29, 1896, 6

Figure 17. Charles O. Morgan

Lawn, he ran for election as a superior court judge as a socialist but was not elected.[34]

Perpetual Care Fund and Cash Flow Problems

C. V. Rowe, the certified public accountant reviewing Forest Lawn's books, determined that $4,616 had been collected for the perpetual care fund, but only $2,454 had been deposited in the fund. He told Morgan, "The Association has to deposit [the difference] as soon as it has funds available." This confirmed and quantified Pop's concern about Lockwood paying operating bills with money that should have gone into the perpetual care fund trust account. Beyond confirming Lockwood's transgressions, Rowe also told Morgan, who now had the ultimate responsibility for the accounting records, that Morgan's entries for the perpetual care fund were wrong—he was "endeavoring to offset one credit on the ledger with another credit item."[35] For accounting books to be in balance, the credits must equal the debits.

Charles Morgan questioned Rowe's accounting principles and disagreed with the CPA's directions. Rowe dismissed Morgan's proposed accounting entries, saying, "As to the question you now ask—it appears to me [it] is one of elementary book-keeping." Even after that, Morgan persisted, sending two letters explaining what he believed to be proper accounting. With Morgan's faulty entries, the books were in disarray. Finally, Rowe instructed Morgan to "open new books according to my statement."[36] Morgan was apparently a better attorney than accountant.

After a month on the job, Charles Morgan understood the inadequate cash flow from the cemetery operation. He wrote TL&I that Forest Lawn had just over $900 in bills and less than $300 in cash. Pop Ross replied to Treadwell with a check from Tom Ross for $500—less than the $600 Morgan had asked for—and a cautionary note to "not pay anything to Lockwood until you have had a talk with Tom on the matter."[37]

At the June 1909 meeting of FLCA's trustees, they learned there was now approximately $2,700 in cash in the perpetual care fund.

The trustees realized that this money should be invested to earn income as soon as possible. After some discussion, a resolution was passed that the perpetual care fund's cash should be used to buy an undivided interest first mortgage on the property owned by Tropico Land & Improvement Company, unless there was a legal issue with the purchase. The motion passed.[38] An undivided interest in a first mortgage means that each co-owner has an unrestricted claim to the entire mortgage investment, in proportion to his or her ownership percentage, but no co-owner has exclusive claim to any specific part of the investment.

Near the end of July, Morgan let Pop Ross know that the shortage in the perpetual care fund had been reduced to $522. Responding to Morgan, Pop directed that the shortage be allocated to Treadwell for $389, Lockwood for $67, and Blain for $67, under the theory that the three men all had some responsibility for the management of the cemetery. Lockwood was sent a bill for what he owed, since he was no longer on the payroll, although Morgan did reveal that the amounts due from both Lockwood and Blain had been "treated by Mr. Lockwood as paid" before he left.[39]

When the trustees next met in November, they were informed there was a legal issue with the perpetual care fund investment that had been authorized at the June meeting. Accordingly, they rescinded the June motion. The minutes do not explain the nature of the legal problem, but it is possible the mortgage note might not have been deemed a prudent investment for the trust fund because the note was secured by property FLCA was buying from TL&I.[40]

Also at the November 1909 meeting, the FLCA trustees were told that the association had total debt of $59,140. This included $32,658 due to TL&I, $15,878 due to Treadwell, $823 due to Blain, and an unspecified amount due to Tom Ross. Secretary Charles Morgan reported that the perpetual care fund had grown to $5,056. The trustees passed a new motion authorizing a loan to TL&I for $5,000 at 8 percent interest, secured by a new mortgage on a portion of TL&I's land. Evidently the legal issue of June had been resolved.

Inadequate cash flow was a constant issue during Forest Lawn's early years. The almost circular flow was an indication of the fragile finances of the enterprise. The funds moved in this manner: FLCA would make a sale, some of the sales proceeds would go into the perpetual care fund, the perpetual care fund would loan money to TL&I, and then TL&I would loan money to FLCA for operations.[41]

Collections on Accounts

Because of the cash flow issues, collections on accounts were frequent topics in correspondence. In August 1910, for example, Pop was told that collections were slower than usual and that, "The bottom seems to have dropped out of business."[42]

Even though some of the discourse recognized the sensitive nature of making collections on accounts involving burials, apparently Charles Morgan thought Pop Ross was encouraging very aggressive collection methods. Some of the letters were very blunt, as is this letter, most likely written by Morgan.

Dear Madam:

We are writing you in reference to the matter of the payment for your late husband's grave, $35.00, for which nothing has ever been paid thereon. Some time ago, we learned that you had received from the contributions of the railroad boys $2230.00 with which to pay the funeral expenses of your late husband, but up to the present time we have never seen the color of any of it to pay for this grave and for the care thereof. To-day we were quite surprised to learn that you had collected a further considerable sum of money from the railroad company, and instead of paying the bills for the funeral expenses, that you should pay, you have taken your father and mother with you, and all have taken a pleasure trip to the far east.

Now we do not like to be treated in this manner, and we expect that you will pay this bill of $35.00 for the grave and the care of the same at once. There seems to be no reason why it should not be paid for at once, and we shall expect a check for the amount by return mail.[43]

New Salesman

After J. J. Lanigan left Forest Lawn, hiring a new salesman was a priority. Dr. George Heath appeared to be the most promising candidate. Heath reported to Tom Ross that he had met J. B. Treadwell, who had taken him to The California Club for a "Royal Lunch" and then out to the cemetery, where they met with Billy Blain. Heath liked what he saw and told Ross, "I hereby most respectfully make application for the position. . . . I have gone to a number of my friends yesterday and today, and started the ball rolling. If you and Mr. Treadwell will talk this matter over <u>seriously</u> . . . I will be glad to . . . get the 'Forest Lawn', on a paying basis as soon as possible."[44]

Heath then received a letter from Pop Ross saying he was being given consideration. Intent on getting the position, Heath replied that he was "working, every day, on the quiet, to help your Forest Lawn proposition." Still angling for the job, Heath wrote:

Now, I am in no position to <u>knock</u> any man; I do not wish to be in the class; yet, I must state the facts, when I <u>see</u> and <u>know</u>, that my friends are burning up their money.

. . . Most of the undertakers are a little off with your representative [Lanigan], as . . . he is too abrupt and uses no tact with his clients; I have had three talks with Mr. Blaine [*sic*] and he fully agrees with me and <u>knows</u> how well you need a <u>live</u> man in place of [Lanigan]—who work[ed] about 3 hr's per day, & play[ed] pool from 11 a.m. [for] the balance [of the day]. I have ascertained, from several undertakers that they can influence about <u>one</u> in <u>ten</u> to bury their loved ones where the U[ndertaker] suggests. . . .

As stated before, I have been on the hustle, every day; I have dug up facts that I can't write; I honestly believe, with Mr. Blaine [sic] at the Cemetery and me on the outside, to round up business, we could soon gather up the loose threads and get this proposition going. . . .

As stated in my former letter, I mean business, and will leave no stone unturned to promote the Forest Lawn.[45]

George Heath landed the FLCA sales job beginning May 1, 1909. He was responsible for selling cemetery lots and looking after the undertakers. In addition, he was to take charge of the office except for bookkeeping and cash matters, which were the province of the bookkeeper. Heath was to receive a guaranteed salary plus commission on multiple-lot sales, but nothing on amounts for perpetual care.

Although always enthusiastic, Heath did not always pay attention to details. For example, only a few days after starting work, Heath wrote Tom Ross to tell him how well things were going. Heath managed to find obsolete Forest Lawn letterhead—it had the old downtown Los Angeles Chamber of Commerce building address rather than the current Wright & Callender Building address. He told Tom Ross he was on the "'war path,' for business, already & will give very best efforts toward the success of the Cemetery."

Auto Expenses

Heath also revealed his infatuation with Forest Lawn's new auto, which was to be used for meeting prospects and bringing them to the cemetery. Less than a week after starting work, he reported to Tom Ross that after taking lessons in "automobiling," he had made his first trip alone to Forest Lawn.[46] A month later, the ever-enthusiastic Heath wrote Tom with a "Dear Sir & Friend" salutation to tell him how hard he was working; three trips with the auto had produced two single grave sales for which he did not earn commission.[47]

Unfortunately, Heath also found that the automobile was not in good condition. He told Tom that he looked for and found a "double rear seat" to increase the passenger capacity. He also hired a car one morning "for two reasons: radiator on our machine was leaking, & four people could not ride in three seats." He did not tell Treadwell of the cost, because Treadwell was focused on reducing expenses to match the incoming cash flow.[48]

When Tom Ross criticized Morgan for not keeping him apprised of outstanding bills, Morgan sent him the auto repair bill that led to this criticism, explaining that "Dr. Heath has had [the bill] in his possession for some weeks, and he turned it in to the office [only] a few days ago." Defensively, Morgan stated he was not to blame for the bill "running along." Furthermore, the expense was incurred in an "unusual manner and for an unusual expenditure, and you Mr. Thomas Ross having known of the matter for months, I cannot understand why you should so write about it to me."[49]

Reacting to Morgan's letter, Tom Ross wrote George Heath that the auto expense was running out of proportion to the value it produced and all expenses had to be kept down. Although the prior month's sales were almost nothing, an "extra large" quantity of gasoline had been used. Tom told Heath to use the machine as little as possible or it would be eliminated. Expenses needed to be cut, and Tom was discouraged that the bills continued to exceed income.[50]

Although Tom Ross received Heath's auto repair bill, he evidently did not authorize payment of it. Two weeks later, E. W. Kelly of Schwaebe-Atkinson Motor Company sent Tom, rather than Morgan, a dunning letter. He explained that they had been patient even though the account had been "running" since May and was "long overdue." He had written a letter to Forest Lawn's city office, but no payment was received. Tom learned that the auto company had reviewed the charges with Dr. Heath and that Heath agreed the charges were correct. Kelly's letter acknowledged that there had been some misunderstanding with respect to the account, but that the "fact of the matter is that the car was down and out and we had to tow it in from somewhere way out in the country."[51]

On the same date as the letter to Tom Ross from E. W. Kelly, George Heath wrote Tom that he had "hounded" the Schwaebe-Atkinson office more than a dozen times attempting to have the bill reduced. All he had accomplished was to prompt Kelly to send the dunning letter to Tom Ross. Heath defended the repairs, saying he'd asked a mechanic to examine the auto before it went into the shop. The mechanic explained that he had found "it in AWFUL shape; it had been run with the belt off, & got too hot." Heath added that the auto "was all taken to pieces & thoroughly overhauled; it is running first class now, & will need very little repair work done to it, for several months. I am saving every $ I can, & will make NO unnecessary expense."[52]

Pop Ross conceded that the auto repair bill would have to be paid, "though Dr Heath informed me [while I was] in Los Angeles that some portions of it were wrong . . . [but] if there is any chance of any allowance to be had or arranged with Schwabe [sic] please do so." Morgan responded that Heath was unsuccessful in getting any reduction in the bill. Not willing to pay the bill without specific instructions from one of the Rosses, Morgan wrote, "An immediate and definite answer is requested." Replying that the bill should be paid, Pop made it clear that the charge should be an expense of FLCA—not TL&I—since TL&I had the responsibility only to "supply the machine but the Cemetery Co [should] pay for all charges during its use."[53]

Pop's irritation stemmed not only from the bill being long overdue, but also from Heath telling him that he had negotiated some reductions in it, which he had not. In exasperation, he told Heath, "Regarding the Schabe [sic] matter[,] any explanation to be given when I come to Los Angeles will be of little use as the bill will have been paid, being long overdue." Pop admonished Heath that the returns from the use of the auto had been small and repeated that expenses must be kept down. Furthermore, Heath was "to use the machine only when absolutely necessary and not at all on Sundays."[54]

Heath and Blain

Never wanting to miss an opportunity to meddle, George Heath wrote Tom Ross of his concern with Blain. Heath said he found Blain to be discouraged, as progress in generating sales seemed slow or nonexistent. Although Heath had tried to encourage Billy Blain, he wanted Pop Ross to do the same, as well as to rush the arrival of a new FLCA president. Heath reiterated his confidence in Blain, but believed he "is on a nervous strain, and we can't afford to have him leave the Co, now; he talked of giving it up yesterday . . . I smoothed him down and he felt better . . . I tell you this in confidence. I am following up every clue, and have lived in hopes of new business coming in."[55]

Although Heath supported Blain, the feeling was not reciprocated. Blain complained to Tom, "I can't see where Heath is doing any good and it strikes me he has developed into a first class joy rider. The machine [auto] is kept busy but I see very little of him."[56]

The Llewellyn Family

Then, as now, companies were often judged by their leaders—board members and officers. Being associated with prominent and successful men from the community was one way to increase an organization's prestige and credibility. TL&I and FLCA believed this was important for the success of Forest Lawn. So when Treadwell returned to Los Angeles from San Francisco in October 1908, he began courting two members of a prominent local family— John Llewellyn and his brother Reese—to invest in TL&I or serve on the FLCA board of trustees.*

The Llewellyn family owned the Llewellyn Iron Works—a foundry, machine works, blacksmith, and boiler works outfit—which occupied a full block in Los Angeles. The Llewellyns had a reputation for

---

* The Llewellyn Iron Works family is not related to Eaton's nephew, Frederick Eaton Llewellyn, nor to John F. Llewellyn, the author of this book.

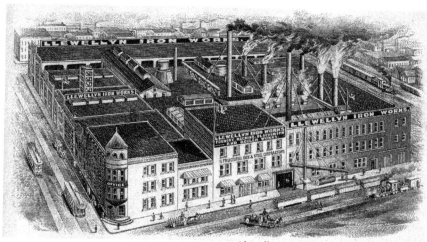

Llewellyn Iron Works letterhead c. 1909

Figure 18. Llewellyn Iron Works Building

The Llewellyn Iron Works occupied a full city block.

being staunchly opposed to labor unions. This made their business a target for violence during a nationwide labor dispute involving the Bridge and Structural Iron Workers Union and the National Erectors Association. A group of employers supporting an open shop were particularly active in Los Angeles, resulting in the Los Angeles Times plant being bombed on October 1, 1910, causing twenty deaths. Sixteen sticks of dynamite had been placed in an alley next to the Los Angeles Times building. When placing the dynamite, Jim McNamara had not realized that he was placing the explosive next to barrels of highly flammable printer's ink.[57]

Motivated by the prominence of Llewellyn Iron Works and the Llewellyns' anti-union stance, a man named Ortie McManigal placed a bomb that damaged the Iron Works building on Christmas Day 1910. McManigal was responsible for several bombings across the country and ultimately went to prison, but McNamara received a life sentence due to the deaths in the Los Angeles Times bombing.[58]

Treadwell met with brothers John and Reese Llewellyn to explain how the two corporations, TL&I and FLCA, worked together.

Because the Llewellyns had extensive bank borrowings, they were quite cautious about getting financially involved with other enterprises. Their concern was that their bankers might fear that the TL&I stock was assessable, meaning it could become a liability in the event that TL&I failed. But they seemed intrigued by the fact that FLCA was "without capital [stock] and that [TL&I was] kept in the background."[59]

Recruiting John Llewellyn

Treadwell met with John and Reese Llewellyn several times, trying to interest them in the cemetery business. Following one of those talks, Treadwell sent Reese Llewellyn an R. G. Dun & Co. report on the Rosedale Cemetery Association in Los Angeles, hoping the report would make cemeteries, particularly Forest Lawn, look like an attractive business. However, the report only confused Reese, who told Treadwell that he wanted an explanation of the report the next time they met.[60]

Not waiting for a next meeting, Treadwell wrote Reese that the report was faulty in that it combined the finances of the cemetery association and the land company (akin to combining FLCA's finances with TL&I's). Additionally, the report mixed up the names of the officers of the two entities. Treadwell further told Reese that he thought Rosedale's claim of having fifteen to twenty acres of unsold lots was exaggerated; he believed they had only five to eight acres, which could not last long.[61]

Furthermore, Treadwell observed that the Dun report stated that Rosedale had purchased nearly 140 acres on the Sherman line of the Los Angeles and Pacific Railroad just north of the Cienaga Schoolhouse, which they expected to use for cemetery purposes. Treadwell did not think that land could be used for cemetery purposes because "in boring for water they ran into oil," making the land more valuable for oil production than cemetery use.[62]

When Treadwell explained the Dun report to Reese, he projected the total sales over the life of the cemetery. He told Reese that

Press Reference Library 1912

Figure 19. John Llewellyn

Rosedale would eventually have almost $2 million in cemetery sales. With that $2 million split evenly between Rosedale and the related land company, Rosedale would have $1 million to be used for improvements and expenses. The land company would have nominal expenses—most of its $1 million would be profit.[63]

Realizing the Llewellyn's sensitivity about their banking relationship, Treadwell met with John and Reese Llewellyn to explain how TL&I and FLCA worked together. Treadwell wanted to persuade one of the brothers to at least become a trustee of FLCA.[64]

The Rosses probably would have preferred the eldest brother, Reese Llewellyn, as a trustee because of his role as president of the Llewellyn Iron Works. However, when it became obvious that Reese would not get involved in any way, the Rosses concluded it would be better to court John Llewellyn.

Though not president of the Iron Works, John Llewellyn, fifth of the seven Llewellyn children, was still a prominent citizen. He was an assistant secretary of the company, but his principal assignment was as head of the elevator department. After the San Francisco earthquake and fire, he was one of the rebuilders of the city and installed the first elevator in a San Francisco building following the disaster. Under his supervision, elevators were installed in most of the tall buildings in Los Angeles, including the Alexandria Hotel, Los Angeles Hall of Records, and Los Angeles Athletic Club. He was quite prominent socially and belonged to The California Club, Jonathan Club, Los Angeles Country Club, and Sierra Club.[65]

In January 1909, Treadwell turned his attention to persuading John Llewellyn to join the FLCA board of trustees. His first proposal was to give Llewellyn shares of TL&I in exchange for a Premier automobile and a horse. The auto was to be used as transportation for the salesman, and the horse was for use at the cemetery.[66]

This draft of the agreement was not signed, and negotiations continued. Blain wrote Pop Ross that they had not yet been able to take possession of the auto or the horse, although he thought they could pick up either of them at any time. Blain believed that Forest Lawn was badly in need of the car because it was "losing valuable time in this season of the year when business should be rushing." Reporting that John Llewellyn had been hard to connect with and that Reese Llewellyn had been away, Blain also told Pop, "Treadwell is still under the impression that they are jollying you . . . so if there is any way of bringing this thing to a head it should be done at once."[67]

In addition to the Llewellyns' concern about what their bankers thought of TL&I stock, there was another problem to resolve. It would be a conflict of interest for an FLCA trustee to also own shares in TL&I. Treadwell had come up with a deceptive means of hiding this conflict of interest. He told John Llewellyn that the TL&I stock could be issued in Treadwell's name. Treadwell would then endorse the shares to Llewellyn, but not record the transfer on TL&I's records. That way no one would know that Llewellyn owned the stock, and he could serve as a trustee of FLCA without damaging his family's standing with the bank.[68]

In April 1909, Pop Ross sent John Llewellyn a certificate for one thousand shares of TL&I stock as a "bonus for services to be rendered to the [TL&I] in the Forest Lawn Cemetery Association." Pop asked Llewellyn to sign an agreement dated January 16 and return it. Although it carried the same date as the first draft, the versions were quite different. The final agreement called for Llewellyn to buy the shares, paid in installments of $250 per month. Ross also sent two certificates for 750 shares each to David Llewellyn—one of John Llewellyn's brothers—as payment for the automobile and requested that a bill of sale be sent to TL&I.[69]

Part of the agreement with John Llewellyn was that the Llewellyn family monument, along with the remains of six Llewellyn family members, would be moved from Evergreen Cemetery to Forest Lawn. This would give visibility to the Llewellyn family's support and inspire confidence in Forest Lawn. In August 1909, Heath wrote Tom Ross that "I think it would be advisable to drop John [Llewellyn] a reminder about moving the monument as it undoubtedly will be a big help to us when we get it up."[70]

By the time Pop Ross sent Llewellyn the agreement and stock certificates, Llewellyn had been elected as a trustee and vice president of FLCA. However, this election was invalid, because Forest Lawn's bylaws required that trustees be "lot proprietors"—owners of at least 200 square feet of burial property. FLCA secretary Charles Morgan pointed out that for John Llewellyn to serve on the board of trustees, he would have to be named on the Llewellyn family cemetery deed. Since no one had thought of this, the cemetery property in Forest Lawn had been deeded to John Llewellyn's wife.[71] This was remedied by adding John Llewellyn's name to the owner records so he would be qualified to serve as a trustee.*

Once this was accomplished, John Llewellyn was legitimately elected to the FLCA board of trustees on January 11, 1910.

Treadwell and the Rosses had achieved their goal of associating one of Los Angeles's most prominent families with Forest Lawn. However, that did nothing to help the immediate problem of expenses exceeding sales income.

---

* The records use "lot proprietor" and "lot owner" interchangeably. "Lot owner" is used throughout this book, except when "lot proprietor" is used in a quotation.

CHAPTER 4

Trouble for Treadwell

THERE IS NO DOUBT that J. B. Treadwell was a major figure in the founding of Forest Lawn Cemetery. He was one of the original group of men who gathered in San Francisco in 1905 with a plan to enter the cemetery business. He served as president of Tropico Land & Improvement Co.—albeit for only two weeks—and was the first president of the Forest Lawn Cemetery Association. But there is also no doubt that Treadwell had a tendency to stir up trouble. His quarrelsome relationships and questionable ethics led him to became a thorn in the side of his Forest Lawn colleagues.

The Wheeler-Dealer

Treadwell was no stranger to controversy, even prior to TL&I. In 1898 he applied for a wharf franchise from the board of supervisors of Santa Barbara County. The ostensible purpose was to load oil and other commodities onto ships for ocean transportation. Once he built the wharf about 400 feet into the ocean, he built 2,000-foot extensions from the end, parallel to the coast line. All of this was done so that he could drill oil wells off shore. The oil-bearing rock formation ran downward from the land into the ocean. So pumping

oil from Treadwell's planned oil wells would soon lower the oil level
on the land-based wells, making them dry.[1]

Although Treadwell had claimed the wharf project was his own,
it was actually a project for a subsidiary of Southern Pacific Railroad.
The drilling and the railroad's acquisition of oil lands led to litigation
between the US government and Southern Pacific. When Treadwell
was called to testify, he said that he "did not know G. J. Griffin [a
Southern Pacific official] and did not remember ever having written
[Griffin]." Called as a rebuttal witness, Griffin testified he had a
close relationship with Treadwell. He repeated many conversations
with Treadwell regarding the Southern Pacific Railroad acquiring
oil lands in California.[2]

Today, J. B. Treadwell would most likely be labeled a "serial
entrepreneur." Less charitably, he would be called a schemer and
"wheeler-dealer." Whatever label applied to him, he always seemed
to be working on multiple business ventures.

For example, just after the January 11, 1906, incorporation of
FLCA—even before FLCA's articles of incorporation were filed
with the state—Treadwell sought to start another cemetery in
San Bernardino, to be named the Ferndale Park Cemetery. The
San Bernardino Sun reported that Treadwell was the head of "an
association which makes a business of laying out and maintaining
cemeteries and has cemeteries all over the country." The Masonic
Building Association had purchased ten acres in the north part of
San Bernardino to establish a cemetery. Treadwell, representing
himself as president of the National Cemetery Association of San
Francisco, acquired options for an eighty-acre burial ground, which
led the Masonic organization to abandon its project in favor of his.
In order for his development plan to succeed, Treadwell would need
to successfully contest the legality of the city's ordinance restricting
where cemeteries could be located. He claimed to have established a
cemetery in Washington City, which had a more restrictive ordinance,

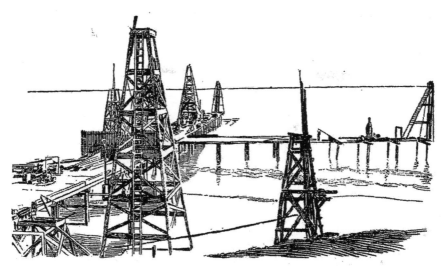

Los Angeles Times, October 26, 1898

Figure 20. Treadwell's Oil Well Wharf
When Treadwell began construction of a lateral extension to the oil wharf at Summerland (Santa Barbara), citizens were outraged.

and boasted that he had "unlimited means with which to make the contest if necessary." Nothing supports that claim of experience, and he apparently did not follow through with the project.[3]

Treadwell's predilection for exploring outside business opportunities sometimes meant that he was unavailable or unresponsive when Forest Lawn needed him. J. J. Lockwood, secretary of FLCA, called attention to this when replying to a letter from Pop Ross, ostensibly to explain why a report had not been sent. He unsubtly expressed his frustration: "As I presume you are aware Mr. Treadwell left here some days ago. . . . I am simply holding my report for his return to O.K. same. I have been looking for him daily, the only information I have received being through Mrs. Treadwell, that he hopes to leave San Francisco to-night."[4]

Several months later, however, Treadwell told Tom Ross that his attention had indeed been focused on Forest Lawn. It was near the end of 1907, when Forest Lawn's sales revenues did not cover expenses. Treadwell expressed his discouragement at the close of a letter to Ross.

> Tom. I am all out of funds. I have the money for the taxes. I don't see how we are going to get through. Rather than have you fail with your friends [I] would let all my stock go to keep it going. I have not made any money out side for over a year, as you know I have been giving my personal attention to this.[5]

Stock Ownership Dispute

Treadwell's questionable ethics were apparent in the initial purchase of land for TL&I, when he didn't reveal that he'd kept some of the land for himself. But that was not a unique situation. A dispute over the ownership of TL&I stock shares provides further illustration of Treadwell's less than honorable character.

The dispute related to a transaction that occurred in 1907. Because there often was not enough cash to pay Blain and Lockwood, shares of stock in TL&I were set aside for the two men. In a handwritten note dated June 3, Treadwell told Lockwood that "I hold for you Five hundred shares of the Capital Stock of the Tropico Land and Improvement Co. of Arizona. . . . Said stock is to be delivered to said J. J. Lockwood when my stock is taken out of the Pool. Which pooled stock is in the hand of Mr. Thomas Ross." The pool of stock consisted of the TL&I common shares that had been set aside in an informal trust when the company was formed. The intent was that key individuals would be given the shares at some future time when the venture was successful.

Twenty years later, Treadwell asserted that he, not Lockwood, owned this stock. When Treadwell was told that the corporate records showed Lockwood as the owner, Treadwell presented a handwritten note, dated June 14, 1909. It appeared to be a receipt signed by J. J. Lockwood for $100 received from J. B. Treadwell "in full for 500 shares of Tropico Land and Improvement stock." Treadwell filed a lawsuit to get a court to declare that he owned the shares, using this receipt as evidence.[6]

Belle, Tom Ross's second wife, suggested that the signatures should be carefully studied. A document expert testified that the words "dollars, in full for 500 shares of Tropico Land & Improvement stock" had been added sometime after the other writing on the paper. The ink color was different in the added wording, and the expert showed that although Treadwell's signature had been written before the paper was folded, the word "dollars" had been added after it was folded.[7] Based on the evidence that the receipt had been tampered with, the court ruled that Treadwell did not own the stock.

Despite the embarrassing testimony and finding, Treadwell appealed the ruling. The Third Appellate District Court of California was not impressed with the validity of Treadwell's appeal. In addition to upholding the lower court's ruling, the Appellate Court's 1932 decision concluded, "The appeal is utterly and obviously devoid of any vestige of merit, so much so that a fine of $100 is hereby assessed against appellant for indulging in this frivolity." Treadwell died in 1931, sparing him the embarrassment of the final court decision.[8]

Concerns about Blain

In early 1907, Treadwell became frustrated with the behavior of cemetery superintendent Billy Blain. Before the cemetery was in operation, Blain had been occupied with the construction of the entry arch, roads, irrigation, and other infrastructure. Once those projects were completed, Blain did not have much to do. In a letter to Tom Ross, Treadwell complained that for the last four days, Blain had been coming to the cemetery but would stay only for an hour or so. Treadwell did not say why Blain did not stay longer.[9]

In September 1908, again frustrated by Blain, Treadwell began a letter to Tom Ross with a formal "Dear Sir" instead of his customary "Dear Tom." Blain had been in the city office on Saturday morning to look up a prospect in the city directory, but he did not appear on Sunday morning as was expected. A sale was lost to Rosedale Cemetery because Blain could not be found. Treadwell was frustrated that he could not rely on Blain, telling Tom, "It seems that Blain goes off [at] just the wrong time. I don't see how we are to make a success of this cemetery business[;] it is surely out of my line. I feel I cannot do any good." Given his frustration with Blain and Forest Lawn's finances, Treadwell wanted out. He offered to give up 24,000 of the 25,000 TL&I shares that had been held in trust for him.

It was only two days later that Treadwell felt compelled to write once again to Tom complaining about Blain. Billy had turned up drunk at the office—so drunk that he fell off his chair. Although he wanted to stay to meet a prospect, Lanigan convinced him to go home. Treadwell tried to stay away from Blain, but wrote Tom:

> I don't object to a man drinking but when he cannot take a drink without getting drunk and then exhibits himself before the public, that will not do for cemetery business.
>
> Had I known Blain's failings I should never have taken hold of this enterprise. My past experience with such men has caused me so much trouble besides loss of money. As soon as I can I will resign as President and Director of the Cemetery [Association].[10]

Treadwell stated that he was giving up his TL&I shares and wanted 500 of them to go to Lockwood. Shortly after sending the letter, Treadwell sent Pop Ross a receipt and assignment that stated, "I hereby assign and sell to T. Paterson Ross twenty-four thousand Shares of Tropico Land and Improvement Co. Stock now held by you in trust."[11]

Tom Ross acknowledged Treadwell's intent to resign, but did not interpret Treadwell's letter as a resignation.

Treadwell continued to express his frustration. He told Tom that he was losing sleep over Blain and believed Blain would wreck the business. Treadwell believed it was well known around Tropico and

Glendale that Forest Lawn had a drunkard for a superintendent. Treadwell feared that the Inglewood people would find out and publicize it. He closed his letter with, "If I could make a million dollars I would not be associated with Blain in this business."[12]

Shortly after sending that letter, Treadwell went to San Francisco. After discussing his concerns about Blain with Tom Ross, Treadwell wrote a letter marked "Private" to Lockwood. "[Tom] Ross wants to keep Blain if we can get along with him on account of his talent in laying out the Cemetery grounds. I told him it was up to him to run it. . . . [Tom] Ross don't want me to get out, but I am going to consult my own ideas and do what is best for my comfort."[13]

Lockwood, like Tom Ross, thought that Blain should be kept as superintendent of the cemetery. He told Treadwell it would be hard for anyone to take Blain's place, as "it is only a matter of holding him down, he in my mind, is the only one to be at the cemetery to meet all parties going out, not only [for] burials but for selection of lots."[14]

In early October 1908, Treadwell planned to stay in San Francisco for a while to complete an oil deal, but perhaps also to avoid dealing with Blain. Treadwell also reported to Lockwood that he had shared his concerns about Blain with Pop and "evidently he don't like to hear it as he has made no reply to me. So I have concluded to let him work it out his own way. It don't interest me any more. Time will show how it will all come out. I cannot say when I will return to Los Angeles as I have not [finished] my oil deal." Treadwell reported that the oil well was progressing nicely; there was just a problem with the well casing that needed to be fixed.[15]

Treadwell returned to Los Angeles but went back to San Francisco at the end of November 1908. When he left, he asked Lockwood to keep him informed of what was going on at Forest Lawn. Lockwood wrote him that Adler, another employee, had to do a burial service, since Blain was not in a condition to do so. Apparently that was not the first time within a week that Adler had to fill in for Blain.[16]

Returning to Los Angeles three days after Lockwood's letter, Treadwell immediately wrote Tom Ross. "I arrived here this morning and went out . . . to the cemetery. I find Blain has been on a toot again, for a week or more and he has not shown up at the cemetery for two days. . . . Now it is up to you as to what you want to do."[17]

Not receiving a response to his letter about Blain, a frustrated Treadwell wrote Tom Ross expressing his intent to resign.

> [From] your silence I concluded you wish to keep Blain regardless of what he does. I am through with Blain and I told him so but don't want to interfere with your ideas on arrangements and management of the Forest Lawn Cemetery and I will now turn it over to you. I shall call the Directors or Trustees meeting and tender my resignation as Director and President. You had better select some one you want in my place. . . . The annual election of Trustees comes on the 11th of January 1909. There is one Trustee to be elected for 3 years. That is the expiration of myself as Trustee.[18]

While Treadwell was complaining to Tom Ross about Blain's problems, Tom and Blain were in direct contact. The same day Treadwell wrote Tom about tendering his resignation, Blain wrote Tom calling Treadwell's actions a "conspiracy" and that he, Blain, was in the process of easing salesman Lanigan out of Forest Lawn.[19]

Treadwell had a lot on his hands in 1909, with Heath and Morgan new on the job as of May 1 and Lockwood moving out of the office on May 6. Meanwhile, Treadwell continued to have fits with Blain's drinking. After typing a letter to Pop Ross, Treadwell scrawled a handwritten postscript on a scrap of paper and taped it to the page: "P.S. I notice that Blain had been drinking last evening and this morning. I don't know how he will do if he will straighten up or not. When he starts he finishes up like a Hog."[20]

Only three days later, Treadwell wrote Pop Ross about another Blain drinking spree.

Blain started his drunk last Monday and kept it up till last night. He is sober this morning and when I needed his assistance [he went] on a drunk. I am giving all my time to get things in running order. Blain could help much if he would. [H]e was going round with Dr. Heath, that's off now.[21]

Although Treadwell was frustrated with Blain and wanted to be rid of him, the feeling was not universal. When George Heath heard that Treadwell intended to call a special meeting of the FLCA trustees to get rid of Blain, he made sure the Rosses knew about it. He wrote Tom that Treadwell was going to "make it hot" for Blain and added, "[We] must not lose Mr. Blain at this time; he is head, foot & trunk, of this Ass'n at the present stage of the game." Heath saw Treadwell's special meeting as an act of revenge: Treadwell was annoyed that his office had been cleaned out before he had resigned and believed Blain was behind that.[22]

Tom Ross, unsurprisingly, was not happy to hear Heath's warning about Treadwell's plans. He wrote John Llewellyn of his concern, giving Llewellyn direction about how to handle the situation.

I understand that J. B. T. is about to call a special meeting of the Forest Lawn Ce. Ass/n and will try to out Blain.

If possible notify me by telegraph and I will come down, in any event be sure to be present and see that Blain . . . is present.

According to the agreement between Tropico Land & Imp. Co and the Cemetery Co it is necessary to get the approval of the Tropico Co in appointing a Superintendent for the Cemetery, so look out for this.

If motion is carried to dismiss Blain consent to it for the purpose of giving notice of reconsideration at next meeting.

Also take same action if any one is appointed and insist on delay until Tropico's approval is obtained, as per agreement.

J. B. T. will shortly resign and we are arranging for his successor, but of this he does not know.

If possible take a run up to the Office and size up the new Secretary and the general situation.

Mr. Heath may be able to give you some points.[23]

It was now apparent that the special services Llewellyn was to provide included guarding TL&I's position and being an information source. Clearly Tom Ross was quite capable of doing some background maneuvering of his own.

Concerns about Finances

In addition to being frustrated by Blain, Treadwell was also concerned about finances. In mid-May he wrote a letter to Pop Ross, marked "Private," in which he explained that he would be in San Francisco the following week and wanted to discuss the automobile and other matters. "We are doing no business. Dr. Heath don't seem to bring any business. How this is all going to end is hard to say. It is worring [*sic*] me. I want to talk of the future. What is best to do."[24]

Treadwell must have shared his concerns with Heath, the opportunist, since Heath quickly wrote Pop Ross, "We are in the thick of the fray." Heath said Treadwell had told him confidentially that he was going to entirely withdraw and give up his interest in TL&I. Heath added, "Don't say a word, but . . . take him at his word; I have a suggestion—to make, should he give up the Presidency, that I think will help make this proposition a sure winner!"[25] No doubt Heath wanted to assume the presidency himself.

Heath then wrote Tom Ross to report that the auto needed still more repairs. He suggested others were the cause of Forest Lawn's problems.

I have done everything, in my power . . . to get some business going for the Co. An outside-salesman has a whole lot of difficulties to overcome, before getting into working shape; the whole Forest Lawn Cemetery Business, has been mishandled, from the start; if you had employed clean people, in this

office, some of the undertakers, who have <u>thrown off</u>, from
F.L.—would have kept sending people this way; Now, I have
to go round, to all of them, and restore confidence, as lies have
been told, right & left.[26]

Writing to Tom again the next day, Heath told him that he was
both busy and discouraged, as he had not produced many sales during
his first month on the job. He had visited several of the undertakers
with Blain and believed that now confidence in Forest Lawn was
growing. Heath confided that he was "encouraging Mr. Blain, all
I can, but I have not had any too much confidence & back-bone
myself, when all these people kick . . . & give all sorts of seemingly
good advice. . . . I want a little encouragement from you."[27]

A Future Successor

By August 1909, Blain and Heath knew who would replace Treadwell
once he resigned as president of FLCA: Norton Chamberlin Wells.
Born in Eureka, Nevada, in 1874, Wells and his family moved to
California shortly after his birth. He was described as tall and stout
with brown hair.[28]

Blain wanted to have Wells on the job soon, and he expressed this
desire to both Pop and Tom Ross. He also told Tom that Charles
Morgan, as FLCA board secretary, was "curious to know what is
going to be done."[29]

Time passed, and Morgan wrote Pop Ross about his concern with
the delay in the arrival of the new president. "I sincerely hope that
the management will soon come to full understanding of what they
are going to do. It is simply unbearable to be continually waiting,
and waiting for you know not what, and I am heartily tired of it."[30]

J. B. Treadwell was a lame duck—still president of FLCA, but
soon to be replaced. Treadwell was unhappy that Blain was going
around him by writing directly to Pop Ross rather than communicat-
ing through him. Also, he did not like Pop Ross giving directions to
Morgan about collections and other matters. Treadwell wrote Pop

Ross, "You say business is business[;] now get down to business and get Wells down here. I don't want to be held responsible for acts of employees whom are held here, over whom I have no control. It's not business, using your own words."[31]

Treadwell asked Pop for guidance about when Wells should become president. Pop responded that Wells should be hired as of January 1 as assistant manager, then would be elected president and manager at the January 11 organization meeting of the FLCA trustees. He told Treadwell that by doing it this way, "it would not be necessary for you to resign at all, but your office would simply be succeeded by Norton on the 11th." Pop also mentioned that Wells was in Los Angeles on personal business and would "look in upon you and have a little talk on the future."[32]

However, seeing Treadwell was not a priority for Norton Wells—most likely because Treadwell had not been successful as president and Blain was to continue as superintendent. When Wells arrived in town, he did not contact Treadwell, but went out to Forest Lawn to see Blain. The following day, Wells went to the office in downtown Los Angeles before Treadwell arrived. Instead of waiting there so he could talk to Treadwell, he told Morgan that he was going out to the cemetery.[33]

Chattel Mortgage

Along with reporting to Pop Ross that Wells had not met with him, Treadwell did not miss an opportunity to make things difficult for Blain. After telling Pop that Blain seemed to want cash rather than a note for salary and other money due him from FLCA, Treadwell advised Pop that TL&I should protect itself before advancing any more funds to FLCA. Treadwell proposed that TL&I should insist on a chattel mortgage on all FLCA's personal property. A chattel mortgage is the personal property equivalent of a mortgage on land. This would be to Blain's detriment if there were a foreclosure on the chattel mortgage, because the mortgage would have a claim before any Blain could make—other than what might be due him as salary. Treadwell's gratuitous advice was not followed.[34]

Compensation for Wells

The cemetery did not generate enough cash to pay Wells a salary that would entice him to take the job. Therefore, in addition to being paid $150 per month, Wells would receive shares of TL&I. As Pop Ross explained to Blain, Wells was to receive 2,500 shares as a bonus when he ran the cemetery for three months "without any call for financial assistance" and another 2,500 shares when he did the same for another three months. Finally, he would receive an additional 5,000 shares when "he succeeds in making the proposition so profitable that the Tropico Co. shall be able to pay a dividend." Pop assured Blain this was the best deal that could be had.[35]

The shares to be given to Wells were to come from the "promotional shares" (stock to be used to raise capital) held by TL&I. Therefore, Pop needed to have the approval of both Blain and Treadwell as part of the original organizing group. In his response to Pop, Blain was clear that he was not too keen on the way this was to be done. He thought the agreement was ambiguous, since it did not clearly state how much promotional stock was on hand.

You gave me to distinctly understand that the stock turned back by Treadwell was to be given Mr. Wells if he would take the management. Now as Treadwell got that stock to promote this proposition and then fell down and turned his stock back it looks to me as if that stock should be given to his successor.

I am willing to do anything that is reasonable, but I can't see my way clear under the circumstances to sign this agreement in its present condition.

You will notice that Treadwell signed this enclosed agreement, but he said, "as I have no further interest in the escrow having given all my stock back to Tom, I will sign anything."[36]

Several days later, Blain told Treadwell he had received a letter from Pop Ross with an agreement approving the transfer of stock to Wells. Treadwell told Pop that Blain had insisted he would not sign the agreement. Attempting to make Blain look unresponsive, Treadwell offered, "I asked him how long he had had the letter. He said several days. I told him he had better answer it one way or the other and not hold it."[37]

The following week, Tom Ross assured Blain that Wells would not receive any TL&I stock until the cemetery had a positive cash flow. Tom, who realized Blain had been wanting Treadwell to depart for over a year and a half, told Blain he was now getting what he wanted "and had been praying for." Tom anticipated that over the coming six months he would need to continue putting up additional funds to keep TL&I afloat, just as he had been doing since the beginning. Tom told Blain he now had "over $25,000.00 invested in coin which I was not supposed to invest at the beginning and had I not done so the Company would have busted long ago." Treadwell had turned his promotional stock over to Tom because Tom continued to advance funds. Tom was willing to do this "pro rata" (proportionally to each person's holdings) to help make TL&I a success, but told Blain he would "not do so if you expect me to give up my stock, put up the money and worry over the financial part and you not do anything."[38]

Tom Ross's letter to Billy Blain confirmed the Rosses' control. Things were now in place for Wells to start work on January 1, 1910, as assistant manager.

Wells Replaces Treadwell

At the January 11 Forest Lawn lot owners meeting, Norton Wells was elected as a trustee. Later that day, at the organizational meeting of the trustees, he was elected as the second president of FLCA.[39] During that meeting, J. B. Treadwell resigned as trustee and president. John Llewellyn offered the following motion:

Resolved, that the sincere thanks of the Association be and they are hereby tendered to Mr. J. B. Treadwell for the efficient manner in which he has administered the office of Trustee, President and General Manager of the Association for the several years last passed.[40]

Norton Wells and Tom Ross signed an agreement which provided that Wells, as president and manager, would hold office for as long as he desired and would have "complete charge of its business, with full power to hire and discharge all employees." In addition to his salary of $150 per month, Wells was to receive shares of TL&I on the basis that Tom had revealed to Blain the previous December.

The agreement between FLCA and TL&I gave TL&I the right to approve the superintendent, but not to hire him. Therefore it was a mistake for Tom Ross, an officer of TL&I with no official capacity in FLCA, to sign the employment agreement with Wells rather than have an FLCA officer sign it. But it left no question about who was in actual control.[41]

Treadwell was out as president and trustee, but he would continue to be around to meddle in FLCA affairs and frustrate Norton Wells.

CHAPTER 5

Billy Takes the Cure

DURING HIS TENURE AT Forest Lawn, one of J. B. Treadwell's continual frustrations was Billy Blain's habitual drunkenness. After Treadwell's departure, it seemed there was hope for Billy after all. Unfortunately, that hope did not come to fruition.

A Possible Replacement

By June 1910, Wells, like Treadwell before him, had reached the end of his patience with Billy Blain. At a meeting of the Forest Lawn trustees, Wells announced that Blain needed to be replaced because he "has been sick for some time past, and is therefore unable to attend to the duties necessary for the upkeep of the cemetery in its usual beautiful condition." The minutes tactfully avoided mention of Billy's drinking. The trustees authorized Wells to "use his own judgement in filling the vacancy caused by Mr. Blain's absence." Only Charles Morgan voted against giving Forest Lawn's president that authority.[1]

The day after the trustees meeting, Wells wrote Pop Ross to tell him that Blain had been on a "bender," so the board of trustees had authorized hiring a new superintendent: Wilton E. Carre, formerly of Cypress Lawn. Wells also told Mrs. Blain of Carre's employment, but said nothing to Billy, since "he was in no condition."[2]

A few days later, Wells reported to Tom that he had talked with Blain. He said Blain had agreed that "if I would not discharge him he would take the cure. So I agreed to give him another chance if he would do it." In the interim, Wells placed Carre in charge at the cemetery, with an understanding that he might be there only two weeks or less.[3]

Farewell to Billy

On July 7, 1910, just over a week after Blain agreed to undergo treatment, Wells sent this telegram:

> BLAIN DIED LAST NIGHT AFTER HAVING
> APPENDIX REMOVED[4]

He followed the telegram with a letter giving a more detailed explanation of what had happened. After a drinking spree, Blain had agreed to take the "liquor cure" prescribed by Dr. Thorpe. The doctor had determined that Billy was suffering from a nervous condition that made him crave alcohol. The cure involved three operations: the first to remove his appendix, the second to circumcise him, and the third to remove hemorrhoids.

The first operation was done on Friday, July 1. Blain's condition began to deteriorate the following Tuesday. Dr. Thorpe determined that his bowels and kidneys were refusing to work and he had developed "uritic" poisoning. Blain died at 9:30 p.m. on July 6.

Wells believed that after his last drinking spree, Blain had not been in any condition for surgery. When Blain entered the hospital, the doctor had assured his wife, Eva, that it was a small matter and her husband would be out in a week. Wells added that the doctor was right; Blain was out in a week, "out in the undertaking parlors."[5]

Tom Ross sent a wire to Wells requesting that he send flowers to Blain's funeral service. Wells reported that he had sent a wreath of sweet peas on behalf of TL&I and a harp of roses on behalf of Forest Lawn. Wells also sent Blain's obituary to the newspaper.

Blain:-At Clara Barton Hospital, from operation; William J., beloved husband of Eva M., and father of Merrill W. Blain. Born in Marshal, Mich., aged 40 years, for the past four years Superintendent of Forest Lawn Cemetery. Services 2 P.M. July 8th, Presbyterian Church, Tropico; Masonic Rites performed, 2:30 P.M., at the Forest Lawn Cemetery Vaults. Friends invited.[6]

Blain's funeral was a large church service followed by rites at Forest Lawn's receiving vault, of which Blain had supervised construction. Eva Blain was pleased with the way Forest Lawn assisted at the cemetery by putting a tent in front of the receiving vault and decorating the interior with ferns. Wells reported that there were "lots of flowers some of which [Mrs. Blain] is going to ship East with the remains."[7]

Mrs. Blain's Requests

Blain's parents wished for his body to be shipped to Detroit for burial in a family plot. They sent the widow money for the transportation of the body, but left it for her to pay for train tickets for herself and her son. Although Blain had left no money, he had a $70,000 life insurance policy. Since it would take at least a month to receive the insurance proceeds, Mrs. Blain asked for an advance on what was due her husband. Wells had not been involved in Forest Lawn's early years but understood that Billy had agreed to take his back salary in the form of stock in TL&I. So he asked Pop Ross for confirmation.[8]

Pop Ross told Wells that Blain's account "stands that what has been credited to him is as a loan same as Mr Treadwell's or Toms [sic] or the Tropico Co and when there is any money on hand to pay anyone after the cemetery is self-supporting then it is to be divided pro rata. This you will see is the only way as otherwise it would be favoring one at the injury of the others." Pop also explained that although there had been discussion of Blain taking TL&I stock for the amount due him, that had not been done, since they "were afraid to do so as he might dump it on the market and hurt the stock of the other shareholders."[9]

Mrs. Blain again asked Wells for money—this time for $100 "on account" as soon as possible, because she wished to return to California. Once again, Wells would not act without confirmation and asked Pop for directions. Pop reiterated that any money to Blain's "credit in the Cemetery Ass'n is in the form of a loan under the conditions agreed to in his own motion" (at a board meeting). He did say Wells could send $25, since only $50 of Blain's last month's salary had previously been sent to his widow.[10]

Finally, Wells wrote Mrs. Blain explaining that he could not give her money because any pay due before November 1909 was treated as a loan to FLCA, just as were funds advanced by Treadwell and Tom Ross. Wells told her that things were so tight that Tom Ross had needed to lend an additional $750 to FLCA the prior month so that bills could be paid. Following Pop's direction, he sent Mrs. Blain a bank draft for $25.[11]

Wells's letter to Mrs. Blain may have crossed in the mail with another letter from her requesting that he wire her $100, since "there is some delay in insurance policy's [sic] [and] I am pressed for funds." Pop told Wells not to be concerned with her second request, since she should have received Wells's letter by then and would understand why Wells could not send more money.[12]

Court Petition

In September 1910, Eva M. Blain filed a petition for letters of administration for the estate of her husband. The estate's principal assets consisted of 17,500 shares of TL&I, a lot in Detroit, Michigan, and an amount due from Forest Lawn for services of $3,553.35, as well as promissory notes for roughly $1,000. No mention was made of the insurance policy.[13]

Treadwell wrote Pop warning that Mrs. Blain would likely try to collect the balance due on Billy's salary. He noted that Billy had not actually accepted a note for the money, although he had agreed to do so. Due to his lack of empathy and his animosity toward Billy, Treadwell advised that TL&I or Tom Ross demand a pledge of all personal property and contracts due as security for any money advances to Mrs. Blain in the future. Treadwell thought this would keep Mrs. Blain from tying up the cemetery and would force her to wait and take a pro rata distribution along with himself and Tom Ross. After suggesting that Wells call a meeting of the trustees to pass a resolution requiring that action, Treadwell closed with, "You don't want to leave anything undone to protect yourselves." Of course, it is likely that Treadwell was trying to protect his own interests rather than the interests of the others.[14]

Tom C. Thornton, the attorney representing Mrs. Blain, asked Wells to come to his office to discuss the amounts due Blain at the time of his death. Apparently Thornton had no qualms about having both Eva Blain and TL&I as clients, though it would seem to be a conflict of interest. One of the issues Thornton wanted to discuss with Wells was the unpaid salary due Blain. According to Thornton, Mrs. Blain had heard there might be someone who did not want her to receive the money because of Billy's drunkenness. Thornton reasoned that the company had accepted Billy's services, so it should make no difference whether he drank or not. Wells tried to deflect the issues to Pop Ross, since TL&I contended that some of the salary due Blain should be treated as a loan to TL&I.[15]

Despite wanting to be left out of the Blain matter, a few weeks later Wells visited attorney Tom Thornton. He was accompanied by Treadwell, who had more firsthand knowledge of the origins of TL&I's position. Although Wells and Treadwell tried to convince the attorney that immediate payment was just not possible, Thornton pressed for payment, since he believed he could obtain a judgment to accomplish everything.[16]

In addition to unpaid salary, there was the issue of TL&I stock. Billy had been promised shares in TL&I that were held in an informal trust for all the original men: Tom & Pop Ross, Treadwell, and Blain. The shares in the pool of stock had not been issued to the individuals to make sure no one could sell them to the detriment of the others. The Rosses did not want to issue Billy's shares to Mrs. Blain out of fear that she would sell them at a low value that would decrease the value of their own shares.

Resolution

The conflict continued until 1914, when Thornton prodded Norton Wells to issue the shares held for Billy and deliver them to Mrs. Blain. He explained that he was writing Wells rather than TL&I because he believed that Wells could be more persuasive with Tom Ross. According to Thornton, Mrs. Blain had received various promises regarding when the stock would be delivered to her, but none of these promises had been kept.[17]

Thornton told Wells that Eva Blain did not intend to sell the stock or even to let anyone know that she had it. Thornton recognized Tom Ross's fear that if Mrs. Blain sold shares, that sale might cause Treadwell or other shareholders to try to sell their shares. Because Mrs. Blain had made up her mind that she must have the shares, Thornton counseled Wells that it would be better to give in gracefully than have a fight.[18]

Eventually, Eva Blain was able to get the money due her husband, and TL&I issued the shares due Billy in her name.

CHAPTER 6

ᏘTTEMPTED ᏟOUP

AFTER COMING TO FOREST Lawn in June 1909, Charles
O. Morgan did not make many waves, other than disagreements
about accounting methods and unpaid bills. However, by the end
of 1910 he was laying plans for a corporate ambush.

TL&I Appoints Morgan

At their February 1910 meeting, the TL&I board of directors elected
Charles Morgan, the FLCA secretary, to serve as an assistant secretary-treasurer of TL&I. Morgan was surprised to learn this. Pop
explained to him that the appointment was made so there would
be an officer of TL&I in Los Angeles to protect TL&I's interest in
money received by the cemetery. This was a precautionary move on
the part of the Rosses. Pop told Morgan, "While it is to be hoped
that there will be no occasion for such action being taken yet it was
considered as desirable to be ready beforehand."[1]

Pop Ross explained that in exchange for providing this oversight,
Morgan would receive 250 shares of TL&I stock on July 1, 1910, and
the same amount on July 1 of the following year. The Rosses must
have believed that someone at Forest Lawn might take an action to
their detriment. Perhaps they were thinking of the experience with

J. J. Lockwood, the former FLCA secretary who had paid the bills with money that should have gone into the perpetual care fund. Or they may have been worried that Treadwell was somewhat unpredictable, or were just being cautious because Wells was new as president. Whatever the Rosses' motivation, they obviously believed that having an officer of TL&I in Los Angeles to represent their interests was a good idea. It was also an indication of faith in Morgan—a faith that would soon prove to be unwarranted.[2]

Morgan Wants More

By December 1910, Charles Morgan did not think he was making enough money. Although he had continued to conduct his law practice while serving as secretary of FLCA, Morgan believed his law practice had dropped off because he was now practicing in a cemetery office—even though it was FLCA's downtown Los Angeles office, not the one on the cemetery grounds. Morgan hoped that he could meet with Pop or Tom before Christmas to discuss his salary, but Pop said that would not be possible.[3]

Morgan then sent Tom Ross a letter requesting that he receive more pay. Wells was not surprised—he had expected Morgan to ask for more money, though the matter had only been hinted about. Wells did not believe the association could afford to pay more. He would be sorry to lose Morgan, as he appeared to be competent, but knew he could be replaced. Wells proposed to Tom Ross that Morgan be kept on as a trustee and as secretary for a nominal consideration. They would then "get a girl for $60.00 to do the bookkeeping." He believed that for ten dollars a month, Morgan "would remain on the board, sign the checks once a month and advise on matters of interest to the association for a time."[4]

Tom thought the matter should be deferred until it could be handled in a face-to-face meeting. He put the matter in Pop's hands, since Pop was planning to come to Los Angeles for the annual meeting of cemetery lot owners in January. Pop told Morgan they could discuss the matter then. Pop had no idea of the fireworks that would result from that annual meeting.[5]

Making His Move

The year 1911 started without a hint of anything unusual in the works for Forest Lawn. Morgan sent TL&I his usual letter with financial reports for December, noting that FLCA had lost a little more than $13,000 in 1910 compared to $9,000 in 1909. In 2017 dollars, the 1910 loss was the equivalent today of about $339,000. The financial situation was not improving.[6]

Morgan was likely pleased to find out that Pop Ross was expected to be in Los Angeles by Tuesday, January 10, the day before the annual meeting of Forest Lawn lot owners. Morgan expected there would be time before the meeting to discuss his request for an increase in pay.[7]

For reasons unknown, Pop Ross, Norton Wells, and trustee George Walker were not in attendance at the lot owners meeting. Only John Black, George H. Heath, Charles O. Morgan, and Hugh S. Wallace were physically present, with forty-six other lot owners present by proxy. The proxies were all in favor of Morgan, allowing him to vote on behalf of those lot owners.[8] Morgan had solicited the proxies so he could control what was to happen at the meeting even if Ross and Wells were there.

The meeting was called to order at 11:15 a.m. The main order of business was the election of three trustees to fill the vacancies of John Llewellyn, J. Schoder, and W. J. Blain, whose terms had expired. John Black, George Heath, and Hugh Wallace were nominated. Each received fifty votes and was duly elected.[9] The new trustees were loyal to Morgan rather than the Rosses, so Morgan had effectively seized control of FLCA by electing his own board members.

Before the lot owners meeting adjourned, Morgan proposed that the Forest Lawn Cemetery Association's bylaws be amended to provide that if the trustees designated someone other than the president to be general manager, that person would have the "power and authority" to take any action the president could take. The motion passed.[10]

After the short lot owners meeting, the organization meeting of the board of trustees convened at 11:30 a.m., with Wells and Walker still absent. As at the lot owners meeting, Wallace and Morgan were chosen as chairman and secretary of the meeting, respectively.

When it came to electing officers, new trustee Black was nominated to be president, but he declined. Then Wallace was nominated and unanimously elected president. Charles Morgan was re-elected as secretary and treasurer. John Black was then elected vice president. As a reward for being part of the overthrow, Wallace was to receive a "nominal salary of $5.00 per month, for his services as President." Previously, none of the trustees had received a monthly stipend, only a small fee for meeting attendance. Morgan would receive $150.00 per month for his services. That was the same amount Wells had received as president and a significant increase from the $100 per month Morgan had been receiving.[11]

Morgan apparently wanted more power in addition to more money. A motion was introduced, no doubt at his behest, to appoint him as general manager. The motion explicitly provided that the general manager would have full authority over the superintendent and all other employees, including hiring and firing. The motion passed.[12]

In addition, at Morgan's request, a resolution was passed to change the long-standing policy that checks had to be signed by both the president and the corporate secretary. Morgan proposed that checks issued in the "usual course of business" would require only the signature of the secretary.[13] The two-signature requirement would be called an "internal control" today, a procedure designed to protect against any individual misusing company funds.

The meeting adjourned with Morgan undoubtedly feeling that he had accomplished a takeover of the management of Forest Lawn. On the same day, Morgan sent Mike Glora, now the acting superintendent, a letter listing the new officers. The letter said that Morgan was now "General Manager, with full powers" and that Glora was "most respectfully requested to govern himself accordingly."[14]

Several days later, Morgan sent TL&I a copy of the minutes of the two meetings, noting, "I trust you will find them in perfect shape, even if the actions recorded therein may not at this time meet your hearty approval. I feel confident that you will be gratified by the final outcome in the matter." Not long after that, Morgan went so far as to write the Los Angeles Chamber of Commerce to cancel Forest Lawn's membership.[15]

Reversing the Coup

Pop Ross, Norton Wells, and Tom Ross were irate with what had transpired at the two meetings. Immediately after the revelation of what Morgan had done, things were set in motion to reverse the attempted coup.

Walker and Wells called for another meeting of the trustees at 11:00 a.m. on January 23. Walker, Wells, Morgan, and Heath attended this meeting. Trustees Black and Wallace were absent. Morgan and Louis Peters were elected as temporary chairman and secretary of the meeting.

The meeting quickly undid many of the actions of the prior meeting. John Black, George Heath, Charles O. Morgan, George W. Walker, and Hugh S. Wallace all resigned as trustees and officers. The resulting openings for trustees were filled by John Llewellyn, Fred V. Owen, Louis H. Peters, William Watson, and Charles O. Winters. The new officers elected were Norton Wells, president and general manager; John Llewellyn, vice president; and Louis Peters, secretary and treasurer.[16]

The new trustees then proceeded to rescind motions passed at the January 11 meeting regarding payments to Wallace and Morgan. They also passed a resolution setting Wells's salary at the same $150 per month level it had been the prior year. Wells was authorized to set the salary for the secretary. After George Heath's resignation as trustee was read, the president was authorized to dispense with the service of Heath as salesman at his discretion.[17]

The day after the trustees meeting, Wells, continuing to undo Morgan's actions, sent a letter to the bank with a new bank signature resolution to replace Morgan's single-signature resolution. The day after that, Wells wrote the Los Angeles Chamber of Commerce that FLCA wanted to remain a member and was in full support of the chamber.[18]

A few days later, Pop Ross wrote Morgan with his reaction to the whole episode.

> I had expected to see you this afternoon as agreed upon but as you did not come I am constrained to write.
>
> HOW HAS THE MIGHTY ONE FALLEN!!!! Seems to be the thought which comes to me. To think of the absolute confidence and trust which I placed in you and which I transferred to those whom you were representing, and of my having on more than one occasion declared the same to you so that you might feel inwardly at least that you and your character and services are appreciated.
>
> Again to think how you and others secretly connived to take advantage of this misplaced confidence and trust to write us . . . requesting us to advance your salary, and calling that communication a "confidential" one, while you had already on the 20th sent out your request for proxies, which were to be used and which you did use improperly and under false pretenses to the injury of the Association. . . .
>
> It is indeed difficult to believe you capable of such treachery and betrayal of us as you did and also to believe you capable of making such motions as you did and still have any faith in you. . . .
>
> For a man of your age, with your reputed character and qualifications, to do these things and to remember that you at one time had a high standing as a Judge of the bench in

this City, once more call up the thought, "HOW HAS THE MIGHTY ONE FALLEN".

Your former friend

Thomas Ross[19]

Heath's Overpayments

Although Charles Morgan and co-conspirator George Heath were now gone from Forest Lawn, they were not yet a part of history. Heath and Wells had a conversation concerning amounts overpaid to Heath.

First, there was an issue regarding a 10 percent commission paid on a "supposed sale to M. Brock" for $200. Believing that Heath had not made the sale and was not entitled to a commission on it, Wells concluded that Heath had been overpaid by $52.50 for January. In addition to the overpayment, Wells discovered that Heath had accepted payment for use of the Forest Lawn automobile during the primary and general elections the prior fall, totaling an additional $45.00. In laying this out to Heath, Peters, the new secretary and treasurer, also noted that Wells had received "reports there are others of a similar nature." Peters concluded that as a matter of honor, Heath should turn over to Forest Lawn whatever he had been paid.[20]

Later, Wells determined that Heath had been overpaid by an additional twenty dollars and requested return of the additional amount. Heath, in turn, hired Charles Morgan to represent him in 1912. Wells duly responded to Morgan's request for details of the 1910 overpayment.

To no one's surprise, Heath was not forthcoming with repayment. Instead, he sent a bill to FLCA for overtime that he had allegedly worked while employed at Forest Lawn. Wells forwarded the bill to Morgan, commenting, "It seems strange that he should wait until called upon to return this amount which was over-paid to him, before presenting such a claim, especially since it is over a year since he performed the services."[21] Wells noted that Heath, a medical doctor, did not give any credit to Forest Lawn for the time Heath had spent treating patients or doing personal business while being paid as a full-time Forest Lawn employee. Additionally, Heath had collected money from other people for the use of Forest Lawn's auto. Eventually, however, Wells concluded it would be pointless to try to collect anything from Heath.[22]

CHAPTER 7

The Partition Suit

When J. B. Treadwell purchased the land that would become Forest Lawn Cemetery from Susan Glassell Mitchell in 1905, he encountered an issue with the property rights of her two daughters. Believing the issue had been settled, Treadwell went ahead and purchased the land. However, the property rights of Susan's granddaughter, Lucile Bedford, would come back to haunt Forest Lawn, leading to a series of lawsuits that plagued TL&I for more than two years.

Background

The land that Susan Mitchell sold to Treadwell had been given to her by her father, Andrew Glassell. The terms of this gift specified that the land would be handed down through the generations, a "life estate" in legal terms. When Susan passed away, her two adult daughters—Lucie Lambourn and Eileen Bedford—would each be entitled to one-half interest in the property. In turn, their rights would eventually be inherited by any children each had, and so on.

At the time he purchased the land, Treadwell believed that both daughters had deeded their property rights to their mother based on advice from Leslie Brand, senior officer of the Title Guarantee

87

& Trust. Thus he thought that Susan Mitchell was free to sell the property to him. What Treadwell did not know at the time was that Eileen Bedford had a daughter, and she had property rights as well. But that discovery would not come until later.[1]

As time passed, other relevant events transpired, unnoticed by anyone at Forest Lawn. In April 1907, Eileen Bedford, suffering from great stress after her divorce, committed suicide. She left behind her daughter, Lucile Richmond Bedford, now three years old.[2] After Eileen's death, Susan Mitchell revised her own will, adding several provisions regarding Lucile's care.

Just a few months later, on December 31, 1907, Susan Mitchell passed away. According to the terms of Susan's will, her granddaughter Lucile was entitled to one-half interest in the land that Treadwell had purchased.[3] Susan's surviving daughter, Lucie Lambourn, was appointed executrix of her estate. Furthermore, after a custody battle with Eileen's ex-husband, Lucie Lambourn became Lucile Bedford's legal guardian in August 1908.[4]

As part of her responsibility as executrix, Lucie Lambourn duly published a notice in the *Los Angeles Daily Journal* on January 25, 1909, calling for any creditors to file their claims with Susan Mitchell's estate. On April 8, 1910—more than a year after the notice to creditors had been published—Treadwell learned of the notice and immediately telegraphed Pop Ross, urging him to come to Los Angeles as soon as possible.[5] Quite likely, Treadwell had found out that a suit challenging TL&I's title was about to be filed. He must have been concerned that anything that challenged TL&I's holdings would pull him into the dispute.

Suits and Countersuits

The next day—April 9, 1910—the Los Angeles Trust & Savings Bank, acting as guardian of Lucile Bedford, filed suit on her behalf (referred to hereafter as the partition suit). The bank asked for a court order declaring Lucile Bedford, now six years old, to be the owner of an undivided one-half interest in the 151 acres sold to J. B.

Treadwell by Susan Glassell Mitchell. The bank believed the deed from Eileen Bedford to her mother, Susan Mitchell, had no effect, since Eileen could not sign away the property rights of her child. An undivided one-half interest means that each co-owner (TL&I and Lucile Bedford) has an unrestricted claim to one-half of the entire property, but neither has exclusive claim to any specific part of the property. If the claim were successful, TL&I (and FLCA) would not have a clear title to any of the property for development as a cemetery without the agreement of the other one-half undivided interest owner, Lucile Bedford. If Bedford agreed to development, she would be entitled to one-half of any proceeds from the development of the property, be it cemetery or some other use.

The suit shocked the Rosses. They knew that Susan Mitchell had given Treadwell a warranty deed, which offered protection against the claims of all persons. Furthermore, Treadwell claimed that he hadn't known of the existence of the granddaughter when he bought the land.

Whether or not that claim was true, Treadwell must have realized that the lawsuit spelled trouble not only for TL&I, but for himself. It was unlikely that the bank would file a frivolous lawsuit. If the bank won the suit, TL&I would lose a substantial portion of land. In addition, the suit would likely expose Treadwell's deception: that after he originally purchased the land, he secretly kept some of it for himself and sold the rest to TL&I for a higher price than he had paid for it. Once that information became known, Treadwell would be vulnerable to legal action brought by TL&I—not only for the land he had kept, but for any land lost to Lucile Bedford.[6]

Caught off guard by the partition suit, the Rosses wasted no time in hiring San Francisco attorney C. C. Boynton—who was also Treadwell's son-in-law—to represent them. On April 14, Boynton filed a petition to initiate a lawsuit against Lucie Lambourn as executrix of the Mitchell estate (TL&I–Executrix suit). The petition requested a court order for specific performance: require the estate to buy Lucile Bedford's interest and then transfer that interest to TL&I.[7]

Several weeks after TL&I's suit against Lucie Lambourn, Treadwell also filed a suit against her as executrix (JB–Executrix suit). He asked the court to direct Lucie Lambourn to convey all rights in the property sold to him, except for the property he had sold to TL&I. Just as TL&I had done, Treadwell hired C. C. Boynton to represent him. By accepting Treadwell as a client, Boynton ignored the potential for a conflict of interest should TL&I decide to take legal action against Treadwell for selling it property with a defective title.[8]

Upon learning of the partition suit, John Llewellyn asked whether "there was any truth in the report that our land title was being attached." Norton Wells made a personal visit to Llewellyn to explain the matter of the "flaw in title." Pop Ross was pleased that Wells had made the visit, realizing that the explanation "was much better to come from you [Wells] or us than thro' any other source." Pop was "anxious to have this settled up as soon as possible as others may get wind of it and cause anxiety." Pop further tried to reassure Wells: "Regarding buying lots in the Cemetery there is no hesitation in the matter as they are claiming only an interest, not all of the property, so do not let that matter affect you in the least."[9]

Neither the TL&I–Executrix suit nor the J.B.–Executrix suit found any traction with the probate court. In August 1910, both suits against the executrix were dismissed without prejudice—meaning that either party was free to file a new action under a different legal theory. The court found that a timely claim should have been filed with Mitchell's estate in response to the notice to creditors, which none of the interested parties (TL&I, Treadwell, and FLCA) had done.[10] Not filing a claim within the allowed time frame made the claim invalid.

On October 21, 1910, the Los Angeles County branch of the Superior Court of California approved the distribution of Susan Mitchell's estate. However, that did not resolve the issue of land ownership central to the partition suit.[11]

J. B. Treadwell refiled his suit against Lucie Lambourn as executrix on November 1, 1910. This time his suit was a call for specific performance, like the unsuccessful suit TL&I had filed in April: the estate should buy Lucile Bedford's interest in the land Treadwell had not sold to TL&I and transfer that interest to Treadwell. This suit was also unsuccessful.

Boynton's strategy was to immediately file a suit against the child, Lucile Bedford. Boynton expected to lose this suit, which would result in giving up half the land. That loss would enable another suit against Lucie Lambourn, as executrix, for the value of the lost land: $28,500 (half of what Treadwell paid for it). It would also provide grounds for a suit against the Title Guarantee & Trust Company for the same amount. However, the title company took the position that its liability ended two years after giving the guarantee, blocking any recovery from it.[12]

Pop Ross believed that if TL&I lost half the land it had purchased from Treadwell, the company had a legal claim against Treadwell for half of the $60,000 it had paid him. According to Pop, it had been a "dubious transaction," and he told Wells that Treadwell should be concerned with the details of his duplicity coming to light. Pop thought it was time to hire an attorney in Los Angeles to represent TL&I's interests, but one who was not too antagonistic toward Treadwell, since they had a common interest in resolving the land title issue. He was concerned that things were progressing slowly, commenting that "delays are always bad and sometimes dangerous."[13]

Thornton Joins the Legal Team

At their March 1911 meeting, the directors of TL&I officially ratified employing Los Angeles attorney Tom C. Thornton& to deal with the land issue. Their intent was to eventually have him replace Boynton.[14]

With Thornton formally retained to represent only TL&I, his first action was to examine the various deeds and other documents related to the several transfers of land. He had no doubt Treadwell would lose his suit against Susan Mitchell's estate, but until then TL&I could not bring its own action against Treadwell.[15]

The tension between Treadwell and the others was growing, and Tom Ross had a "fall with Treadwell." When Wells shared this with Thornton, he just smiled at the report.[16]

Trying to keep a spirit of common interest, Pop Ross told Boynton that he wanted the two attorneys to work in harmony. Boynton agreed to send Thornton his notes, as well as the brief that was almost finished. The Rosses' interest in settling the case was both practical and financial because, as Pop told Thornton, settling would "enable us to do some business[,] as at present we cannot sell any shares and consequently there is no income."[17]

Because of the potential for litigation between Treadwell and either TL&I or FLCA, Norton Wells asked Thornton how to interact with Treadwell regarding the various suits. Thornton advised that the two men should not discuss the matter, since any conversation might prejudice TL&I's demurrer in the partition suit that was to be heard the following week.* Saying there was a "strong equity case for both sides," Thornton advised that if Boynton's demurrer was successful, then all would be good, since the partition suit would be dismissed. On the other hand, if the court rejected the demurrer, the partition suit would proceed to trial. However, TL&I would still have the option of filing a lawsuit against Treadwell for selling it property with an undisclosed encumbrance.[18]

Thornton thought it foolish that Treadwell had not tried to settle the partition suit for about $5,000 to protect himself, since Treadwell was liable for "a good sum of money." Although Thornton was optimistic about recovering what TL&I had paid for any land lost, he did not think TL&I would be able to recover the excess paid for the

---

* A demurrer is the legal equivalent of "so what?" It is an objection claiming that even if an allegation is true, there is no basis for a lawsuit.

land Treadwell had kept for himself. Even with that limitation, he believed that Treadwell should at least pay all the attorneys' fees.[19]

At the suggestion of Boynton, Treadwell visited Thornton to ask if Thornton could represent TL&I and Treadwell at the same time, but he "was given a stand off reception." After learning of this meeting from Thornton, Wells told Tom Ross that "after going over the case in a general way, one point at a time, the question was asked of our old friend [Treadwell] if he had ever considered his responsibility to the company, and it was like a cold bath, he, in a modulated voice, said he had, and was satisfied with his position." Thornton and Treadwell apparently agreed that the case needed to be settled. But in a veiled reference to Treadwell, Wells also said he believed that "someone is walking around on a hot iron this morning, and I do not need to tell you who it is."[20]

Several days later, when Treadwell arrived in San Francisco—by boat, since his railroad pass had expired—he had another hostile meeting with Pop Ross. Treadwell told Pop that Thornton had threatened him with a lawsuit, but after talking with Boynton, Treadwell thought he had nothing to fear, because Thornton did not know California law. Treadwell had told his daughter Lillian (who was also Tom Ross's wife) that if Oscar Souden—the banker who held the mortgage on the cemetery property TL&I had purchased from Treadwell—knew the way Treadwell was being annoyed, he would probably foreclose the mortgage. When Lillian told Treadwell that the Rosses believed the mortgage was actually Treadwell's, "he immediately shut up and got red in the face."[21]

Pop Ross was concerned that Boynton seemed anxious to withdraw from the matter. But he thought Treadwell would find it difficult to find other legal representation, since "no one will handle his work[,] as he is too well known and very stingy in paying attorney fees."[22]

Thornton was also concerned that Treadwell and Boynton might be engaged in a "rather foxy dodge" to force Thornton to go to trial without getting the information he needed. Thornton also seemed to be wary of a potential conflict Boynton might have as the attorney of record, but did not want to force the issue by a substitution of attorneys at the last minute, if that could be avoided.[23]

Boynton did indeed want to accomplish the substitution of attorneys. He told Pop Ross that upon execution of the substitution, he would send the papers in the case to Thornton as he had previously agreed to do. Although Boynton told Pop that he'd sent a letter requesting the substitution, Pop had not received it and, with a bit of skepticism, suggested he "would not be surprised if [Boynton] omitted to mail it."[24]

Several weeks later, Boynton gave Pop Ross a substitution of counsel letter in the suit against Lucile Bedford. When asked why it did not also include the TL&I–Executrix suit, Boynton explained there would be a substitution on each case, but did not explain why both were not presented at the same time. Forwarding the unsigned document to Thornton, Pop also reported that when the cases were due to go to court, Boynton was willing to come to Los Angeles to review them with Thornton, since, according to Boynton, the cases were identical.[25]

Deed Discovery

While investigating the partition case, Thornton made a "rather unsatisfactory discovery." When Treadwell had bought property from Susan Mitchell, he had received a warranty deed, but when he sold a portion of the property to TL&I, he gave them a grant deed. A warranty deed would have required Treadwell to defend title on the property against all claims. A grant deed guaranteed only that the property had not been sold to anyone else and did not have any liens or restrictions that had not been disclosed. Thornton's assessment was that the weaker grant deed raised a "severe question about [Treadwell's] liability." Sharing his opinion of Treadwell, Wells wrote Pop Ross, "You will see by this fact that he schemed from the beginning. The old rascal."[26]

Although the original warranty deed was probably binding on the Glassell estate at the time it was given, the deed to TL&I did not use the warranty language. As a result, it would be almost impossible to get a judgment requiring the estate to honor the old, original warranty deed provisions.[27]

Pursuing Settlements

Susan Glassell Mitchell's brother, Hugh Glassell, had been involved in negotiations with Treadwell for the purchase of land from Mitchell. As the senior member of the Glassell clan, Hugh was believed to be able to influence acceptance of any settlement proposal. For this reason, Thornton met with Hugh Glassell to tell him that a settlement offer would be forthcoming. Thornton was thinking that something in the range of five or six thousand dollars should settle the case, but admitted that he did not know if that figure would be acceptable. Although he thought none of the other related cases should go to trial, he was skeptical of the possibility of a settlement in the partition suit. However, Wells opined to Pop Ross that if Treadwell and Glassell were ready, he couldn't "see why an amicable settlement [could not] be made in the near future."[28]

When discussing the possibility of a settlement with Thornton, Hugh Glassell stated that he would ensure that seven-year-old Lucile Bedford "would be protected, as Mrs. Lambourn had always robbed the little one." Pop Ross did not agree that aunt Lucie Lambourn had "always robbed" her niece, since Lucie "keeps her and is very fond of her which she would not do if she wanted to rob her. It simply is illwill [sic] on the part of Hugh Glassell to Mrs. Lambourn. . . . Mrs. Lambourn has stated that if she could get the case amicably settled that she would make the child her heir, showing her love for the girl."[29]

Up to this point, Treadwell and TL&I had acted as though there were some common interest in getting the land issue resolved. But with the possibility raised of an action by TL&I against Treadwell in early April 1911, things changed. After receiving a continuance from the court, Thornton learned that Boynton now intended to represent only Treadwell. It appeared to Thornton that everyone wanted to settle the case—Treadwell had even agreed to contribute toward the settlement amount—but Boynton had not made much of an effort to do so.[30]

Despite his frustrations with Treadwell and Boynton, Thornton continued to have frequent meetings with Treadwell, who at times seemed anxious to help achieve a settlement. Perhaps he thought he might have some liability from his sale to TL&I. Thornton changed his instructions to Wells, now asking him to "work with Treadwell in a harmonious manner in seeing the other attorneys" in the hope of moving settlement along.[31]

Thornton and Treadwell thought little of each other, but Thornton described the situation as "the lion and the lamb are lying down together, or at least lying." Treadwell seemed interested in helping reach a settlement, so Thornton had resolved to "treat him fairly and meet him half way and use him, to put it plainly, as far as I feel our interests will permit but not a step further."[32]

Lucie Lambourn evidently felt some moral obligation to make up for the defective title her mother had given J. B. Treadwell. To encourage settlement, she offered to give her niece, Lucile Bedford, one-half of her estate if the child—meaning the bank as trustee—would disclaim any interest in the Forest Lawn cemetery property. This offer would have required approval of the Los Angeles Trust & Savings Bank as Lucile's guardian. Thornton thought the proposal was so good that either Lucile's "friends or enemies would recommend this settlement."[33]

A month later, Thornton still thought Lucie Lambourn and her advisors were amenable to a settlement. However, the "animosity" (Thornton's word) of others stood in the way. Mrs. Lambourn had agreed to sweeten her prior offer and to deed her niece nearly $25,000 more in property than could be received from the one-half interest in the Forest Lawn property. However, she wanted to add a condition that the property would come back to her if her niece died before she was eighteen. Those representing the niece balked at the proposal, since it might precipitate something happening to Lucile Bedford.[34]

Although there was more correspondence that seemed optimistic regarding the prospects for reaching a settlement, that possibility had dimmed by the end of May. Thornton believed there was little chance of getting Judge Cyrus F. McNutt, who was hearing the case, to agree with TL&I.[35]

Even though no settlement seemed to be forthcoming, Lambourn did fulfill her earlier promise to provide for her niece. In September 1911, Treadwell sent Tom Ross a copy of a newspaper article reporting that the Superior Court had approved Lucie Lambourn's adoption of Lucile Bedford. During the proceedings, Lucie Lambourn had promised to give her new daughter a proportionate share of her grandmother's estate. Lucile Bedford had been effectively cut out of the estate because her grandmother's will left only five dollars to Lucile's mother, Eileen Bedford.[36]

Although Treadwell occasionally seemed to be trying to help, at other times he was working behind the scenes to cause trouble. He pushed Souden to request that TL&I make a principal payment on the mortgage and pressed Boynton to ask for early payment of his bill.

Treadwell also criticized Thornton, telling Pop Ross that Thornton should have waited for Treadwell's suit against Lambourn to conclude before bringing the case against Lucile Bedford. Pop, however, agreed with Thornton that they had to bring the case against Lucile Bedford so they could go on to the next move. Pop also told Thornton that he did not know whether Treadwell had actually filed suit against Lucile Bedford, the child, or was only preparing to file one. Pop was annoyed that Treadwell "shoved a few more remarks . . . to try to make us feel that he would have done better."[37]

The Foreign Corporation Argument

As 1911 drew toward its close, the attorneys on all sides continued their legal maneuvering. The Mitchell estate's attorney in the
TL&I–Executrix suit, Horace Wilson, believed he could obtain
dismissal of that suit by showing that TL&I should have known
of Susan Mitchell's death and thus could have made a timely claim
against her estate. This strategy would require Wilson to prove that
TL&I was a California corporation governed by California laws.

To counter Wilson's strategy, Thornton explained to Pop Ross that
it was vital to prove that TL&I was a foreign (out-of-state) corporation. He planned to emphasize that TL&I's corporate home was the
state or territory of Arizona, its annual shareholder meetings were
held there, and its officers were all elected there. This, he thought,
would allow him to argue that the company had not had reasonable
notice of Mitchell's death and therefore could not have made a timely
claim to the estate. Furthermore, Thornton now thought Mitchell's
warranty deed should apply to and protect TL&I.[38]

In a deposition taken in the TL&I–Executrix suit, Pop Ross testified that no business had been conducted outside of California. This
concerned Thornton, since Pop's testimony made it more difficult to
sustain the position that TL&I was a foreign corporation.[39] Pop Ross
clearly understood Thornton's concern, but defended himself by saying,
"I considered it safest to give straight answers and nothing else."[40]

Anticipating a Loss

The year 1912 began where 1911 left off, with the land litigation
foremost on everyone's mind. Thornton believed that TL&I had
lost the property even before it knew of Mitchell's death, since
the time for presenting a claim to the estate had already passed.
With that view, he thought settlement unlikely. Nevertheless, he
approached one of Lucie Lambourn's attorneys, Oscar Mueller, to
discuss the possibility of a private settlement of the TL&I–Executrix
suit. Mueller promised to discuss this with Lambourn and attorney
Horace Wilson. As expected, no settlement was made.[41]

Thornton was similarly pessimistic about the prospect of suing the Title Guarantee & Trust Company under the theory that its negligence caused TL&I's loss. The title company would argue that even if it had been negligent, the loss was TL&I's fault for not filing an estate claim during the required period.

Pop Ross was disturbed with Thornton's candid assessment of the litigation and thought Thornton did "not feel very sanguine of a favorable result." Thornton recommended, and Pop Ross fully supported, bringing on additional counsel. Pop wrote Los Angeles lawyer Max Loewenthal, encouraging him to join the fray because Loewenthal had "made a very exhaustive investigation of the whole matter" and had advanced an additional theory regarding the case.[42] It turned out that Loewenthal did not have a new theory, but he became affiliated with the case nonetheless.[43]

In anticipation of losing the partition suit and having the land divided, Wells discussed the possible outcome with Loewenthal. Wells was told it was likely that TL&I would receive the northern part of the land in a partition judgment, since FLCA had already made improvements on it. Lambourn's attorneys did not want to cause damage by disrupting the cemetery, so they agreed with Norton Wells to allow FLCA and TL&I to continue to issue deeds for burial rights as lots were sold. They could easily agree to this because the selling activity was entirely on the northern part of the property. Any split of the property could be accomplished without being concerned about burials or previous sales of cemetery lots..[44]

Court Ruling

As expected, the Los Angeles Superior Court ruled against TL&I in the partition suit in January 1912. Although TL&I's lawyers asked for reconsideration of the decision, that was denied. For the record, the complaint, which had been filed on behalf of Lucile Bedford, was amended to include Lucie Lambourn as executrix.

With half the cemetery property at stake, the Rosses believed the ruling should be appealed, even if it was a long shot. When

Loewenthal, Thornton, and Wells met, they agreed that Loewenthal should seek a thirty-day extension for an appeal while Thornton and Tobias Archer, a Los Angeles attorney, worked on the appeal itself. Wells pointed out to Pop Ross that it would take a considerable sum of money to continue the lawsuits, since Loewenthal believed that the appropriate fee to his firm, Dennis & Loewenthal, should be equal to those paid Thornton and Archer.[45]

The negative judgment in the partition suit determined only that Lucile Bedford was the owner of an undivided one-half interest in the property sold to Treadwell. northeast of the railroad line. The actual division of the property still needed to be agreed on by all parties and approved by the court.[46]

Dividing the Property

Near the end of September 1912, agreement was reached on how the property would be divided and an interlocutory decree was entered.* Oscar Souden, the banker who held the mortgage, needed to approve the division because the mortgage covered the entire property. Wells believed Souden would have no objection, since the banker's attorneys were satisfied with the referee chosen to propose the division line. However, Souden did not like the proposed land division. Wells asked him what the problem was, "and in his usual way, he evaded my direct questions, saying everything would be alright and said that if so and so was so and so, it might be so and so, and that he wanted to do everything he could for us, and would so instruct his attorneys, etc. etc." That was all Wells could draw out of him.[47]

Souden finally came around and agreed to the division line and how his mortgage would be treated. This cleared the way for the final decree to be issued.[48]

---

* An interlocutory decree is a court judgment which is temporary and not intended to be final until either a) other matters come before the judge, or b) there is a specified passage of time to determine if the judgment is "working" and should become final.

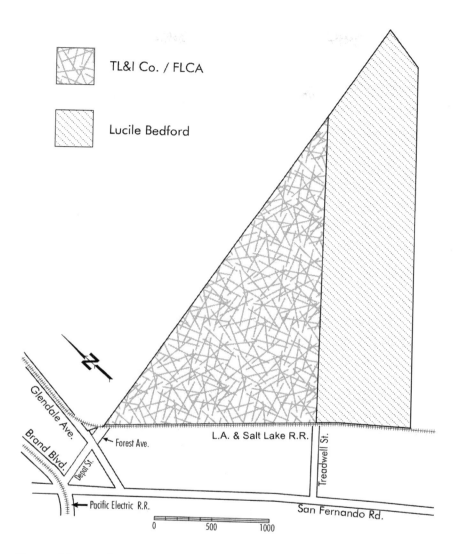

Figure 21. Land Partition Map

With the litigation lost, the land was divided between TL&I and Lucile R. Bedford.

The property was partitioned by a final decree signed by Judge Walter Bordwell on October 28, 1912. TL&I and Lucile R. Bedford each received one-half of the property TL&I had acquired from Treadwell. The two loans to TL&I—the mortgage from Oscar Souden and the loan from FLCA's perpetual care fund—were now secured by one-half of the real estate that had previously been security for the loans.[49]

TL&I Files Appeal

Tom Thornton, Tobias Archer, and Max Loewenthal duly filed an appeal with the Second Appellate Court of California. After deliberation, the appellate court was unable to reach a decision. As a result, the appeal by TL&I was kicked up to the California Supreme Court.

The loss of acreage from the land partition suit was a blow to all involved. Although many had believed that Lucile Bedford's aunt, Lucie Lambourn, would have been willing to settle before the judgment, the trust company had refused to agree to that. However, with the judgment rendered, there were now negotiations to sell the partitioned property back to TL&I. Although Wells received proposed terms for a purchase, no agreement was reached because the appeal of the partition suit was still pending.[50]

When summoned to Loewenthal's office in early May 1915, Wells found that the California Supreme Court had decided en banc (all justices present) against Forest Lawn and TL&I in the appeal of the partition suit. Having all the judges hear the case, rather than a panel of judges selected from them, showed that this case dealt with significant, potentially precedent-setting issues. Disappointed with the news, Pop Ross lamented, "We have not had justice but only LAW, we will await quietly and hopefully for equity before giving up." Pop cautioned Wells to "not mention it to any one, not even to Eaton, as it does not do any good and lets them know inside matters of no interest to them."[51] (By that time, as discussed in later chapters, Hubert Eaton was in charge of Forest Lawn's sales program.)

Several days later, Pop Ross pondered, "It certainly seems hard to get justice in this country[,] as the Attorneys and Judges seem to apply more value to a precedent than to equity."[52]

The Aftermath

After Loewenthal's petition for a rehearing was denied, he made plans to go after the Title Guarantee & Trust Company, which had provided Treadwell with the title guarantee in his 1905 purchase of land from Susan Glassell Mitchell. In preparation for the suit, Loewenthal and his associate, E. C. Griffith, began to gather documents from Treadwell's land purchase. The lawyers also wanted to interview Treadwell to find out whether he had any correspondence or other evidence that would help build a fraud case against the trust company. Pop Ross wanted to talk with Griffith before Treadwell was interviewed, since Pop could "make statements verbally which would be better than in writing."[53]

Ultimately, no one was willing to incur the legal costs of the long-shot claim against the title company. Nor was anyone willing to pursue a claim against Lucie Lambourn as an individual rather than as executrix—partly because recovery of any money from her would be difficult, since her late husband had squandered much of her wealth in a failed business deal.[54]

It would have been equally difficult, back when J. B. Treadwell purchased the land for the cemetery from Susan Mitchell, for the founders of TL&I to predict what was to come. A single real estate transaction in 1905 led to court cases that occupied much of TL&I's attention from 1910 through 1912 and lingered until 1915. Although the outcomes were not as favorable as TL&I wanted, Tom and Pop Ross must have been relieved that the litigation—at least regarding this issue—was finally over. The storm cloud of the title dispute was gone, and an obstacle to Forest Lawn's success had been removed.

CHAPTER 8

WELLS MAKES HIS MARK

DURING THE YEARS 1910 through 1912, a lot was happening at Forest Lawn. Billy Blain's "cure" for drunkenness led to his death; Charles Morgan attempted, and failed, to take over FLCA; and TL&I was occupied with the partition suit. But through it all, the ordinary business of the cemetery still needed to be conducted. Norton Wells, the president of FLCA, was always seeking opportunities to improve Forest Lawn's operations.

Gaining Visibility

When he started at Forest Lawn, Wells continued to look for ways to gain visibility and status in the community. Because of these efforts, he was invited to be an investor and board member in the formation of the Tropico Bank. TL&I provided the $500 to make this possible. Wells wrote Tom Ross, "To have one of the bank directors also president of the Cemetery, will help the Cemetery and to have the President of the Cemetery a director of the bank will help the bank; many of the big men in San Fernando Valley are interested more or less and it will give us a standing in that section."[1]

Wells's efforts to establish himself in the Los Angeles business community continued to bear fruit. The fifth club of Rotary

International had been formed in Los Angeles about a year before Wells came to Forest Lawn. Though a new club, it endeavored to admit the "best" businessman in any given field, so Wells considered it prestigious when he was invited to join in September 1910.[2]

Protests Over Expansion

Public controversy came to Forest Lawn for the first time in early 1910. One of the issues involved plans for expanding the cemetery by developing land already owned by TL&I and committed to FLCA for expansion. A group of citizens not only protested the expansion of the cemetery but went so far as to ask that the cemetery be removed. Dr. C. S. James and J. Mills Davies were appointed to a committee to prevent the conversion of land between Elysian Park and Tropico into a cemetery.[3] The possibility of a new cemetery was blocked, but FLCA succeeded in keeping the right to use all the TL&I land for cemetery purposes.

The Hillside Sign Controversy

Citizens living near Forest Lawn were also unhappy over a large sign carved on the hillside above the cemetery. Norton Wells revealed plans for the sign in early January 1910 and had it laid out by mid-February. The words "Forest Lawn Cemetery" were cut into the hillside in two rows of fifty-foot letters, each of which was filled with whitewashed rock. The sign measured one thousand feet in width and about one hundred feet in height.

The *Los Angeles Times* reported that neighbors did not appreciate the sign.

Probably the largest sign in Southern California, and possibly one of the biggest in the country, figured in the proceedings of the North, Northeast and Northwest Improvement Association, at its meeting yesterday. A delegation of citizens was present to ask the assistance of the association in eliminating from the landscape, beyond Tropico a graveyard sign that was declared to be one of the wonders of the world. On a beautiful green hillside across San Fernando Valley, there appears a sign, "Forest Lawn Cemetery," cut in the ground, the letters filled with broken rock, and then whitewashed. . . .

One of the visiting delegation described it as "the greatest and most monstrous thing in Southern California." Those who are obliged to look at it by day and dream of it by night are stirred to a lively opposition.[4]

There was an uproar over the new sign. E. Forbes expressed his displeasure in a letter to the editor of the *Los Angeles Express.*

To the Express: Will you not kindly lend the weight of your influence in ridding the beautiful San Fernando Valley of the hideous defacement placed upon it through the selfish greed and utter lack of taste shown by some cemetery association? In utter abandonment of good taste, to say nothing of the proprieties and completely disregarding the frightful disfigurement of a most beautiful landscape, these people are endeavoring to thrust their melancholy place upon the notice and consideration of tourist, visitor and resident alike. With their monstrous "ad" placed in full view from the trains they invite the pleasure-seeking tourist and the health-seeking visitor to get ready for death, and in huge letters which can be read miles away they announce the location of their burial grounds.[5]

When the sign was completed, Wells sent Pop Ross a newspaper article regarding the sign, proclaiming that it paid to advertise. He wrote, "Gee, but our sign is 'waking the dead!' To-day . . . the Express has had its artist out to take photographs. . . . All want to know what we mean by putting a sign up on our own land before asking permission from everybody in L. A. Sure this is ducks, for the first thing we know everybody will be talking about Forest Lawn and we won't have to lay out money monthly for ads."[6]

Members of the Civic Association of Los Angeles were so distraught over the sign that they presented a petition to the Los Angeles County Board of Supervisors, urging them to "enact an ordinance prohibiting the displaying of billboards and advertising throughout the county." According to a news report, "Supervisor [Henry D.] McCabe stated that the board had no power as to the regulation of the placing of signs on private property and the county already has an ordinance relating to that subject."[7]

Unrepentant, Wells reported to Pop that "our publicity still continues. All three morning papers were giving the big sign a boost to-day. I had [a meeting] to-day and sent [the protestors] on their way without hurting their feelings but still they had nothing for their troubles."[8]

Later the same day, Wells wrote Pop another letter regarding the sign. "The Park Commissioners have written me and . . . now I will appear before the Supervisors and make the talk of my life."[9]

The sign stayed on the hillside. Soon it was time to think about Decoration Day—the precursor of Memorial Day—when many cemeteries held remembrance ceremonies. With the holiday approaching, Wells reported to Tom Ross that Blain was having trouble keeping up the grounds because everything grew so fast. However, Wells seemed more concerned with maintaining the hillside sign, which had faded. He planned to hire two extra men for a week to put whitewash on the letters. Since several hundred visitors were expected on Decoration Day, Wells wanted to be sure they were greeted with the giant sign.[10]

The whitewash did not last through the summer. As it faded, Wells thought the letters looked like "nothing more than dust." A faded sign was not acceptable to Wells, so a new solution was needed. Pop Ross suggested that Wells try a new product called "Liquid Stone" paint, which could be brushed on. However, one gallon would cover only ten square feet. Wells calculated that the letters of "Forest Lawn" covered 7,857 square feet, so almost 800 gallons of paint would have been needed to repaint them. Wells thought that if the new paint could be applied with a "white-wash spraying machine," it would save labor in refurbishing the sign. That did not turn out to be practical.[11]

A Rival Sign

Although Norton Wells did not seem troubled by insulting the sensibilities of citizens with the big hillside sign, he was quick to take action on others. Writing the county road overseer, Wells complained that the Lawrence B. Burck Co. real estate firm had erected a large sign, including a blackboard with chalk entries for property listings, on the street leading up to Forest Lawn's entrance. In addition, the real estate firm had "mutilated one of the Golden Cypress trees that were growing there, by cutting the limbs off for some 6 or 8 feet above the roots." Wells pointed out that the street had recently been deeded to the county—making it a public highway—and the tree was in the street right-of-way, so the firm should be fined $100 for damaging the tree.

Of course, Wells's main objective was to have the sign moved or removed. So he wrote, somewhat disingenuously, "I do not wish to make a complaint such as to cause the firm annoyance at this time, for no doubt the firm . . . is ignorant of the law in such matters, and would not willfully break such law, but I would like to have you request them to remove the black-board off the lawn back to the property line."[12]

The Price of Newspaper Ads

Although Wells was willing to spend money on a big sign for advertising, he had a sharper pencil when dealing with the local newspaper. As would have been expected in a small community, Forest Lawn advertised in Tropico's small and relatively new paper, the *Interurban Sentinel*. Wells balked when the paper wanted to increase the price of ads in 1912. Responding to N. C. Burch's solicitation for advertising, Wells said, "I cannot consider it . . . for we derive no benefit from an ad[vertisement] in your paper . . . because everyone in the

Figure 22. 1912 Advertisement.
In an ad in the *Interurban Sentinel*, Forest Lawn emphasized it was among the foothills of Tropico. The ad also used the term "memorial park" before Eaton gave it a specific meaning and punctuated it with a hyphen.

community knows of our Cemetery, but are only interested in it when compelled to use it." He went on to say that Tropico needed a newspaper and he wanted it to thrive, but he felt that Forest Lawn's advertising was "more of a contribution to the public good" than an advertisement on which he could expect returns.[13]

Designing Letterhead

Wells's marketing efforts extended to designing a new letterhead for Forest Lawn in June 1910. He left a copy of his proposed design with Tom Ross for comment, but received no reaction. Following up, Wells wrote, "I am looking for a 'letter head' I left while in [San Francisco]. If you have criticized it, I wish you would send the same down to me at your earliest convenience."[14] The response from Tom, through Pop, speaks for itself.

Regarding the letter head sketch which you sent, Tom thinks it is all right except the four little flyaway things which he supposes are representative of four lilies in a pond but which look like (#1) a mosquito with his sting all ready for action, (2nd) a bumble bee rushing for a drink, (3rd) a butterfly or some other fly nosing around after something, and (4th) another bumble bee getting a last drink; that is to say he doesn't like anything below the "Los Angeles" but might have that a little to the right so as to show the roadway. He thinks the rest is too showy for a Cemetery heading.[15]

This ended Wells's attempts to design letterhead. Sadly, no copy of the proposed letterhead seems to exist.

Designing letterhead was not Wells's only venture into aesthetics. After receiving a critique from Tom Ross about a "rustic cobble flower bed," Wells explained that it was an experiment and to Wells's eye was "very pretty." Acknowledging that he was not an artist, Wells agreed that "stone work adds to the agony" of the design. He told Tom, "I believe I catch your point that it is not good landscape gardening to mix artificial with natural, but, of course, the common herd does not always know these fine points and ordinary things many times look beautiful to this class of people." Wells went on to say that he would put no more of the bed in because he wanted Forest Lawn to be "above criticism, particularly by people who know" good design.[16]

Wells could not help himself and, over the years, periodically made other suggestions to Tom Ross that were not implemented.

Moving the Llewellyn Monument

When John Llewellyn was being recruited to join the FLCA board of trustees, part of the negotiations involved moving the Llewellyn family monument, along with the remains of six Llewellyn family members, from Evergreen Cemetery to Forest Lawn. The family's lot in Evergreen was to be sold and the proceeds put into the Forest Lawn perpetual care fund. It was important to have this prominent family's monument be seen in a visible location in Forest Lawn to promote Forest Lawn's credibility. The family was to receive additional burial property for future use.[17]

J. B. Treadwell had been unable to accomplish moving the Llewellyn monument to Forest Lawn, so Norton Wells inherited

April 2018

Figure 23. Llewellyn Monument

As part of the effort to identify Forest Lawn with prominent citizens, the Llewellyn family's monument was moved from Evergreen Cemetery to Section C in Forest Lawn in 1910.

October 2014

Figure 24. Evergreen Cemetery

Evergreen Cemetery was one of Los Angeles's early cemeteries. October 2014 photo with downtown Los Angeles skyline in background.

the unfinished project when he took over as president of FLCA. At first he thought everything was set for the move. But when he went to pick up the deed, he learned that Reese Llewellyn, John's brother, had not understood that the Llewellyns were to pay for a new stone base and the actual moving of the monument. Reese did not think that was fair, since Forest Lawn would reap the most benefit of the monument being moved. The Llewellyns and Wells finally reached an agreement: the Llewellyns would pay $275 for the new base for the monument, but Forest Lawn would have to pay for disinterment and reinterment of the Llewellyn relatives, as well as the installation of the monument.[18]

Wells also found out that the deed for the Llewellyns' Evergreen Cemetery lot had never been recorded. Once he fixed that, John

Llewellyn's brothers, Reese and William, were able to sign the deed turning lot 92 in Evergreen Cemetery over to TL&I on February 15, 1910, for the sum of ten dollars.[19]

By mid-March Wells could report, "The Llewellyn monument is lying on the ground to-day in our Cemetery." With the monument finally placed in Forest Lawn, Wells let Pop know they also had "moved the Llewellyn bodies Wednesday last."[20]

Calling on Undertakers

Maintaining good relationships with undertakers was an important way to get referrals. Wells worked on these relationships just as Treadwell and Blain had done previously. Wells wrote Pop that he and Blain had called on Mr. Wheat of Pierce Brothers Undertaking and "gave him the 'bush-wah.'" They also "called on Sharp and Goodman & Martinoni scattering little seeds of business among them all." Wells added,

> Martinoni has asked me to open the cemetery for them on Sunday as they are writing all the lodges* that they will conduct Sunday funerals. On sounding the undertakers, I find it would raise a bigger noise than the sign did, so until Inglewood breaks the ice we won't consider it. Then if Inglewood does, why we won't and will get the organized undertakers on our side. Really, I would prefer Sunday funerals as it would advertise us through the larger crowds which would attend, but we won't make the first move for awhile yet.[21]

Wells continued his calls on undertakers, reporting in April 1910 that he had "been treated fine in making my proposition to them. Called at Pierce Bros., Bresee [Brothers & Todd Undertaking Company], W. H. Sutch's [Undertaking Company] and Overholtzers

---

* A lodge is a fraternal organization, e.g. Kiwanis, Knights of Pythias, Lions, Shriners, or Masons.

[Undertaking]." He added a note that his proposition included a 10 percent commission on plots sold from the undertakers' referrals.[22]

Auto Expenses

The saga of George Heath and the automobile, which began when Heath arrived in 1909, continued into 1910. In February, Norton Wells told Pop Ross that "Dr. Heath had an accident Friday with the machine . . . after leaving me at the office. . . . The steering-rod broke and the machine veered off and ran into the sidewalk. It broke both springs in front, so we had to send it to the shop."[23] Not too many days later, Pop reported, "Auto expense for Jan. $84.10 including another new tire which makes one tired!!! Hope it is not so expensive in February."[24]

Wells understood the pun and shared the news with Pop that Heath had the auto in the shop again. Apparently a clip that held up the body broke, and Heath was up until two in the morning working on it. The fenders would have to be replaced because they were dropping off—there was just one problem after another. Wells huffed, "I am afraid to ride in it. There is no emergency brake on it and it would cost $8 or $10 to put one on[,] so we go without and I am scared of my life. It is just disintegrating and falling apart. If Dr. H. wasn't the best natured man I ever saw he would have run it into the L. A. River months ago, and forgotten where he left it."[25]

In April, Wells wrote Pop that he had "told Dr. Heath to get a machine, as ours is still in the shop" so he could take a party out to look at cemetery property. The rented auto was returned after Forest Lawn's car was repaired, but the car continued to be unreliable. Pop learned that Heath and Wells were cruising at Fifth and Spring Streets when a bolt came out and stripped the gearing before they could stop the vehicle. The car was in the shop four or five days. Wells wrote Pop, "O my! Damn our old automobile."[26]

George Heath was not the only one who liked autos. In February 1911 Forest Lawn purchased a new Hupmobile Runabout, and Wells told Pop of his pleasure with the new machine.[27]

I took a run out in the new automobile yesterday to the cemetery and it runs like a bird. Twenty-five miles an hour is like "duck soup", thirty-five miles an hour is like that proverbial sewing machine in Kentucky, — it is going some. However, I have put the limit to twenty miles an hour, as that is plenty fast enough for anybody to ride, and at that speed we can very nicely get from the [downtown] office to the cemetery in thirty minutes or less. The machinery is still new and stiff and it will need running for a couple of hundred miles to really loosen the bearings up, so tomorrow afternoon I am going to take Lou Peters and his wife out to the cemetery and kill two birds with one stone, first, to exercise the machine, and second, show our cemetery to our new secretary and his better half.[28]

Avoiding Annexation

In the spring of 1910, Glendale civic leaders supported a plan by the Glendale Improvement Association to consolidate the territory between the Glendale city boundaries and San Fernando Road, including Eagle Rock Valley, Forest Lawn Cemetery, and the foothills beyond Casa Verdugo, into one city. They adopted the theme "Bury politics and boost for consolidation!"[29]

Wanting to avoid potential taxes on land not yet developed for cemetery use, the Rosses did not want Forest Lawn to be part of the area annexed to Glendale. Yet Wells was in the thick of the movement. Somehow he managed to have himself appointed as chair of the Glendale Special Committee on Annexation, although his first priority was to keep Forest Lawn out of the area to be annexed.

As chair of the committee, Wells was able to draw the preliminary annexation line to leave the cemetery entirely out of the planned annexation. However, that action was contested at a meeting of the group.

Wells then worked with J. B. Treadwell to negotiate a compromise. Treadwell shared Wells's desire to remain out of Glendale, since he owned property along San Fernando Road, south of Forest Lawn.

This was the property he had purchased from Susan Glassell Mitchell and kept for himself, while selling the rest to TL&I. Although his ownership was common knowledge, the financial details of his acquisition were not yet known to TL&I or FLCA.

In the compromise negotiated by Wells and Treadwell, the "ornamental area" fronting Glendale Avenue was included in the area annexed to Glendale, but the cemetery proper was not. The "ornamental area" was the land TL&I owned west of the railroad right-of-way, which was not part of the original cemetery boundaries. The compromise gave Glendale control of Glendale Avenue all the way to San Fernando Road, so the city could make an "oiled road" out of it. Wells also believed that if Forest Lawn made a single interment on the west side of the railroad tracks, an amended map could

Figure 25. Tropico Annexation

Wells was instrumental in keeping Forest Lawn out of the area of Tropico being annexed to the City of Glendale. In this sketch, the dotted line is the annexation boundary, avoiding most of Forest Lawn Cemetery. Wells's penciled notes say, "All that will be in the city of Glendale will be about 300 feet of land East of Glendale Ave west of red dots."

Forest Lawn archives

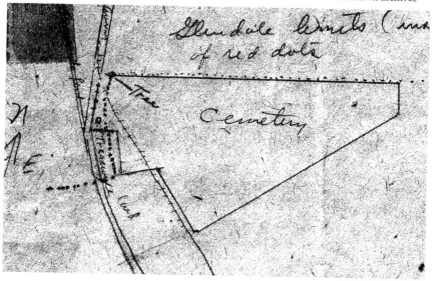

be filed to make that area part of the cemetery.[30] It would then, as cemetery land, become exempt from property taxes.

In connection with the Tropico annexation, Treadwell tried to give Wells a bill for the legal services of an attorney by the name of Hass. Treadwell expected TL&I to pay one-half of the amount. Wells told him he could not pay it, since he did not have the authority to represent TL&I, so Treadwell should present it to the Rosses himself. Wells told Pop Ross that Treadwell "is a keen old grafter, but his day of graft with me is ended." Wells believed that Treadwell had "doubled up" on the bill, trying to trick TL&I into paying the full amount of the actual charges.[31]

Tropico Becomes Independent Municipality (1911)

After rejecting annexation to Glendale, Tropico began to contemplate incorporating as a city. Forest Lawn was not within the boundaries of either Glendale or Tropico, and the original lands that Wells kept out of Glendale in 1910 eventually became part of Los Angeles. With Tropico flanked by Glendale and Los Angeles, both cities eyed Tropico as a candidate for further expansion of territory.[32]

Because Treadwell still had land interests near Forest Lawn, he continued to have frequent contact with Wells. In 1911, a movement started for incorporation of the remaining part of Tropico as a city. Treadwell made it clear in a series of phone calls to Wells that he was "very desirous that [Forest Lawn] knock out the incorporation of Tropico." Nonetheless, Tropico became an independent municipality on March 17, 1911.[33]

Along with the issues related to annexation, Wells learned that Pacific Electric might change the location where cars stopped, moving it to a place north of the intersection of Brand Boulevard and San Fernando Road. This would have made street car riders walk a greater distance to get to Forest Lawn. So Wells suggested changing the alignment of Depot Street to continue direct access to the cemetery. The re-alignment, which would have required cooperation from the Richardsons, as adjacent landowners, never took place.[34]

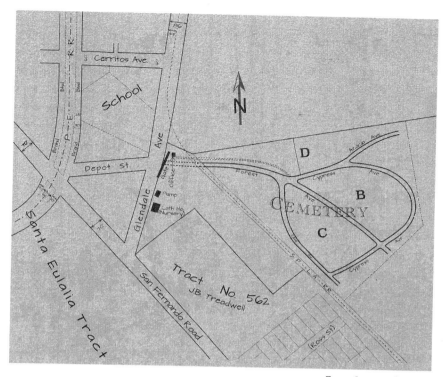

Forest Lawn archives

Figure 26. Forest Lawn Cemetery Plan, c.1911
The road layout and section letters changed from the 1906 version (Figure 11).

Relations with Other Cemeteries

New to the cemetery business when he came to Forest Lawn, Wells sought information regarding successful sales strategies from cemeteries in other parts of the country. Since cemeteries compete with one another only when nearby, he found many willing to share ideas with him.

Wells received a response from Loudon Park Cemetery Company in Baltimore that clearly described an early "preneed" sales document. The cover of the brochure read, "You have insured your house.

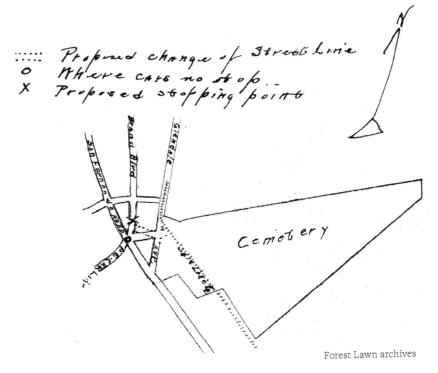

Forest Lawn archives

Figure 27. Sketch of Depot Street Realignment

You have no doubt insured your life." When opened, it read, "But have you provided your family with that which soon or later will be necessary?" The document continued with pictures of the cemetery and concluded with a page that suggested, "If not, why delay in these days of sudden deaths? Our representative will call upon request, or full information in regard to prices and terms may be obtained at the Cemetery grounds."[35]

In addition to Loudon Park Cemetery, Wells corresponded with various cemeteries across the United States, including Spring Grove (Cincinnati), Lorraine (Baltimore), Mount Greenwood (Chicago), Mount Olivet (Colma, California), Mountain View (Prescott, Arizona),

Oakwood (Sharon, Pennsylvania), Westminster (Philadelphia), and Utica (Utica, New York).[36]

In April 1910, when returning from out of town, Wells found that "a crowd had been trying to close Hollywood Cemetery." He reported to Pop Ross that Heath had been able to sell lots to a family who had planned to buy in Hollywood Cemetery, but had changed their minds after reading about the cemetery in the newspaper.[37]

Pop found the Hollywood Cemetery situation interesting. He replied, "I notice where the Hollywood people say the ground is particularly suitable for burying[,] where it is well known that when the rainy season is on[,] the clay so absorbs the moisture that it is absolutely shameful to use it for graves." Pop told Wells to work behind the scenes to convince opponents of Hollywood Cemetery to make the argument that the ground was unfit for burial. Even if that did not change the minds of city council members, Pop thought it would at least result in adverse publicity for Hollywood Cemetery that would help Forest Lawn. After ten years of existence, the Hollywood Cemetery had made only 950 interments, so the developers of the cemetery would do better to sell the land for other purposes. Pop prompted Wells to "study this up[;] there are so many points to it that it will certainly do them a lot of harm[,] and the more there is of talk on the matter the worse it will be."[38]

The Hollywood Cemetery situation heated up when a paid advertisement appeared in the *Los Angeles Record* in July 1910 to protest the expansion of the cemetery. It carried the headline, "Should the City Discriminate in Favor of the Hollywood Cemetery?" The ad was placed by Seward Cole, the son of former US Senator Cornelius Cole and a trustee of a local water company, as was his father. The ad explained that the ordinance allowing burials in Los Angeles cemeteries "left out all unoccupied land, and included only the ground actually occupied by graves." When a new ordinance had been passed on the last day of 1909, replacing the prior one, it used precisely the same boundaries for Evergreen and Rosedale Cemeteries as the previous ordinance. However, Hollywood Cemetery received more generous treatment. It was now described as a hundred-acre tract, of which more than three-fourths was vacant land.[39]

Cole's ad also said that opening large areas for burials amid a growing city was a mistake. Los Angeles, like other cities, had previously restricted cemeteries to small areas. The new ordinance had been passed without appropriate consideration or discussion, and "the reasons for excluding burials from the large unoccupied portion of this Hollywood concern are too numerous and cogent to need repeating."[40] As TL&I already had a cemetery, anything that limited competition was undoubtedly welcomed.

Though the cemetery industry was (and is) relatively small, by 1912 Forest Lawn and Wells were earning a reputation as a successful startup operation. Wells received a letter from Stephen L. Richards, an attorney representing the Wasatch Land & Improvement Company in Salt Lake City, asking about various issues related to starting a cemetery. Their questions included whether it was necessary to employ a landscape architect to lay out the cemetery, whether an expert caretaker or superintendent should be employed from the beginning, what was the best way to advertise, and whether they should sell lots before the grounds were laid out and prepared for burial.[41]

Now a veteran of almost three years in the cemetery business, Wells freely offered advice to Richards. He advised against hiring a landscape architect, since he would probably charge a large fee. He recommended hiring a superintendent from the very beginning and cautioned against selling lots before the cemetery was ready. He explained that advertising could be placed in streetcars and newspapers but should be done in a dignified manner, and advised them not to start advertising unless the company had sufficient cash for a six-month campaign.[42]

After answering the questions posed by Richards, Wells offered additional advice on how to develop a cemetery.

Do not allow any body who lays out your cemetery, to make the mistake of using the ground close to your entrance for interment purposes. A modern cemetery tries to keep the grewsomeness [sic] of monuments, mausoleums, etc., covered up from public view, by planting, etc., as they approach the entrance. It is far better to have your funeral cortiege [sic], when entering your gate way, pass along over a road surrounded with beautiful lawns and trees without monuments, rather than to have masonry slap them in the face as they enter your grounds. . . .

Another mistake is to plant trees too near your [driveways]. Keep them back at least ten feet from the drive. If you do not, people will want to hitch their horse to your trees. Do not allow seats in the cemetery so people can loiter around your grounds, for if you do they will bring their lunch and scatter their papers around your grounds. . . .[43]

When giving advice to other cemeteries, Wells neglected to mention Forest Lawn's cash flow issues.

CHAPTER 9

Settlement with Treadwell

Even after he left Forest Lawn in January 1910, J. B. Treadwell continued to require attention from those involved with the cemetery. One of the ongoing issues had to do with whether money and stock shares were owed to him.

Back Pay

In the fall of 1911, J. B. Treadwell wrote FLCA asking for payment of the amount due him from his time as president. Norton Wells responded that the compensation owed to Treadwell was offset by a shortage in the perpetual care fund account that occurred during Treadwell's tenure. Thus he was due less than forty-four dollars, which Wells would send him if he agreed.[1]

Wells did send Treadwell the money, but Treadwell did not agree that he had owed the cemetery anything for the perpetual care fund. The following year he filed suit against FLCA to collect the money withheld from his back pay. While Treadwell's deposition was being taken, a stipulation was agreed to whereby FLCA would file a demurrer stating that the claim was barred by the applicable statute of limitations—that is, he had waited too long to make a claim.[2] The effect was that Treadwell was agreeing to allow his suit to end with the court rejecting his claim. FLCA would owe him nothing more on his claim for back pay.

Promissory Notes

Although the issue of compensation due Treadwell was resolved, he still had promissory notes from FLCA for expenses not reimbursed to him when he was president. When TL&I paid off Oscar Souden's mortgage on December 23, 1912, Treadwell must have assumed that FLCA would also have cash. He reacted by having his attorney, Carroll Allen, write FLCA asking for payment. After Wells met with Allen, he reported to Pop Ross that Allen "was as nice as a basket of chips." Allen seemed to understand that Forest Lawn was not then in a position to pay the notes. The matter was left at that.[3]

Pop Ross was irritated that Treadwell had hired Carroll Allen to collect on the promissory notes. He dashed off a letter to Treadwell complaining that continuing to make remarks about Norton Wells "caused [Wells] annoyance." He suggested Treadwell "refrain from making any reference to or about [Wells] so that this irritation cease for the good of both parties." Pop told Treadwell that hiring Allen was not necessary. The various promissory notes FLCA issued had been renewed with new due dates, and the same could have been done with Treadwell's notes if he had only asked. Pop assured Treadwell that renewing the notes would eliminate "any chance of [the notes] being outlawed"—uncollectible due to the passage of time. Pop closed the letter assuring Treadwell that he would be paid when the funds were available and would "get a square deal in every way."[4]

Although Wells thought he had placated attorney Allen, it was not long after Pop's letter to Treadwell that Wells received another letter from Allen demanding immediate payment. Wells countered to Allen that the $432.58 sought by Treadwell was offset by a $388.85 shortage in the perpetual care fund. Because this had happened before his tenure, Wells suggested that Allen contact Pop Ross for an explanation of the offset.[5]

Norton Wells met with Allen again, but just as before, he referred Allen back to Pop Ross. That still did not resolve the issue. One day Wells was greeted by a process server, who handed him a complaint seeking payment. Wells gave the complaint to attorney William Hazlett and wrote Pop, "We are in for a scrap."[6]

Allegations of Illegal Loans

Unexpectedly, in January 1913 W. B. Scott, one of the original trustees of FLCA, threatened to send the state a complaint alleging that Forest Lawn had made illegal loans to TL&I. The law did not allow for loans to officers or trustees of the cemetery. Therefore, if any officers or trustees of Forest Lawn were also shareholders in TL&I, the loans of perpetual care funds to TL&I would have been a violation of the law.[7]

Pop Ross believed that Treadwell was behind Scott's threat to lodge a complaint with state officials, since Treadwell had recruited Scott as a trustee of FLCA. Pop reassured Norton Wells that the allegations were unfounded and that the directors of TL&I and trustees of FLCA were independent of one another. FLCA trustee John Llewellyn owned 1,250 shares of TL&I, "but he is not an officer, only a stockholder." Pop Ross's attempt to distinguish between corporate officers and stockholders was futile, since a loan to a company was, in effect, a loan to the shareholders. But when Llewellyn saw Pop in late January, he told Pop that he was not a stockholder, since he had given his shares to his sister and his brother had given his to his wife. Wells was a trustee, but he had not yet received any shares of TL&I because Forest Lawn had yet to meet the targeted three months of positive cash flow necessary for him to receive his first allotment.[8]

Thinking that Scott's allegation of illegal loans had damaged the reputations of TL&I and FLCA, Pop Ross asked Wells to find out if a suit for defamation could be brought against Scott and Treadwell. Wells queried William Hazlett "about the blackmail in the case of Scott, et al," and was told that such a suit was a possibility. Hazlett went on to tell Wells, "We have Treadwell and there is no doubt about it, so that we can make him pay back the money and the acreage he took for his own in that land transaction. His having accepted the promotion stock puts him in on the ground floor as a partner, therefore, we have him."[9]

Hazlett's reference to "that land transaction" goes back to Treadwell's original purchase and sale of property in 1905. During the partition suit, it came to light that Treadwell had purchased more land from Susan Mitchell than he had led TL&I to believe and that he had, in Pop Ross's words, "retained secretly 21 acres of the best land fronting on San Fernando Road." Furthermore, by misrepresenting the amount he had paid for the land, Treadwell had effectively caused TL&I to pay for the land he now owned. And he had also received 100,000 shares of TL&I stock as part of the bargain. The undercurrent through much of the partition suit was that Treadwell was responsible for any problems with the purchase and for any loss that TL&I might sustain. Once TL&I lost the partition suit, it was time to negotiate some sort of settlement with Treadwell.[10]

Settlement Negotiations

In March 1913, Pop Ross let Wells know that negotiations were underway to settle the issue regarding the promissory notes that Treadwell held. Pop asked Wells to send him two new notes, one for $5,000 and one for $4,200. The notes were to be properly stamped with the association's seal and signed by the president and secretary. Wells learned that if the new notes were used in the settlement, the older two notes currently held by Treadwell from Forest Lawn would be returned and the suit between TL&I and Treadwell would be dismissed. Pop further instructed Wells to not make any accounting entry for the new notes until a settlement was reached—Pop would give him the correct entries later.[11]

Wells ended up sending signed notes to Pop, but left the amounts blank to leave room for negotiation. Pop thought the blank notes were a good idea. He asked Wells to follow up on the ownership of some shares of stock in TL&I that were recorded on the stock

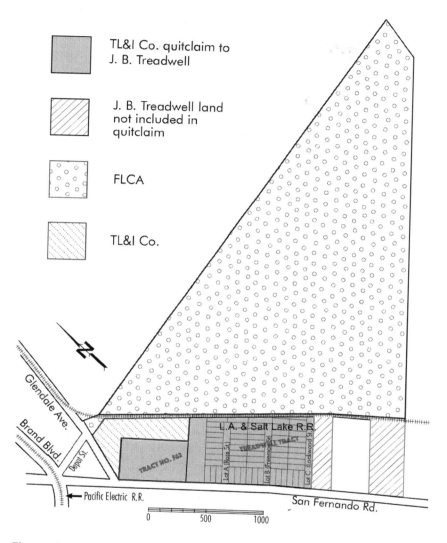

Figure 28. Area Quitclaimed to J. B. Treadwell

As part of the settlement of claims between J. B. Treadwell, TL&I, and FLCA, TL&I quitclaimed any interest it had in land Treadwell had purchased from Susan Mitchell but not sold to TL&I, as well as any interest it had in a small parcel of land Treadwell had previously sold TL&I.

ledger as belonging to Treadwell, but which Pop believed had actually been transferred to "certain undertakers." Pop's goal was to avoid having to pay future dividends to Treadwell when others actually owned the shares.[12]

Treadwell now cut a deal that would end any claims he might have against TL&I or FLCA, as well as end any claims either of the corporations might have against him. He would give back an additional seven thousand five hundred shares of TL&I stock and would receive a quitclaim deed on property he purchased from Susan Glassell Mitchell and did not sell to TL&I. The area TL&I was quitclaiming also included a small portion of the land it had purchased from Treadwell. (See Figure 28. "Area Quitclaimed to J. B. Treadwell.") A quitclaim deed is used to relinquish all rights in property but makes no representation about what, if any, property rights the person giving the quitclaim deed might have. By quitclaiming land already in Treadwell's name, TL&I was foregoing any possibility of taking action against Treadwell for the land he "retained secretly." As damages for his deception in the 1905 land purchase, Treadwell would assign, with interest, the two original promissory notes from FLCA that had been placed for collection: a note for $5,000 would be assigned to Tom Ross and a note for $4,356 to TL&I. With the notes now transferred out of Treadwell's hands, the suit over collection would also be cancelled. Pop Ross believed the settlement terms would also end the risk of any lawsuits like the one W. B. Scott had brought.[13]

Surprised to learn that Treadwell's notes had been assigned, Wells wanted Pop Ross to tell him how it was done. Hazlett, too, wanted to know how the deal was accomplished. Unfortunately, none of the existing correspondence describes the negotiations.[14]

At its March 1913 meeting, the TL&I board of directors approved the settlement. Wells thought TL&I was now "foot loose" and everyone could sleep peacefully with the matter put to rest.[15]

CHAPTER 10

Eaton and Sims Arrive

In July 1910, Norton Wells received a letter from a man named Charles Sims concerning the "promotion and sale of cemetery lots."[1] This seemingly routine correspondence—to which Wells did not even bother to reply—heralded a major turning point in the history of Forest Lawn Cemetery.

Charles Sims

Charles Blackburn Sims was clearly an early pioneer of selling interment property before death occurred—often referred to as "preneed" or "before need." Sims did not make an outright claim to being the first to offer preneed sales; in fact, he acknowledged that some cemeteries "had made a friendly effort to interest people in purchasing lots in a very limited way for a very limited time . . . but no scientific plan of sales campaign had ever been used until . . . 1905."[2] Therefore, he just claimed that he was the first to put in a "scientific sales campaign" for the purchase of cemetery property before death occurred.

Sims took a roundabout path to his career in cemetery sales. He was born in Leroy, Illinois, to Dr. William B. Sims and Sara Jane Sims, both natives of Tennessee. After graduating from the University of Illinois and the Illinois College of Law in Chicago, he became the elected city attorney of Urbana, Illinois, at the age of twenty-one. He then moved to Chicago and practiced law for twelve years, until he fell thirty-two feet from the step of a railway car to the road below. After a year of recuperation from the accident, he moved to Mobile, Alabama, where he headed the bond department of a large bank. Not enamored with a future in banking, he sought other lines of work.[3]

In 1905 Sims purchased land on the outskirts of Mobile and opened Pine Crest Cemetery. It was here that he began selling cemetery property on a preneed basis—before a death had occurred.[4]

Twenty years later, a newsletter published by Valhalla Cemetery in Milwaukee, Wisconsin, extolled Sims's importance.

> No man in the world enjoys the place in cemetery history that is held by Charles B. Sims. For twenty years Mr. Sims has devoted his entire time to the scientific study, and betterment, of cemeteries in larger communities, and is the originator and founder of practically all of the basic principles accepted and used by the modern cemetery.[5]

In 1925, Sims claimed to have directed the establishment of twenty cemeteries between 1912 and 1924, including Fairlawn in Decatur, Illinois; Forest Lawn in Los Angeles; Oak Hill Cemetery in Bloomington, Illinois; Valhalla in St. Louis, Missouri; Valhalla in Milwaukee, Wisconsin.; and Washelli in Seattle, Washington. In addition to the cemeteries Sims claimed to have established, he trained managers who were operating cemeteries for other interests. Sims was exaggerating. For example, Forest Lawn opened in 1906 without his involvement. The Washelli Cemetery started in 1884 and was known as Oak Lake Cemetery. In 1912 it was purchased by American Necropolis Company and renamed Washelli. Sims was president of American Necropolis. It may be more accurate to say that he was involved in creating sales programs in these properties. Sims was primarily a promoter and salesman involved in real estate

Ancestry.com 2017

Figure 29. Charles B. Sims

sales of various sorts, in addition to cemetery lot sales.[6]

Sims was quoted as saying, "There is not a single promoter of cemeteries that could solve scientifically the amount that he must receive for a cemetery lot in order to operate on a scientific basis, nor is there a single promoter that could tell what percentage of the sales should be used for overhead, development, maintenance, perpetual care, etc. . . . A great number of cemeteries [have been] promoted in the United States by people who have no knowledge of cemetery work."[7]

Clearly, Charles Sims accumulated much knowledge of cemetery work over the span of his career. But that was yet to come. In 1910, when Norton Wells received Sims's letter, he took little notice of it.

Correspondence with Wells

Having failed to receive a response to the letter he had written to Wells in July, Sims wrote again at the end of August. In regard to "taking up the sale of your Cemetery near Los Angeles," he told Wells, "it is possible that we would take an interest with you in this property if you were so disposed."[8]

When Wells finally responded in September, he provided details about Forest Lawn, describing it as consisting of 125 acres of land located just six miles from Los Angeles and outside the city limits. With the cemetery surrounded by foothills, "the city in its growth for the next 100 years will not be inconvenienced by our location." He said the cemetery was located on San Fernando Road, "main artery for wheel-traffic between Los Angeles and Northern California." Though the cemetery was only four years old, Wells reported, it had made over 550 interments, and Wells believed it was now known as one of the prettiest cemeteries in Southern California.[9]

Wells had a number of questions for Sims, which Sims answered in his next letter on October 1. Wells wanted to know whether Sims was interested in becoming an investor. Sims replied that his company would be in a position to take either a selling contract or a financial interest, or both. However, it would be willing to take a financial interest only after investigation, and based on being the "most favored stock-holder."[10]

Wells also wanted to know what would be required of Forest Lawn other than a one- or two-year contract with a 40 percent commission. Sims's expectation was that the Forest Lawn property would be in "good selling condition," and, if not, that Forest Lawn would put it in salable condition.[11]

Wells asked how Sims could sell cemetery lots in California when he was headquartered in Alabama. Sims explained that the selling force might come from Alabama, or he might hire a portion of it in Los Angeles. He also explained that American Securities Company of Georgia—a company that Sims was involved in—had successfully developed similar cemeteries and had created a demand for cemetery property in advance of need. He represented that he would have "high-class" personnel, and his organization would first make a careful study of Forest Lawn and the conditions in Los Angeles. Furthermore, Sims himself would probably remain in Los Angeles for six months to ensure that the "machinery of selling [was] in order." After that, an experienced person would be left in charge to continue the program. Sims declined to give specifics of how their program worked, but claimed his organization was the only one in the country that could do this. The company could handle only one location at a time, but if employed by Forest Lawn, "practically all of our machinery would be in your service. . . . [We] would expect to work, of course, from your office."[12]

Once again, Wells did not answer. A week later, Sims sent another follow-up letter saying he had expected a prompt reply. He wanted to find out whether Wells had any interest in the proposal and offered to come to California to finalize details and begin sales.[13]

Almost five months passed. In March 1911, Sims followed up on his prior correspondence with Wells, once again offering to visit Forest Lawn. Wells responded that he would be pleased to meet with him. He also noted that he was writing to several banks for references on Sims. Wells followed through with letters to the Bank of Mobile, City Bank & Trust Co., and Union Bank & Trust Co. for their "judgment as to [Sims's] ability in handling cemetery promotions."[14]

Hubert Eaton

By this time, Hubert Eaton had begun working with Sims. The son of James Rodolphus Eaton and Martha Lewright Eaton, Hubert Lewright Eaton was born in Liberty, Missouri, in 1881. Hubert's father, who was a professor, died on a trip to the Holy Land in 1897, leaving Martha and her two surviving children, Hubert and Mabel, in a precarious financial position. Overcoming adversity, Hubert graduated from William Jewell College—the school where his father had been a faculty member—in 1902. Eaton liked to tell people that in the front of all two thousand books left by his father were the words *Perseveranita omnia vincet* (Perseverance conquers all things) and that he, Hubert, had succeeded because he followed those words.[15]

Having studied chemistry and metallurgy in college, Eaton found his way into the mining industry. For four years, he worked for the Boston & Montana Copper and Silver Mining & Smelting Company in Great Falls, Montana. He began as an assistant assayer, then worked his way up through a series of promotions from tenth assistant chemist to first research chemist. He moved on from the chemist position to a job that involved traveling to do mine examinations and sell the Boston & Montana company's "electric mud."[16] "Mud" is the byproduct of one of the steps in the smelting of copper and contains small amounts of valuable metals. So the "electric mud" must have been a proprietary method of producing the "mud."

Forest Lawn Archives

Figure 30. Hubert Eaton, c. 1913

Eaton briefly worked with the Teziutlan Copper Company near the village of Aire Libre in Pueblo, Mexico. He was asked to resign by Sam Barron, the general superintendent, for leading a crusade against long hours for his department. After that, Eaton spent time selling mining stock in Liberty and Kansas City, Missouri. He then worked as a metallurgist at the Lodi Mines Company before teaming up with his cousin Joseph Eaton to form a new venture.[17]

The Eatons started the Adaven Mining and Smelting Company to explore a newly discovered silver vein in Nevada. They hit it big with their new mine, taking out more than a million dollars' worth of ore in the first year. They poured all the money into the infrastructure necessary to expand the mining operation: roads, housing for employees, and a new smelter. But after all their preparations for growth, the vein ended abruptly. The Eatons exhausted their remaining funds searching for the resumption of the silver vein, but never found it.[18]

The failure of the mine in 1911 led Hubert Eaton to St. Louis, where he dropped in on a former college friend, Charles S. Marsh. In addition to being vice president of the Bankers Trust Company,

Marsh was also a vice president of the National Securities Company of St. Louis, one of Charles B. Sims's companies for cemetery and real estate promotions. Marsh introduced Eaton to Sims. Intrigued with Sims's idea of selling cemetery property before a death occurred, Eaton tried it himself. He was soon convinced that cemetery sales had good prospects and teamed up with Charles Sims.[19]

Getting to California

Like Sims, Eaton was interested in selling for Forest Lawn and began to correspond with Norton Wells. He made plans to come to Los Angeles to see the cemetery and discuss a selling contract, but failed to come as planned.[20]

In July 1911, Eaton made a second commitment to visit Forest Lawn on behalf of Sims's American Securities Company. But Eaton was once again detained—this time by a cemetery in St. Louis. The owners of that cemetery had been wanting to expand their operation for several years, and Eaton had promised to organize the expansion. He assured Wells that doing so would not interfere with taking on Forest Lawn, and he would still be happy to meet in Los Angeles to discuss a contract.[21]

Neither Eaton nor Sims made it to California in 1911. However, they were still interested in Forest Lawn. Sims wrote Wells that Hubert Eaton would be leaving for California in March 1912 and planned to call on Wells to discuss the sales proposal. If Wells was still interested, Eaton would make a proposition that would bring $200,000 in sales in the next two years. Sims boasted this would make Forest Lawn the "leading cemetery" in Los Angeles.[22]

This time, Eaton arrived as planned. In March 1912 he met in San Francisco with Pop Ross, and perhaps with Tom Ross as well. Pop reported to Norton Wells that "Mr Eaton was here and we have had quite a talk over his proposition and have told him that at present we think favorably of the matter and will consult with you regarding details and be ready to decide on his return in about 30 days with Mr Sims. He leaves for Reno today."[23]

In April, Wells wrote Motley H. Flint, vice president of Los Angeles Trust & Savings Bank, asking him to "obtain whatever information can be had regarding some business people in St. Louis, Missouri." Flint was asked to ascertain information regarding the "honesty, integrity, ability and the financial standing" of Charles B. Sims, W. E. Tally, Charles S. Marsh, E. R. Kinsey, and L. B. Pendleton, all of whom were involved with the National Securities Company. Wells also asked for information relative to "a Hubert L. Eaton connected with the Bankers' Trust Company." He went on to explain that six or eight months prior, Sims had been president of Southern Investment Company, which was a holding company for Pine Crest Cemetery in Mobile, Alabama; Greenwood Cemetery in Montgomery, Alabama; and Peach Tree Hills Cemetery in Atlanta, Georgia.[24]

Although Sims and Eaton were expected to be in San Francisco in June 1912, neither could make it. Sims was delayed by the death of his wife, and Eaton was detained by business—most likely the closing of the Adaven Mining & Smelting Company.[25]

A new date was set for Sims or Eaton to arrive in San Francisco, but once again, the target arrival date was not met. This time they were delayed by closing contracts in Pittsburgh and New York. Apparently Sims had changed his mind since his 1910 letter to Wells, when he insisted his company could handle only one cemetery location at a time.[26]

The Selling Contract

Sims and Eaton finally came to California in July. While in San Francisco, they negotiated a contract for the sale of cemetery property with the Rosses. Officers of TL&I signed it on July 11, 1912. Wells then brought the contract to Los Angeles, where the FLCA trustees were meeting to discuss and approve its terms. After some discussion, John Llewellyn moved to approve the agreement between FLCA, TL&I, Charles B. Sims, and H. L. Eaton. The motion passed unanimously.[27]

The following day Wells sent Sims a telegram at the St. Francis hotel in San Francisco:

CONTRACT PASSED AND SIGNED CONGRATULATE YOURSELF A GOOD JOB DONE[28]

Wells also sent a letter to Sims at his St. Louis address to confirm the telegram's news of the contract being approved.

It was truly a good job, and I must congratulate you on picking up what, in my judgement, is one of the cleanest and prettiest spots for a cemetery in all of Southern California. I only hope that success will be obtained commensurate with the beauties of the ground for yourself and associates, as well as for ourselves also.[29]

Figure 31. Organization Structure 1912

In July 1912, a contract was signed by TL&I, FLCA, Hubert Eaton, and Charles Sims allowing Eaton and Sims to sell Forest Lawn cemetery property to consumers. FLCA retained limited rights to continue sales on the cemetery grounds.

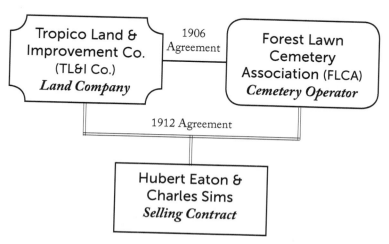

The five-year contract, scheduled to go into effect on October 1, 1912, specified that Sims and Eaton were to manage sales of lots in Forest Lawn. FLCA reserved the right to sell up to $30,000 of cemetery property each year without paying them a commission. Otherwise, during the first two and a half years, Sims and Eaton were to receive 50 percent of the money from sales. For the remaining two and a half years, they were to receive 40 percent of sales. Money paid for perpetual care was excluded from the calculation. If Forest Lawn's sales exceeded $30,000, then Sims and Eaton would receive the same commission on the excess as if they had made the sale. FLCA could not sell cemetery lots for less than fifty cents per square foot.[30]

The contract provided that the amount to be put into the perpetual care fund was 25 percent of the gross sale price of any lot and would be taken from the last payments received on any contract. For example, on a $100 sale, the last $25 received would be put into the perpetual care fund.[31] The remaining $75 would be split evenly for the first two and a half years of the contract: $37.50 would go to Eaton and Sims, and $37.50 would go to TL&I and FLCA. The latter two organizations would then split the $37.50, with each getting $18.75.

Figure 32. FLCA Letterhead, c. 1912

In 1912, FLCA letterhead retained the image of the entrance arch, but added "A Memorial Park" to the Tropico location. It would be another five years before Hubert Eaton would adopt the term, assign a specific meaning to it, and add a hyphen to distinguish it from prior uses.

Forest Lawn archives

A MEMORIAL PARK. TROPICO. CAL.

The contract also provided that Sims and Eaton were to be responsible for advertising and employing the sales force, but FLCA had the right to approve both the advertising and the people hired.[32]

FLCA was obligated to keep the "cemetery property in good selling condition at all times and to keep [Sims and Eaton] supplied with an assortment of lots for sale"—a minimum of four hundred, "equally divided as to values."[33]

The contract specifically allowed Eaton and Sims to sell property on an installment basis. They were entitled to charge interest on installment sales at a rate agreed to by TL&I and FLCA and keep the interest for themselves. In the event an installment sale was cancelled, Eaton and Sims were to receive the first 25 percent of the amount paid in. If more than 25 percent had been paid on a contract, the amount received in excess of 25 percent would be split evenly—half going to Eaton and Sims and the other half to TL&I and FLCA.[34]

After signing the selling contract with Eaton and Sims, FLCA and TL&I amended their agreement with each other. To conform to the terms of the selling contract, they decreased the minimum sales price from seventy-five cents to fifty cents per square foot. The even split of proceeds between FLCA and TL&I would be determined after deducting amounts due the perpetual care fund and any commissions paid Eaton and Sims.[35]

American Securities Company

The contract between Sims and Eaton, TL&I, and FLCA contemplated that a new corporation would be formed to be the selling agent and that the selling contract would be assigned to the new entity. On September 9, 1912, the American Securities Company was incorporated in Maine by Charles Sims, Charles Marsh, and Hubert Eaton. Although this new company had the same name as Sims's American Securities Company incorporated in Georgia, it was a separate, distinct entity.

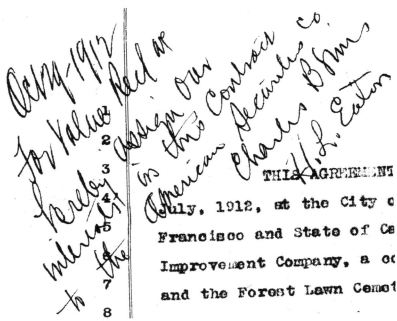

Figure 33. Contract Assignment

In 1912 Eaton, Marsh, and Sims incorporated American Securities Co. in Maine. Eaton and Sims signed the assignment of their selling contract to the new company.

In a contract signed by Sims, Marsh, and Eaton, they agreed that the new company would be assigned the new Forest Lawn selling contract, the Mount Hope selling contract, and two pending mausoleum patents. Eaton, L. C. King, Marsh, and Sims each received 250 shares of stock in the new company. The four men were to solicit investors to buy additional American Securities shares at par ($100 per share) and would receive an additional share for each share they sold.[36]

L. C. King would be paid 1,500 shares in American Securities for the Forest Lawn contract, Mount Hope contract, and the mausoleum patents. No explanation was given for King's interest in any of this.[37]

Initially, Sims was president and Marsh was secretary of the new company. Soon after incorporation, Marsh resigned as secretary and was elected vice president, and Eaton was elected as corporate secretary.[38]

American Securities Company's certificate of organization contemplated that the company could buy land to subdivide for "residence, cemetery, parks or other purposes, and for the improvement, development and handling of real estate generally, and act as Trustee for fund for permanent maintenance thereof." It also provided that the company could "conduct general undertaking business and maintain and conduct undertaking and funeral parlors." In the style of the times, the document included an extensive list of other businesses the company could conduct, ranging from manufacturing to logging to railroads and, finally, "any lawful business transaction or operation undertaken or carried on by capitalists, or financiers."[39]

Sims was quite upbeat when he wrote B. F. Edwards, president of the National Bank of Commerce in St. Louis, that "there are several good openings on the Pacific Coast for cemetery propositions at a fairly minimum cost." Of course, that was just the introduction. Sims's purpose was to interest Edwards in buying stock in the new American Securities corporation. He included a summary of the financial side of the Forest Lawn contract, concluding they could produce a profit of $25,000 a year on $100,000 in sales.[40]

Norton Wells also received a letter, apparently from Sims, telling him of the incorporation of the American Securities Company, "composed of representative bankers and business men of St. Louis and Kansas City." The letter proposed that American Securities would control Forest Lawn's perpetual care fund "on a fair contract." In return for this, the Rosses could buy five thousand shares of stock in American Securities for $2,500 in cash. Twenty percent of that amount would be paid on receipt of the stock. The balance would be paid in installments of 20 percent, payable on fifteen days' notice from American Securities. The letter said the Rosses would have to decide on the stock purchase very soon, because the stock was already fully subscribed—meaning that other buyers (subscribers) had committed to purchasing all the shares. To accommodate the Rosses, Sims would have to leave out some of the other subscribers. Wells told Sims by telegram that the Rosses would communicate directly with him regarding the stock.[41]

Preparing to Sell

During the months when American Securities was being organized, the parties began to get ready to start selling. Norton Wells sent Eaton photographs of Forest Lawn to share with various associates in St. Louis. Eaton returned to Reno to continue with the shutdown of the Adaven mine.[42]

The partition suit was still pending in July, so Eaton wrote Wells to make every effort to resolve the title problems of the suit and related mortgage issue so that selling could commence. On August 17, Wells wrote Sims that the attorneys seemed to have come to an agreement and that the partition suit should be settled within three weeks. Sims responded that if that happened, operations could begin in October. By the end of August, however, Wells could only report that things were progressing, but resolution still eluded them.[43]

Wells became concerned that selling activity might not be able to begin on time. In September, Eaton assured Wells that they still intended to start on the first of October, subject to the final decree being issued in the partition suit. But Wells had been told so many times that finalization was imminent that he began to lose confidence in the lawyers.[44]

Near the end of September, Wells sent a Western Union night letter to Sims saying that agreement had been reached on how the property would be divided.[45] Further delays followed, however, because of objections made by Oscar Souden, the mortgage holder.

On October 11, Wells told Sims he had good news: the attorneys had convinced Lucile Bedford's guardian, the Los Angeles Trust &

Savings Bank, to agree on the property division, and an engineer would have the map drawn by the following week. He reassured Sims and Eaton that "Thursday should see matter closed then we can talk business."[46]

This time, Wells's prophecy was right. A judge signed the decree partitioning the property on October 28, 1912.[47] The next day, Wells wired Sims that resolution had been reached:

FINAL DECREE ENTERED EVERYTHING NOW READY FOR
YOUR COMING[48]

Sims immediately replied that Eaton had left for the West and would stop in Reno and Sacramento on his way, arriving in Los Angeles around November 15. Sims was expected to arrive at about the same time. Eaton met with an accident while in Reno, delaying his arrival, but Wells received assurance that Sims would be there soon.[49]

Near the end of November 1912, Wells asked Sims if he wanted an office in the same building where FLCA's "city office" was located. Wells had previously offered to find office space for Eaton and Sims, but because they did not respond, he had lost the ability to rent two offices. When Sims again failed to respond, Wells telegraphed that the office could be held only a few more days.[50] Sims responded by wire.

EATON WILL BE IN LOS ANGELES MONDAY. IS NOW IN
SAN FRANCISCO. THINK IT WOULD COMPLICATE MATTERS
TO HAVE AN OFFICE ADJOINING YOURSELF AS THERE
WOULD BE A POSSIBILITY OF CONFLICTION AS TO
BUSINESS PORDUCED [sic]. WE ARE TRYING TO INDUCE
ROSS TO LET US HAVE MANAGEMENT OF LOS ANGELES AS
WE NEED YOU VERY MUCH IN OUR WORK IN OTHER LINES
AND WE THINK TO YOUR ADVANTAGE.[51]

The last comment is a reference to aspirations Sims and Eaton had for developing other selling contracts. The two men hoped to use Wells in the investigation of other sales projects—some of which would extend beyond cemeteries, although they had apparently not divulged this to Wells.

Wells was surprised by the comment regarding the management of Forest Lawn, and perhaps concerned about his job as president. He responded that this was the first he had heard of the matter and hoped Eaton would give him more information when he arrived.

January 1913 came, and selling efforts still had not begun. Pop Ross was waiting for word that Sims had arrived in Los Angeles, as he was presumed to be the heart of the selling effort. However, Hubert Eaton and E. D. Getzendanner, the sales manager, were in Los Angeles preparing for selling, including finalizing printed materials for the salesmen to use.[52]

Getzendanner was also working on recruiting a sales force, hiring Lyons & Beavis as "employment specialists" to find applicants. Although Lyons & Beavis's letterhead proclaimed "Proficient Help Supplied for Any Commercial Position," they finally wrote Getzendanner that they regretted not having been able to send better candidates, but it had not been for lack of trying. Many of the people they contacted were just not interested in sales positions like this.[53]

Although the contract had called for commencement of sales activity by Sims and Eaton in October 1912, it was not until February 1913 that selling efforts actually began.

Other Cemetery Opportunities

Between the signing of the selling contract in July 1912 and the spring of 1913, Forest Lawn was not the only cemetery on the minds of Eaton and Sims. Being the promoters that they were, they were investigating the purchase or establishment of cemeteries in other California cities, including San Diego, Sacramento, Oakland, and Berkeley.[54] Norton Wells and Tom Ross were involved in some of these opportunities.

San Diego's Greenwood Cemetery was not a good candidate for a selling contract with Sims, since it was already doing well. However, the city owned a cemetery with approximately one hundred undeveloped acres. Sims saw that as an opportunity.[55]

At the end of July 1912, Sims wrote Wells asking if he would be willing to help investigate the San Diego City Cemetery. He suggested Wells go to San Diego to represent Sims and his associates. Sims assured Wells that although the subject had not been raised yet with the "appropriate people" (city officials), when it came time to close, he would come to help. Wells replied that he would be pleased to assist with the project. In fact, he had already started using some of his Los Angeles contacts to arrange for contacts in San Diego. When Sims asked what compensation Wells would expect, Wells told him he wanted only to be reimbursed for expenses. He thought developing contacts in the San Diego area would be valuable and hoped there would be other opportunities after the San Diego and Los Angeles projects were underway.[56]

Wells proceeded to make several trips to meet with officials, including L. A. Blochman, a local banker and president of the San Diego Cemetery Commission. From Blochman, Wells learned that the city mayor, James E. Wadham, believed the cemetery land was part of the original Pueblo land grant creating San Diego. It was likely that any transfer of the unsold cemetery land by the city council would require ratification by the California legislature. Sims stroked Wells's ego by telling him, "I want to congratulate you upon the nice way in which you have handled this very delicate mission and you are the only one outside of myself that I would have trusted it to."[57]

In August, Sims wrote Mayor Wadham, offering to "take over the unused [San Diego cemetery] land . . . [because] it is never profitable for a City to operate a cemetery, as it is a technical matter regarding which few have a thorough knowledge." If the city could not sell the land, Sims offered the alternative of taking over operation of the cemetery, effectively paying the city the same amount that would have been paid if the land were sold to Sims and his associates.[58]

Though Norton Wells made multiple trips to San Diego, he had been unable to negotiate a final deal for the San Diego City Cemetery on his own. So in April 1913, Wells and Eaton traveled south from Los Angeles so that Wells could introduce Eaton to the "City Bosses" of San Diego. After the trip, Wells reported to Pop Ross that "Eaton did not accomplish anything of note, owing to the City being in preparation for a Municipal Election, yet, he laid the wires for some future work down there."[59]

Eaton reported to Sims that he had returned from San Diego and felt "more like a lobbyist or politician than anything else. The deal in San Diego is a question of politics." He went on to say he thought they could close the deal, but it would take a lot of "wire-pulling." The cemetery was governed by a commission appointed by the mayor. However, the commission had little authority, and the city council had to approve what the commission did.[60]

I took Mr. Wells down with me, and he introduced me to the Mayor, "Mr. Wadham", Mr. Blochman, and another friend who later introduced me to Mr. Kavannah. Said Mr. Kavannah is a quiet owl-like person who wears blue spectacles, and has his finger-tips on everything political in San Diego, and right here, I want to remark that I take my hat off to the political machine of San Diego; it works very quietly and denies its own existence, and it was only after closer acquaintance with some of the members thereof, that I finally knew that such a steam-roller was in existence. . . .

All steam-rollers as you know, need a little fuel, and while I would be the last one to suggest such a thing, I have been wondering if the question were hinted at, just the best way to meet it.[61]

Eaton also learned that some of the information Wells had reported regarding Greenwood Cemetery was wrong. The president and part owner of Greenwood, Ralph Granger, lived in San Diego, not Los Angeles. Wells had been correct that he was a banker; Granger was president of San Diego's Merchants National Bank. A local undertaker, James E. Connell, was the largest shareholder in the cemetery.[62]

Wanting to begin building relationships in San Diego, Eaton retained Terence B. Cosgrove, who was Mayor Wadham's partner in the law firm of Wadham, Cosgrove & Titus, to represent American Securities. Eaton also contacted Los Angeles attorney William Hazlett and asked him to give his opinion about the matter.[63]

After reviewing the situation, Hazlett wrote Cosgrove expressing doubt about the possibility of a sale of the cemetery. However, he was somewhat confident that a selling contract could be possible if it did not "result in the delegation of powers of an arm of the city government which is not warranted by the law or by the charter." Cosgrove responded that a selling contract was impossible. Because American Securities Company would make improvements costing up to $15,000, it would need a contract of at least twenty years to protect its investment, but that would violate legal limitations on the length of city contracts.[64]

Hazlett then wrote Eaton, providing a summary of Cosgrove's position without acknowledging the source. In closing, he cautioned there was danger in such a contract and investing money in upgrading the cemetery. If the contract were successfully attacked as exceeding the powers of the cemetery commission, there would be no recovery of the investment or compensation for time spent. With this opinion, the lawyer killed any possibility of a contract for the San Diego cemetery.[65]

Meanwhile, Sims had his eye on cemeteries in other cities. In mid-September 1912, he told B. F. Edwards, the St. Louis banker, that he had "a deal on with the owners of a cemetery in Sacramento, California, which we expect to close on exactly the same basis, as Los Angeles." However, nothing indicates that he was actually able to win that contract or one for a San Francisco cemetery he was also negotiating with. Sims told Edwards that American Securities was working on a cemetery contract with the City of San Diego and would need approximately $35,000 to start that venture. He concluded his letter by saying that he had "spent considerable time investigating the Western field and believe that it is wise to get a foot-hold there so as to be fairly well established by the time we get our present property on a basis where it will not require my personal attention."[66]

Sims was also interested in starting a new cemetery in Oakland. Tom Ross was actively involved in the search for land for the project. Ross wrote Sims in February 1913 that their option on a sixty-five-acre tract had been extended by a few days, and that no conclusion had been reached on a second parcel. Ross and Sims wanted to drill on the lot to determine whether well water would be available, but were concerned that if they did, the land price might be raised because the owners would think someone was anxious to buy the property.[67]

Although the Oakland project was of interest, it was not a high priority, so the project would lay fallow for some time.

In the coming years, Eaton continued to keep looking for other cemetery deals. When he learned at a social gathering that Forest Hill Cemetery in Kansas City, Missouri, might be up for sale, he wrote its secretary regarding a possible purchase.[68]

George Law, secretary of Forest Hill Cemetery since 1892, replied with a rather lengthy letter extolling the virtues of the cemetery. Concerning its availability, he told Eaton, "Our capital stock is $300,000 and I presume, Mr. Paul would sell it for par, though the property is not offered for sale and I have no authority for saying this."[69] Since the property was not actually on the market, Eaton chose not to pursue a purchase.

Although Sims and Eaton believed that the population growth of the West Coast would offer them many opportunities for expansion of cemeteries under their control, their efforts were not successful. It was time to stop the distraction of looking for new cemetery deals and focus on making the Forest Lawn selling contract a success.

CHAPTER 11

Property Management Challenges

From 1912 to 1915, managing the Forest Lawn property required Norton Wells to deal with problems ranging from storm damage to gopher infestation. Some of the issues he faced led to clashes with Burt Richardson, the neighboring landowner and nephew of W. C. B. Richardson, whom Wells may have thought was more pesky than the gophers.

Street Improvements

With Forest Lawn's growth and increased visibility, Norton Wells became concerned with the appearance of the entrance to the cemetery. Since no city had plans to make street improvements, in the spring of 1912 Wells independently sought bids for improvements to Glendale Avenue in front of Forest Lawn. He received a proposal from general contractor Peter L. Ferry to grade the street, put in curbing, and pave it with oil and macadam (a mixture of broken stone and asphalt).[1]

The grading proposal covered only the east half of the street, the side next to Forest Lawn. Improvements on the west side of the street were to be paid for by Burt W. Richardson, who owned property across from the cemetery. The son of W. C. B. Richardson,

Burt was a vice president of the First National Bank, a prominent citizen, and reportedly a millionaire. However, he did not agree to pay for the work on his side, so the project adjacent to Forest Lawn was postponed. Property owners on both sides of the street north of Forest Lawn were willing to pay for the work, so Glendale Avenue north of the cemetery was improved.[2]

About a year later, an attempt to close Depot Street was started by Burt Richardson. He was willing to give the railroad right-of-way across his property for free if the city would close Depot Street to give the railroad access to his property. Wells met with city officials to protest the action. He told them that closure of the street would irreparably harm Forest Lawn, since Depot Street was the prime access to the cemetery from the streetcar line on Brand Boulevard.[3] Depot Street remained open despite Richardson's influence.

In May 1913, a large storm sent quantities of water south past Forest Lawn, damaging Glendale Avenue and eroding a three-foot-deep gouge in Depot Street. The city took care of the immediate problem with Depot Street by filling the rut with oil chips taken from the torn-up streets. However, that did nothing to appease the property owners north of Forest Lawn, who were irate because traffic was being diverted to Central Avenue due to the condition of Glendale Avenue.[4]

Wells concluded that he needed to proceed with curbing and a sidewalk on Glendale Avenue all the way to San Fernando Road, in addition to road improvements, which he duly proposed to the board of trustees of the city of Tropico. This plan would have improved the Forest Lawn entrance. However, Wells thought it might further irritate Burt Richardson, since road improvements on Forest Lawn's side of the street would have no benefit to him.[5]

The plan for Glendale Avenue road improvements in front of Forest Lawn was taken up at the Tropico board of trustees meeting in late May 1913. Although Richardson had not filed an official complaint regarding Forest Lawn's application, Wells felt Richardson had manipulated things to make things difficult for Forest Lawn. Wells described the board chair, C. A. Bancroft, as an "agent of Richardson."[6]

After the meeting, Wells reported to Pop, "We had a great scrap Thursday night at the Trustees meeting over the side walk, it having occupied the greater part of the evening up to 10 o'clock."[7]

The issue with the sidewalk was its location. The city required all sidewalks to be put in at the property line, a setback from the street. However, as Wells had been told earlier in the month, Forest Lawn's stone entry arch was improperly placed. The north end of the three-arch structure encroached on the city's right-of-way by as much as six feet.[8] Installing the sidewalk at the property line would require removing the arch from city property.

Wells told Pop that Bancroft held out on every point possible. But "every time an argument was put up, the expression of the Board in favor of [Forest Lawn] confronted him until he called for a meeting of the Committee as a whole in a private session." Wells was excused from the meeting.[9]

Half an hour later, Wells was invited back in. He was told that the board was now proposing to seek bids only for the road and curb and would not build the sidewalk. Moving the arch was to be

Figure 34. Wells's Sketch of Entry Arch Location.

The arch encroached on the city-designated area for sidewalk along the east side of Glendale Avenue. An accompanying note read, "Pencil is arch as put in—Red ink is where arch will have to be moved to" and "You will note that the south colums [sic] is where the center was moved which placed the North wing outside our line."

Forest Lawn archives

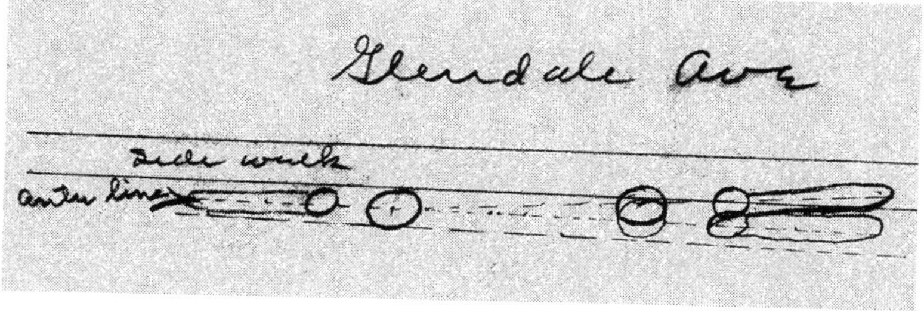

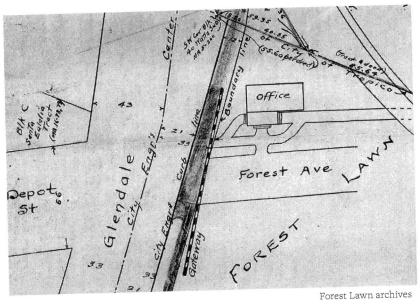

Forest Lawn archives

Figure 35. Engineer's Entrance Drawing
Detail of entrance area including office and misaligned entry arch.

dropped (for the moment), and Forest Lawn would be allowed to put in decomposed granite between the curb and the property line. This was a big win for Wells. He thought the sidewalk was unavoidable but did not feel it would be of much help to Forest Lawn.[10]

Moving the Arch

The location of the entrance arch came up again a year later. After storms early in 1914, Glendale Avenue was in poor condition. In May of that year, Norton Wells had an informal meeting with the newly elected City of Tropico board of trustees, who indicated that pressure was being put on them to extend the improved portion of Glendale Avenue south to San Fernando Road. The trustees intimated that they were considering filing a lawsuit to compel Forest Lawn to move its arch off city property. The adjacent property owners, including Burt Richardson, were taking the position that

Engineering News 1915

Figure 36. Arch and Wing-Wall Move

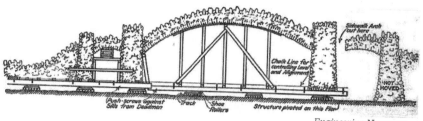

Engineering News 1915

Figure 37. Shoring and Support for Arch Move

they would not pay for the road improvements "even if the work is put for public contract, nor will they sign for private work, unless the arch is moved."[11]

During the meeting with the Tropico trustees, a compromise was suggested that if Forest Lawn moved its arch, Richardson might be persuaded to agree to paying for part of the street improvements—grading and installing curbs. That would have left the construction of sidewalks to be done a year later.[12]

Before agreeing to move the arch, Wells wanted to know what the project would cost. When he consulted Harry Stocks, the contractor who originally built the arch, he was told the north arch would have to be torn out because it was misaligned by approximately six feet. If it had been put in straight, it would have been well within the property line. According to Stocks, he had told Blain and Treadwell it was laid out "off line," but he was instructed to "build it that way" anyway.

Engineering News 1915

Figure 38. Moving the Arch on 20″ X 20″ Beams

Wells mused, "What reason they had I do not know, but as everything seems to have been with an unterior [*sic*] motive in mind, I presume this work was constructed [this way] for a reason." Wells added that Forest Lawn's entrance appearance would be improved if the road were graded and oiled.[13]

On June 8, 1914, Wells asked Pop to approve a contract between the City of Tropico and FLCA regarding moving the arch. Wells thought the contract should really be between TL&I and the city, since TL&I owned the arch. Pop Ross replied that Wells should do the best he could to reach an agreement "as amicably as possible and do not have any fight over it as we are in the wrong."[14]

When a month passed without the contract being signed, the city referred the matter to its attorney, Henry P. Goodwin, who then sent a demand letter to FLCA. Goodwin's July 1914 letter reiterated what everyone already knew: the arch had been built encroaching on a city street. Since the city now had plans to improve Glendale Avenue, it wanted quick action on arch removal. Goodwin added that if something wasn't done quickly, he would start legal action.

The contract was finally signed on June 1, 1914, giving FLCA one year from that date to remove the arch from city property.[15]

Almost a year went by before there was any progress on Glendale Avenue improvements or moving Forest Lawn's arch. In April 1915, Wells reported to Pop Ross that grading on Glendale Avenue had been completed and the road improvements would be completed in about three weeks.[16] In May, city attorney Goodwin sent Wells a reminder that the one-year anniversary of the agreement was only weeks away and the arch needed to be moved by that date.[17]

Realizing that time was running out, Wells wrote Goodwin to ask for an extension in order to avoid blocking the cemetery entrance on Decoration Day. Goodwin took the matter up with the City of Tropico's board of trustees and was able to obtain a one-month extension for Forest Lawn to remove its arch from city property.[18]

Although a settlement had been reached with J. B. Treadwell, he still dropped in on Wells from time to time. Treadwell suggested to Wells that TL&I, rather than FLCA, should protest moving the arch, because FLCA had actually signed the agreement with the city. Pop Ross characterized this suggestion as "useless," since it might prompt others to object. Treadwell also claimed that one of the City of Tropico trustees had assured him the arch would not need to be moved, but there was no evidence to prove that claim. Pop did not believe it was physically possible to move the arch, and thus he thought it would be necessary, but disagreeable, to take the arch down and rebuild it.[19]

Meanwhile, Wells consulted a contractor, Kress House Moving, at the suggestion of cemetery superintendent Mike Glora. The contractor believed it might be possible to brace the main arch and then swing the north end back onto TL&I's property. Wells suggested that at the same time, the iron letters on the front face of the arch could be moved to sit on top of the arch and be gilded. Doing this, he said, would solve the problem of the letters being covered up by the vines that grew their way up the pillars and across the face of the arch. Tom thought that moving the letters would spoil the arch, so told Wells that he would just have to trim the vines around the letters from time to time.[20]

Norton Wells often wanted to push decisions off to the Rosses, or at least obtain their concurrence before acting. Such was the case with moving the arch. With just under a month to go before the deadline for moving the arch off the city right-of-way, Wells wrote that he wished Tom would come down and consult on whether to move or rebuild the arch.[21]

Having received bids on tearing down and reconstructing the arch, Wells attempted to persuade Kress House Moving to lower its price for moving the arch, which was fifty dollars higher than the cost of rebuilding. He told J. C. Coleman, secretary of Kress, that he preferred moving the arch to rebuilding it because of the "litter" that would result from construction. Furthermore, he concluded, the higher cost for moving the arch "naturally cuts considerable figure with members of the board of trustees."[22]

Coleman declined to lower Kress's price for moving the arch. He reminded Wells that the job had originally been estimated at $500, but the price had been lowered to $450 to win the work. On June 21, shortly after Tom came to Forest Lawn to review the moving project, Wells sent a very short letter accepting the proposal.[23]

In mid-July, Wells was in San Francisco when his secretary, Eva B. Cole, wrote Pop Ross about the arch. She reported that the arch had been moved, and Kress was installing the necessary foundation and repairing "torn parts" of the arch. The move took ten days and was completed well before the end of the month deadline. In a letter of commendation to Kress—requested by them for marketing purposes—Tom Ross praised them for saving money as well as completing the job in one-fourth the time that demolishing and rebuilding the arch would have taken.[24]

Other Property Issues

In addition to the street repairs and the arch, Wells had to deal with other challenges affecting the cemetery property.

The winter of 1913–1914 hit Los Angeles with a series of storms because of an intense El Niño season. Rivers overflowed and thousands of acres were flooded. Bridges washed out along the Los Angeles River, leading to suspension of railroad service for almost a week and causing more than $10 million in damage.[25]

Wells reported to Pop Ross that one of the January rainstorms inflicted damage on the railroad right-of-way adjacent to Forest Lawn. He thought the Los Angeles River had so much water that it looked "like a branch of the Mississippi River."[26]

After further investigation, Wells told Pop Ross that the cemetery had not suffered as much storm damage as was originally feared. However, the road into the cemetery did not fare well. In addition, the Los Angeles and Salt Lake Railroad track running adjacent to the cemetery, and which had to be crossed to enter the cemetery, suffered severe erosion where its trestle crossed the waterway. One of the bents (supportive piers) was torn out and another was left hanging.[27]

In late February, Wells was caught in one of the largest storms to hit Southern California. He just beat a flood in Cajon Pass. The flooding was so bad that Wells and his party were marooned in San Bernardino and had to spend a night at an orange grower's ranch. The following day they made it only as far as Covina, where they found many bridges washed out. It was not until the third day that the group made it back to Los Angeles.

After describing his trip to Pop, Wells reported on damage to Forest Lawn. Once again the railroad trestle was damaged, resulting in the need for a temporary footbridge to the cemetery. Although there was no damage to the cemetery's lawns, Wells believed it would be expensive to fix the culvert that crossed near the railroad track. The lawns had been saved from serious damage because ditches had been dug to control the water runoff.[28]

After the terrific storms of January and February 1914, Los Angeles was hit with unseasonably warm weather in March. According to Wells, it was the warmest weather in thirty-five years.

Just as the hot weather came, Forest Lawn's well casing collapsed. Learning that it would take three weeks to drill a new well, Wells needed a temporary source of water. J. B. Treadwell was willing to provide a temporary connection from his adjacent property, but Wells did not like the idea of working with him. Once again, Wells sought direction from Pop Ross. With assurance that attorney William Hazlett could draft an agreement to protect TL&I and FLCA, Pop told Wells to make the best deal he could without delay. Wells arranged to buy some water from Treadwell's adjacent property, but was not sure it would be adequate.[29]

Indeed, after pipes from Forest Lawn were connected to Treadwell's system, it turned out that Treadwell's pump motor was not strong enough to provide pressure to the upper areas of the cemetery. Consequently, Wells rented a larger pump, and for the first time in two weeks he could water the grass in the Iona, a newer section of the cemetery.[30]

The well replacement and installation of the new pump went slowly. At the beginning of May 1914, Wells reported that the new machinery had been shipped, but it was another two weeks before Wells could finally write Pop Ross that the new pump had been started. After making considerable noise because of air in the line, it was yielding three times as much water as the previous setup.[31]

A year later, Eaton sent a note to Wells concerning the cemetery's gopher infestation. While he admitted that driving the rodents out was hard, he implored Wells to keep at it constantly. He suggested hiring a little boy to shoot them and trying "gopher guns."[32]

When little progress was made with the eradication efforts, Eaton sent Wells a note that he had been at the cemetery with prospects who were disgusted by the gophers. According to Eaton, "At one time there was a little drove of about ten that scurried across the front of our auto." One of the prospects said they had used poisoned grain with great success.[33]

Wells quickly responded to Eaton that cemetery superintendent Mike Glora had succeeded in getting a "gas pump" designed for killing ground squirrels, and he anticipated the gophers would soon be eliminated. The gopher problem was not new, nor was it surprising given the rural nature of the area. Several years earlier, in an eradication program, gophers had been gassed using the pump.[34]

The End of Burt Richardson

In early December 1915, two "monumental" men visited Wells, wanting to find a location near Forest Lawn's entrance for their cemetery monument business. Wells did not like the idea, nor did Burt Richardson. With Richardson's hatred of all things cemetery, Wells was sure that between Richardson and Forest Lawn, "any objectionable feature, like having a stoneyard at [Forest Lawn's] entrance," could be avoided.[35]

Nevertheless, local businessman Thomas Mizar planned to rent a triangle of land for a "tombstone yard" to sell monuments on Brand Boulevard in Tropico, just a block from Forest Lawn. Richardson was quite unhappy with the prospect of having cemetery monuments sold so near his real estate holdings,

Los Angeles Evening Herald,
December 23, 1915

Figure 39. Burt W. Richardson

believing the sight of the tombstones would be depressing.[36]

One of Burt Richardson's brothers, E. W. Richardson, later said that Burt had openly opposed Mizar's proposed tombstone business location, believing it would spoil the beauty of Brand Boulevard. E. W. also maintained that "the cemetery does not spoil the beauty, as it is hidden from view of the boulevard and the houses by a small forest of trees and shrubbery."[37]

Richardson's opposition to the monument yard location did not sit well with Mizar. His animosity toward Richardson—whether due to this disagreement or the fact that the banker had turned down Mizar's request for a loan—led to tragic results.

On December 23, 1914, Wells was at the cemetery with Mike Glora,

Los Angeles Evening Herald,
December 23, 1915

Figure 40. Thomas Mizar

Forest Lawn's superintendent. They heard a loud noise, which Glora thought sounded like two bombs exploding on the streetcar track. When they looked down Depot Street, they saw a man lying on the ground. Glora ran to the man, who turned out to be Burt Richardson. Running up the street, Wells and Glora met Deputy City Marshal E. C. Fairfield, who had arrived at the same time. Fairfield told them that Thomas Mizar had shot Burt Richardson and then run up Glendale Avenue.[38]

According to the *Los Angeles Evening Herald,* Fairfield was one hundred yards away from Richardson, seated on his motorcycle, and "watched the murder under the impression that it was a moving picture rehearsal."[39]

Glora, who was a deputy sheriff, went back to Forest Lawn so he could grab his gun. He and Wells then climbed into an auto and went up the street. They caught up with Mizar at Palmer Avenue, half a block from his house. Mizar had his gun in hand and was ready to fight. Glora called to him to surrender, but Mizar just cut across a vacant lot. Wells and Glora jumped out of their car and found shelter behind some trees. Wells told Glora to shoot, but Glora could not because several children were on the sidewalk. Mizar took that as an opportunity to run into his house.[40]

Glora kept the house covered while Wells scrambled back in the auto and headed for city hall. On the way, he met Deputy Fairfield and another officer, Marshal Gould. After leading the lawmen back to where Glora was stationed, Wells sought out the nearest phone to call for the sheriff's posse. Wells also tried to collect men with rifles, since the handguns were no match for the Winchester rifle Mizar was now using. By the time Wells was able to return with the rifles, the sheriff's posse had arrived and surrounded the house, and Mizar, realizing he was outnumbered, had surrendered.[41]

A coroner's jury found Mizar guilty of murdering Burt W. Richardson.[42] With Richardson's death, the conflicts between Forest Lawn and Richardson also died.

CHAPTER 12

Startup Tensions

In February 1913, the selling of plots in Forest Lawn Cemetery by American Securities salesmen finally commenced. Pop Ross, Tom Ross, and Norton Wells had been waiting a long time for Hubert Eaton and Charles Sims to implement their selling program at Forest Lawn. However, it did not take long for tension to cloud the new relationship.

Settling Accounts

The first dispute between American Securities, TL&I, and FLCA had to do with how money was divided as it was received after someone purchased a cemetery lot. Although the contract between the three parties defined the portion that each would ultimately receive, they did not always agree on the process for splitting the money.

Each organization wanted to get cash as soon as possible. Pop Ross and Norton Wells wanted to receive cash as payments were made for cemetery lot sales. American Securities also wanted to receive all cash on sales as it came in—up to the commission specified in the contract—to offset the sales force commissions and other selling expenses.

When Wells told Sims that TL&I and FLCA would like to receive their portion of proceeds as soon as it came in, Sims countered that this would cause extra work. Therefore, Sims said, TL&I and FLCA should accept payments based on a monthly accounting. The contract called for an accounting and settlement of amounts received by the tenth of the following month, so Pop and Wells had little choice but to accept Sims's position.[1]

Handling Installment Payments

The contract terms for a paid-in-full sale were not in dispute. If a $100 sale was paid in full, $25 would go to the perpetual care fund,

Figure 41. Differing Cash Distribution Methods

The two methods of cash distribution gave the same final result, but the difference was when cash was received. Here is the cash distribution on a hypothetical $100 sale.

Eaton & Sims's Method				
Payment Number	Payment Amount	To Be Split between TL&I and FLCA	Commission to American Securities	To Perpetual Care Fund
1	$10.00	–	$10.00	–
2	$10.00	–	$10.00	–
3	$10.00	$2.50	$7.50	–
4	$10.00	$5.00	$5.00	–
5	$10.00	$5.00	$5.00	–
6	$10.00	$10.00	–	–
7	$10.00	$10.00	–	–
8	$10.00	$5.00	–	$5.00
9	$10.00	–	–	$10.00
10	$10.00	–	–	$10.00
Total	$100.00	$37.50	$37.50	$10.00

$37.50 would go to American Securities, and $37.50 would be equally divided between FLCA and TL&I.

Although this calculation seemed clear, there was disagreement about how to distribute cash received from installment sales. When Pop wondered how partial payments on accounts would be treated, he asked Wells to get some examples from Eaton to "see how it works."[2] He did not like what he found out.

Pop Ross and Wells took the view that when the first installment payment came in, half would go to American Securities and the other half would be divided between TL&I and FLCA. These amounts would be paid by the tenth of the month following receipt. As more payments came in, this pattern would continue until all three parties had the money due them. After that, the remaining payments would go to the perpetual care fund.

Ross & Wells's Method				
Payment Number	Payment Amount	To Be Split between TL&I and FLCA	Commission to American Securities	To Perpetual Care Fund
1	$10.00	$5.00	$5.00	—
2	$10.00	$5.00	$5.00	—
3	$10.00	$5.00	$5.00	—
4	$10.00	$5.00	$5.00	—
5	$10.00	$5.00	$5.00	—
6	$10.00	$5.00	$5.00	—
7	$10.00	$5.00	$5.00	—
8	$10.00	$2.50	$2.50	$5.00
9	$10.00	—	—	$10.00
10	$10.00	—	—	$10.00
Total	**$100.00**	**$37.50**	**$37.50**	**$10.00**

Sims and Eaton, on the other hand, took a different position. According to the contract, if buyers defaulted and the sale was cancelled, American Securities would get the first cash received, up to 25 percent of the contract price. Any additional cash received would be evenly split between American Securities and TL&I/FLCA.[3] For example:

- A customer signs a contract for $100 and makes payments of $46 before cancelling. American Securities would be entitled to $25 (25 percent of the $100 contract price), plus one-half of the remaining $21 that was received ($10.50), for a total of $35.50. TL&I and FLCA would split $10.50 and each would receive $5.25.
- A customer signs a contract for $100 and cancels after making payments of $24. American Securities would receive the entire $24; TL&I and FLCA would receive nothing.

Sims and Eaton took the position that since they never knew which contract might end up in cancellation, the initial installment payments should go entirely to American Securities until it had received 25 percent of the sale price. After that, receipts would be split evenly between American Securities and TL&I/FLCA until American Securities had received its full share. TL&I and FLCA would then receive the rest of their share, and the final payments would go to the perpetual care fund.

There was no disagreement about how much each party should ultimately receive. The dispute related to the timing of when they received it. But with cash so tight for each of the parties, the timing of receipts was critical to survival.

Monthly Letters

In May 1913, Pop Ross, on behalf of TL&I, and Wells, on behalf of FLCA, began sending monthly letters to American Securities protesting the method of calculating cash distributions. Wells attempted to get something from Sims explaining American Securities' position.[4]

When Sims finally did respond, Pop Ross was not satisfied and sent a letter to Sims pointedly asking for a change in the method of distribution of cash. Wells described Sims's response as being "just about as good a dodger of the question as any epistle I ever read."[5]

Sales were now going so well that Pop thought it would be more damaging to escalate the conflict to legal action than to endure the problem. He also recognized that the success of American Securities's selling organization was essential to Forest Lawn's success. Pop told Hazlett he would wait for Sims's reply and consider what action to take.[6]

No response to the letter was forthcoming, and Wells learned that Sims had left the country.

Saturday, the American Securities Company's office learned that Mr. Sims had been married and on June first was leaving for Europe. Now, what do you know about that! I believe he has a young wife of some twenty-two or three summers. I asked Mr. Eaton what would be the conditions of our affairs therefrom, and he said he thought it would be better than before, because everything will be left to he and Mr. Marsh, Vice-President, so, I do not contemplate anything but concerted action.[7]

Pop Ross was surprised to hear of Charles Sims's marriage, but nevertheless hoped Sims would finally agree to follow TL&I's interpretation of the contract and that the matter would be settled quickly. "We do not want another statement on the lines of the last three and shall insist upon its being decided in that manner. Please find out from Mr Eaton if he has had any word from Mr Sims regarding this[,] as our patience is about exhausted."[8] Wells's letter also raised the question of who was now actually in charge at American Securities.

More Contract Disputes

In response to TL&I protesting the calculation for dividing receipts, American Securities raised its own issues with contract compliance. In June, Hubert Eaton wrote Wells complaining that FLCA was not providing enough interment property to sell, and reminded Wells he had repeatedly brought this matter to FLCA's attention over the previous four months. Under the terms of the selling contract, FLCA was obligated to keep at least four hundred burial spaces available for sale by American Securities. To be available for sale, the burial spaces had to be developed. FLCA would need to do final grading, install irrigation, plant grass, and make whatever roadway improvements were necessary for access.[9]

Eaton sent a letter to TL&I and FLCA reporting that after getting contracts signed, salesmen were finding out that the "cemetery office" had already sold the lot. He went on to complain of the general lack of cooperation from the cemetery office staff, particularly the bookkeeper. At the same time, he took pains to make sure the criticism did not apply to Norton Wells, saying they had always "found him affable and sincere in his efforts to promote harmony between the two companies[,] but we regret that we cannot say this much for his employees."[10]

When Wells did not indicate disagreement with the letter, Eaton wrote a note on the bottom of it: "9/1/13 This letter shown to Wells and he promised to adjust matters."[11]

In a letter to Wells, Eaton noted that they had begun the selling operation at the first of the year and had averaged over $9,000 each month, compared to only $2,000 a month before then. "We feel we are doing our part and trust you will co-operate with us in putting this proposition in shape whereby we may sell it according to the plans, which through hard experience we have found to be most advantageous."[12]

Before sending the letter to Pop Ross, Eaton had given Wells a copy of it. Wells had told Eaton not to send the letter to Pop until the dispute over dividing receipts was resolved, as it would only irritate Pop more. Despite Wells's suggestion, Eaton did send the letter. Wells wrote Pop Ross, "I know that letter of Eaton's has stirred you. . . ." Eaton thought of the letter as a "tit for tat," while Wells characterized it as "more boys play than a serious complaint."[13]

Pop may have been a little more than "stirred" by Eaton, and reported to the TL&I board of directors that American Securities was "not carrying out the terms of [the] contract satisfactorily." On June 5 the board instructed Pop to consult with FLCA and to take any legal action necessary.[14]

The next day, Wells wrote Pop about the status of the payment dispute. Eaton had written Sims, who was in New York, but did not expect a quick reply. However, Wells believed Eaton had indicated that TL&I's and FLCA's demands for calculating payments would be met. [15]

> As for his letter, I have talked over plans to put in new sections with [Eaton] . . . which I believe suits him especially now that he has gotten the bile off his stomach thro' the letter. I really don't feel that our positions are serious especially as he has shown no disposition not to comply with our request by the 10th. He even told Hazlett that he expected to comply with our wishes.[16]

Waiting for Sims to return to resolve the payment matter did not sit well with Pop. Although he seemed to be resigned to waiting, he told Wells he was thinking about options for action if a satisfactory understanding could not be reached. Pop's dilemma was that legal action would undoubtedly stop sales until things were settled. His view was that litigation would be far more damaging to American Securities than to TL&I or FLCA because the latter two would be in the same position as before Eaton and Sims were on the scene. American Securities, on the other hand, would risk that the dispute would be reported in the papers and prospective buyers would be put off purchases. Pop told Wells he had no desire to enter litigation and that they would not be forced into legal action.[17]

A month later, in a postscript to a letter to Pop, Wells related, "Mr. Eaton received a wire from Mr. Sims this morning and he has just returned to St. Louis. Said he would write soon. That is the first word Mr E[aton] had had from him."[18]

Strained Relationships

As tensions grew between TL&I and American Securities, TL&I faced a dilemma. Eaton and Sims had dramatically increased sales, so if TL&I pushed too hard or took legal action, all momentum of the increased sales could be lost. Also, Eaton appeared to be dodging responses until Sims could be present.

Acknowledging he had been told Sims would soon be in California, Pop Ross wrote Eaton, reiterating TL&I's reluctance to take action that would cause disturbance with American Securities and its salesmen or with purchasers, but noting that it could not continue the status quo. He told Eaton that TL&I was not being treated courteously or in a businesslike way, and this treatment created more strain in the relationship.[19]

The stress of the situation apparently was taking its toll within TL&I. Albert Burgren, Tom Ross's partner, resigned as a director of TL&I in early October 1913. Concurrently, he told Pop he wanted to sell his 8,500 shares in TL&I to the company for $500, and requested that Pop "place my offer before the meeting of the Directors and oblige."[20]

When Sims showed up in California, he worked on settling things with Eaton rather than letting TL&I or FLCA know of his intentions regarding the method for dividing cash received. Since Sims did not volunteer information regarding what would be done, Pop Ross wrote Wells that when the monthly accounting was received it would be clear whether Sims had altered his position. Pop still wanted to settle things amicably, but told Wells he might have to travel to Los Angeles to discuss legal options with attorney Max Loewenthal. He warned Wells that he would not let Sims or Eaton know if he were to come to Los Angeles, because "it is always desirable that one's opponent should know as little of our movements as possible, or our intentions, so that we may be all the more free to act as circumstances direct."[21]

When Wells could see Eaton and Sims at the same time, they told him they were not going to put any more money into Los Angeles because they were not making as much money as they would in a property they owned themselves. Wells postulated that they were "planning to bluff [TL&I and FLCA] then try and work us for either more commission . . . or to scare us into leaving the contract to go on as it is now."[22]

Perhaps because of the conversation with Wells, Sims asked the Los Angeles law firm of Williams, Goudge & Chandler for a legal opinion relative to the interpretation of the 1912 contract between TL&I, FLCA, and American Securities. Sims had also learned of TL&I's referral of the matter to Loewenthal. In Sims's letter to his attorneys, he explained his understanding of the contract but added, "[We] have in mind that Mr. Ross intends to use every avenue open to him to force us to settle on his construction." He further noted that although he and Eaton had opened their sales office in Los Angeles in January and it was now October, the inventory of four hundred lots had never been provided as called for in the contract. Sims also expressed indignation at Pop's characterization of the Eaton-Sims method of calculation as "misappropriation."[23]

Herbert J. Goudge responded in short order with an analysis of the contract wording and the conclusion that "your interpretation of the contract and your manner of making monthly settlements is certainly proper and correct." Goudge also reassured Sims that the "circumstances do not in any way justify the use of the word [misappropriation]."[24]

Meanwhile, cash was running low for everyone.

In early October, Pop Ross wrote Wells that as soon as American Securities made its monthly payment, TL&I's portion should be sent immediately, because they wanted to close their books in preparation for the annual meeting. Primarily concerned with closing the books and getting cash, Pop did not mention the calculation issue.[25]

Wells promised he would send everything as soon as he received it, but as payment had been late the prior month, he might not be able to send it as soon as Pop wanted. He further noted that FLCA and American Securities also were short of money, but he would do the best he could.[26]

Clearly wanting to move things along, but feeling some frustration at the lack of progress, Pop Ross thought all the back and forth talk covered everything except resolving the issue of dividing receipts. He was not interested in what American Securities would like to do or anything but getting the money due TL&I and FLCA. Pop saw it as a matter of restitution, while Sims had riled him by saying American Securities was simply the custodian of funds.[27]

After receiving a legal opinion supporting their position, Eaton and Sims intended to keep going the way they had been.[28]

Of course, Pop Ross was frustrated with Eaton and Sims's intractability. His solution was to instruct Wells to protect against the nonpayment, but Pop did not explain how Wells was to do so.[29]

Tensions mounted when Eaton sent a letter indicating that he and Sims now believed that FLCA and TL&I had been overpaid in the past, and the overpayment had been deducted from the current payment that was enclosed. Eaton must have known that closing the letter with "Hoping that this will be satisfactory to yourselves" would only infuriate the Rosses.[30]

Sims wanted a meeting with Pop Ross, but their respective schedules made that difficult. This bothered Eaton, as he believed that once Sims left for St. Louis, it would be unlikely that he would return. Sims was disenchanted with the Forest Lawn operation and told Wells that American Securities had not made any money on it, but now had new deals in the East that were more promising. Tom Ross—or perhaps Pop—thought Sims was bluffing. Nevertheless, Pop once again cautioned Wells to be careful, saying, "The main thing for us is to take the utmost care that we do not make any slip, which could give them a cause to say that we have not fulfilled the contract in any way."[31]

Eaton and Sims traveled to San Francisco to meet with Pop Ross. In a preliminary meeting, they explained to Pop how they had arrived at their method for dividing receipts, and they shared the letter from their attorney, Herbert Goudge. Although they postured that they had just handed the agreement over to their attorneys without comment, Pop believed they had told their lawyers what result they were seeking. Pop did not tell them of his suspicion; he just reported that Goudge's opinion did not agree with William Hazlett's. Eaton and Sims took the position that if they could not receive enough to cover their expenses before any payments were made to TL&I, they would terminate the agreement, since they had invested some $2,800 more than the 25 percent already received (an amount equivalent to $73,000 in 2017). No common ground was found in the meeting.[32]

When they reconvened for a second meeting, Pop Ross restated TL&I's position that the handling of payments had not been according to the contract—using Eaton and Sims's method, it could be six or seven months before TL&I and FLCA would receive cash from a sale. Pop told them that there was no "equity or justice" in what was being done.[33]

Pop's Compromise

As a last resort for settlement, Pop offered a compromise: American Securities would receive the first 25 percent of money received, but after that TL&I and FLCA would share three quarters of the following payments and American Securities would receive one quarter. Under Pop's proposal, the two sides would then receive their full share at the same time. The final money received would continue to go into the perpetual care fund.[34]

Pop Ross assessed his proposal in a letter to Wells: "I don't think they have any ground to state that we are not meeting them on more than equitable grounds; and if they resolve to retire, it will not be on our account but on some differences among themselves." Pop seemed to sense that friction was developing between Sims and Eaton. He cautioned Wells to "not be too confidential with Mr Eaton as I am not sure what position he occupies in the matter."[35]

Although Pop Ross's letter did not indicate there had been agreement on the terms, Wells seemed to think the matter was settled. He wrote, "I was glad to get your explanation of the settlement between Mr. Sims, Eaton, and yourself, although it be brief. I knew you would adjust the matter all right." Eaton had returned to Los Angeles, but had little to say. Wells—who, like Pop Ross, seemed to sense some dispute between Eaton and Sims—merely reported to Pop that Eaton was getting ready to leave for St. Louis, and he did not know where Eaton stood on the issues.[36]

Eaton received a letter from William Hazlett reaffirming the position of TL&I and FLCA on the issue of dividing receipts. Hazlett concluded that when cancellations occurred, some repayment to American Securities might be required. Until a sale was cancelled, though, the money received should be split as though the account would be paid in full.[37]

Perhaps Hazlett's letter shook Eaton's confidence in Goudge's opinion, since he then asked for an opinion letter from a Reno attorney, Prince A. Hawkins. According to Hawkins, there was not an issue with the contract as written; the issue was with the selling method. Hawkins noted that the problems had arisen because the lots were being sold on time-payment terms, a method of sales that was not anticipated in the contract. American Securities could have used another method of sales to protect itself from cancellations and at the same time live up to the provisions of the contract with TL&I and FLCA. His conclusion was that American Securities had a right to adopt the practice of having buyers pay in installments, but the risk of cancellation coupled with that practice did not give the company the right to change the terms of payments to TL&I and FLCA.[38]

No doubt, Eaton chose not to share Prince Hawkins's opinion with anyone at TL&I or FLCA. However, he may have shared the opinion with Sims, since it showed that the selling system relied on payment terms rather than cash sales for success.

Eaton Contemplates Parting Ways

With Eaton left mostly on his own to manage and improvise, the tensions of the start of the selling operation must have been stressful. Sims was mostly absent, working on other deals. Eaton began to think he would be better off on his own than with Sims.

On the way to St. Louis in November 1913, Eaton stopped in Mexico, Missouri, where his sister, Mabel Llewellyn, lived (no relation to the Llewellyn Iron Works family). From there, he wrote Pop and Tom Ross indicating that he might break away from the "St. Louis crowd." Because Sims had spent little time in Los Angeles, Eaton had a much deeper understanding of the Los Angeles operation and felt more connected to Forest Lawn.

In anticipation of a possible breakup, Eaton began getting powers of attorney from friends who were stockholders of American Securities—including the Rosses, who now were also stockholders—telling everyone this would be their chance to throw their lot in with him. The powers of attorney would enable Eaton to negotiate a separation from Sims on behalf of other stockholders. Eaton cautioned, however, that he was only considering parting ways with Sims, not committed to it.[39]

Proposed Contract Changes

A break between Eaton and Sims appeared to be more likely when Eaton sent a Western Union night letter to Pop Ross from St. Louis on November 3. He told Pop that the Forest Lawn contract had not been profitable for American Securities, so its stockholders were going to vote to cancel the contract. Eaton told Pop he thought the contract could be saved if TL&I agreed to a 50 percent commission rate for five years, net of perpetual care.

He admonished Pop to "think this over carefully as upon your answer will depend my own decision." He asked Pop to wire him Tuesday at the Planters Hotel.[40]

Eaton was proposing that American Securities would continue to receive a commission of 50 percent of the net sales revenue for the entire five years of the contract, instead of receiving only 40 percent during the last two and a half years, as the original contract stated. This was a separate issue from the question of which method to use for dividing installment payments.

Pop wired back that TL&I would agree to continue American Securities' 50 percent commission only if Eaton agreed to divide installment payments according to the Rosses' interpretation of the contract. Pop Ross had been careful to write Eaton as secretary of American Securities rather than as an individual. If Eaton was representing himself rather than the company, Sims could have claimed that Eaton was acting to the detriment of American Securities. Once again Pop cautioned Wells that if Eaton sent any more telegrams that seemed to "be handling two ends of the proposition" rather than clearly representing American Securities, Eaton would have to indicate who could represent the company.[41]

Wells believed Eaton's statement that American Securities was not making money, and he certainly knew TL&I and FLCA were not doing well either. He told Pop Ross that if American Securities did not want to go on, he would not "nurse them" by changing the contract. Wells was frustrated with the uncertainty of the evolving situation.[42]

Impatient that Pop Ross had not agreed to his terms, on November 5 Eaton wrote from the Planters Hotel in St. Louis. He stated that the Los Angeles "city office" would likely be closed unless he personally took over the Forest Lawn contract by paying American Securities the amount it had invested in establishing the Forest Lawn selling program. Eaton determined he would need to put at least $4,500 more capital into American Securities if he were to agree to the

Rosses' method of dividing installment payments. He concluded it "was too much—all told—to pay for a 'pig in poke.'"

Eaton went on to explain that if cash receipts were divided using the Rosses' method, American Securities' profit margin would be too small to cover expenses in months with slow sales. He made the case, as he would many times during his life, that each contact—even when a sale was not made—would go to the future benefit of Forest Lawn. Eaton reiterated that he wanted to do whatever was right. Having a sense of urgency, he implored the Rosses to respond quickly and meet him halfway. Halfway, of course, meant his interpretation of how to divide receipts.[43]

Wells and Pop each had different views of the situation. While Pop Ross was suspicious of the other men's motive, believing that Eaton and Sims were working together to manipulate the situation, Wells believed Eaton was acting independently. Despite being less cynical than Pop regarding the negotiations, Wells believed that Pop's tough stand was the correct position.[44]

Eaton made another, final attempt to get the contract terms he wanted with a November 10 telegram to Pop Ross.

DEPENDENT UPON MANNER YOU MEET SUGGESTION
CONTAINED MY LETTER... I CAN CONSUMMATE DEAL HERE
WHEREBY PRESENT CONTRACT AND BILLS RECEIVABLE
AND ALL OTHER PRIVILEGES OF AMERICAN SECURITIES
IN CALIFORNIA ARE ASSIGNED TO MYSELF AND FRIENDS
IMPOSSIBLE FOR ME TAKE CONTRACT UNLESS YOU MEET
HALF WAY... WIRE ME FRANKLY AND FINALLY TONIGHT[45]

Pop Ross immediately responded with "Cannot do better than our last." He continued to believe that Eaton was really acting on behalf of Sims and was only trying to negotiate better contract terms. He also doubted they had put as much money into the operation as they claimed.[46]

The End of a Partnership

What neither Pop Ross nor Norton Wells knew was that things had changed dramatically in St. Louis during the previous seven days. Two days before his November 10 telegram to Pop, Hubert Eaton had negotiated and signed a contract with Sims for Eaton to take control of American Securities.[47]

The Forest Lawn selling program had been in place for slightly less than ten months, but the Eaton and Sims relationship was finished.

Eaton and his associates owned just under one-third of the stock in American Securities. Sims and associates held the balance of the stock. Although the company had assets in both California and Missouri, the only liability was in California. The Missouri assets were primarily the selling contract with Mount Hope Cemetery and a pending patent application regarding mausoleums. The principal California assets were the selling contract with FLCA and TL&I and related accounts receivable. The Sims group agreed to turn over all their shares to Eaton's group in exchange for the Missouri assets. In addition to gaining control of all stock in American Securities, Eaton's group received $500 in cash, a $25,000 bond to indemnify Eaton's group against loss, and an agreement preventing Sims from competing in California for five years.[48]

The plan for ending Eaton's relationship with Sims was fair, because the Mount Hope contract had preceded the Forest Lawn contract and was closer to Sims's Missouri base of operations. Additionally, Sims had spent little time in Los Angeles once selling began—his role was more of a rainmaker than manager. Eaton had carried the primary responsibility for the Forest Lawn contract since selling began and had continued to make adaptations to the sales system that he and Sims had brought to Los Angeles.

It was not until November 17 that Eaton wrote Wells from Kansas City to tell him of the change in control.

Myself and immediate friends are now in absolute control of the American Securities Company, but the sales have been dropping off in Los Angeles and I am not sure whether we want to be [in Los Angeles] or not, but more of this when I see you.[49]

The transaction with Sims had not actually closed, but Eaton now felt he had control of the selling organization. He still did not have a new compensation arrangement with TL&I—he was only obtaining control of American Securities.

Sims Moves On

After his relationship with Eaton was over, Sims continued to work on cemetery deals around the country. In 1916, N. P. Dodge & Company wrote Wells for confirmation that Forest Lawn had been "promoted" by Sims. Wells replied that Eaton and Sims had entered into a contract to sell lots in Forest Lawn, but Sims had been associated with that effort for only "about six months" before he separated himself from the contract. Wells added that he did not feel Sims was entitled to list Forest Lawn as a cemetery he had promoted, because Sims had been in Los Angeles for only one month at the time selling started and for only two or three additional weeks before separating from Eaton.[50]

Similarly, in 1917 Charles Werner, an attorney from Evansville, Indiana, wrote Wells attempting to obtain a copy of Forest Lawn's contract with Sims, or to at least find out as much as he could. He wanted to know how lots were sold, what compensation was paid, and whether Sims or his new partner, a man named Bennett, had any role in the development of the property. Probably annoyed by the fact that Sims continued to use Forest Lawn as a reference, Wells replied, "Sims and Bennett have never acted as sales agents or fiscal agents in promoting the organization of Forest Lawn Cemetery." Furthermore, Wells informed Werner, he did not have the right to divulge the terms of the contract to other parties.[51]

Less than a year after Eaton and Sims began a sales program for Forest Lawn, the two had parted ways. Sims had not spent much time in Los Angeles, so it was not surprising that Eaton remained. However, the split between the two men did nothing to resolved the conflict between TL&I, FLCA, and American Securities. A formula for success of each of the three organizations had not been found.

CHAPTER 13

TRYING TO COOPERATE

THE END OF THE relationship between Eaton and Sims simplified the decision-making process for American Securities, but did not resolve the conflicts with TL&I or FLCA over division of cash. Nevertheless, the three organizations were dependent upon on another, and divorce was not practical. So, the struggle to mend the relationships continued.

Continuing Conflicts

Following his severance from Sims, things in Los Angeles were much the same for Hubert Eaton as they had been before.

TL&I continued to protest monthly over American Securities' method of splitting cash received. Pop Ross asked Norton Wells to let him know when the timing or amount of payments varied from what was expected so that a protest could be issued.[1]

By the end of November 1913, Eaton was back in Los Angeles and, according to Wells, was "elated" with the deal negotiated with Sims for control of American Securities. Also, Eaton planned to continue negotiations with TL&I over the division of receipts and alluded to Wells that there was a possibility of the "new parties" acquiring an interest in TL&I.[2]

185

During the process of finalizing the separation of American Securities' interests between Eaton and Sims, Pop Ross met with the two men several times in early December. Pop thought Eaton seemed to be upset rather than "elated," as Wells had reported. Eaton was still trying to figure out how to restructure the financial arrangement. Pop reminded him that TL&I had made an offer in November for a modification of the method for dividing receipts but that American Securities had rejected it. So nothing had changed. Eaton tried, once again, to refer to the opinions of the various attorneys who supported his position—never disclosing the negative opinion from Prince Hawkins. Pop merely replied that TL&I was "perfectly satisfied" with the legal advice it had been given. Pop wrote Wells that Eaton seemed to have placed himself into a predicament and did not know what to do. Eaton agreed to look over the situation and write Pop concerning what actions he might take.[3]

In the following months, Pop Ross and Hubert Eaton continued to spar over the division of receipts. In one of their exchanges, Eaton apparently mused of possibly restructuring the sales program in a way that did not involve American Securities, implying that he might be representing not the company, but himself. Fearing that Eaton might not always be solely representing American Securities, Pop expressed concern about "unofficial" communications from Eaton. That struck a nerve, and Eaton fired back that Pop would "hereafter receive no communications, either verbal or written, from this Company that you cannot consider official." Pop Ross had also referred to the statements provided by American Securities, saying the figures were "presumably correct"—again annoying Eaton, who interpreted Pop's statement as meaning "if amounts were correct." Eaton retorted that TL&I could look at American Securities' books at any time.[4]

Eaton's reaction to Pop Ross's letter surprised Pop. He replied to Eaton that he regretted offense had been taken to some of his words—particularly the statement relative to figures being "presumably correct." Pop tried to calm things by telling Eaton, "Now do not let us get into a condition of irritation on matters on which we are both desirous to handle in a friendly way same as usual."[5]

When Pop sent his regular protest letter over the January 1914 division of receipts, Eaton fired back a four-page letter extolling the sales results American Securities had achieved, while lamenting that "Up to date we have received but small return for the immense amount of work and money we have spent on your behalf." He noted that he was "surprised and grieved" about Pop's attitude of constantly wanting a "pound of flesh." Eaton went on to complain that TL&I and FLCA had not kept American Securities supplied with an inventory of cemetery property to sell as called for in the selling contract. Additionally, they had failed to keep the cemetery in good condition.[6]

Pop Ross cautioned Wells about the handling of receipts on accounts that were near the point where money should go into the perpetual care fund. He believed that the correct handling of this matter was "distinctly called for in the contract so please see that they do not break this contract any more than they have done."[7]

Tiring of the protest letters, Eaton sent a rebuttal letter in February 1914 reminding Pop Ross that sales had tripled under his selling program. Eaton lamented that they had not yet recouped their investment and suggested TL&I and FLCA could and should solve the difficulties American Securities was working under. The difficulties included inadequate inventory and a poor variety of cemetery lots, poor maintenance of the cemetery, and slow repair of rain damage.[8]

Shortly after Eaton's letter of complaint enumerating the alleged failings of TL&I, Eaton told Wells he wanted to reduce the price on some interment property further from the road. Wells interpreted this to mean that Eaton was asking him for permission to do so. He told Pop of Eaton's request, but said, "It don't appeal to me!" Pop was of the same mind; he thought the request was ridiculous after Eaton's most recent letter. However, he assured Wells that even though the request seemed out of place, anything that would help all parties should be considered. He told Wells to go ahead with Eaton's proposal.[9]

Several days later, Pop explained to Wells why he had decided they should agree with the request. The Los Angeles economy was in rough shape in 1914, and he did not want Eaton to be able to say that TL&I had not helped American Securities during these difficult economic conditions. To promote growth, the Los Angeles Chamber of Commerce formed an "Industrial Bureau." The city's leading newspapers supported the effort to expand industry and promote job growth. The Chamber's goal was to make Los Angeles "not only big but busy; make it bustling and bread-winning as well as beautiful."[10]

When Pop Ross notified Eaton of TL&I's acquiescence to the request, he received a prompt reply that would only add fuel to the flames of the disagreement. Eaton retorted that it had not been a request. He was only informing TL&I of what he was doing; he was not asking for approval—the notification was just a courtesy.[11]

Pop Ross was angry that Eaton thought he could unilaterally offer the discount. He told Wells that if he had understood Eaton's position, he would not have consented—he had only done so because of Wells's recommendation. Pop scolded Wells, telling him he had been used again.[12]

In early May 1914, Eaton once again complained to TL&I and FLCA that there was an inadequate assortment of cemetery lots. He reminded them that "one of the fundamental principles of our selling scheme is a range in prices, the prices to advance just as rapidly as we have new sections to take their place." Eaton concluded the letter with the admonishment, "We trust that you will remedy this negligence on your part immediately, in order that any further loss on our part in this matter may cease."[13]

American Securities, TL&I, and FLCA were essentially in a stalemate. No one was happy with the situation, but none of the parties were willing to rock the boat. So the conflicts just carried on from month to month.

Eaton Wants to Buy TL&I

Meanwhile, Eaton began to court the Rosses with a goal of taking over TL&I. Eaton urged Tom and Pop to give him financial information regarding TL&I so that he could figure out how much it would cost to buy the Rosses' TL&I stock. He told the Rosses he wanted to have things settled, once and for all, relative to devoting his full attention to Forest Lawn and putting off further pursuit of an Oakland cemetery.[14] If Eaton were able to buy the Rosses' stock, then he would obtain control of TL&I and end disputes over distribution of sales receipts.

When Pop visited Los Angeles in August 1914, Eaton believed the visit had given Pop "a closer insight into our various difficulties." Apparently, Eaton believed he had demonstrated the potential for increasing Forest Lawn's market area and the challenges of doing so.[15]

After Pop's visit, Eaton received letters from Tom and Pop Ross that he "read with a grin that stretched from ear to ear.[16] Presumably this meant Eaton had received positive feedback about the possibility of gaining control of TL&I.

In response to the letters, Eaton gave an enthusiastic assessment of the prospects for a sales campaign "in the territory adjacent to the towns of Van Nuys, Lankershim, Newhall and San Fernando." However, Eaton believed that such a campaign could be successful only if he furnished the salesmen with a "machine"—that is, an automobile. He estimated that the cost of a Ford auto plus operating expenses would reach nearly $1,000 for six months. Given that cost, Eaton explained that he could not afford to provide the needed auto if the commission rate was reduced to 40 percent in August 1915, as called for in the 1912 contract. If no modification to the contract could be agreed upon, Eaton told the Rosses he planned to end his relationship with Forest Lawn and move on to other opportunities.

Eaton also noted that World War I was having a depressing influence on economic conditions and thus on sales.[17]

As a follow-up, Eaton wrote Tom asking him to come to Los Angeles, just as Pop had. Eaton wanted to show Tom his ideas about the opportunities for Forest Lawn and the difficulty of realizing those opportunities. Eaton believed that if Tom could thoroughly understand what was being done and should be done, there would be "no trouble in finally working out something that will place Forest Lawn at the head of cemeteries in Los Angeles. So be a good fellow and come on down and look things over."[18]

Tom was busy working on plans for an apartment house, so he declined the invitation to come south. Eaton wired that if Pop and Tom couldn't come to him, he would go to them. He planned to first visit Oakland—a not subtle reminder of his interest in a cemetery there—and then go to San Francisco the following day.[19]

Out of the loop on negotiations, Wells wrote Pop Ross that Eaton arrived back in Los Angeles on an August Saturday morning and, though he had seen Eaton twice, he had not learned anything from Eaton about what transpired in San Francisco. Wells asked Pop to bring him up to date on what happened when Eaton visited the Rosses in San Francisco. Given the sensitivity of the conversations with Eaton, Pop did not reply to Wells.[20]

In a follow-up letter to the Rosses after the visit, Eaton said he was pleased with the discussions because the Rosses had been willing to share new information with him about the cemetery land. The next time either Pop or Tom Ross came to Los Angeles, Eaton hoped they would be able to meet, as the recent visit to San Francisco was "productive of a more confidential understanding between us. I am a firm believer in the constant meeting of executives, in order that friction may be thoroughly eliminated."[21]

Although it appeared there had been some progress in talks between Eaton and the Rosses, Pop Ross continued to send his monthly objection letter protesting the way Eaton was dividing receipts. While Eaton may have thought friction was being reduced,

Pop told Wells that "Mr. Eaton will be specially displeased at my sending the usual protest . . . as it will always remind him [that we believe he is not following the contract] and prevent his slipping us another [false interpretation of it]."[22]

Extending the openness of the August meetings, Eaton sent the Rosses a copy of American Securities' income and expense statement for August 1914, since the Rosses had said they did not understand how the company had lost so much. Eaton closed with, "I trust you will not think I am making any bid for sympathy, but simply to show you that I have something to worry about, as well as you." The statement showed net sales of $1,203, of which American Securities' share was $451, based upon Eaton's calculations. With expenses for the month running $1,793, American Securities lost $1,342 in August.[23]

Eaton continued to press for some sort of deal between American Securities and TL&I. In October, he told the Rosses he needed to know the exact number of shares they could sell and at what price, so that he could determine when to approach "financiers" about purchasing control of Forest Lawn Cemetery and buying adjacent land. Once again, he told the Rosses that if they had not made up their minds to sell, he would turn his attention to other things.[24]

When Pop Ross was in Los Angeles in November 1914, he and Eaton discussed the possibility of Eaton acquiring Tom's shares in TL&I. When Pop pressed the issue with Tom, he found Tom unwilling to listen, despite Pop's assertion that his own age and health were a large factor in his interest in the sale. Finally, after more discussion, Tom agreed to leave the matter in Pop's hands, with the stipulation that the deal should not take longer than three months. Securing Tom's agreement, Pop finally sent Eaton the financial information he had been requesting.[25]

Soon after sending the financial information, Pop Ross wrote Eaton that they were endeavoring to put TL&I into the "highest possible condition" by paying off all indebtedness, and that the last of their debt was owed to Tom Ross. Once Tom was paid off, a dividend could be declared. Paying a cash dividend would allow the release of the unissued sixty thousand shares of TL&I. These shares could then be sold, which would raise cash for the repurchase of the sixty-five acres that had been lost through litigation. Pop pointed out what Eaton already knew: if Eaton controlled the land company, the 50 percent commission could be continued and all other matters that caused friction between TL&I and American Securities would be eliminated. Pop's assessment was that Eaton could gain control by buying at least fifty-thousand shares of TL&I at a dollar a share.[26]

Just before Christmas, Eaton told the Rosses that he had some friends who wanted "to put some more funds into the Treasury of American Securities Company with the intention that these funds shall be used primarily for securing a cemetery here [in Los Angeles] or in Oakland. He indicated that he had "Oakland figured down to [his] finger tips." However, he had not received any response or information from the Rosses that would help him reach a conclusion regarding the purchase of Forest Lawn.[27] Eaton was trying to pressure the Rosses to make a decision about selling their interest in TL&I.

1914 Finances

The income and expense statement for Forest Lawn for the year 1914 showed the cemetery was still not doing well financially. FLCA lost over $6,000 in 1914. After general labor, the biggest expenses were salaries for the manager and the office, followed by interest on loans necessary to continue development of cemetery property. Under the assumption that any loss must have resulted from development of the cemetery, the full amount of the loss was capitalized by charging it to cemetery improvements.[28] This was a convenient but erroneous way to look at the loss, and it overstated the value of the company.

Perpetual Care Funds Bill

In early 1915, a number of California cemeteries began working together because of a bill introduced in the California Assembly to expand liability for investment losses in perpetual care funds. Norton Wells first learned of Assembly Bill 646 from Jo J. De Haven of Mount Olivet Cemetery in Colma, California. De Haven asked Wells if he knew who was behind the bill, suspecting it may have been instigated by cemeteries in the south of the state, since its author, Grant Conrad, was from San Diego.[29]

Wells responded to De Haven that he thought all cemeteries should be concerned about the bill because it would make cemeteries absolutely liable for any loss on an investment in a perpetual care fund, even if the loss was caused by a bank failure. He told De Haven he would explore the matter. Wells also sent a copy of the bill to Pop Ross, W. H. Eckley of Inglewood Cemetery, and Harry W. Watson of Hollywood Cemetery, explaining the background of the bill and conveying his concern over its content.

Wells believed the bill was influenced by the dramatic failure of the Los Angeles Investment Company in 1913, which had severely impacted the Los Angeles economy. When the investment company's president, Charles A. Elder, was convicted of fraud, the stock price plummeted, bringing many of its investors to insolvency. In addition to the economic damage, one of the byproducts of the failure was greater regulatory scrutiny of investments, including those of perpetual care funds.[30]

Some cemetery operators speculated that the bill was a result of competition between the City of San Diego's cemetery and a private cemetery. However, Wells found that the city was not the catalyst for the bill. He told Jo De Haven that the San Diego Cemetery Corporation apparently had been in the hands of speculators who had bought its stock with the intent of raiding its perpetual care fund. Over one-half of that fund had allegedly been dissipated by investments in largely worthless mortgages. Wells believed that "as the beneficiaries and original investors mostly are among the dead, there is frequently no one to bring suit." There were allegations of similar things happening in the San Francisco area. Based on the belief that none of the beneficiaries would hold cemeteries accountable, the bill called for broad liability of the cemetery trustees in the event of an investment loss.[31]

Once Wells received information explaining the trigger for the proposed law, he shared that information with De Haven, Eckley, Watson, William Cleaver of the Los Angeles Cemetery Association (operator of Evergreen Cemetery), and Bishop Thomas J. Conaty of the Los Angeles Catholic Diocese.

De Haven replied to Wells that he would take the matter up with Northern California cemeteries "in a casual way" but that he, personally, did "not see any great objections . . . [and] any opposition we might suggest might be more harmful than good."[32]

One month later, in March, De Haven reported to Wells that he still could not see harm in the measure and that one of the northern cemeteries was "very much in favor of the bill in all its particulars."[33]

The bill failed. However, the cemeteries interested in legislation were the stirring of a movement that would eventually result in a statewide association for cemeteries and future cooperation among cemeteries in legislative matters.

More Division Disputes

A new conflict over the division of receipts arose in March 1915. When American Securities wrote an additional sale to the fraternal group Knights of Pythias, a new agreement was written that included the prior sale. This, according to Eaton, reset the measure of who received what money when.

Pop was quite irritated. If the old sales agreement had been left undisturbed, the money received would have been divided equally between American Securities and TL&I/FLCA—even under Eaton's disputed interpretation, since American Securities had already received its first 25 percent. Under the new, consolidated agreement, the money already received was less than 25 percent of the higher total price. So American Securities would continue to get all the cash until it had received 25 percent of the new total, and until then TL&I and FLCA would receive nothing. Wells believed that although the purchaser requested the consolidation, under Eaton's interpretation the fifty-fifty split would not have come into play anyway. Pop disagreed, noting that Eaton always protected himself without regard to impact on TL&I, but did not hesitate to ask for concessions for his own benefit. Nevertheless, Pop was willing to "let it go."[34]

In April, Eaton took umbrage at Pop Ross's monthly protest letter, which characterized the American Securities method of splitting receipts as being "arbitrarily adopted." Eaton maintained they were splitting the receipts according to the contract, and insisted once again that their attorney had advised them they were correctly interpreting the document.

Furthermore, Eaton pointed out that whereas TL&I's protests dealt with receipts, TL&I's failure to provide inventory of burial lots according to the terms of the contract had resulted in actual, material damage to American Securities. Eaton emphasized that his organization had increased sales by over 400 percent, and that Forest Lawn was the ultimate beneficiary of the 95 percent of contacts in which no sale took place. His belief was that even if a sale was not made, the prospect now knew of Forest Lawn and its many positive attributes and would be almost certain to choose Forest Lawn when a death occurred. He postured, "You could well afford to give us every cent we make from sales during the life of our contract, in exchange for the greater work we are doing in preparing future customers for your cemetery."[35]

Commission Negotiations

Since American Securities had not agreed, back in November 1913, to divide receipts from installment payments according to the Rosses' method, the Rosses had not agreed to continue American Securities' 50 percent commission rate beyond the first two and a half years. Therefore, the rate was scheduled to drop to 40 percent on August 1, 1915. In late June, Eaton wrote TL&I and FLCA asking to extend the higher rate to January 1, 1916. He emphasized how much progress had been made in sales. During 1913 and 1914, each year's sales were more than double the sales for the entire two years before American Securities came on board, and sales by American Securities in the first five months of 1915 were almost equal to sales for the entire year of 1911. Eaton cajoled the companies, quoting an old saying that "the servant who does not receive a just compensation for his services soon begins to look for a place where he can do so."[36]

The Rosses considered Eaton's request and called a meeting of the TL&I board of directors. They approved the contract modification, as did the FLCA trustees. Thus, Eaton was successful in his efforts to extend the higher commission rate to December 31, 1915.[37]

Despite this victory, Eaton believed that American Securities was still not receiving the proper amount of commission. The issue had to do with the way contract language was being interpreted regarding single-grave lots.

The custom of the day was that families would purchase a lot that contained multiple burial spaces. Some buyers, however, purchased a single grave. The selling contract between American Securities, TL&I, and FLCA referred only to "lots," with no definition and no differentiation between single and multiple burial spaces. The contract had been interpreted to mean that no commission would be paid on single spaces. Although that may have been the original intent, the interpretation could be contested because "lot" was not defined. Eaton wanted to interpret "lot" to include all burial spaces, including single graves. In late October 1915 he wrote FLCA and TL&I jointly, saying he now had legal advice that American Securities was entitled to receive the same commission on single spaces as for multiple spaces. He requested an accounting of the commission due on single-grave lots.[38]

Wells irritated Eaton by not responding to the accounting request. He had fallen into his usual pattern of avoiding confrontation with Eaton and deflecting decisions to the Rosses.

In his letter, Eaton asserted that American Securities had a contractual right to a full 50 percent commission on single burial spaces. However, he was willing to waive that right if TL&I and FLCA would also be willing to compromise. He knew that undertakers and others were paid at least a 10 percent commission on single graves, but noted that undertakers did no advertising for Forest Lawn and had no other expenses in relation to the sale. Eaton was willing to accept an amount somewhere between the undertakers' 10 percent commission and the 50 percent commission to which he believed American Securities was entitled.[39]

Although Pop Ross believed the issue of commissions on single graves had not been raised previously, Eaton insisted it had been brought up to Wells as TL&I's "resident agent." According to Eaton, Wells had been asked repeatedly to discuss this with TL&I, but no response had been forthcoming. American Securities' position was that because a commission was being paid to others for the sale of single-grave spaces, it should receive at least the same commission. Eaton expressed resentment at the unequal treatment.[40]

Wells admitted to Tom Ross that Eaton had brought the matter up several months earlier, but Wells had not taken Eaton seriously. Wells believed Eaton wanted to call single burial spaces "single-grave lots" because these spaces then would neatly fit within the wording of the contract, which called for commission to be paid on the sale of "lots."[41] This was a minor issue compared to a division of receipts or commission rates, so it would not be resolved until those two issues were put to rest.

Cancellations and Trade-Ins

The issue of the division of receipts became even more confused in late November 1915, when attorney Ben S. Hunter wrote William Hazlett, who represented TL&I and FLCA. Hunter had reviewed both the contract between TL&I, FLCA, and American Securities and the purchase agreement used with buyers, apparently at the request of Hazlett. Hunter reached the conclusion that under the cancellation provision of the purchase agreement, American Securities was not entitled to "the payment of any moneys on account of terminated contracts, until such time as the statute of limitations shall have run under the sale agreement." He believed that a buyer who defaulted was entitled to have any money paid applied to a future purchase of cemetery property. In other words, the purchase agreement changed the character of the money received from being forfeitable to being a deposit that could be applied to a future purchase.[42] If Hunter's opinion was correct, then funds would have been held in limbo to the detriment of all three companies.

Eaton, of course, did not like Hunter's position. He once again sought the opinion of Prince Hawkins, the Reno attorney he had consulted previously. He told Hawkins that he wanted an explanation of both when and how cancellations could be made under the terms of the agreement with lot purchasers. Eaton also wanted to know what the proper division of money should be if a sale involved a trade-in from a prior lot purchase. TL&I and FLCA had taken the position that only the actual money received should be divided under the terms of their contract with American Securities, and that the lot turned in should merely be turned over to TL&I and FLCA.[43]

Just before the end of 1915, Hawkins sent a six-page response to Eaton. His letter reasoned that the answer to the "when" question was clear. When a cancellation occurred under the purchase agreement with the buyer, it should be construed as a cancellation under the terms of the contract between TL&I, FLCA, and American Securities. Furthermore, in answer to the question of how to cancel a sale, he believed that because American Securities entered into the agreement with the purchaser, as agent for FLCA, American Securities should be the corporation to determine and send a notice of cancellation.[44]

However, Hawkins did not agree with FLCA, TL&I, Eaton, or Hunter on the matter of how to divide funds. He interpreted the contract as giving because American Securities had the right to set prices—subject only to the "not less than fifty cents per square foot" provision of the contract. However, Hawkins noted that American Securities also had control of what it received in compensation.

American Securities could decide to accept or not accept a trade-in lot as part of a sales transaction. According to Hawkins, TL&I and FLCA were entitled to their share of receipts on lots sold at the listed prices. If American Securities decided to accept something other than cash as payment, that was fine, but the other two companies would be entitled to their portion in cash.[45]

Another Extension

Shortly before the end of 1915, Eaton once again wrote TL&I and FLCA requesting another six-month extension of American Securities' 50 percent commission that was due to expire in just over two weeks. Eaton included a schedule showing that American Securities had lost $4,600 in the first ten months of the year. He reiterated that if forced to retreat to a 40 percent commission, American Securities would end the contract. He told TL&I and FLCA that it would be up to them to decide whether American Securities would continue.[46]

> We are in the position of the little boy who grabbed the calf's tail and found that when the calf galloped madly down the field, he had to hang on to keep from being dashed to the earth and severaly [sic] hurt. The only thing we can do is keep holding on in hopes that the financial condition will lift and we can begin to recuperate our loss.[47]

The Rosses were persuaded by Eaton's letter and agreed to extend the 50 percent commission rate through December 31, 1916.[48]

1915 Audit Report

During 1915, TL&I was able to reduce the amount borrowed from Tom Ross by $6,500, as well as invest in a new pumping plant and other improvements by borrowing with an additional mortgage. This was positive news, and Pop Ross told Eaton about it in a transmittal letter accompanying the annual audit report issued in October. Pop also pointed out that TL&I did not record its share of accounts receivable on its books, some $21,000. If that amount were included in TL&I's assets, he said, the company would be worth more than its financial statements showed. Pop was trying to raise the value of TL&I because he and Eaton had been discussing the sale of the company to Eaton.[49]

In a second letter to Eaton accompanying the audit report, Pop laid out the Rosses' conditions for use of the report. He emphasized that it was to be kept "absolutely confidential"—Eaton should not even look at the report unless he agreed the information was private. Furthermore, Pop was providing it under the assumption that Eaton was sincere about desiring to purchase the Rosses' TL&I shares and for the sole purpose of Eaton determining a purchase price of the stock. Copies were not to be made, nor could information be shared with anyone else. The copy was to be returned to TL&I whenever requested.[50]

The audit report prepared by C. V. Rowe showed assets of TL&I of just over $246,000, with nearly $43,000 in mortgages and bills payable, resulting in a net book value of just over $200,000. Eaton thought the statement put too high a value on the unsold land. This was partially justified by the land being valued based on shares of stock given J. B. Treadwell rather than on an appraisal or what had actually been paid for it.[51]

Slow Progress

TL&I and FLCA were quite aware that Eaton was trying to position his affairs for a deal with TL&I but the effort was moving slowly. In mid-November 1915, Wells commented that Eaton had told him that nothing would happen soon, since "one of his confreres was in the east and would not return until December."[52]

Meanwhile, FLCA was making other changes. Norton Wells notified local undertakers that Forest Lawn would be discontinuing commissions to them effective January 1, 1916.[53]

Although Eaton remained steadfast regarding the calculations for dividing receipts, he also realized that the relationship with the

Rosses was important if he were to accomplish his goal of acquiring control over TL&I. After thanking Pop Ross for facilitating the extension of the 50 percent commission through the end of 1916, he also said he regretted that Pop had not stayed longer on his last trip to Los Angeles, since the visit had been productive. Eaton believed "all perplexing questions" could be resolved if there were more frequent contact between principals of the various companies.[54] Nevertheless, several more months would go by before Eaton and TL&I would begin serious negotiations leading toward a change in the structure and control of Forest Lawn.

CHAPTER 14

EXPANDING SALES EFFORTS

ALTHOUGH HUBERT EATON WAS not part of the start of
Forest Lawn Cemetery, he was certainly instrumental in improving
its financial condition. Always on the lookout for ways to promote
the cemetery and attract buyers, he developed, through trial and
error, an effective sales system that "brought in the bacon."

Spreading the Word

Early in his tenure at Forest Lawn, Eaton began to collect quotes
from families who had purchased cemetery property before need.
He desired to have prominent citizens proclaim the virtues of Forest
Lawn and in some cases suggested what they should say. The quotes
were intended to explain why buyers should choose Forest Lawn over
other cemeteries and why they should purchase cemetery property
before need. Eaton published these quotes in a booklet titled "The
Reasons Why."

Eaton also believed that an esprit de corps should be cultivated
with lot owners so that they would discuss Forest Lawn with their
friends. Periodically telling lot owners of the various improvements
and how Forest Lawn kept moving ahead and becoming more beautiful, he believed, would encourage them to tell their friends of

203

Forest Lawn's advantages. He proposed to Wells that five hundred newsletters be sent to lot owners, but only if Forest Lawn would bear half the expense.[1]

Wells agreed with Eaton, and the plan proceeded. Letters were sent out in May 1914 inviting people to Decoration Day at Forest Lawn, encouraging them to visit and see "how much more beautiful your cemetery has become" and "to learn of our plans for the future."[2]

But when he found out the cost, Eaton lost his enthusiasm for the newsletter idea. He wrote sales manager Getzendanner, "Much to my disgust, I find that the cost of putting out 500 letters to the lot owners will be just about $30.00, and if I had known this before I started, I do not think I would have gone to the expense on such an advertisement that is of doubtful results to the American Securities Company."[3]

Lot Repurchase Offer

One of the skills important to any salesperson is the technique for closing a sale. The most controversial idea for a closing tool that Eaton came up with was a lot repurchase offer, which he proposed to FLCA in June 1913. His idea was that five years after a lot was paid for in full, a purchaser could elect to have Forest Lawn buy back the lot at the price paid plus 6 percent interest. Eaton told Wells that he would expect to use this offer only with people "who are looking at the purchase from an investment standpoint and are hard to close up with a contract."[4]

Pop Ross told Wells it was "impossible to even consider" the lot repurchase offer. Nevertheless, Wells apparently did not think Pop's response was an absolute rejection of the idea. He sent Pop a copy of a memo written by Eaton and sales manager E. D. Getzendanner that explained the plan to buy back lots five years after the sale. Although he realized that at first glance the plan did not look good, Wells contended that FLCA had been selling lots at a higher price than American Securities. So if the lots were taken back, they could be resold at a much higher price than American Securities had sold them for. He went so far as to include his calculation of what it might look like financially.[5]

Pop Ross was uncomfortable with the proposals from American Securities and its method of presenting the proposals through Wells. He once again cautioned Wells to be very careful in dealing with Eaton and his associates. Pop directed Wells to commit to nothing, "as they might get the advantage of you accidentally on some matter," and to refer all proposals to the Rosses.[6] Pop believed that Eaton knew how to manipulate Wells.

Pop Ross gave Wells a lengthy analysis of why the buy-back proposal wasn't a good idea. He even questioned the legal validity of such a program and thought it might require approval of TL&I's stockholders. Pop clearly thought the proposal would be good only for American Securities by providing a closing tool when making sales, but would cost TL&I money in the long run. Saying there were even more reasons not to accept the proposal, he closed his rejection with, "Cheer up, give us something better next time."[7]

Wells did not agree with Pop Ross's figures, since he believed that any profit made on the resale of the lot should be included in the calculation. Furthermore, he believed that since Eaton did not plan to offer the repurchase option on all sales, there could be a limit on the number of sales with the option, reducing the risk. He acknowledged that the question of agreeing to the repurchase plan was entirely in Pop's hands.[8]

Firmly slamming the door on the issue, Pop Ross wrote, "The matter of the re-purchase is entirely closed as the Directors positively will not consider the question further. I may be able to give you further satisfaction in the consideration of such a proposition when I next see you, but there is no reason to write further about it at present."[9]

Insurance Ideas

Early in 1914, Eaton added a phrase to the American Securities Company letterhead: "The only corporation devoting itself exclusively to the scientific study of mortuary conditions throughout the globe, and the practical application of these researches to the development and safe-guarding of the modern park-cemetery." The letterhead described the company as "fiscal agents" for "park-cemeteries and cemetery securities." By May, Eaton had changed the letterhead to identify American Securities as "Fiscal Agents" for "park-cemeteries and mortuary securities." Additionally, it now proclaimed it was "operating Forest Lawn Burial-Park" in Los Angeles, California.[10]

The phrase "mortuary securities" was intended to cover the possibility of selling a contract to cover funeral and burial costs. Eaton described this to Pop Ross and Wells as a purchase on monthly payments that would provide a cemetery lot, monument, funeral service, and flowers. Eaton told the men that he had been working with Pacific Mutual Life Insurance Company to underwrite this plan and it would "absolutely [do] away with all risk on our part."[11]

After Wells and Eaton had more conversations about the idea, Wells told Pop how it would work. A salesman for American Securities would sell a Pacific Mutual policy by explaining that at the time of death, Pacific Mutual would pay American Securities the face amount of the policy. Then American Securities would arrange with the undertakers for the funeral and with Forest Lawn for the cemetery lot.[12]

Although Eaton had told the others about Pacific Mutual, he also sought other sources for the insurance. He sent one of them, Metropolitan Life Insurance Company, a rather detailed letter describing the policies he wanted to sell. Since his conversation with Pacific Mutual had apparently been just that—a conversation—he sent that company a letter similar to the one sent to Metropolitan, hoping to find an insurance company interested in his proposal.[13]

The question of whether funeral insurance made sense never became an issue between Eaton, TL&I, and FLCA because neither insurance company wanted to issue the type of policy Eaton envisioned. Pacific Mutual replied that such a policy would not be profitable for their company. A. S. Theberge, superintendent of Metropolitan

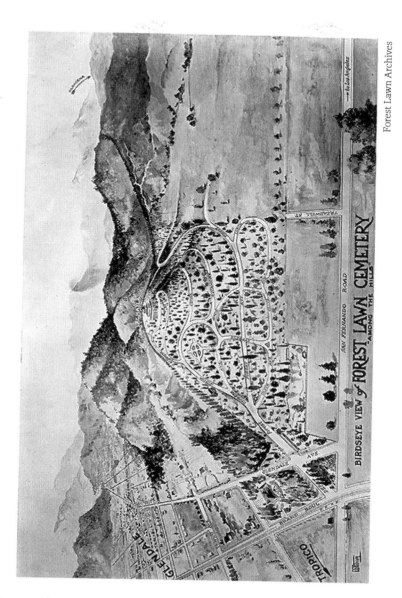

Figure 42. Cemetery Plan c. 1914

An artist's conception of how Forest Lawn would be developed. It includes a Valhalla-style mausoleum placed at the top of the hill, despite Hubert Eaton's apparent dislike of community mausoleums.

Life's Los Angeles office, let Eaton know that the matter was referred to the company's officers, who would consider the issue. After not receiving any response from Theberge, Eaton tabled the idea for the time being.[14]

<hr />

Eaton's insurance plan would have linked Forest Lawn to the undertaking business. Wells had heard, and shared with Pop, that attempts to expand beyond the cemetery business had been tried and failed in other parts of California. For instance, he had learned that when George Fletcher, superintendent of the Odd Fellows Cemetery, entered the undertaking business, the Odd Fellows cemetery business fell off substantially. When undertaking firm N. Gray & Co began offering an insurance product like the one Eaton proposed, its sales literature recommended Calvary and Cypress Lawn cemeteries. The other undertakers were furious and made things so difficult

Figure 43. Valhalla Mausoleum

Some Forest Lawn promotional literature used the same rendering of a mausoleum that Sims had used at other cemeteries.

Forest Lawn Archives

for Cypress Lawn that Hamden Noble had to "work hard to stop the knocking." Wells wondered whether it was a good idea to have undertakers "coupled with Forest Lawn."[15]

In spite of the risks, insurance-like products appealed to Eaton. In August 1915 he learned that Woodlawn Cemetery in Chicago had a "cemetery bond" that protected any purchaser buying on an installment plan. If the purchaser died before the contract was paid in full, the balance would be forgiven. Eaton wrote for samples of documents, but was particularly interested in what "safe-guards" the cemetery would "throw around in order to be insured that a majority of the purchasers do not die within a short time" of making the purchase.[16]

Mausoleum Pros and Cons

From the beginning of American Securities' involvement in Forest Lawn, Charles Sims had envisioned a community mausoleum atop the hill above the cemetery. A community mausoleum is intended for the above-ground entombment of many families, in contrast to a private mausoleum, which is intended for members of one family.

After Sims's exodus, Wells apparently continued to believe that building a community mausoleum was a good idea, as evidenced by his sending Tom Ross a set of plans for a "combination crematory, Columbarium, Mausoleum and office." A columbarium is an above-ground structure with individual spaces for urns containing cremated remains (ashes).[17] The plans Wells sent envisioned that the multiuse building would be placed either "between the pump house and the railroad . . . [or across] the railroad tracks in that section of parking opposite the Llewellyn monument."[18]

Meanwhile, Eaton must have feared competition from other cemeteries that already had community mausoleums, as well as public mausoleums not owned by cemeteries. In August 1914, when he received a circular from the National Retail Monument Dealers Association attacking the concept of community mausoleums, it seemed like a good sales tool to him.

The flyer described community mausoleums as promoters' schemes and tenements for burial—buildings intended for profit and only incidentally for burial. It alleged that their foundations were too weak to support the buildings and that brick or stone veneer was used to hide the cracks that would inevitably appear as the buildings settled. The roofs were made of concrete but had only a thin coating of asphalt for waterproofing. The monument dealers described the perpetual care fund of community mausoleums as their most ridiculous feature, since the promoter would lead the purchaser to believe the buildings could be kept in perpetual repair.[19]

Eaton replied to the Monument Dealers Association that he commended them for their action on this issue and had instructed his salesmen to describe mausoleums in much the same way. Eaton asked that copies of the circular be sent to several prominent people in Los Angeles, since the letter would have more weight coming from someone not in the cemetery business locally.[20]

In a letter to Carl Price, secretary of the Ohio Retail Monument Association, Eaton wrote, "It has just occurred to us that it would be an excellent plan to give a copy of one of these circulars to each one of our salesmen, in order that they may have it to refresh their memories from time to time."[21]

Shortly afterward, he sent Forest Lawn's superintendent, Mike Glora, a copy of the circular with instructions to memorize the points and pass the information on "to the poor, deluded public."[22]

The monument retailers were not primarily interested in protecting the public, but themselves. Every crypt sold in a community mausoleum was a lost opportunity for them to sell a monument. This competitive feud between the monument sellers and cemeteries continued for decades. In some cases the battle was in state legislatures, with attempts to pass laws that would prohibit cemeteries from selling monuments. In other instances, the dispute made its way into the court system; there were allegations that cemeteries had violated antitrust laws with their rules and requirements regarding monument installation.

Monument sellers were not the only ones to disapprove of community mausoleums. In defense of their businesses, cemetery superintendents were condemning stand-alone community mausoleums that were not part of cemeteries. An early book on cemetery management proclaimed, "Practically without exception, superintendents condemn the public mausoleum idea. If allowed at all, the public mausoleum should by all means be erected, owned and controlled by the cemetery association."[23]

In December 1914 Eaton received a letter from mausoleum builder Frank Church asking why he had not received a reply to the set of mausoleum plans Church had sent Eaton in July. According to Church, the selling of mausoleums—probably individual family mausoleums—was "a business that offers good chance of profit and handled in the right manner offers no chance of loss."[24]

Although Eaton wanted FLCA to develop interment property that could "meet the requirements of those purchasers who express preference for mausoleums," he had something else in mind. He described an underground vault for burial of family members—much like a flattened sarcophagus. He wanted it to be as impressive to buyers as a mausoleum crypt, but less expensive. His vision was for the top of the vault to be made of either "granite concrete" or a natural granite block. He thought FLCA should decide whether the vault would have a flat top, "placed flush with the ground or slightly raised above the ground in the form of a sarcophagus." He went so far as to have a concrete company prepare sketches and quote prices, although he believed that Forest Lawn would "be in better shape to do this work than the concrete company."[25] Either these underground vaults proved not to have appeal or they were too expensive, as none were built.

A less elaborate alternative to a mausoleum crypt was proposed by Jay D. Brunner of the Pacific Coast Concrete Company. Brunner tried to persuade Eaton to sell concrete burial vaults—outer burial containers—as an alternative to a community mausoleum as well as an opportunity to enhance revenue. Eaton was willing to give the vaults a try if Pacific Coast set up samples at the cemetery without cost to Forest Lawn or American Securities. Brunner had suggested that a drawing be included in promotional literature that showed how graves could collapse when burial vaults were not used. When Eaton talked to his salesmen

Figure 44. Vault or Outer Burial Container

concerning this, they balked at the illustration of a collapsed grave, believing it might cool potential customers to burial and become an argument for cremation.[26]

Eaton eventually changed his mind about a community mausoleum, realizing that a segment of the population would prefer above-ground interment. He realized that the arguments the monument dealers made about construction were a question of design and not of inherent flaws in the concept of a community mausoleum. It would be several years before Forest Lawn carried out plans to add a community mausoleum and other structures.

Getzendanner Resigns

In August 1915 E. D. Getzendanner resigned as sales manager of American Securities. He did not give Wells an explanation for a rather abrupt departure, but it appears to have been on good terms, since Eaton wrote him a complimentary reference letter.[27]

When Getzendanner left American Securities, he did not return to working for Charles Sims. Rather, he ended up working for the Whittier Heights Cemetery (now Rose Hills Memorial Park) in

Whittier, California. Upon learning of this, Eaton wrote to remind him that he was bound by a five-year noncompetition agreement that kept him from engaging in cemetery sales without the approval of American Securities. Eaton initially took the position that because Getzendanner had never asked for approval, he was inclined to enforce the noncompetition clause. However, he told Getzendanner he was willing to let him make his case for not enforcing the clause.[28]

Getzendanner sent Eaton a blueprint map of the cemetery where he was now working. Eaton did not feel it gave adequate information to determine whether Getzendanner was working in competition with American Securities, so he wrote that he would look at the cemetery some weekend. Later that same day, however, he had second thoughts and wrote Getzendanner another letter granting a waiver of the noncompetition clause, but only for the Whittier Heights Cemetery.[29]

Possible New Selling Agent

Near the time that Getzendanner left, Wells received an unsolicited letter from Paul Sacks of the Eagle Development Corporation of Saint Louis asking to replace American Securities as the selling agent for Forest Lawn. Sacks's pitch was similar to Sims's original pitch: Eagle was "familiar with establishing modern perpetual care cemeteries" and selling on a before-need basis. Sacks also noted that Eagle would pay all expenses pertaining to its sales of lots. The letter explained that the company had been able to put cemeteries "on a highly profitable and dividend paying basis."[30] Given the ongoing squabbles with Eaton over the division of receipts and the inventory of lots for sale, this must have had some appeal to Wells as an alternative selling organization to Eaton's American Securities Company.

Wells forwarded the letter on to San Francisco, where Pop Ross was not so sanguine. He returned it to Wells, saying the "circular" should be kept for possible future reference. He believed either Sims or someone who had worked for him had started a new company. Pop suggested that Wells reply with questions regarding selling

Figure 45. Prospect card c. 1916.

Front of card had details regarding the prospect.

Back of card had record of follow-up calls and activity.

Forest Lawn Archives

PROSPECT'S RECORD

Name .... (Write plainly and write surname first.)

Res. address .... phone ....

Bus. address .... phone ....

Occupation .... No. in family .... No. years here ....

INTERVIEW—Husband. Wife. Relative .... Length of talk .... min.

BELIEF—Catholic. Protestant. Jewish. Scientist. Cremation. Mausoleum. Burial. Ship body away. Investment. Superstitious.

AGE—Old. Medium. Young. Married. Single.

PROSPECT'S ATTITUDE—Good. Fair. Indifferent. Poor.

FINANCIAL CONDITION—Rich. Well off. Medium. Poor. Own home.

Send Literature as follows:

1st Letter, R. W. .... 191....

2d Letter, Views .... 191....

Follow up .... 191....

.... 191....

Have lot or ....single graves at .... cemetery. Date call again .... 191....

Chief objection made and other remarks: ....

Salesman .... District .... Date .... 191....

NOTE.—Be sure to fill in all blanks and put check mark (√) through all words that are descriptive of prospect.

SECOND CALL Date .... 191....

Remarks: ....

Date will call again .... 191....

THIRD CALL Date .... 191....

Remarks: ....

Date will call again .... 191....

FOURTH CALL Date .... 191....

Remarks: ....

Date will call again .... 191....

Final remarks on subsequent calls:

On ...., 191...., I hereby relinquish all claim to above prospect.

Signed ....

OFFICE MEMORANDA:

methods and names of cemeteries with which the company was affiliated—questions that might lead to information concerning what individuals were behind Eagle Development.[31]

Eagle did not take long to reply, but their response did not tip their hand regarding their past affiliations. They told Wells what expenses they would bear and the expected commission (50 percent), and generally discussed how successful they were. They did not disclose any past affiliations. If the proposition in their letter looked acceptable, they would send a contract and only then would give references.[32]

When Wells responded, he asked again for names and financial references. He also noted that the commission rate of 50 percent was excessive.[33] Of course, TL&I and FLCA had just agreed to an extension of American Securities' 50 percent contract, so that comment was a bit disingenuous. Eagle apparently took Wells's comments as the end of the discussion and did not respond to his letter.

Eaton's Sales System

Although Sims and Eaton had originally come to Los Angeles together to install a "system" for sales, Sims did not spend much time in Los Angeles. It was mostly left to Eaton to experiment, modify, and fine-tune the system to make it work at Forest Lawn. Some things worked. Some did not. The result was a sales system that evolved over time. Eaton's system is not documented per se, but its essence and evolution can be seen from comments in correspondence, promotional material, and various forms in files.

To Eaton, the fundamental difference between what his sales system had evolved to and what he had first seen of Sims's system in St. Louis was philosophy. Sims had stressed the sale as a financial transaction—buy now for the prices are surely to go up. Eaton doubted the ethics of selling based on price speculation. His sales system was based on what he would describe as moral concepts—more like the premise of life insurance. Yes, purchasing today would lock in the price, the importance of the purchase was the protection the family from making decisions under the stress of death having occurred.[34]

Today we would describe Eaton's sales system in terms of lead and customer relations management. Because the system was based on door-to-door selling, Eaton had salesmen keep rigorous records of prospects contacted, including family details, dates and times of contacts, and other information. The sales manager would keep track of the leads the men were working and make sure they were following up in a timely manner.

Recruiting and Training Salesmen

Eaton aggressively sought salesmen to help him achieve his goals. He used newspaper advertisements as one method of recruitment.

> WANTED—Salesmen, by well known corporations, to work in Los Angeles. No competition. Work is permanent and opportunity for advancement is better than other lines for men of ability. We want clean-cut forceful men only of 30 years or over. No others need apply. Commission basis. General offices 609-11 L. A. Trust and Savings Bldg. Ask for Mr. McJennett between 9:00 and 12:00 A.M. Monday.[35]

A weekly "sales school" was held each Saturday morning for the entire sales staff. It included presentations on various topics as well as role playing practice sessions on the presentation of cemetery property. Topics would usually be announced prior to each week's school. Role-playing of sales presentations was a common training tool. Here are some sample agendas sent by sales manager George Emery, who came to Forest Lawn in the spring of 1917:

> November 3, 1917
> The opening argument or introduction - Mr. Hathaway. Second call - Mr. Raymond. This call is supposed to be made at the house, and an appointment made to visit the Park. . . .

Mr. Harding will take the prospect through the Park, going carefully into all the details and this prospect practically decide on some particular lot or lots. Mr Stuart will take the prospect from there and endeavor to close.

November 17, 1917

Saturday morning's school first will be a general resume of the business of the past week. Afterwards, Mr. Stuart will proceed to close a sale with Mr. Mason as a prospect. Supposedly, Mr. Mason has visited the Park and has selected No. 91 in "Iona." So all that is necessary now, is to get the contract.

If there is any time left, it will be occupied by opening arguments.

November 27, 1917

. . . Afterwards each Salesman will be allowed fifteen minutes on a first call interview. He may select his prospect from those present at the meeting.

December 8, 1917

At Saturday's School, we will have two sales: one a Mausoleum sale, and one a Cemetery Lot sale. Mr. Dougher will sell Mr. Harding a Family Section of three compartments. Mr. Perkins will sell Mr. Mason a Family Lot in Section "B."

Their sales will be preceded by the usual reports on your different districts.[36]

In another exercise for the salesmen, a sample letter from a prospect was produced and each salesman was asked to write a response.

Sales Letters

The puffery of the sales force seemed to be almost without bounds. One example is Charles Harding's October 1917 letter to William

Stephens, a prospect for a before-need purchase. Harding congratulated Mr. Stephens for recognizing that he owed "a duty" to his dependents to provide "a suitable resting place" and to do so "while . . . in possession of your normal faculties and while you have the earning capacity to make such provision for the future." In keeping with the vision that Eaton had developed by this time, Harding stressed that Forest Lawn was a memorial-park and not a cemetery. He claimed that one of America's most famous landscape architects had designed

Forest Lawn Archives

Figure 46. Hubert Eaton c. 1917

it (nothing supports that claim) and proclaimed that an investment in Forest Lawn property was as safe as a government bond. Furthermore, cemetery property would only increase in value. The hardest work, according to Harding, was to convince prospects they should buy before need and "not wait until the undertaker knocks at the door."[37]

Harding went on to tell Stephens of Forest Lawn's great topography with gradual slopes on all sides, differing from an ordinary flat cemetery, which "allows seepage of water into the graves." Forest Lawn's location was such "that it will never be disturbed by the encroachments of municipal life. . . . Its topographical location is such that no force of nature will ever affect it; no flood may destroy nor any earthquake mar its natural beauty[,] for it is built upon a rock as solid as Gibralter [*sic*] itself."[38]

Harding used what is known as a "presumptive close" to end his letter: "Shall I mail your contract or bring it in person?"[39] Despite his enthusiasm, Harding did not make the sale.

The use of exaggeration and misinformation in Forest Lawn sales letters was not new. Years earlier, a letter had been sent to Right Reverend H. J. Johnson of the Episcopal Church in Los Angeles, offering to establish a dedicated "Churchyard in our Cemetery, where the clergy and communicants may assemble to enjoy the sublime rite of your church . . . an entire section . . . to be named Iona Churchyard.[40"]

The letter stretched the truth. It described the Forest Lawn Cemetery location as being selected after many months of consideration. It stated that William Blain had come from Michigan to lay out Cypress Lawn Cemetery in San Francisco "at its inception," and after overseeing Cypress Lawn, he was then hired by the Masonic Cemetery Association of San Francisco to lay out its cemetery as landscape engineer and superintendent. The truth is that Cypress Lawn in San Francisco was designed under the direction of Hamden Noble in 1892, and Tom Ross designed its Noble Chapel. Blain had worked at Cypress Lawn, but as assistant superintendent. The letter stated that "as a landscape engineer, mr. [sic] Blain had no peer." It also stated that Blain had been persuaded to come to Los Angeles to "select our land and lay out our grounds." Blain's objective, it said, was to find land that was dry but with sufficient water for irrigation, in a location with no possibility of roads or other incursions affecting it in the future.[41] However, there is no evidence that suggests Blain was involved with J. B. Treadwell in the selection of land for Forest Lawn Cemetery.[42]

Managing Ineffective Salesmen

Eaton gave salesmen a relatively short time to become productive, and he aggressively managed salesmen who did not perform. For example, Eaton wrote salesman W. M. Holden that he was wasting his time in an endeavor to learn to sell cemetery property and that Eaton did not believe he could be successful. If Holden agreed with

Eaton's conclusion, he should leave his maps and sales materials at the office.[43]

Bradbury, another salesman, replied to a similar letter that it was "not my fault that I have been unable to close any prospects in the last two weeks." He went on to say he had been ill, an old gentleman had put him off, and someone should talk to contacts he had made previously to show that he had been hard at work. Several weeks later, Eaton replied that some of Bradbury's customers had been misinformed relative to payments; at least one customer reported paying Bradbury thirty dollars more than showed on the books. There were other irregularities too. Eaton concluded that he could not see "where any particular good can be accomplished by your again entering the field."[44]

Hubert Eaton believed the reputation of all involved with Forest Lawn was important to the success of the cemetery. Thus when he learned that salesman and former temporary superintendent Wilton Carre was behind in support payments to his ex-wife, he was concerned that Carre might be arrested, which would reflect poorly on Forest Lawn. In a letter to Mrs. Carre's attorney, A. E. Campbell, Eaton pleaded that Carre had no income other than that from Forest Lawn, so his arrest would not help her receive money due her. He also asked the attorney to give him notice before an arrest of Carre was planned. With advance knowledge of Carre being taken into custody, Eaton asserted he would "sever Mr. Carre's connection with [Forest Lawn] beforehand, and publicly announce that such connection has been severed."[45]

Contacts with Other Cemeteries

Despite his bravado about his long, scientific study of cemeteries, Eaton often exchanged promotional material with other cemeteries, looking for new ideas. Although Eaton was no stranger to San Francisco, he apparently had not spent much time in Colma—just south of the city—where cemeteries had started after a 1902 ordinance was passed banning burials in San Francisco. When sales manager Getzendanner was in San Francisco in June 1915, Eaton wrote him, "Please be sure and beg or borrow a kodak [*sic*] somewhere, and go out to Cypress Lawn and adjoining cemeteries, and take many pictures of anything and everything that we may need or is instructive."[46]

Other cemeteries also asked Eaton to share ideas with them. After receiving a letter from William Pierce of the Fairmont and Riverside cemeteries in Denver inquiring for details of Eaton's selling methods, Eaton replied with a copy of "The Reasons Why" booklet. He explained it was impossible to describe the selling method questions by letter, since it would take hundreds of pages. He told them that it had taken years of experience and experimentation to perfect a system that "brings in the bacon" and that sales had increased by 400 percent since he arrived at Forest Lawn. He offered to send one of his sales executives to Denver to assess the situation and make recommendations, as "each cemetery situation is a problem in itself."[47]

Even though his selling program was successful, Eaton was not willing to settle for the status quo. He continued to experiment to fine-tune the program and to think about alternative ways of structuring the relationships of the three corporations: TL&I, FLCA, and American Securities.

CHAPTER 15

EATON THE ENTREPRENEUR

HUBERT EATON ALWAYS PORTRAYED Forest Lawn
as his singular focus. In reality, this was not true. During 1915
and 1916 he looked into two entrepreneurial opportunities: selling
residential lots in Orange County and starting a cemetery in Eagle
Rock. Although the latter did not come to fruition, Eaton used
the possibility of a new cemetery as a negotiating ploy to get what
he wanted out of the Forest Lawn related companies—FLCA and
TL&I. Eventually he succeeded in orchestrating the formation of
a new corporation that would absorb TL&I.

Selling Residential Lots

American Securities organization documents allowed for involvement
in residential subdivisions as well as cemeteries. Accordingly, when
Eaton sought an agreement to sell residential lots in Orange County,
California, it was clearly within the purposes of the company. In
early 1915 Eaton reached an agreement with the Huntington Beach
Company to be the exclusive sales agent for residential lots in the
area including and around Anaheim and Santa Ana. The Huntington
Beach Company was a land development firm owned by Henry E.
Huntington, the railroad magnate for whom the present-day city

of Huntington Beach is named. The company owned about two thousand acres.[1]

Eaton formed a new, additional company to be used to establish a "chain of agencies" to sell subdivision lots. He planned to use the umbrella name "Columbia Realty Co." for these sales efforts. The letterhead for Columbia Realty identified it as the exclusive agent for Huntington Beach and "Bullard Lands" as well as dealing in "city property," "farm lands," and "exchanges." O. E. Darling was the sales manager. Employing Eaton's sales strategy, Darling used door-to-door prospecting, just as Eaton's Los Angeles group did for cemetery lot sales.[2]

As Eaton became more and more immersed in the Forest Lawn selling project, his interest in Huntington Beach faded, and nothing became of expanding Columbia Realty.

Scouting for a New Cemetery

Given the tension between American Securities, FLCA, and TL&I, Eaton wanted to hedge his bets regarding his Forest Lawn sales program. So in April 1915 he sent E. D. Getzendanner, who at that time was still Forest Lawn's sales manager, on a quest to find other parcels of land that might be good locations for a new cemetery. Getzendanner reported that he and O. E. Darling had found possible property north of Foothill Boulevard near the Altadena Country Club, and another tract on Colorado Boulevard in Eagle Rock. Both parcels were a short distance northeast from Forest Lawn and close to Pasadena.[3]

While Eaton made no secret of the possibility of starting another cemetery and had told Pop Ross of a possible property in Long Beach, he did not reveal all of his plans. Pop thought Eaton was bluffing, telling Wells he would not listen to talk of a Long Beach cemetery. To Pop, it was just another Eaton maneuver. Pop may have been right, but only insofar as Long Beach was not Eaton's first choice. Eaton had looked at a parcel in Long Beach, but he had not decided whether to buy it, so he told Darling to keep the land owner "on the fence."[4]

The real estate agent representing Eaton was certainly taking the investigation of properties seriously. He wrote Frank Schumacher, the owner of a parcel in Eagle Rock, to inquire whether an offer of $43,000 for the twenty-seven acres, with a $5,000 down payment, would be accepted. Schumacher responded that he thought the deal could be put through if the down payment were $10,000.[5]

Darling learned that an alternate parcel in Altadena was tied up in a lawsuit. However, he was told that if American Securities offered enough cash for a down payment, a deal might still be possible. Darling proposed terms like those being negotiated for the Eagle Rock parcel, and received a reply that it would take at least $20,000 down to make the deal happen.[6]

Planning a New Company

While pursuing alternate cemetery sites, Eaton began to think of forming a new corporation to own the land. He explained to several American Securities stockholders that it was desirable for the organization to be formed by local people to enhance acceptance. Furthermore, if American Securities started a competing cemetery, there might be issues because of the Forest Lawn contract with TL&I and FLCA. A new company could avoid those problems.[7]

The American Securities stockholders would be given an opportunity to purchase stock in the new company at an unspecified "bed-rock original price." Eaton expected to receive shares in the new company in exchange for the option on the new cemetery land and his system of cemetery management and sales. He planned to divide the shares of the new company proportionately among the American Securities shareholders. As a result, all American Securities shareholders would also own part of the new company, even if they did not purchase additional shares.[8]

In July 1915 Eaton left Los Angeles for Kansas City, Missouri, where he had business contacts he wanted to bring into his new company. Wanting to keep things moving, he wired his office that any correspondence from Carroll Gates or William Hollingsworth, his associates in forming the new company, should be forwarded to him by special delivery. When he received nothing, he wired his secretary, Estelle McDonald, of his concern. It was ten days before McDonald replied that everything was proceeding as expected.[9]

Carroll Gates was a prominent Los Angeles industrialist and real estate investor. He was also a director and president of the Huntington Beach Company, which owned the residential lots that Eaton and O. E. Darling were selling on a commission basis. William Hollingsworth was an early Los Angeles industrialist and real estate investor who owned an office building on the southeast side of Pershing Square in downtown Los Angeles.

At least one American Securities shareholder, Merritt Llewellyn, was not pleased with the proposed change. Merritt's brother, Frederick William Llewellyn (not related to the Llewellyn Iron Works family), was married to Eaton's sister, Mabel. Merritt wrote Eaton that if the same directors were to be elected and no dividends were declared, he wanted to sell Eaton his stock at its original price.[10]

It was almost a month before Eaton responded, mostly with quotes from the last American Securities annual president's report. He explained to Merritt that things were progressing toward the formation of a new company that would own cemetery land. He turned down Merritt's request that he buy his stock, saying he would need to put all his available cash into the new venture. Encouraging patience, he expressed confidence that Merritt would realize a greater return than if he had invested his money at 6 percent compound interest.[11] Eaton's explanation was justification for his current plans.

> As everyone knows, it was the original intention that [American Securities] should actually own a cemetery or cemeteries, as well as selling contracts. . . .
>
> It takes an original investment of $50,000.00 to $100,000.00 to finance a cemetery, and experience has taught me that most of this amount should come from stockholders living in the vicinity. . . . If we start a cemetery in Los Angeles

or Pasadena . . . at least one-half of the original investment should be secured from Los Angeles or Pasadena people. . . .

Recently two or three wealthy and influential men in Los Angeles have spoken to me in [a] manner which leads me to believe that the time above has arrived for us to start a new cemetery.

After his first response to Merritt Llewellyn, Eaton had second thoughts. In a second letter of the same date, he noted that the shares were originally owned by Frederick William Llewellyn, Eaton's brother-in-law. He tried to reassure Merritt that he was committed to protecting the investment in American Securities. If the investment were not protected, he told Merritt, it would be only because Eaton had lost everything. Eaton assessed the situation: "At present the future seems very bright that I shall make quite a little money."[12]

Meanwhile, Wells had heard that Eaton was starting a cemetery. He asked Eaton if it was true, but Eaton said nothing had been done so far.[13]

Toward the end of February 1916, Eaton—concluding that he would need a new company to either make a deal with TL&I or start a new cemetery—drafted a memo outlining the formation of this new company. Though ultimately not used, it indicated Eaton's initial intent. Hubert L. Eaton, J. M. Elliott, Carroll W. Gates, and William I. Hollingsworth would form the new company and share the expense of starting the business. In addition to owning cemeteries, it would sell "mortuary and other kinds of insurance." The company would be incorporated in Arizona, with residents of Arizona as the first five directors. Subsequently, they would resign and elect as directors Eaton, Elliott, Gates, Hollingsworth, and "one other individual who shall be named at that time."[14]

In exchange for his "System of Cemetery Sales, and the management and general knowledge of mortuary affairs," Eaton was to receive three thousand shares of stock—2,000 common and 1,000 preferred. Preferred shares have fixed dividend payments that must be paid before any dividends can be paid to the common shareholders. Also, upon liquidation of a company, preferred shareholders must be paid before common stock shareholders.

The remaining common and preferred shares were to be held by a mutually agreeable trustee. The trustee would sell 1,000 shares of common stock at a price determined by the board of directors, and 1,000 shares of preferred stock at par value—$100 each—with the proceeds going to the corporation. Eaton agreed that as the stock sold, Gates, Hollingsworth, and Elliott would each receive 250 common shares from Eaton's common stock holdings.[15]

Taking the Next Steps

Pop Ross may not have believed Eaton was serious about starting another cemetery, but he was wrong about that. In April 1916 Eaton, Gates, and Hollingsworth signed a memo agreeing they would each put up one-third of the $800 option price for land in Eagle Rock Valley. Each of them had the right to drop out of the agreement before the option expired on July 10, 1916, as long as someone else took his place and refunded the money paid by the exiting partner.[16]

Another memo of agreement, dated May 19, 1916, specified how the new corporation would be set up once it was formed. This memo replaced the draft that Eaton had developed in February. It was signed by Eaton, Gates, and Hollingsworth. J. M. Elliott was not mentioned in the memo. In a corporate structure similar to that between TL&I and FLCA, Eaton's group would incorporate a second new company to operate the cemetery. It would be known as the Valhalla Cemetery Association.[17]

According to the agreement, the corporation would act as the selling agent and holding company for cemeteries and also sell various kinds of insurance. The new company would purchase land for a cemetery in Eagle Rock Valley—specifically, a parcel of land on which Frank D. Hamilton held an option. Although Eaton's associates had been searching for the land for a new cemetery, Hamilton had been the one to purchase the option. It appears that Hamilton's role was that of a financier and that Eaton was the actual architect of the plans for the new cemetery.

Hamilton, like Eaton, had attended William Jewell College in Liberty, Missouri. Although Hamilton was two years older than Eaton, they may have met at the college. Hamilton was affiliated with the Liberty Bank of Liberty, Missouri, but in describing the plan, Eaton just referred to him as "an Eastern Banker."[18]

The second agreement called for the same capital structures as the previous draft: 4,000 shares of common stock and 1,000 shares of preferred stock, all with a par value of $100 each. Gates and Hollingsworth would each receive 500 common shares, and 1,000 common shares would go to Eaton. An additional 500 shares would be used to buy the assets of American Securities. All the preferred shares were to be sold to raise cash. A "common fund" would be established with the other 1,500 shares of common stock. Buyers of the preferred stock would receive one share of stock from the common fund for each share of preferred stock they purchased. The remaining 500 shares in the common fund would be used for the "general purpose of paying for the services rendered by persons other than Gates, Hollingsworth and Eaton, in the securing of cash, stockholders or other benefits necessary to the complete financing and wellfare [sic] of said corporation."[19]

By June 1916, Eaton reported to Merritt Llewellyn that the first payment had been made on the new tract of land. He also reported that plans were being made to form the new corporation within a few months, with investments by Gates and Hollingsworth. Eaton said he already had commitments for $55,000 in stock purchases, although he had not yet started a campaign to sell shares.[20]

When Eaton outlined the plan to Merritt Llewellyn, no mention was made of TL&I or FLCA. Llewellyn was told that the new company would purchase American Securities' assets. The accounts

receivable would be collected over time and applied to the debts of
American Securities. Eaton believed that over time, all debts would
be extinguished and enough cash would be left over to return some
money to American Securities shareholders.[21]

Encountering a Roadblock

Although Eaton and associates had located land they wanted to
develop into a cemetery, they were surprised to find that the City
of Eagle Rock had an ordinance prohibiting the sale or purchase of
property for burial purposes and the burial of human bodies. George
Pratt, who would become a director and secretary of Eaton's new
company, wrote Herbert Goudge for a legal opinion on the validity of
the statute. Goudge replied to Pratt's inquiry by sending Eaton, along
with a bill for ten dollars, an opinion that a municipality could impose
reasonable restrictions but that if a cemetery could be conducted so it
would not "endanger the safety, health or comfort of a community,"
the city should not be able to simply prohibit the activity.[22]

Eaton was not bluffing concerning the new organization or the
new cemetery, but the City of Eagle Rock restriction made that
option problematic.

Tension with Glora

In July 1916, Eaton complained of tension between the cemetery and
American Securities, primarily due to superintendent Mike Glora's
unhelpful attitude towards Eaton's men. This lack of cooperation
created an "air of inharmony" that was detrimental to the sales force.[23]

When Wells tried to discuss the matter with Mike Glora, he
learned that Glora believed Eaton had written Pop Ross a deroga-
tory letter about him. Eaton denied ever writing such a letter to Pop
and went so far as to authorize Pop to send Wells anything Eaton
had written against Glora. Wells asked to see the letter because he
wanted to have things straightened out but admitted to Pop that
Glora had been quick to jump to judgment. Despite Eaton's verbal
complaint about Glora, Wells told Pop he had never heard Eaton

speak negatively about Glora. Wells was sure that Eaton had nothing but high regard for the superintendent.

Glora was not reassured by Wells and refused to believe Eaton had not written a critical letter. He also accused Wells of lying to him about matters related to the cemetery—for example, Glora believed the American Securities contract had ended, which it had not. Wells's conclusion was that it would be best to overlook the burst of temper and try to restore harmony to the situation.[24]

Proposed Stock Deals

At some point, Eaton told Pop Ross details of his plans to start a new company and open new cemeteries. This resulted in serious negotiations for Eaton to acquire TL&I. Eaton's motivation had been clear for some time: combining the land company with the selling company would reduce friction and create flexibility. Although he was willing to start a competing cemetery, his aim was to stay involved with Forest Lawn. The Rosses would now have a chance to exchange their interest in TL&I for cash, a good move for them because of Pop's age and to allow Tom to focus on his architectural practice.

In July 1916, Pop signed an option agreement that would allow Eaton, Gates, Hollingsworth, and Pratt to buy 39,015 shares of the Rosses' stock for a dollar a share. Once that purchase was made, the Rosses could exchange their remaining 5,000 shares of TL&I stock for a like amount of par value common stock in Eaton's new corporation. As part of the option agreement, Pop agreed to help the others obtain the majority of the shares of TL&I so that the group would own a majority of the TL&I shares. Pop also committed to urging the Tropico shareholders to exchange the shares they held in TL&I for an equal number of shares in the new corporation.[25]

On August 7, the terms of the transaction were changed. Now the stock held by Pop Ross and Tom Ross would not be purchased until Gates and Hollingsworth had acquired 27,000 shares of TL&I stock. Additionally, the Rosses would now receive only fifty cents per share for their stock, but Pop would receive a commission for his continued cooperation equal to another fifty cents a share. Thus the Rosses would receive the same total amount of money. Gates and Hollingsworth could then offer the other TL&I shareholders a choice: they could receive the same fifty cents a share in cash, or trade each TL&I share for one common share in the new corporation with a par value of one dollar each. They believed this offer would encourage people to take the new shares.[26]

Keeping his commitment to support the deal, Pop Ross wrote the TL&I shareholders two weeks later, saying he was writing as an individual stockholder and not as an officer of the corporation. He said he had learned that a group of men were planning to start a new cemetery and were negotiating with American Securities to be the selling agent for the new cemetery. The American Securities sales system had been developed over time and was superior to any other. Having locally influential people start a new cemetery with that system would create a very strong competitor.

Pop told the shareholders that he believed American Securities was now planning to use its sales system only for cemeteries it owned. The contemplated new cemetery, he said, would eclipse all cemeteries in the Los Angeles area, including Forest Lawn. To compete with this new organization, Forest Lawn would need to build a chapel, crematory, columbarium, and mausoleum at a cost of thousands of dollars that TL&I did not have. He finally came to the point and told his fellow shareholders that this group of "financiers" could be interested in acquiring TL&I as a means of controlling a cemetery as an alternative to starting a new cemetery. Without directly saying so, Pop was suggesting that this would be a better alternative than having a new, competing cemetery. Giving no details, Pop directed the shareholders to Frank Hamilton—the banker who apparently was acting as Eaton's financier—for further information.[27]

Impatient to learn what had been happening since his last correspondence in June, Merritt Llewellyn wrote Hubert Eaton again at the end of August, inquiring whether Eaton's plans for a new corporation and new cemeteries were coming to fruition. After summarizing how American Securities and TL&I would be absorbed by the new company, Eaton told Merritt, "I should advise all of those to whom I am personally responsible to hold their [TL&I] stock as I think it is going to become very valuable."[28]

Only three weeks after writing the TL&I shareholders, Pop Ross told Wells to explain to Max Loewenthal that a deal would likely be made between TL&I and American Securities. Therefore, Loewenthal, as TL&I's attorney, would need to prepare a statement describing the legal condition of the corporation. Pop also told Wells to have Loewenthal collect all the papers belonging to TL&I so that Hubert Eaton could review them.[29]

Eva Blain's Shares

One of the TL&I shareholders who received Pop Ross's letter was Eva Blain, the widow of William "Billy" Blain, the late superintendent of Forest Lawn. There had been some difficulty with Mrs. Blain concerning Billy's shares in the years immediately following his death. Upon receiving Pop's letter, she sought counsel from Los Angeles attorney Tobias R. Archer, who had previously worked for TL&I on the Susan Mitchell estate issue.

Archer wrote Pop to tell him that his letter "purporting" to be from a stockholder rather than an officer of TL&I was questionable posturing. Archer pointed out that Pop was obliquely suggesting that stockholders sell to Hamilton, but did not come out and say it. Archer wanted Pop to give him an assessment of the value of Mrs. Blain's shares.[30]

Pop's response dodged the valuation question. He could not reveal the deal he and Tom had already cut for the sale price of their shares plus commission. If Pop told anyone what he and Tom were to receive, it would undermine Hamilton's plan to pay other shareholders half that amount. Instead, Pop advised Archer that he had referred stockholders to Hamilton so they could learn the terms from him. Since Mrs. Blain had been unable to contact Hamilton, Pop suggested that she call Hollingsworth, and he would fully explain the proposal. Pop did tell Archer that shareholders had three options to dispose of their TL&I shares: sell them for fifty cents each, sell some for fifty cents each and exchange the remaining shares for shares in the new company, or exchange all their TL&I shares for shares in the new company.[31]

Pop noted, "Of course the cash price is a low one but the buyer always wants to get his stock as low as possible and unless Mrs Blaine [*sic*] or any shareholder is in need of the coin there is no occasion for selling but just make an exchange. Each shareholder must decide that matter for himself or herself, being an entirely personal matter and depending upon their circumstances." Pop's letter closed with a postscript suggesting that Eaton be contacted for information concerning what the new company would do or for more details regarding the purchase or transfer of stock.[32]

Protecting Eaton's Selling System

With the likelihood of a deal between TL&I and American Securities increasing, Eaton realized the value he brought to the consolidation of the two companies was his system of selling, as it had evolved from what Sims had used in St. Louis.

The success of Eaton's selling system is apparent in the requests he periodically received to take on additional cemetery sales programs. One such request came to him in September from W. E. Pearson, who was on the board of directors of the Mt. Scott Park Cemetery Association in Portland. Pearson wanted to know what Eaton would charge to run a program to "dispose of enough property to pay the bonded indebtedness, selling lots on reasonable terms."

Eaton did not reply until a month later. He apologized for the delay, saying he had been considering a cemetery in San Francisco. He was interested in exploring Pearson's proposition, but was "deeply engrossed in plans which contemplate the development of our Forest Lawn Cemetery here to a point where it will bury a person in any way in which they desire to be buried." Eaton went on to say it would be impossible for him to go to Portland to evaluate the situation until after the first of the year. He also told Pearson, "We ordinarily do not take on selling contracts alone. We generally insist on an interest in the property." Apparently Eaton thought he could take on even more cemeteries once he completed acquisition of TL&I.[33]

Because his selling system was an essential part of the rationale for the consolidation, Eaton realized it was important to protect it. When it looked like the consolidation was likely to go ahead, Eaton asked his attorney, Herbert Goudge, for an opinion.

> We are very desirous of protecting the System under which we operate, develop, and sell cemetery property. The System has been gradually built up through years of experience, and the perfecting of it has cost us immense sums of money. We are consequently very desirous that this information does not fall into the hands of competitors. The main way in which this information could be carried to other people is through the medium of some salesman who has been discharged by us or has voluntarily quit our employ.[34]

Eaton enclosed a form of contract he wanted to use with salespeople and asked the attorney to review it to see if it gave adequate protection to the system. If a salesman parted company with Forest Lawn or American Securities, Eaton wanted to stop him from taking that knowledge to another cemetery.

Goudge's reply included some suggested changes, but he also opined that the agreement probably gave as much protection as possible to Eaton's trade secrets. The attorney pointed out, however, that restrictions in state law made it difficult to prohibit a salesman who left Eaton's employ from working for another cemetery or selling organization.[35]

AS&F Formed

In November 1916, the new corporation was finally formed. Rather than any of the names Eaton had proposed in February, it was initially called American Trust & Security Company. As is custom-

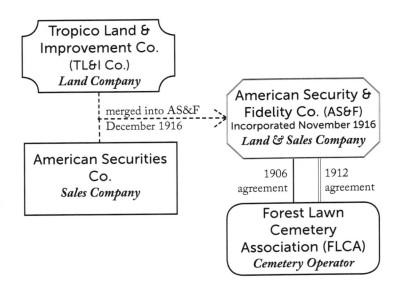

Figure 47. American Security & Fidelity Co.

TL&I and American Securities merge into the new American Security & Fidelity Co. (AS&F). Existing contracts are moved with the mergers.

ary, temporary directors and shareholders fulfilled the statutory requirements to activate the corporation. I. J. Lipsohn, H. M. Harrison, M. A. Pickett, E. J. Doyle, and G. F. Allen each gave the corporate secretary one dollar and received one share of stock, making them shareholders and eligible to vote for and be elected as directors. At their first meeting on November 23, 1916, the directors changed the name of the corporation to American Security & Fidelity Co. (AS&F).[36]

Proposal from Frank Hamilton

With the improved likelihood of a deal between American Securities, AS&F, and TL&I, Frank Hamilton submitted a formal proposal on November 25 to merge TL&I and American Securities into AS&F and raise working capital to finance improvements to the cemetery.

Hamilton's somewhat disingenuous explanation was that he had long wanted to be in the cemetery business due to his exposure to

Valhalla Cemetery in St. Louis. His search for a suitable cemetery site in Los Angeles had led him to buy an option on land in the Eagle Rock district (most likely the land that the Eaton team had found). Hamilton also said he had consulted Hubert Eaton, whom he considered a cemetery expert who had studied both the financial and technical sides. Given the additional knowledge of cemeteries Eaton had acquired from his "Eastern associates," Hamilton wanted Eaton and the selling system to be part of his cemetery venture. He found that Eaton was receptive to the idea, because he had been unsuccessfully trying to secure a financial interest in TL&I for some time. According to Hamilton, Eaton was now willing to resign from American Securities and join forces with Hamilton in a new cemetery.[37] With all the puffery about Eaton in Hamilton's proposal, and Eaton's instigation of investigation of a new cemetery, it seems much more likely that Eaton was responsible for the form of the proposal than Hamilton.

Hamilton went on to say that once those in control of TL&I learned of the situation, they concluded that a new cemetery with Hubert Eaton's system would be a formidable competitor. To prevent Hamilton from proceeding with his plans, the Rosses had offered to sell their stock to Hamilton. At the same time, Hamilton had arranged to buy all the stock in American Securities, giving him control of TL&I's land and American Securities' selling operation.[38]

Hamilton proposed that Eaton would be paid a small salary by AS&F in addition to what Eaton would be paid by Hamilton. Eaton would install his system for cemetery development and management, and devote his "entire time" to AS&F until he was satisfied that others could "competently manage" the operation.[39]

Under the proposal, all the preferred stock and 150,000 shares of common stock of AS&F would be placed with a trustee. These shares were to be sold for one dollar per share or more, with the proviso that any unsold shares as of January 1, 1919, would be returned to Hamilton. The cash from the stock sales prior to January 1, 1919, would go to AS&F.[40]

Additionally, the proposal obligated Hamilton to try to acquire the remaining 24,785 shares of TL&I within six months, by purchases or exchanges for AS&F stock. He could resell any of these TL&I shares to AS&F for one dollar per share. For each TL&I share Hamilton bought for cash, he was obligated to put one additional share of his AS&F stock into the trust to be sold for one dollar or more until January 1, 1919, when any unsold shares would revert to Hamilton. If Hamilton exchanged AS&F shares for TL&I shares, the AS&F shares would come from Hamilton's holdings.[41]

Several times in Hamilton's proposal letter, he emphasized that he was making money at each step of the way.[42]

By the end of November 1916—just a few days after he wrote his letter—Hamilton had acquired 116,838 shares of TL&I and 380 shares of American Securities Company through purchase or options. In addition to the shares in the two corporations, he had an agreement with Hubert Eaton for "his services, cemetery System of lot sales and improvement and influence." Hamilton wrote AS&F offering to exchange his stock holdings in TL&I and American Securities as well as his contract with Eaton for all the stock in the new AS&F—500,000 shares consisting of 400,000 common and 100,000 preferred, all at one-dollar par value.[43]

Clearly, Eaton wanted this transaction to work. He sent a telegram to on of his friends, L. E. Wyne, encouraging him to take action.

FORWARD STOCK TO BANK IMMEDIATELY . . . I AM NOT RUNNING THIS SHOW AM ONLY THE GOAT WHO IS DOING THE WORK AND TRYING TO PROTECT HIS FRIENDS PRESENT EXCHANGE ARRANGEMENT IS CONSIDERABLY TO YOUR ADVANTAGE[44]

Preparations for Merging

In mid-December, Pop Ross and Tom Ross wrote George Pratt—now secretary of the new AS&F—a letter supplementing Hamilton's proposal. AS&F was to have the use and income from the receiving vault. The promissory note due Tom Ross from FLCA was confirmed to be $23,529 due in December 1926, and AS&F was to guarantee the payment of the note. In return for $37,000, the Rosses were to deliver 43,045 shares of TL&I and 50 shares of American Securities. The Rosses also promised to give their "hearty cooperation and assistance in [the] endeavor to place Forest Lawn Cemetery and American Security & Fidelity Co. on a paying basis." The Rosses further agreed to use their influence with the stockholders of TL&I and AS&F, as well as the lot owners of Forest Lawn, "to the end that you will not be troubled with annoyance and that friction may be eliminated."[45]

Ten days later, when K. L. Crowley, AS&F's cashier, sent 116,836 shares of TL&I to Pop Ross to have them reissued in the name of AS&F, the big actions necessary for the merger had been accomplished.[46]

Everything was falling into place. To prepare for closing the Hamilton transaction, American Security & Fidelity borrowed $68,000 from the Citizens Trust and Savings Bank—$66,000 to pay Hamilton and $2,000 to set up a bank account to pay immediate expenses. Hamilton, with William Hazlett acting as his attorney in fact,* put the 100,000 shares of AS&F preferred stock and 150,000 shares of common stock into trust, also with Citizens Trust and Savings Bank. B. E. Marks, AS&F's agent in Phoenix, was directed to publish the notice of sale before the end of the year.[47]

At a December 18, 1916, meeting of the board of directors of AS&F, Frank Hamilton's proposal was formally accepted. Eight days later, TL&I's board of directors passed a resolution calling for a special meeting of stockholders to authorize the "sale, transfer or exchange of all the Corporate assets of every description of this Co." Although there were still things to be done, the major players had agreed—other than FLCA, which had no real say in what was happening.[48]

---

* An attorney in fact is a person who is authorized to perform business-related transactions on behalf of someone else.

Merritt Llewellyn's Stock

Not wanting to have anything to do with the new AS&F, Merritt Llewellyn wrote a letter to the company—not Eaton—saying that he wanted to sell his stock. He asked what commission would be charged on the sale.

It was not long before Crowley replied that AS&F was "not in the business of selling stock and accepts no commission for same."

Merritt Llewellyn then wrote Hubert Eaton. He noted that Eaton had previously told him that half of the stock issued by AS&F would be preferred and the other half would be common stock, but "the new stock is all common. Is there any market for it and what can you sell it for? Mine is for sale & what will your commission be to turn it?"[49]

Taken aback by the letter, Eaton told Merritt that the request was "certainly very sudden as the Company is just formed and as yet has not appeared before the public, consequently there is no market for your stock." Explaining that 100,000 shares of preferred stock had been issued, Eaton reported that it would be used to generate the cash needed "for new improvements such as a mausoleum, crematory, columbarium, chappel [*sic*] and receiving vault that are needed in Forest Lawn Cemetery." Although there was no market for the stock yet, Eaton believed there would be one in 1917. He also had no doubt that although the value of the stock had been debatable, the outlook was now positive. He told Merritt that he must have patience. Eaton ended with, "I know that you feel you have given them time[,] yet if the final outcome is 100% increase for you, you really have no kick coming."[50]

Eaton closed the letter by chiding Merritt, "I have never sold a share of my own stock and do not intend to because I realize now that it is going to get better every year and I want to realize on it to the very fullest extent."[51]

Everything was now set for the first stages of Eaton's transformation of Forest Lawn from a cemetery to a memorial-park. But the challenges were far from over.

CHAPTER 16

Building for the Future

Considering all the correspondence, negotiations, and agreements regarding the organization of Forest Lawn, the concerns over its finances, and the seemingly endless lawsuits, one might think little progress was being made. But Hubert Eaton now had a vision for a new kind of cemetery—a place of beauty, inspiration, and solace that would exceed all previous cemetery experiences, and it needed to be built.

The Builder's Creed

Hubert Eaton often told the story of standing on the hill above Forest Lawn on New Year's Day 1917 and dreaming of what Forest Lawn should become. As the story went, Eaton wrote down his thoughts about what Forest Lawn should becom, calling his vision The Builder's Creed. These thoughts became Eaton's guide for building Forest Lawn. Even now, this creed continues as a core statement of Forest Lawn's values and goals. The Builder's Creed has now set the tone for Forest Lawn for over one hundred years. It has been used in countless publications, and Eaton had it inscribed in stone for all to see.

Forest Lawn Archives. c. 1950

Figure 48. The Builder's Creed

Hubert Eaton seated in front of The Builder's Creed which he had carved into stone when building the Memorial Terrace entrance to the Great Mausoleum in 1931.

The Builder's Creed

I believe in a happy eternal life.

I believe those of us left behind should be glad in the certain belief that those gone before, who believed in Him, have entered into that happier life.

I believe, most of all, in a Christ that smiles and loves you and me.

I therefore know the cemeteries of today are wrong because they depict an end, not a beginning. They have consequently become unsightly stoneyards, full of inartistic symbols and depressing customs; places that do nothing for humanity save a practical act, and that not well.

I therefore prayerfully resolve on this New Year's Day, 1917, that I shall endeavor to build Forest Lawn as different, as unlike other cemeteries as sunshine is unlike darkness, as eternal life is unlike death. I shall try to build at Forest Lawn a great park, devoid of misshapen monuments and other customary signs of earthly death, but filled with towering trees, sweeping lawns, splashing fountains, singing birds, beautiful statuary, cheerful flowers, noble memorial architecture, with interiors full of light and color, and redolent of the world's best history and romances.

I believe these things educate and uplift a community.

Forest Lawn shall become a place where lovers new and old shall love to stroll and watch the sunset's glow, planning for the future or reminiscing of the past; a place where artists study and sketch; where school teachers bring happy children to see the things they read of in books; where little churches invite, triumphant in the knowledge that from their pulpits only words of love can be spoken; where memorialization of loved ones in sculptured marble and pictorial glass shall be encouraged but controlled by acknowledged artists; a place where the sorrowing will be soothed and strengthened because it will be God's garden. A place that shall be protected by an immense Endowment Care Fund, the principal of which can never be expended—only the income therefrom used to care for and perpetuate this Garden of Memory.

This is the Builder's Dream; this is the Builder's Creed.[1]

Eaton had now outlined his vision. When he later had this vision carved in stone, he simply had it signed as "The Builder."

Sharing His Vision

Wanting to impress potential customers, Eaton continued to solicit statements to include in a new version of the promotional booklet "The Reasons Why" (Appendix D). For example, Eaton asked an acquaintance, Dr. William Watson, to write favorable comments for use in the booklet. Eaton even suggested specific comments that Watson could make: that after investigation, he had found Forest Lawn to be less expensive and more beautiful than other cemeteries, that Forest Lawn had a water supply "large enough to run a city", that it had "quiet efficiency," and that it had an ideal location between Los Angeles and Pasadena. Eaton told Watson's assistant that he hoped some of these suggestions would be incorporated and that the doctor could "clothe . . . them in his own diction which we have occasion to know is most scholarly."[2]

While Eaton believed that quotes about Forest Lawn were important, he also believed that it was important to portray the visual side of the cemetery. Accordingly, in addition to "The Reasons Why," he planned a book with photos of Forest Lawn. Part of Eaton's vision for Forest Lawn's future was contained in the final paragraph of copy sent to publisher Young & McCallister for inclusion in this book:

Forest Lawn is more than a park-cemetery because vast improvements are now being added which, when completed, will give to Forest Lawn the distinction of being the ONLY INSTITUTION IN SOUTHERN CALIFORNIA IN

WHICH OUR LOVED ONES CAN BE LAID AWAY
AT REST IN ANY MANNER THAT THEIR WISHES
SO DICTATE—be it earth burial, mausoleum crypt, cremation, columbarium niche, private vault or any other way that
they may wish. The word "Memorial-Park" has been coined
to embrace all those different forms of burial. These various
departments are all under one management and operated
under one over-head expense, thereby making an immense
saving of money which is shared with the purchaser.[3]

Eaton was now poised to make Forest Lawn different from other
cemeteries. Little did he realize that he also would change the
way cemeteries were viewed throughout the country and even in
foreign lands.

Time to Build

Visible changes were needed to move Forest Lawn from being just
a cemetery to the memorial-park that Hubert Eaton envisioned.
During 1917 and 1918, plans proceeded to build a church, an adjoining crematory, new receiving vaults, and a mausoleum-columbarium.

The idea of adding these improvements to Forest Lawn was not
a new one. From the time he arrived, Charles Sims had envisioned
a community mausoleum on the hill above Forest Lawn. Norton
Wells supported this idea and sent Tom Ross a set of plans in January
1914. Hubert Eaton, on the other hand, instructed his salesmen to
point out the supposedly shoddy construction of the community
mausoleums provided by other promoters. He explored less expensive alternatives for Forest Lawn, but they did not come to fruition.
Eventually, however, Eaton saw a community mausoleum as an
essential part of his vision for the memorial-park.

One of the earliest references to crematories in Forest Lawn
files—other than their being specifically mentioned in FLCA's articles
of incorporation—was in a 1914 letter from Norton Wells to Frank
Gibson, who supplied crematory equipment to cemeteries. Wells asked

Gibson to introduce Hubert Eaton to the operators of a crematory in Portland, Oregon. Gibson obliged by writing to J. C. Bratten at the Portland Gas & Coke Company, asking him rather than the crematory operators to arrange for Eaton to inspect the installation. Gibson wrote the manufacturer rather than the crematory operator because he had had a "falling out" with the crematory operator. Gibson believed that if the crematory operator knew Eaton was acquainted with him, Eaton would get little information, as they would "shut up like a clam."[4] Eaton had planned to look at the new Portland crematory on his way home from a meeting in Reno and was encouraged by Wells to "accumulate a mass of information to be digested later." However, Eaton skipped the Portland leg of the trip, did not stop in San Francisco to see the Rosses, and telegraphed his office that he would be home but that no one should be told of his arrival.[5]

Nevertheless, by November 1914 Pop Ross was aware that Eaton had plans to construct improvements such as a crematory and mausoleum at Forest Lawn. In early January 1917, Eaton told Merritt Llewellyn that preferred shares of AS&F stock would be sold to generate the cash for these improvements.[6] The time had come to build.

Pratt's Report on Plans

In March 1917, TL&I shareholders—soon to become AS&F shareholders—learned that Forest Lawn Cemetery would have a new name: Forest Lawn Memorial-Park. AS&F secretary George Pratt told them of the new philosophy:[7]

> The future policy of American Security & Fidelity Co. will be to specialize along lines of natural beauty. . . . We shall build a park for the living—we believe the only gruesome thing about death is the misconception given to it by human thought. In fashioning our architecture we shall depart from the old conventional ideas of stiff, cold, severe lines and make Forest Lawn a cheerful spot of sunlight, birds, flowers, doves and color.[8]

Also in March, Pratt wrote a letter to AS&F stockholders describing the improvements that were planned. The first significant structure to be built would be a church known as the Little Church of the Flowers.* With a design inspired by Thomas Gray's "Elegy Written in a Country Churchyard," the Little Church would be unique. Pews would be flanked by conservatories—a glass roofed addition with flowers and plants. Birds in cages would be added to the conservatories "to warble their sweetness during the funeral services." A modern pipe organ was to be installed, and the plan was to hold organ recitals on Sundays. Pratt acknowledged that FLCA's officers had "worked under great handicaps," and explained that with the new Little Church, AS&F was "throwing around it a romantic atmosphere." Other planned construction included receiving vaults for bodies and cremated remains (ashes), as well as a crematory with two retorts.[9]

Crowning all of this, Pratt said, would be a mausoleum, which would be unequaled in the world. It was to be the only mausoleum lit with electric lights, emitting a soft glow at night that could be seen for miles. According to Pratt, the plans were being drawn to avoid "the dark and gruesome ideas of death and substituting therefore light, warmth, color and a soothing peacefulness"—Hubert Eaton's new memorial-park concept.[10]

In addition to reacquiring the sixty-five acres that had been lost through the partition suit—a purchase that would be completed a few months after Pratt's letter—the new American Security & Fidelity planned to purchase additional land for the expansion of Forest Lawn. Pratt's letter estimated that the improvements would cost at least $300,000—equivalent to more than $5 million currently. The result of the expenditure, the letter said, would be a "consolidation of all forms of burial [that] will place Forest Lawn in a class absolutely by itself. This fact, when advertised through salesmen, literature and newspapers, will result in bringing a wealth of patronage to Forest Lawn that it has never dreamed of."[11]

---

* Originally it was called just the "Little Church." The name was expanded to "Little Church of the Flowers" after conservatories were added to the plans.

In his letter, Pratt claimed that AS&F had entered into a contract with George Emery, "whose specialty is that of conducting mausoleum sales campaigns," and was willing to assign that contract to FLCA "without any profit on our part, you simply assume our position in the contract." FLCA would have the use of the Little Church of the Flowers free of charge if it paid for the repair and upkeep. FLCA would be responsible for "the entire administering and selling authority for the mausoleum-columbarium and crematory," while AS&F would build and equip the church and mausoleum.[12] FLCA would now have complete responsibility for all sales and would continue to develop the cemetery—other than the mausoleum.

Choosing a Crematory Manufacturer

With the word out that Forest Lawn would build a crematory as part of its new church complex, Norton Wells started receiving solicitations from manufacturers. Frank Gibson, of Houston, Texas, wrote Wells that he was "still in the Crematory game, better qualified than ever to render the very best service obtainable in that particular line of work." Furthermore, he declared that he had "successfully designed, constructed and personally operated . . . more crematory retorts than any other individual or firm in the U. S. or for that matter the entire world." Gibson was particularly proud of installing retorts in Kansas City for D. W. Newcomer's Sons Undertakers, and, acting as "consulting architect and engineer," designing twelve "oil burning mortuary Retorts" for the City of New York. He also enclosed letters of commendation from the Denver Crematory and Harry Watson of the Bonney-Watson Co. of Seattle. Gibson also advised that crude oil was preferable to gas for crematory fuel.[13]

Occupied with other things, Wells took several weeks to return Gibson's letter, only to tell him that Tom Ross was investigating "different forms of incineration" and was "waiting [for] final tests on a process that he [had] been investigating." Norton Wells suggested that Gibson write Tom directly regarding his company.[14]

Undaunted by Wells's tardy reply, Gibson immediately followed up with a letter expressing his regret that Wells had not seen fit to have his firm come at once for the crematory and mausoleum construction. With prose reminiscent of George Heath's flamboyance when applying for the FLCA sales job, Gibson extolled the virtues of his company, proclaiming that he would give better service than anyone could, as well as save the cemetery money. Frank Gibson claimed to have had "the pleasure of a personal acquaintance with [Tom Ross] for a number of years," so he had written Tom as Wells had suggested.[15]

Gibson was not the only one to take note of Forest Lawn's plans for a crematory. Jo J. De Haven, who knew Wells from their 1915 communications concerning legislation, also wrote him wanting to bid on the installation. De Haven reported that Mount Olivet, where he was secretary, had built a new crematory that burned oil. He could provide Eaton with detailed information relative to the cost of operation and stressed the value of Mount Olivet's experience in the field.[16] Despite the relationship, De Haven did not win the job.

Not much later, Eaton received a pitch from Lawrence F. Moore, president of the Crematory Supply Company in Piedmont, California, for the construction of the crematory and the columbarium. Not sure to whom the proposal should be sent, Moore also wrote Norton Wells, enclosing his business card as manager of the California Crematorium in Oakland. Eaton gave his letter to Wells for reply, and Wells simply told Moore to contact Tom Ross.[17]

Moore contacted Tom Ross and then followed up with Wells, suggesting changes in plans—suggestions that should have been sent to Tom Ross, the architect. Moore claimed he could eliminate the underground smoke flue, high stack, and compressor room, which would save cost by reducing the building size.[18]

I am glad to find that you will be opposed to cremation by direct assault upon the body (the Honolulu, Sacramento and

Cypress Lawn way). . . . You have seen enough . . . to have a very decided opinion about lowering caskets through floors, stripping off the metal and shooting them into white hot furnaces. . . .

We will give you retorts the public will approve: they are smokeless, odorless and almost noiseless. The casket goes in cold retort with flowers and handles on just as in the vault in cemetery. . . . You will never have to chop corners off of fancy caskets and best of all, you will cremate in 45 to 90 minutes . . . by indirect heating, starting cold.

We have seen every retort there is—our's [sic] is a development of all features calculated to satisfy the public and line the owner's pockets with dividends earned by high class service.[19]

Moore convinced E. H. Neuhrenberg, secretary of Cypress Lawn, to write Wells with an "unbiased" opinion of Moore's cremation equipment. After witnessing a cremation from start to finish, Neuhrenberg said it was the best crematory retort he had ever seen. Despite his praise of the product, a handwritten postscript on the letter indicated that his recommendation was confidential—no doubt because Cypress Lawn had previously chosen different equipment.[20]

Still another purveyor of crematory equipment, Henry Brett, a mechanical engineer with several "crematory furnace" patents, pitched his Brett-Benton Type D-2 retorts. He claimed that the equipment could be adapted to use either fuel oil or natural gas, with hydraulic cylinders for raising the large furnace doors quickly. However, he also disclosed he "would prefer that you have the masonry work and mechanical plant for operating the burners done under separate contracts."[21]

About two months after sending his previous letters, Lawrence Moore made another plea for the business, writing, "When can I come down and close with you?" He made his last pitch for the business, boasting that Neuhrenberg of Cypress Lawn would advise the use of his equipment. He also claimed, "[Sandy] Davidson's new retorts will not deliver. Poor old Sandy has built his last retort. I believe they have caught the chaffeur [*sic*] who ran him down. . . . I am selling a $250 niche and an Urn to a lady who will never go near one of those direct-fire retorts again. Really, it pays to get the ideal apparatus."[22]

Despite Moore's many efforts, Henry Brett's company was ultimately awarded the contract for the crematory retorts.[23]

Mausoleum Sales Manager

With word out in the industry that Forest Lawn would be building a new mausoleum, a man named Herbert Webber approached Eaton, wanting to become the manager of the mausoleum sales operation. Eaton turned to Getzendanner, now with the Cemeteries Improvement Corporation. which was operating the Whittier Heights Cemetery, for any background information he might have regarding Webber.[24]

Getzendanner's reply quashed any thought Eaton might have entertained about hiring Webber. Although Webber had claimed he oversaw selling for California Mausoleum Company, headquartered in Pasadena, it turned out that he was only a "verifier of contracts" and had never overseen the selling effort. As for Webber's claim of involvement with promotion of the Riverside Mausoleum, Getzendanner reported that during Webber's ten months with the project, he "never turned in a contract for a single crypt and I understand constituted himself as dictator of the proceedings . . . but his appointment to this particular position was never authorized or recognized by the company. I believe this is Mr. Webber's long suit." Getzendanner said Webber had also failed in promoting a mausoleum in Santa Ana and was currently rumored to be trying "to secure a foot-hold" in a new cemetery and mausoleum project in Fresno.[25]

Webber was not hired. Instead, the man who became sales manager for the mausoleum was George Emery. Although Pratt had told the AS&F stockholders on March 1 that AS&F already had a contract with Emery, this apparently was not so. On March 28 Emery wrote Eaton to ask for the mausoleum sales job. Extolling his "extensive experience in the business of selling crypts, family vaults and burial space in mausoleums," he also assured Eaton that he firmly believed he could produce gross sales of $250,000 within six months of the time he started.[26]

Emery was hired but could not produce sales volume anywhere near his boasts. In fact, he did not produce enough sales for his commissions to cover the $250 advance that he received each month. When renegotiating his contract in September 1917, the revised agreement acknowledged that his account was overdrawn and that he would no longer receive a monthly advance. Furthermore, 25 percent of the commissions he earned would go toward repaying the deficit in his account.[27]

Design Decisions

By early February 1917, Eaton was well on the way to transforming Forest Lawn Cemetery. Although Tom Ross was selling his entire TL&I stock holdings, he continued to have a professional relationship with Forest Lawn as an architect. Eaton reported to the American Security & Fidelity board that Ross had agreed to prepare the plans for the church, crematory, mausoleum, and columbarium as well as "specifications, complete drawings and blue prints for the sum of $2000.00." Eaton had already made a $500 payment to Ross to put things in motion. He was further authorized by the directors to pay Tom Ross "such further sums as are in [Eaton's and corporate secretary Pratt's] minds commensurate with the services received."[28]

By March 1917, Tom sent Wells blueprints for the foundation, along with specifications for the Little Church of the Flowers and crematory, to file with permit applications. Ultimately, Tom Ross decided that it would be best to file for a permit just for the foundation of the church rather than for the entire building. When it was time to apply for a permit for the balance of the work, Tom would then go "before the board to explain any matters they may wish."[29]

Correspondence between Norton Wells and Tom was frequent and filled with details needing resolution from the architect. In a few instances, Wells offered suggestions for design. In a postscript to a letter, he suggested alternatives for placement of the walkway and toilets. One of his options was to have the walk lead to the door of the conservatory that the Building Department had required.[30]

Tom did not like Wells's idea for the location of the toilets, because he thought they should not be seen immediately as people left the chapel. However, he agreed he would look at the suggested location when he next came to Los Angeles.[31]

Although Tom Ross was an experienced architect, he was not familiar with the operational side of designing mausoleums. One of the design issues was how to keep marble fronts on mausoleum crypts in place but still have them removable for making entombments.

Figure 49. Little Church Toilet Location

Wells and Tom Ross had different ideas regarding the toilet location. This sketch shows Tom's proposal.

Forest Lawn Archives

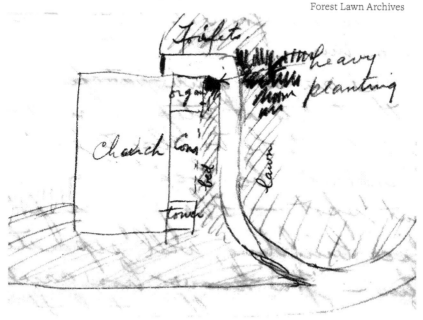

The marble contractor asked Wells how this was to be done without having hinges on the crypt fronts. The contractor suggested that the "front slab slide forth and back, allowing a bevel on one edge, so that the marble can be pulled past the jamb and to have two handles on each slab so that it can be lifted away from the crypt opening at will." The handles would have been aesthetically awkward, to say the least. After examining how other mausoleums dealt with the issue, the mausoleum was designed with stiles and rails construction—stiles being the vertical elements between crypts, and rails the horizontal elements at the top and bottom. With this method of construction, the crypt fronts are recessed. In future construction at Forest Lawn, the crypt fronts would be flush, allowing the use of removable, ornamental "rosettes" to keep the marble in place.[32]

The Grand Tour

Construction of the Little Church of the Flowers began in May 1917. Shortly afterward, Hubert Eaton and Tom Ross departed for a month-long grand tour of American cemeteries, seeking the best

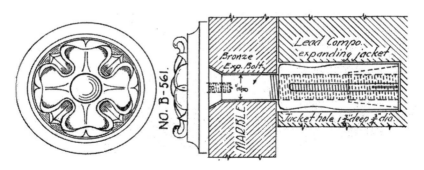

Detroit Mausoleum Equipment Works

Figure 50. Mausoleum Crypt Rosette

As Forest Lawn and AS&F planned construction of a mausoleum, many vendors contacted them with product literature, such as this ad for "Standard Bronze Rosettes for marble catacomb fronts."

ideas for cemetery and mausoleum development to incorporate into Forest Lawn's expansion plans. Eaton wired Wells on July 2.[33]

NOW LEAVING OMAHA TWO HUNDRED THOUSAND
INHABITANTS, SEVEN CEMETERIES, ONE MAUSOLEUM,
ONE CREMATORY. FIND ROSS SPENT TWO DAYS HERE.
MEET HIM CHICAGO TOMORROW. FOREST LAWN [OMAHA]
BEST MODERN CEMETERY HERE BUT CANT [*sic*] HOLD
CANDLE TO OUR FOREST LAWN.[34]

In addition to the telegram, Eaton wrote a letter with additional detail, saying he believed he was learning more about what not to do than what to do. Although he thought the countryside around Omaha was perfect for cemeteries, he was quite critical of the Forest Lawn cemetery in Omaha (no relation to Eaton's Forest Lawn), saying management had "ruined the cemetery through extensive admission of monuments and head-stones at any place and of every size and description." Although the cemetery had an expensive chapel, Eaton found it to be "cold, inartistic and uninviting."[35]

Eaton had similar issues with Omaha's West Lawn cemetery. Although Eaton thought the mausoleum was its crowning glory, Tom Ross was not impressed. Seeing the mausoleum the day after Ross, Eaton was impressed that the mausoleum was placed so that it had wonderful views of the countryside. But that was the only nice thing Eaton observed concerning it. He described it as being built entirely of white marble, and the architect had "religiously remembered every cold, severe, dark and grewsome [*sic*] idea he ever had or read of burial and inculcated these beliefs into the designing of his building."[36]

Eaton continued on to Chicago, where he met up with Tom Ross. They found that this city of two and a half million people had thirty-five cemeteries, three crematories, and one mausoleum. Believing that only ten of the cemeteries were worth looking at, they finally decided to visit only two due to time constraints.[37]

Graceland Cemetery, near what is now Wrigley Field, was the first place Eaton and Ross visited. They found it filled with monuments and private vaults. They concluded that the cemetery's superintendent must not have wanted visitors to see large vistas of monuments and tombstones; the solution was dense planting that created "landscape rooms." Eaton wrote Wells,

> The observer can not at any place see beyond a few feet and the cemetery is thus broken up into a thousand and one little nooks and garden spots and fanciful arbors. The total result is not so pleasing as the vistas, or the outlook in the theoretically perfect park cemetery, but it was most interesting to observe how planting done correctly could overcome the stone yard effect of too many monuments.[38]

Eaton was impressed that the crematory used kerosene and the retort had an electric motor to open and shut the door.[39]

The second Chicago stop was Rosehill Cemetery, about three miles north of Graceland Cemetery. Eaton was impressed that Rosehill "had lots of money spent on it and must have made a bunch of profit for its stockholders." They found that the cemetery had many beautiful private vaults and that the designer now lived in Los Angeles. The mausoleum was the highlight of the visit. Eaton and Ross were particularly interested in the mausoleum having two levels, and were told by the superintendent that the public did not object to it. It was interesting to them that an elevator had been installed in the structure but was going to be torn out as it was not used. Stained-glass windows, particularly one by the Tiffany studio, added to the grandeur of the mausoleum. However, Eaton thought the building had a the large amount of wasted space. Despite that comment, he found some useful ideas relative to electric lighting in the mausoleum.[40]

Eaton concluded his report to Wells with the assessment that the trip was worthwhile and they had gleaned many ideas that might be applied to Forest Lawn's mausoleum.[41]

From Chicago, Eaton and Tom Ross went on to Detroit, Buffalo, Boston, and Brookline, Massachusetts, all the while expanding their knowledge of developments at other cemeteries. Near the end of their trip, Eaton reported to Wells by telegram:

```
WE HAVE EXAMINED EVERY COMMUNITY MAUSOLEUM
[OF] ANY IMPORTANCE IN UNITED STATES. WE FOUND
ONLY TWO WHERE SOMETHING COULD BE LEARNED.
ALL OTHERS SHOW TOO PLAINLY WHAT NOT TO DO.
VOLHOLLA [sic] MAUSOLEUM ST LOUIS IS MOST
EFFICIENT AND ROSEHILL CHICAGO IS LARGEST AND
MOST MAGNIFICENT. THERE IS NOW NO DOUBT THAT
OUR BUILDING AND PERFECTED [PLANS] WILL SURPASS
ALL OTHERS AND BECOME THE GREATEST EXAMPLE OF
MAUSOLEUM ARCHITECTURE IN THE COUNTRY. IF THE
PUBLIC COULD ONLY UNDERSTAND THE FACTS AS WE NOW
DO OUR SPACE WOULD BE SOLD TEN TIMES OVER. HAVE
ALSO SOME PERTINENT FACTS REGARDING CEMETERY
AND CREMATORY BUT HAVE BEEN PROUD TO FIND THAT
OUR ORGANIZATION STANDS FOREMOST IN ORIGINAL
[AND] SCIENTIFIC METHODS FOR HANDLING ALL
MORTUARY NEEDS.[42]
```

Tom Ross made several visits to Cypress Lawn Cemetery in Colma, where he had designed the Noble Chapel, to work out details of the mausoleum design he was creating for Forest Lawn. Eaton accompanied him on at least one such visit, immediately following their grand tour of cemeteries.[43]

Construction Decisions

While Eaton and Ross were on their grand tour, Norton Wells kept relaying progress reports and decisions needed on construction. Many of these dealt with the crematory, since the plans were evolving around the crematory equipment rather than architectural design.

It appeared that elements of the crematory were being designed on the fly—particularly the chimney.

Wells explained to Tom Ross that the chimney would be visible from the cemetery office (near the entrance) but not from the side of the church. Wells's idea was just to plant a "tall growing bamboo in such a way that the end of [the crematory] will not be seen." Similarly, he thought, if the chimney were not turned into an architectural feature, they could "plant shrubbery on the roof" to hide it.[44]

When Wells suggested that the crematory should be enlarged for the possible addition of more retorts in the future, Tom wired a reply that the expansion possibility was "too remote" to be considered and the "chief aim should be keep chimney invisible therefore original site according to plans seems best." Ross ignored Wells's landscaping ideas.[45]

Although Eaton respected Tom Ross as an architect, he often felt frustrated by Tom's lack of follow-through. Wells had written and telegraphed Tom regarding several matters involving decisions needed on the construction of the Little Church of the Flowers, but had received no response. While traveling with Tom, Eaton finally wrote Wells, "Anything you wish to ask Tom you had better send in my care, and I will attend to it and forward [the decisions] to you as soon as possible. I will notify you by wire his itinerary after he leaves me in order that you may communicate with him direct."[46]

Operating Practices

Just as Tom Ross and Hubert Eaton sought to gain understanding and inspiration from visiting other cemeteries, Norton Wells sought information from other cemeteries regarding operating practices.

For example, when Wells asked Jo J. De Haven of Mount Olivet about the process for making cemetery arrangements, he learned that they required all arrangements to be made with the cemetery. If purchasers could not come to Mount Olivet's city office or the cemetery, a representative was sent to see them. This was done to ensure that purchasers were fully informed of what was available from the cemetery. Prior to this, arrangements had been made through the undertakers, and according to De Haven, people were frequently unhappy with the lot and complained to the cemetery regarding the undertaker and the location of the burial property. He also told Wells that having direct contact with the family eased collection problems, since the cemetery could receive immediate payment rather than relying on the undertakers, who were "very timid about requiring sufficient cash."[47]

In August, Norton Wells once again reached out to Cypress Lawn, asking H. Neuhrenberg for a copy of its rules and regulations governing the operation of the crematory and mausoleum. In particular, he was interested in how Cypress Lawn treated mausoleum crypt owners. Since 1859, California law had specified that in order to be a voting member of a nonprofit cemetery association, a plot owner needed to own at least two hundred square feet of cemetery property. A single interment space would usually be less than thirty square feet. Thus the law as written at the time did not provide a way for crypt or niche owners to become members. California law would not eliminate the two-hundred-square-foot provision until 1931, and even then, cemetery associations were not required to change their eligibility requirements for members.[48]

Annexation and Building Codes

In August 1917, the citizens of Tropico voted against annexation to Los Angeles and for annexation to the City of Glendale.[49] Not long after the merger of Tropico and Glendale, the area that included Forest Lawn and J. B. Treadwell's property was annexed to the City of Los Angeles. Thereafter, Forest Lawn was subject to the Los Angeles building permit system.

Wells's reaction to the city's requirements was similar to how business people today might describe the process: "It seems we are delayed with one thing after another . . . but of course we have to learn the ropes of how to prepare to build in Los Angeles and I suppose we cannot learn younger."[50]

Church Nears Completion

By mid-September 1917, construction of the church and its adjoining structures had progressed to the point where the end was in sight. Wells was able to report to Tom that although they were "held up on the marble mosaic floor and the electric current . . . when these are in we will be pretty near completed."[51] Once the church, crematory, and receiving vaults were finished, the plan was to tear out the original receiving vault. This would allow a road to be built to connect the older part of Forest Lawn with a new entrance north of the original entrance on Glendale Avenue.

Throughout the construction of the Little Church of the Flowers, Wells suggested various details to Tom Ross, who, confident in his own opinion, usually just ignored Wells's ideas.

As the church neared completion, Wells asked Tom to find out how Cypress Lawn placed ferns on marble shelves in the receiving vaults. He wanted to know the dimensions of the boxes and whether Cypress Lawn used pots of ferns or filled the boxes with soil. Ross sent a detailed reply with specifications and drawings. He indicated that the boxes should not be lined with galvanized metal because they needed to have "free seepage." Furthermore, he suggested that the boxes for ferns be alternated with pots of flowers. He closed with, "The next time you want this kind of information don't send up for it during a [street]car strike as no cars are running to Cypress Lawn & I had to take an auto. Forgive you this time."[52]

The original plans for the Little Church of the Flowers called for a pipe organ. Murray Harris was chosen to prepare the specifications for the organ and had expected to supervise the installation. When asked what his fee would be, Harris had responded that AS&F could pay him what it thought was right. After receiving a $6,000 quote for an Estey organ, Harris reported he thought he could obtain one at a lower price. In a conversation with Wells, the two agreed that Harris would be paid whatever amount of savings he obtained. However, the organ purchase ended up being postponed because of the war effort. Wells told Harris that it would not be possible to

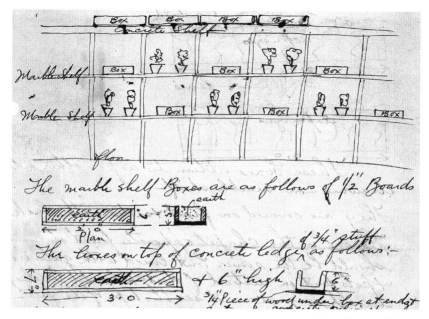

Forest Lawn Archives

Figure 51. Cypress Lawn Receiving Vault Detail

Tom Ross replied to Wells's request for details of how Cypress Lawn handled flowers in its receiving vault: "The following is a sketch of Cypress Lawn boxes of pine. . . . The planting in the boxes is asparagus with fern in & enclosed leaf in the other with asparagus – The entire top concrete ledge is asparagus – The asparagus & ferns are planted in the earth in the boxes."

borrow the money for the organ because that would not be considered patriotic—the organ would be "'non essential', and not necessary for the prosecution of the war." Learning of the organ deferral, Harris complained of receiving nothing for his efforts. Eaton sent him a check for fifty dollars as a gesture of settlement.[53]

Crematory Publicity

After crematory construction was completed in January 1918, Forest Lawn sent a letter to local undertakers announcing the opening, with more than a little bit of puffery.

We desire to announce the formal opening of our Crematory for business.

We believe we have the most improved and efficient crematory in the United States. This is a broad statement, but we make it for this reason: Our architect, in company with our officials, recently made an extensive trip, visiting practically every crematory in the United States. Our Crematory thus represents the sum total of all the excellent points we gathered from the crematories that are now in operation in the United States.

Our prices and terms are as follows:

Still Born Babies - - - - - - - - - - - -	$10.00
Children up to 2 years, Inclusive - - -	15.00
" " " 12 " " - - - - -	25.00
Adults - - - - - - - - - - - - - - - - - -	50.00[54]

With publicity making the new crematory quite visible, it was inevitable that someone would eventually make an "extra-ordinary" request for cremation of the family pet and placement of the pet's remains in a crypt with the owner. George Emery rejected the request, telling the prospective purchaser, Ernest Layrock, that as far as he was concerned, "there is no disposal of the remains to be bestowed upon as faithful an animal as a dog that are too dignified. Forest Lawn's rules and regulations prohibited burial of animals." He told Layrock, "It is a regrettable that Los Angeles, like many of the other large cities has no adequate place, especially dedicated to this purpose. This is rather astonishing, when one considers the vast number of people in this community that are intensely interested in dumb animals."[55]

Mausoleum Construction

When Eaton received a copy of the booklet "Community Mausoleums" about Cecil E. Bryan, an early builder of mausoleums,

Figure 52. Azalea Terrace in Great Mausoleum

Azalea Terrace was the first unit of what would become known as the Great Mausoleum in Forest Lawn-Glendale.

he was so impressed by it that he wrote Bryan and requested eighteen copies for sixty cents each (the cover price was two dollars). Eaton was interested in Bryan's philosophy and wanted to share the various images of mausoleums from the forty-page brochure with Tom Ross and others. Bryan had worked for Frank Lloyd Wright for a year, then for Ralph Modjeski, who specialized in precast concrete. Bryan saw community mausoleums as "beautiful and everlasting temples surrounded by well kept lawns and parks" as an alternative to landscapes "disfigured by the . . . unkempt and unwholesome graveyard." The description of the structures as being "as permanent as any work of man can be" was quite different from the description in the National Retail Monument Dealers' flyer of 1914. Bryan built as many as eighty mausoleums around the United States, including the Sunnyside Mausoleum in Sunnyside Memorial Gardens in Long Beach, California, in 1924.[56]

Figure 53. Azalea Terrace Entrance

The new mausoleum at Forest Lawn was a threat to the local undertakers. They realized that any family choosing a mausoleum crypt could not be sold an outer burial container (vault) and might be tempted to put money into a nice, visible crypt rather than an expensive casket that would not be seen after the entombment. Norton Wells wrote one of the undertakers, C. R. Vesper, to assure him that Forest Lawn's sales campaign would impress crypt purchasers that "a body should be embalmed and that a casket commensurate with their investment in the crypts should be kept in mind. In this way, we feel that the undertaker will be protected."[57]

Forest Lawn's new mausoleum was to feature electric lighting—something just becoming common. When Tom Ross first asked Wells to find out the voltage, phase, and cycles (Hertz) of the electrical supply to Forest Lawn, Wells first responded that the subject was so complicated it would need to wait until Tom was in Los Angeles. Apparently it was not that complicated, because only two days later Wells managed to find the electrical specifications and send them to Tom Ross.[58]

Although mausoleum sales had begun earlier in the year, it was October 1917 before Forest Lawn sought a building permit for the new mausoleum. Bids began coming in, with the concrete work bids ranging from $15,800 to $25,000.[59]

Figure 54. Forest Lawn Mausoleum Rendering c. 1918
Forest Lawn Archives

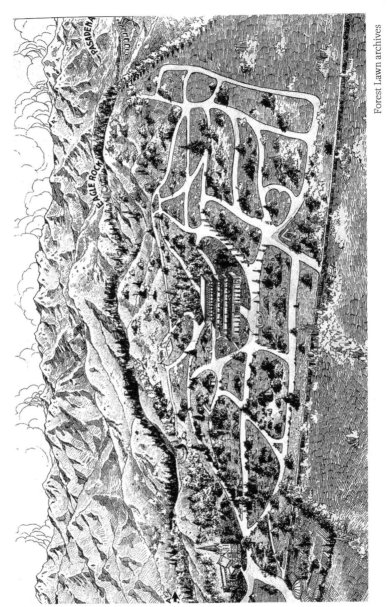

Figure 55. Forest Lawn Cemetery Plan c. 1918

New plans for the cemetery moved the location of the mausoleum
from the top of the hill to a place nearer current development.

Figure 56. Little Church of the Flowers 2017

After the United States entered World War I in April 1917, the federal government began taking incremental steps to support its war efforts. Fearing restrictions on construction materials for the church or mausoleum, Eaton telegraphed AS&F from San Francisco. He asked them to phone Wells immediately and have the contractor rush the building permit, because the "government will soon order all permits stopped.[60]

The threat of the war causing construction problems continued to trouble Eaton. The following day he sent another telegram, this one expressing concern over the potential price increase for cement and directing that a tentative agreement be entered into for price protection. Only an hour and a half later, Wells responded by telegram that he would get the permit immediately.[61]

Wells contacted the Llewellyn Iron Works to secure structural steel. He was told that if he wanted to procure it at all, he would have to commit to a size somewhat larger than specified, because the shipyards were getting most of the steel for war-related production. Similarly, the studio that was to produce the art glass and skylights would take much longer than expected, as skilled labor was very hard to find due to the war effort.[62]

Mausoleum construction progressed rapidly. A formal dedication of Azalea Terrace was held on May 20, 1920, although the first entombment had been made a year earlier, in April 1919. A bronze plaque commemorating the dedication listed the members of the FLCA board of trustees.

Neither George Pratt nor Hubert Eaton could envision how this building would grow over the coming decades. The mausoleum would eventually expand from one story to ten staggered terraces that climbed up the hill like steps. Each new terrace was named after a plant or flower: Azalea, Begonia, Coleus, Dahlia, Evergreen, and so on. The structure would eventually be known as the Great Mausoleum.

Despite the various challenges caused by the war, Wells continued to promote Forest Lawn in advertising. A half-page ad, featuring line drawings of the Little Church of the Flowers and the new mausoleum, was placed on the back cover of the Los Angeles County telephone directory published by the Southern California Telephone Company.

Church Dedication

With the dedication of the Little Church of the Flowers on May 12, 1918, Forest Lawn Memorial-Park reached another milestone. The event began with a male quartet, followed by an invocation by Reverend W. E. Edmonds and a solo by prima donna soprano Miss Helen Newcomb. The dedicatory address was delivered by J.

Figure 57. Little Church Dedication Announcement

Newspaper advertising invited the community to the dedication of the Little Church of the Flowers.

Forest Lawn Archives

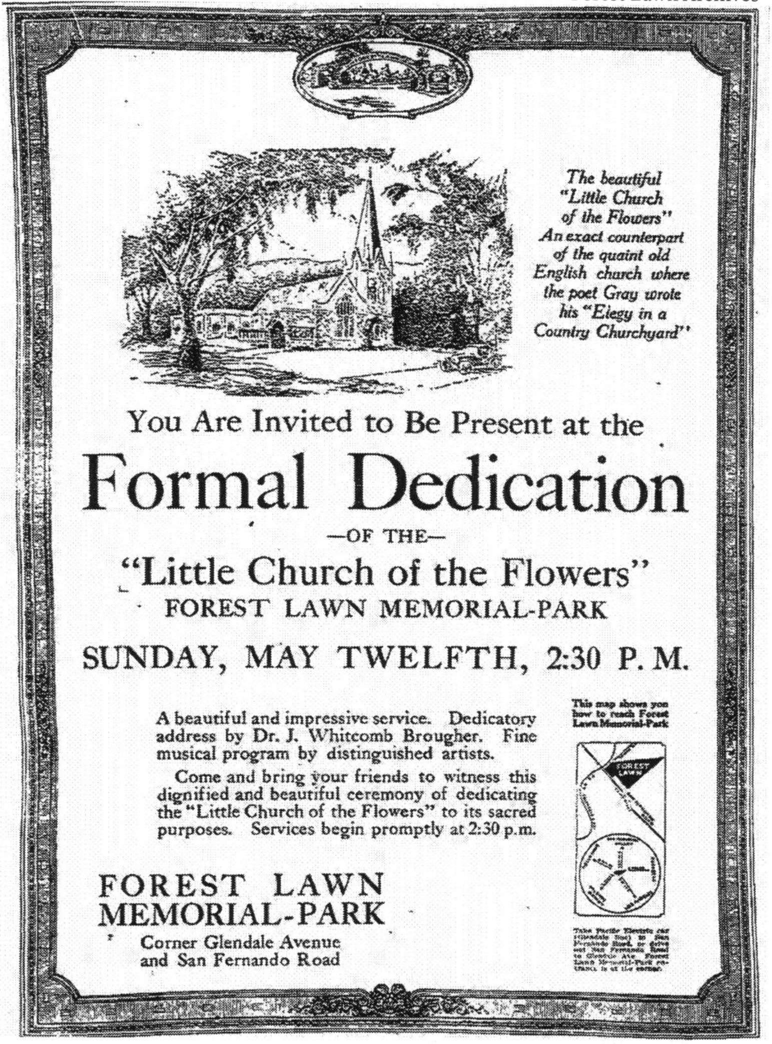
The beautiful "Little Church of the Flowers" An exact counterpart of the quaint old English church where the poet Gray wrote his "Elegy in a Country Churchyard"
You Are Invited to Be Present at the
Formal Dedication
—OF THE—
"Little Church of the Flowers"
FOREST LAWN MEMORIAL-PARK
SUNDAY, MAY TWELFTH, 2:30 P. M.
A beautiful and impressive service. Dedicatory address by Dr. J. Whitcomb Brougher. Fine musical program by distinguished artists.
Come and bring your friends to witness this dignified and beautiful ceremony of dedicating the "Little Church of the Flowers" to its sacred purposes. Services begin promptly at 2:30 p.m.
This map shows you how to reach Forest Lawn Memorial-Park
FOREST LAWN
FOREST LAWN MEMORIAL-PARK
Corner Glendale Avenue and San Fernando Road

Figure 58. Little Church Dedication Plaque Sketch

Tom Ross sketched the design of a dedication plaque for the Little Church of the Flowers.

Whitcomb Brougher. As part of the dedication ceremony, Hubert Eaton delivered an address titled "The Birth of a New Era," which included his vision for Forest Lawn as a new concept in cemeteries, a "Memorial–Park."[63]

The lead sentence in an article in the *Los Angeles Times* heralded the Little Church of the Flowers, which was "said to be the finest example of memorial church architecture in America." The article read like a press release and proclaimed that the church was "an exact counterpart of the old English church wherein the Poet [Thomas] Gray wrote his immortal 'Elegy in a Country Churchyard.'" The article went on to explain that a "magnificent pipe organ is soon to be installed in the church, and organ recitals will be given on Sunday afternoons by well-known artists." The final paragraph of the article—parroting some of Eaton's words—highlighted how Forest Lawn would be different.

Figure 59. Little Church Bronze Dedication Plaque

The dedication plaque as it was cast in bronze and placed in front of the church.

The general plan on which this organization is operating, marks a new era in mortuary affairs, the rules regulating and prohibiting the more grewsome [*sic*] symbols of death, resulting in a beauty spot of luxuriant foliage, green-sward, singing birds and thousands of flowers.[64]

Although Eaton did not mention the The Builder's Creed in his dedicatory speech, the concepts and many of the phrases he used demonstrate that he did have a consistent vision for Forest Lawn.[65] (See Appendix E, Little Church Dedication Speech.) His address included many phrases and sentiments similar to those in The Builder's Creed, such as the following:

- a hope of a greater life beyond
- no grewsome [*sic*] emblems and depressing ceremonies
- a park of endless vistas
- singing birds
- a moral uplift to our neighborhood, and personal pride to our community
- the place where the works of our great sculptors shall be gathered together
- protected by a gigantic perpetual care fund

Hubert Eaton was on his way to make Forest Lawn Memorial-Park something different from any other cemetery.

CHAPTER 17

Consolidation and New Roles

For Forest Lawn, the years 1917 and 1918 were pivotal in more than one way. Not only were new buildings being constructed, but organizational changes were being made behind the scenes. The relationships between TL&I, AS&F, and FLCA needed to be defined in new ways.

Consolidation into AS&F

When American Security & Fidelity was formed in November 1916, the plan was that its predecessor, American Securities, would be absorbed into it. This was accomplished by the end of 1916, when all outstanding American Securities shares had been exchanged for AS&F shares.[1]

TL&I also needed to be consolidated into AS&F. At a special meeting on January 17, 1917, TL&I stockholders unanimously passed a resolution to accept American Security & Fidelity's offer to purchase all assets and assume the liabilities of TL&I Co.[2] Another term of the consolidation was fulfilled on February 10, when TL&I executed a bill of sale conveying "all of its personal property and personal assets, rights, interests and demands" to American Security & Fidelity.[3]

Frank Hamilton and AS&F had previously agreed that Hamilton would exchange his stock holdings in TL&I and American Securities, as well as his contract with Eaton, for all the stock in the new AS&F. Accordingly, 100,000 shares of AS&F preferred stock and 150,000 shares of AS&F common stock were issued to Frank Hamilton to be put into trust. Those shares were then to be sold, with the proceeds going to AS&F as capital to fund its operations. In February, Hamilton assigned his rights to the shares held in trust at the Citizens Trust and Savings Bank to Hubert Eaton. This allowed Eaton to sell the shares to raise capital for AS&F without involving Hamilton. However, Hamilton retained his right to receive any shares that were not sold by January 2, 1919.[4]

American Security & Fidelity acknowledged TL&I's acceptance of the terms of the transaction with Frank Hamilton. It also verified that it was holding 24,785 shares of AS&F common stock, obtained from Hamilton, to be traded for the remaining shares of TL&I when those shares were tendered. Any shareholders who had not been able to sell their TL&I stock now had no option but to exchange their TL&I shares for AS&F stock.[5] TL&I stockholders who had not already exchanged their shares received a notice from George Pratt, secretary of AS&F, that AS&F shares were being held for them.

On March 1, George Pratt reported to FLCA that the transfer of assets and liabilities had been completed.[6] The next day, Tom and Pop Ross sent a letter to FLCA formally notifying them that AS&F had replaced TL&I.[7] Although the Tropico Land & Improvement Company and American Securities had not yet been dissolved, FLCA was now dealing only with American Security & Fidelity.

The ability to sell AS&F shares to raise capital for the planned Forest Lawn improvements was an essential part of the restructuring. In a letter to a prospective buyer of shares, Eaton explained that the strategy was to sell small amounts of stock throughout the community so that some of the "best and most influential citizens"

would have an interest in Forest Lawn. The plan was to sell only $100,000 of stock and to allocate half of that for Pasadena, to be sold in as small blocks as practical.[8] This was to provide geographical distribution of shareholders as well as to keep any individual from having a large block of stock. Eaton wanted to make sure that he would be able to maintain control.

However, in the end, the plan did not work out as Eaton had hoped. The AS&F stock did not sell as quickly as he would have liked. Any stock not sold by January 2, 1919, would become Hamilton's and not be available to raise funds for AS&F. One year before the deadline Eaton drafted a letter to Hamilton explaining the need for an extension: "We believe [that] an extension of this time will ultimately benefit your stock holdings to a greater degree than if you insist on the exact terms of your agreement."[9] Eaton sent the draft to William Hazlett, asking him to rewrite the letter with the goal of extending the original two-year period to ten years.

Eaton also asked Hazlett whether AS&F could use the stock held in trust as collateral for a loan, or whether Hamilton could write a letter negating the need for AS&F to issue him the required dividend on the preferred stock.[10] None of the preferred stock that had been placed in the trust had been sold, so technically it still belonged to Hamilton. Thus, Hamilton probably had the right to forego the preferred dividend, which would conserve cash for AS&F. Ultimately, no extension was needed.

Hazlett replied that he did not think it advisable for the stock to be used in a loan for the benefit of the company. As far as suspending the preferred stock dividend, Hazlett reminded Eaton that dividends could be paid only from net income. Because Hazlett believed AS&F had no net income, he believed the dividend issue was moot.[11]

The archives do not include a copy of a letter sent to Hamilton requesting the extension of time, nor of any agreement between Hamilton and AS&F. However, the files do show that by 1924, only 675 shares appeared in Hamilton's name. In that same year, records show 106,354 shares in Eaton's name.[12]

As far as the question of borrowing against shares held in trust, Frank Hamilton's shares in TL&I were used as collateral for a loan to AS&F from Citizens Trust & Savings Bank. The assets of TL&I had already been transferred to AS&F, so it was not surprising that the bank examiner questioned the shares being adequate collateral. AS&F shares were substituted for the TL&I stock as an interim measure. By February 1919, AS&F arranged for a $27,000 loan from Los Angles Trust and Savings Bank as well as a $10,000 from Ann Munger Eaton, Hubert Eaton's wife.[13] Ann Eaton's family owned a prominent plumbing business in Pasadena.

Dissolution Procedures

Although American Securities and TL&I had transferred all their assets and liabilities to AS&F, the corporations still existed and needed to be legally dissolved. Just days before the end of 1916, Eaton had asked Williamson, Burleigh & McLean—attorneys from Maine, where American Securities was incorporated—to tell him the "most economical and at same time legal way of putting American Securities Company out of existence."[14]

A few weeks later, Eaton wrote the Maine attorneys again, notifying them that all but one share of American Securities would be transferred to American Security & Fidelity. The single share of American Securities stock made it possible to take any actions that required shareholder approval. He asked the law firm to "kindly advise me if it is necessary for me to remain President of American Securities Company—that is, will it be feasible to leave K. L. Crowley, Secretary, as the only remaining officer. I am desirous of accepting the presidency of the American Security & Fidelity Co. as soon as you inform me that such acceptance would offer no embarrassment to the dissolution of American Securities Company."[15]

After being advised there was no law prohibiting him from simultaneously being president of American Securities and American Security & Fidelity, Eaton was given detailed instructions for a special meeting of the American Securities shareholders to authorize dissolution. By the end of March, the stockholders meeting had been held. The directors were told that in sixty days, the board of directors would be automatically disbanded by order of the court, effecting the final dissolution of the American Securities Company.[16] Eaton did not become president of AS&F until April 6, 1917.

Meanwhile, steps were taken to begin the dissolution of TL&I. At a special meeting of TL&I stockholders on January 17, 1917, a resolution describing the transaction was presented and passed with the unanimous vote of all shares represented. Barnett E. Marks, the Arizona attorney who handled TL&I's corporate legal affairs, acted as chairman of the meeting. He declared that "there was no further need of the Tropico Land & Improvement Company remaining a legal corporation after said transfers [as called out in the resolutions and agreement] have been completed." A resolution was then passed to allow the filing of papers for dissolution of TL&I with the authorities in the state of Arizona.[17] However, due to later developments, it would be quite some time before the dissolution became final.

Pratt's Plan for New Roles

In his March 1 letter to FLCA, George Pratt shared his ideas for how FLCA and AS&F could best work together. He began with an analysis of what had gone wrong in the past—why TL&I had never been able to realize enough accumulated profit to declare a dividend and Forest Lawn had not been self-supporting. He gave three reasons. First, TL&I was based in San Francisco, so Forest Lawn did not have the benefit of stockholders who were "prominent financially and socially in Los Angeles." Second, during Forest Lawn's first eleven years of operation, not enough money had been spent on improvements. Third, until the contract with American Securities, the cemetery had not had a system for selling except when deaths occurred. Pratt also correctly identified the problem with the previous corporate structure: too many organizations were claiming a portion of the sales dollars.[18]

Pratt then stated that American Security & Fidelity had decided "the proper method by which these various departments can be administered most economically and efficiently." With the consolidation, AS&F was now the land-owning company as well as the sales agent for the cemetery. Pratt proposed that the selling responsibility should be transferred to FLCA, making it the selling organization as well as the cemetery operator.[19]

AS&F had already turned over its "sale methods, prospect lists and follow up system" to FLCA. AS&F proposed to cancel all the selling rights that had been transferred from American Securities to AS&F in the merger with TL&I. FLCA would now manage the sales effort. Cancelling the sale contract and moving the sales effort to FLCA would simplify the structure of each sale. A plot sale would now involve only AS&F as the land company and FLCA as the cemetery operator and selling agent. A change to a two-way split would result in an immediate increase in FLCA's income from each sale.[20]

The plan contemplated that Eaton would be under contract to AS&F, at no cost to FLCA, with an obligation to give his full time and attention to Forest Lawn.

Borrowing from the Perpetual Care Fund

At the June 7, 1917, meeting of the FLCA trustees, following a general discussion of the progress of Forest Lawn, Eaton read a letter indicating that AS&F desired to borrow money from the perpetual care fund, with the loan to be secured by a mortgage on AS&F's real estate. Wells and other trustees had concerns about the amount of security FLCA would receive if it made the loan. Eaton wrote a lengthy letter to Wells, providing his analysis of the value of the land and urging cooperation.[21]

> [In] this new consolidation the future of Forest Lawn Cemetery depends upon the fact that the most economical and efficient methods be adopted; we must save a nickel wherever possible. . . . If you and your trustees can formulate [better methods] we

will be the first to say "Let's adopt them." A spirit of intense co-operation between [AS&F and FLCA] is absolutely necessary for the working out of the cemetery's future.[22]

Because the perpetual care fund loan would be secured by a mortgage, if AS&F defaulted, FLCA would receive title to the AS&F property by foreclosure. Eaton argued that if this happened, FLCA would own the property "at a price of at least one-tenth of its present value." Eaton maintained that there were two methods of determining the underlying value of the secured property: a "legal view" and a "practical business man's view." The "legal view" yielded a value of $8,375 per acre, and, according to Eaton, "there is no doubt but what this valuation would be sustained by any court of law."[23]

Eaton's second method of valuation was based on "the value that a practical business man would place on this land, who does not know the cemetery game and is therefore not so firmly impressed with the value of a particular cemetery site and the adequate supply of water needed."[24]

This second method of valuation resulted in a value of $4,750 per acre. Thus, Eaton maintained that loaning AS&F $2,000 per acre would only be "asking [the trustees] to act in a most conservative manner" under either method of valuation.[25]

Several days later, when the FLCA trustees reconvened, the discussion resumed regarding the possibility of loaning money from

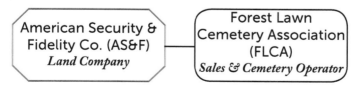

Figure 60. FLCA Takes Over Selling
Selling contract between AS&F and FLCA is cancelled. The contract with George Emery is assigned to FLCA, leaving FLCA responsible for all sales.

Figure 61. Eaton's "Legal View" of TI&I Valuation.

Valuation Factors	Value
Prevailing prices of land sales in the area, coupled with the large amount of frontage on Glendale Avenue: $1,500 per acre	$ 60,000
Incremental value because the land is a cemetery under the belief that it was difficult to get approval to use land for a cemetery.	25,000
Value of water rights: "at least 100 miner's inches of water," valued by Railway Commission at $1,500 per miner's inch (a unit for measuring water flow rate)	150,000
Value of improvements: FLCA had already spent nearly $300,000 on the cemetery, and "at least one-third must have gone into improvements"	100,000
Total	$335,000

Figure 62. Eaton's "Businessman's" Valuation

Valuation Factors	Value
Prevailing prices of land sales in the area, coupled with the large amount of frontage on Glendale Avenue: $1,500 per acre	$ 60,000
The value of this cemetery site over other possible cemetery sites	10,000
Value of water rights: If the cemetery did not have water rights, the water cost would be "at least" $200 per month or $2,400 per year. A yield of $2,400 a year at a 6 percent return would require a principal amount of $40,000.	40,000
Value of improvements: Estimated at $2,000 per acre for forty acres. "We believe this far too low but we wish to be conservative."	80,000
Total	$190,000

the perpetual care fund to AS&F. The trustees decided that after American Security & Fidelity paid off the existing $42,500 loan to TL&I, the perpetual care fund would loan $80,000 to AS&F. The terms were similar to previous loans to TL&I. The loan was to be secured by a mortgage on approximately forty acres of land owned by AS&F that were adjacent to, but not yet part of, the cemetery. However, the perpetual care fund did not have the full $80,000 on hand, so only $68,500 could be loaned initially, with the balance to be "advanced monthly as it accrues, until the full amount" was loaned.

The trustees also decided they needed additional security. They asked AS&F to indemnify FLCA from any liens that resulted from construction of the Little Church of the Flowers and crematory. Furthermore, at least $25,000 of the amount loaned would have to be spent on improvements to the cemetery.[26]

As requested, AS&F provided a guarantee against liens. Hubert Eaton, Carroll Gates, and William Hollingsworth also provided personal guarantees.[27]

This circular arrangement of FLCA loaning perpetual care funds to AS&F was a continuation of the practice followed in the TL&I–FLCA relationship. The perpetual care fund was supervised by the trustees of FLCA, but not owned by them, since it was a trust fund. One of the few legal investment options for the perpetual care fund was mortgages. That meant FLCA could loan money from the perpetual care fund to AS&F in the form of a mortgage. AS&F could then loan the funds to FLCA itself, as distinct from the perpetual care fund, so that FLCA could make improvements to the cemetery. Thus it is not clear which organization was really the "banker"—the source of loan funds. Though apparently legal at the time, this practice stopped in the 1940s and is currently prohibited in California.[28]

Where's the Auto?

Also at the June meeting of FLCA trustees, during a discussion following a trustees' inspection tour of the cemetery, Wells was asked what had become of the Hudson automobile that TL&I had owned.

He answered that TL&I had loaned it to the cemetery association. Upon AS&F's acquisition of TL&I, the car had been exchanged for an auto now used by one of the sales managers, and Wells was temporarily using a Ford. Apparently a Ford was not a fitting image for Wells, since the minutes recorded that "it was the sense of the meeting that the President of Forest Lawn Cemetery Association be supplied with a machine in keeping with his position as such, for the reason the Trustees had heard uncomplimentary comments made about the President riding in a Ford."[29] It must have been easier to make a decision about a car than to work on defining the best structure for the new relationship with AS&F.

Purchase of Bedford Property

Since early 1917, negotiations had been quietly proceeding with Los Angeles Trust & Savings Bank, which was still the guardian for the property interests of Lucile Bedford, who had won the division of the cemetery land in 1912. Eaton was relieved to see a notice in the *California Independent* newspaper that the Los Angeles County Superior Court would hold a hearing to allow the sale of the real estate and that bids were now being accepted. Eaton promptly sent the clipping to attorney Max Loewenthal and asked whether he needed to be present at the hearing. Loewenthal explained that the hearing was only an "application for leave to sell," meaning that the bank "must show to the court by proper evidence that the best interests of the estate require that the property should be sold."[30]

American Security & Fidelity submitted the only bid on the property. The bank dutifully returned to court and received permission to accept the bid and sell the sixty-five acres to AS&F for $31,500, a slight increase from AS&F's $31,150 bid.[31]

New Agreements

Despite everything that was going on, the trustees of FLCA waited until October 1, 1917, to meet again. The meeting was called to consider a proposed new contract with American Security & Fidelity.

When TL&I was absorbed into the new AS&F, the parties had continued to operate under the terms of the TL&I–American Securities agreement. That contract had not contemplated the sale of crypts or niches. An agreement outside of the contract had been reached for fixed amounts to be paid to AS&F for these sales, rather than the percentage arrangement called for in the original TL&I–American Securities contract. During review of a new contract with AS&F, the trustees became concerned with the legality of paying the fixed amounts. The meeting adjourned without a new contract, and trustee Glenn Ely was charged with investigating the law governing the power of trustees and reporting back at the next meeting.[32] However, when the trustees next met in January 1918, Glenn Ely did not make a report on the legal question.

That was not the only issue regarding how to best structure the new relationship between AS&F and FLCA. Prior to the formation of AS&F, FLCA was responsible for all cemetery development, American Securities had been the principal selling agent, and TL&I had just provided raw land. However, the sales management had now moved to FLCA. If AS&F built the crematory and mausoleum on land that AS&F was under contract to sell to FLCA, the responsibility for development would not be clear.

In February 1918, Eaton wrote Wells that the new plans for Forest Lawn raised many legal questions, and that he had asked Max Loewenthal to consider them from a "practical and legal" standpoint.[33] Although Eaton positioned the current structure as being inadequate for "modern and up-to-date methods," his real concern was with FLCA's inability to pay what was due to AS&F. FLCA's only sources of income were the sale of cemetery lots, monuments, boxes, and flowers; charges for opening graves, cremations, and incidentals; and income from the perpetual care trust fund. Eaton was concerned that this revenue would not be enough to pay off indebtedness to AS&F, maintain the cemetery, and fund needed improvements. To cover the negative cash flow, FLCA had continued to borrow from AS&F as it had from TL&I.

When Loewenthal had studied the matter and was ready to report his findings, Eaton invited Wells to be present at a luncheon at the Jonathan Club to discuss the matter with the trustees of FLCA and the directors of AS&F. Eaton cited it as "by far the most important meeting that has been held for some time by Forest Lawn."[34]

That meeting did not produce an agreement between AS&F and FLCA—it only led to months of continued negotiations about how the relationship should be structured.

At last, when the trustees met again in October 1918, they approved new agreements with AS&F.[35]

The first agreement allowed FLCA to borrow up to $250,000 from AS&F to improve and embellish the cemetery. The trustees required that the notes arising from that loan could be repaid only from sales and not from perpetual care fund income. As security for the loans, AS&F received an assignment of all contracts of sale and related receivables, with any money collected thereon to apply to FLCA's indebtedness to AS&F.[36] This last point left little room for FLCA to pay ongoing operating expenses.

A second agreement addressed the issue of sales of interment property in the new mausoleum. It gave FLCA a commission of 25 percent of the selling price of niches, crypts, and vaults.[37]

AS&F's borrowing from Forest Lawn's perpetual care fund was addressed in the third agreement. Just months earlier, in June, FLCA had agreed to loan AS&F $80,000 from the perpetual care fund. This new agreement raised the amount of potential borrowing to $130,000, to be secured, like the existing loans, with a first mortgage on AS&F's land holdings.[38]

The fourth agreement stated that American Security & Fidelity owned the "Selling System" and had originated many of the improvements made over time. The system was defined to include lists of prospective purchasers, booklets, pictures, paintings, photographs, and all other literature that might be used as "Salesmen's Aids."

Although FLCA was given the right to use the system, any additions to the system became the property of AS&F. Either party could end the use of the system by giving written notice to the other.[39]

In a fifth agreement, American Security & Fidelity agreed to turn over the operation of the crematory to FLCA in return for 50 percent of the gross proceeds. Additionally, FLCA received the use of the Little Church of the Flowers and adjoining receiving vaults in exchange for being responsible for the maintenance of the facilities.[40]

The sixth agreement recognized that the crematory, Little Church of the Flowers, receiving vault, and mausoleum were built on land that FLCA was under contract to buy from American Security & Fidelity as successor to TL&I. To clear this up, FLCA agreed to quitclaim the land under these facilities to AS&F because the cemetery association benefited from the construction of these buildings.[41] The quitclaim deed transferred any interest FLCA might have in the property. FLCA was not giving up much—it was only giving up its right to purchase land. Although there was now one less company involved, the structure was even more complicated than before. The right business model had not yet been discovered.

Figure 63. New Revenue Split

Changing from a three-way split to a two-way split would provide an immediate benefit to FLCA.

	Previous three-way arrangement	Proposed new arrangement	
		Ground burial	Mausoleum
Gross sale amount	$100.00	$100.00	$100.00
Perpetual care fund	25.00	25.00	5.00
To FLCA	18.75	37.50	25.00
To American Securities	37.50	N/A	N/A
To TL&I	18.75	N/A	N/A
To AS&F	N/A	37.50	70.00

TL&I Dissolution

Meanwhile, during the months when the agreements between AS&F and FLCA were being negotiated, the matter of dissolving TL&I also had to be dealt with. By May 1917, all TL&I assets had been moved to American Security & Fidelity, so a special meeting of TL&I directors was called to authorize proceeding with the "necessary legal steps to dissolve and disincorporate." Following passage of a resolution to that effect, all shareholders received a notice that a special meeting of shareholders would be held to enable final closure of the corporation.[42]

One of the shareholders who received that notice was J. B. Treadwell, one of the founders of TL&I and first president of FLCA. Not willing to go away quietly, Treadwell wrote Pop Ross that he did not understand why the corporation was to be dissolved. Furthermore, Treadwell believed that disincorporation should not be possible without approval from every single stockholder. He asked what would become of the corporation's property after dissolution—ignoring the fact that there would be no property left, since all was to be transferred to AS&F. He closed his letter with a protest of the action and asked that his protest be filed with the company and stockholders.[43]

Pop Ross replied to Treadwell that all TL&I shareholders had received the notice of the January 17 special meeting, which stated there would be a request to authorize the sales and transfer of all assets of the company to American Security & Fidelity.[44]

Although Treadwell had not attended the special meeting, he tried to block the required exchange of TL&I stock for AS&F stock by filing suit in Arizona opposing TL&I's voluntary dissolution. His petition argued that adequate notice had not been given. Furthermore, AS&F's incorporation documents allowed more common shares than did TL&I's, so the one-for-one share exchange could damage shareholders by diluting each share's ownership percentage. He argued, "If such proceeding can be carried out in this manner, where does the minority stockholder 'get off.' This is surely 'high financeering.'"[45]

Phoenix attorney Barnett Marks wired Eaton that Treadwell's protest had been filed but that he knew nothing more about the matter than what was in the protest. Although a hearing had been set for the coming Monday, that was now to be postponed to an unspecified future date.[46]

Two days later, Marks telegraphed that the hearing was now set for Friday, June 15, at 1:00 p.m. He closed the message by asking plaintively, "Can't you buy Treadwell's Stock?"

Eaton was in Chicago when he received word from Wells of Treadwell's action. He wired instructions to Wells to consult with Hazlett about when would be the best time to interview Treadwell.[47]

As directed, Wells consulted William Hazlett. The attorney replied that although he was in a "quandary" regarding interviewing Treadwell, he was inclined to do so sooner rather than later unless Eaton wired him promptly with reasons not to proceed. There was no quick resolution of this. Eaton commented to Wells in early July, "As regards the Treadwell matter, I confess I am at a loss whether to do it now or later. It is my general principle to let a sleeping dog lie. If that trial does not come up until September why not tell Hazlett let the Treadwell matter wait until I return."[48]

AS&F responded to Treadwell's petition by stating that AS&F and TL&I had offered every shareholder the same deal, so it should not "be possible that a single shareholder in a corporation . . . prevent the sale of all its assets when necessary." The response acknowledged that the majority of shareholders had an obligation to act in good faith, but that Treadwell had not alleged any breach of that duty or alleged any sort of fraud. Additionally, AS&F had added thousands of dollars of improvements since the transfer was consummated in January, making the transaction difficult, if not impossible, to unwind. Finally, the TL&I response concluded that Treadwell's "purpose is evidently to hold up the new company and force them to buy his stock at his figure and the Court should not aid him in this."[49]

Barnett Marks, TL&I's Phoenix attorney, had filed briefs on the matter in June but reported that the judge, having gone on vacation, had not looked at the briefs yet. Marks told Eaton, "I dare say he will take it up immediately upon the resuming of court work early in September." Marks also suggested that if TL&I should lose the court battle, the company could either file an appeal to the Arizona Supreme Court or just let matters sit until Treadwell took "some aggressive steps looking towards setting aside what had been done." So Eaton waited.[50]

By the end of October 1917, no resolution had been reached in the dissolution of TL&I. Although Pop Ross had always been meticulous in scheduling and holding annual meetings of stockholders, doing so for TL&I was not on Eaton's mind, even though TL&I had not yet been dissolved. When Eaton realized on October 31 that the TL&I bylaws called for the annual meeting to take place November 1, he hastily sent a telegram to Barnett Marks asking for guidance on what to do. Marks replied that since all assets of TL&I had now been turned over to AS&F, and Treadwell was the only stockholder to protest the dissolution, no meeting was needed. The attorney added that he had spoken to the judge hearing the dissolution matter, who had made the frustrating suggestion that the matter "be re-argued so as to refresh his mind as to our several contentions."[51]

Several days later, Eaton wrote Marks and, without explanation, told him he wanted to defer the dissolution of TL&I by delaying the arguments before the judge by two or three weeks. Marks replied that would be easy to do, since Judge Lyman had ruled against the demurrer filed by Marks. With the demurrer unsuccessful, the lawsuit would proceed.[52] No doubt Eaton hoped that he could persuade Treadwell to drop his suit.

The legal wrangling over the dissolution carried on for years. Finally, on March 25, 1921, the Arizona Superior Court ended the dispute by issuing a final decree of dissolution to Tropico Land & Improvement Company.[53]

A Boom in Burials

According to a Forest Lawn Salesman's Kit circa 1928, in 1918 a milestone of activity was reached: for the first time, more than one thousand burials were made in one year.*

With so many burials, and with the war effort disrupting the labor market, Eaton wondered whether a machine for digging graves existed. O. H. Sample, editor of Park and Cemetery and Landscape Gardening magazine, responded to Eaton's query that he did not know of such a machine, but "that something like this would be a great invention." It is noteworthy that it was Eaton—not FLCA president Norton Wells, who was responsible for cemetery operations—who was concerned with being able to make burials efficiently. It would not be until 1928 that Forest Lawn tried a "mechanical grave digging machine."[54]

Good news came on another front in November. Like all California cemeteries, Forest Lawn was exempt from property taxes. In order to ensure that this would not change, an amendment to the California constitution was proposed to exempt cemeteries from taxation. Charles Dingley, secretary of Mountain View Cemetery Association in Oakland, wrote Wells stating that he was placing a "Vote Yes" ad in the *San Francisco Examiner*, the *Chronicle*, and the *Oakland Tribune*. He asked Wells to do likewise in Southern California. The amendment passed.[55]

---

* A current review of interment data shows that only 800 interments were made in 1918. The 1,000 interment level was not reached until 1920.

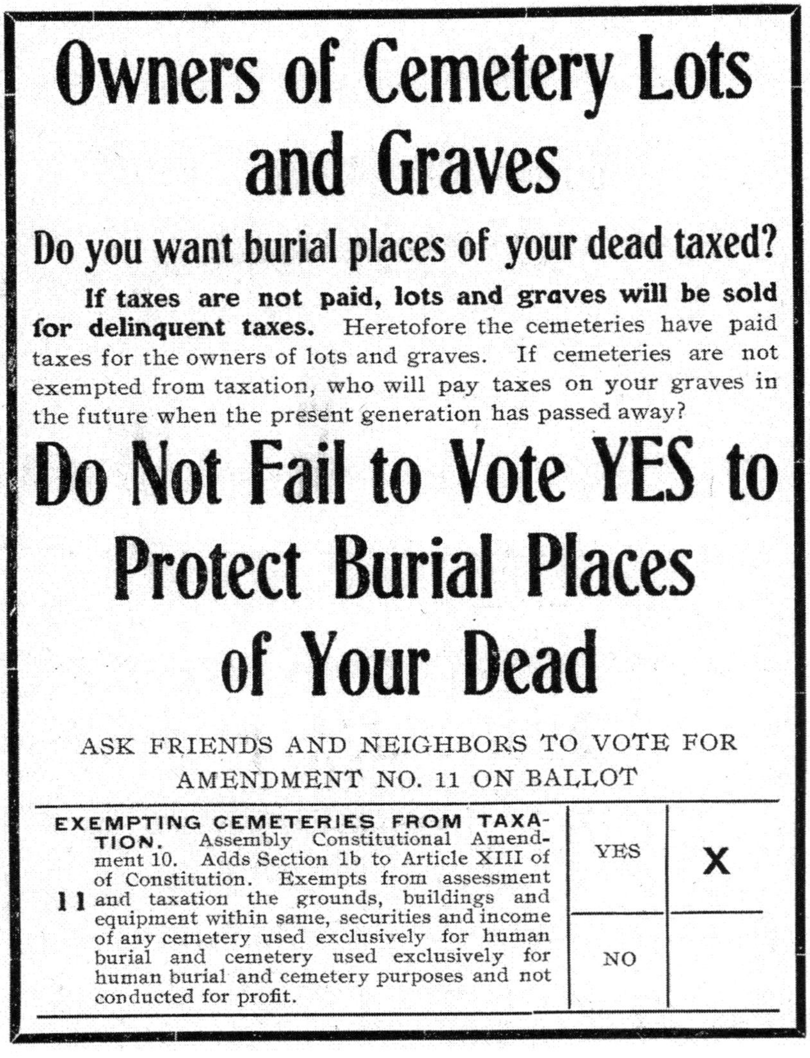

Owners of Cemetery Lots and Graves

Do you want burial places of your dead taxed?

If taxes are not paid, lots and graves will be sold for delinquent taxes. Heretofore the cemeteries have paid taxes for the owners of lots and graves. If cemeteries are not exempted from taxation, who will pay taxes on your graves in the future when the present generation has passed away?

Do Not Fail to Vote YES to Protect Burial Places of Your Dead

ASK FRIENDS AND NEIGHBORS TO VOTE FOR
AMENDMENT NO. 11 ON BALLOT

	YES	X
EXEMPTING CEMETERIES FROM TAXATION. Assembly Constitutional Amendment 10. Adds Section 1b to Article XIII of Constitution. Exempts from assessment and taxation the grounds, buildings and equipment within same, securities and income of any cemetery used exclusively for human burial and cemetery used exclusively for human burial and cemetery purposes and not conducted for profit.		
11	NO	

Figure 64. "Vote Yes" for Cemetery Exemption

Mountain View Cemetery Association in Oakland placed this ad to encourage voters to approve the amendment exempting cemeteries from property taxes.

CHAPTER 18

Eaton Versus Wells

As 1918 drew to a close, those involved with managing Forest Lawn had many accomplishments to be proud of. The cemetery had become a "memorial-park" with a new church, receiving vaults, and crematory. The mausoleum was under construction. New agreements had been reached between the Forest Lawn Cemetery Association and American Security & Fidelity. But in spite of all the progress, it would soon be apparent that Forest Lawn's financial and organizational problems were not over. A storm was brewing on the horizon.

Illusion and Reality

Although things seemed to be going well, some of that impression was illusory regarding FLCA. Almost no payments were made in 1917 from FLCA to AS&F for property purchases. Monthly "settlements" were effected by producing monthly statements of the amount due from FLCA to American Security & Fidelity. When AS&F received a check for the correct amount, FLCA would immediately borrow from AS&F the same amount in a round number. FLCA needed to borrow from AS&F because it still had the responsibility of developing ground interment property as well as paying ongoing operating expenses. Its share of sales revenue was not enough to cover these expenses. During 1917, FLCA issued checks to AS&F totaling $29,414 but borrowed $29,167 from AS&F—resulting in only $247 actually being paid toward what AS&F was owed.

The financial model was still not working.[1]

The new agreements between FLCA and American Security & Fidelity did not solve the basic structural problems with Forest Lawn. In 1918 FLCA paid AS&F the full amount due—$33,037—and did not borrow any further amounts. By paying the full amount, FLCA depleted its cash. The FLCA secretary noted that "many bills, which had accumulated, were left to be paid in 1919, including some money which had been collected which was not [FLCA's] to retain."[2]

At the end of 1918, Norton Wells was concerned with the financial situation. He was also suspicious of Eaton, because he thought FLCA was ceding too much control to AS&F. The storm clouds were gathering.

In 1918, as Eaton told his biographer, Adela Rogers St. Johns, Eaton fell in love at first sight of divorcee Ann Munger Henderson. A graduate of Mills College, and from a "prominent" Pasadena family, she had a child, Roy, from her prior marriage. Not many hours after meeting her, Eaton told Henderson that, "as soon as she would permit him, he wanted to ask her to marry him." They were married on December 10, 1918. Ann would be important financially as well as being a supportive spouse.[3] Eight years after the marriage, Hubert Eaton formally adopted Roy.[4]

Eaton's Proxy Votes

Hubert Eaton was making progress at Forest Lawn, but he continued to have conflicts with Norton Wells. The solution for Eaton was to elect a board of trustees of FLCA more sympathetic to his views than those of Wells.

Forest Lawn Archives

Figure 65. Forest Lawn Phone Book Ad, 1918

In addition to newspaper advertising, many other media were tried.

Prior to their annual meeting, Eaton wrote Forest Lawn lot owners to explain the role and importance of American Security & Fidelity. As a mutual organization of lot owners, FLCA had no way of raising money. Thus a company like AS&F was needed to provide the necessary capital to purchase land and develop the cemetery. When Eaton had negotiated the AS&F acquisition of TL&I, he knew that Forest Lawn had not made needed improvements due to lack of funds. To put Forest Lawn Cemetery ahead of other cemeteries, Eaton told the lot owners he had decided to create a "memorial-park"—creating a specific definition of a term as a different kind of cemetery. He explained that the construction of a church, crematory, mausoleum, columbarium, and enlargement of cemetery land was essential to accomplish this. AS&F was making those improvements, he wrote, but relied on the cooperation of FLCA to have "Forest Lawn Memorial–Park . . . stand without an equal, unique and splendid." Eaton's letter did not ask the lot owners to sign a proxy.[5]

After the letter from AS&F, lot owners received a second letter. This one was from five lot owners—Motley Flint, George Walker, E. U. Emery, Thomas Ogg, and M. M. Kauffman—saying they had investigated the information in the AS&F letter and had found everything to be true. The letter contained a proxy form to be signed and returned. Signing and returning the proxy would allow M. M. Kauffman to vote on a lot owner's behalf.[6]

Prior to the annual FLCA lot owners meeting, Norton Wells learned of the letters to lot owners and discovered that Eaton had instructed the salesmen to secure proxies from lot owners for the benefit of AS&F. This convinced Wells that Eaton was gathering votes through proxies because he planned to have people sympathetic to him elected as trustees of FLCA. Attempting to counteract this plan, Wells addressed a letter to the "Salesmen of Forest Lawn Cemetery Ass'n," directing them to discontinue any further solicitation of proxies.[7]

Wells shared his concern about Eaton's intentions with the other FLCA trustees. The result was that trustees then sent their own letter to lot owners urging them to attend the annual meeting—even if they had given a proxy allowing someone else to vote for them. If they appeared in person, the letter told them, any proxy they had given would be invalid. Although the letter acknowledged the efforts of American Security & Fidelity, identified as the "landholding and profit making company," were appreciated for making costly improvements to the cemetery, the FLCA proxy solicitation was a struggle for control. According to the FLCA trustees, the only question now for the lot owners was whether AS&F should have some representation on the board of trustees—a position the trustees opposed. The FLCA trustees told lot owners that it would be improper for anyone with a financial interest in AS&F to be on the FLCA board.[8]

Lot Owners Meeting

On January 20, 1919, Norton Wells opened the lot owners annual meeting as he had in prior years. This time, however, the minutes show that there was an objection to him acting as chair of the meeting, "and the meeting proceeded to organize from among its members." J. W. Kemp, an Eaton ally, nominated George H. Storer to chair the meeting. The motion passed unanimously. Storer appointed a committee of P. B. Chase, W. A. McIntosh, J. H. Geiger, C. T. Larabee, and George W. Walker to "examine the proxies and to determine also the question of what constitutes membership and voting right." Since the turnout for the meeting was greater than expected, the meeting had to be adjourned to a large auditorium in Berean Hall.[9]

When the annual meeting reconvened at 2:00 p.m., the committee on credentials was not ready to report its findings, so Storer called on Norton Wells to give the president's report. According to the minutes, Wells explained that "a complete [financial] report could not be made, partly because the Auditor's annual report had not been received until the day before the meeting. Conditions precluded an analysis of that report or any satisfactory understanding of the condition of the business."[10]

Once the committee on credentials completed its work, the following were nominated to serve as trustees: P. B. Chase, Glenn M. Ely, John Llewellyn, Wilbur J. Filley, Motley H. Flint, M. M. Kauffman, F. V. Owen, L. H. Peters, Howard L. Rivers, William Watson, and Norton C. Wells. Kauffman was an obvious Eaton supporter. He had been a director of AS&F until the previous week and had resigned from the AS&F board so he could serve as an FLCA trustee without a conflict of interest. Flint was also an Eaton supporter.

After the names of the nominees were written on a blackboard, someone raised the issue of whether three directors would be elected for three-year terms, or the entire board should stand for election each year. So the meeting was adjourned to the following day to seek legal advice.[11]

When the meeting reconvened on the following day, the opinion of the attorneys was reported: "The law contemplated that an entirely new board of seven trustees should be elected at each annual meeting." FLCA had cumulative voting, so because there were seven positions to fill, each lot owner could cast seven votes—all for a single candidate or spread out among multiple candidates. According to a roll call of those present and a report of the proxy committee, twenty-nine lot owners were present in person and another 350 were represented by proxy. Out of the 379 lot owners represented, Norton Wells held 350 proxies, plus a single vote for the property he owned. Eaton held one proxy and one vote for property he owned. Eaton supporter M. M. Kauffman had ninety-five votes in person or by proxy.[12]

Before the vote was called, Chase asked that his name be removed; William Hollingsworth requested the withdrawal of Rivers's name, though he had nominated him. Ballots were cast and tabulated. The top seven vote getters—Flint, Kauffman, Wells, Watson, Llewellyn, Owen, and Ely—were declared elected to serve as trustees for the ensuing year, and the meeting was adjourned.[13]

Wells had far more proxies, and thus more votes, than Kauffman, but spread his votes out over his preferred slate of seven trustees. So when Kauffman split his seven votes per proxy between only two candidates—himself and Flint—both were elected. Wells's concern about Eaton gathering proxies was correct, but he did not foresee the effect of using cumulative voting.[14]

The organizational meeting of the trustees was held immediately after the meeting of lot owners. Wells was again elected as president and manager, Owen as secretary, and John Llewellyn as vice president.[15]

Special Meeting

Less than a month after the FLCA annual meeting, on February 15, 1919, a special meeting of the trustees convened. After the minutes of the prior meeting were approved, trustee John Llewellyn's letter of resignation was submitted and accepted. John N. Smalley was elected to fill the vacancy.

The principal business for the meeting was to receive a more complete explanation of the causes for the president's report being late. Wells explained that the volume of work and the office manager's illness had put the staff behind.

He went on to say that he still did not have as much detail as he would like, but it was clear that the financial structure of the two corporations was not working.

Wells reminded the trustees that FLCA had lost over $15,000 the prior year. He said he believed it was incorrect accounting to treat the loss as an increase in the value of cemetery improvements—it was an operating loss, not an increase in value. This method of accounting for losses was not new; FLCA had used it since its inception and during Wells's entire tenure as president. Wells believed the 1917 consolidation of the FLCA and American Security & Fidelity accounting departments had resulted in a direct loss to FLCA and that the transactions between the two had become so intermingled that he questioned the accuracy of the financial records. He told the trustees that an "exhaustive study and investigation of details is necessary to arrive at any satisfactory and comprehensive audit of the Cemetery business."[16]

Although he had not had enough time to consider everything he wanted to, Wells told the trustees he had taken up an investigation of some departments to determine what bearing they might have on the organization as a whole.[17]

Wells first reported on the selling office. Although two years had passed since the consolidation of American Securities and TL&I into AS&F, his analysis included only the results for 1918. He reported that sales, net of perpetual care receipts, were just over $26,000. After the equal split with AS&F and inclusion of other sales, FLCA had a little better than $17,000 in revenue. The problem, though, was the sales room cost—over $23,000. This meant that the selling operation lost $6,100 without including any proportionate amount of other overhead or depreciation. The result of moving the selling operation to FLCA had hindered rather than helped FLCA's financial position.

The second part of Wells's analysis related to costs of the city office, which FLCA and AS&F shared. Wells believed American Security & Fidelity should be shouldering more of the expense of the space. The total amount he thought would be fair was $1,900—a portion of staff salaries and one quarter of the rent for the entrance room and telephone bill.[18]

Wells also estimated he had spent nearly one quarter of his time acting as superintendent of construction on the crematory and Little Church of the Flowers, both of which were owned by American Security & Fidelity, although used by FLCA.[19]

It was clear to Wells that something had to change, since the current organizational structure was not working. After presenting his analysis of the situation, Wells recommended terminating the sales campaign and firing the sales force that FLCA had taken on in 1917. This proposal would cut the costs of the sales operation, but likely would mean no revenue either. He also wanted to move FLCA's general office and accounting departments to the cemetery, where a "proper" accounting system would be implemented, including a complete audit as of March 1, 1919. Additionally, Wells wanted to cancel the mausoleum-columbarium contract and the 1918 agreement that FLCA operate the crematory and Little Church of the Flowers. By these actions, Wells wanted to force AS&F to negotiate a new contract with FLCA that would be "fair and equitable."[20] His proposal was something like I'll-take-my-ball-and-go-home, only in this case the ball (unsold cemetery property) belonged to AS&F.

The only recommendation adopted by the trustees was to end the sales campaign, which meant termination of the sales force that had been organized under the Eaton–Sims contract.[21] This returned the selling operation for ground interment property to what it had been prior to the arrival of Sims and Eaton.

Trustee Motley Flint, a newcomer to the board, moved that a committee of three trustees be appointed to consider Wells's report and to consult with officers of American Security & Fidelity and FLCA concerning the situation. When the motion passed, Wells appointed trustees Ely, Kauffman, and Smalley to the special committee.[22]

The trustees reconvened twelve days later, on February 27. John Smalley, chairman of the special committee, reported that the committee had been unable to agree on recommendations and wished to be "discharged from further activities." That left the remaining recommendations from Wells's president's report up for consideration by the trustees. Each was considered in turn, and all were approved.[23]

Salvos and Volleys

On the following day, Fred Owen, FLCA secretary, duly notified Eaton of the cancellation of the various agreements and other actions. Eaton responded that since the sales force had been terminated, the prior year's agreement regarding FLCA's use of Eaton's selling system was "discontinued." He reminded Owen that the selling system, including prospect lists, booklets, and other literature, was the property of American Security & Fidelity and requested immediate return of the material.[24]

Although the trustees had adopted his recommendations, Wells decided to document the many issues he had with Eaton. He drafted a "survey of the reasons conveyed individually from time to time by certain members of the Board of Trustees of the [FLCA], for their apparent indifference, refusal and unwillingness" to find a mutual basis for easing the strained relations between FLCA and AS&F. The "certain members" comment was aimed at Flint and Kauffman.

Wells began the document by declaring that Eaton had never been of any benefit to FLCA and questioning his qualifications as a "cemetery man." FLCA, he said, was pushed into taking the salesmen of American Securities, who were incompetent and "in a degree antagonistic towards" Wells. Furthermore, Eaton had allowed salaried employees to be paid commissions without telling Wells, and American Security & Fidelity had loaded FLCA with expenses, resulting in deficits. Wells thought every act of Eaton's should be investigated because it might embarrass FLCA. Eaton treated the new trustees, Motley Flint and M. M. Kauffman, so well that Wells questioned whether they could legally serve as trustees. The concerns had intensified to the point that Flint was asked to resign during a trustees meeting but did not do so. Wells summarized the atmosphere: "That the (pithy) personalities and the graver acts, caused Mr. Wells to gradually develop a feeling, mind and spirit that prevents him from dealing in a manner necessary for the promotion of harmony."[25]

AS&F was not in a conciliatory mood either. Upset with FLCA's cancellation letter, AS&F's secretary replied that FLCA had failed to "immediately pay to [AS&F] all sums received in the perpetual care fund." Previous agreements allowed AS&F to borrow from perpetual care funds to AS&F, up to a maximum amount. However, by not turning over perpetual care funds to FLCA as money was collected, the perpetual care fund did not have as much money to

Figure 66. FLCA Notice About Hubert Eaton

Trying to rein in Eaton, FLCA printed a card to hand out to the public pronouncing that Eaton was not an officer of FLCA.

Forest Lawn Archives

FOREST LAWN CEMETERY ASSOCIATION
1800 S. GLENDALE AVE.

Los Angeles. Cal., March 13, 1919.

Notice is hereby given that Hubert L. Eaton, President American Security and Fidelity Company, is not an officer of the Forest Lawn Cemetery Association, and has no authority to sign contracts for or on its behalf, nor to transact any business in its interest. This notice becomes necessary by reason of the fact that said Eaton has assumed authority to act on behalf of this Association without its knowledge or consent.

FOREST LAWN CEMETERY ASSOCIATION
NORTON C. WELLS, President.

loan AS&F. AS&F also complained that FLCA had not forwarded AS&F's share of sales proceeds for January and February, and thus AS&F would not issue deeds to buyers as requested by FLCA.[26] Deeds to cemetery property required signatures from both FLCA and AS&F, as successor to TL&I, to convey burial rights to purchasers.

On March 13, letters started to fly back and forth between American Security & Fidelity and FLCA.

Wells fired off the first letter, telling Eaton that he had improperly "assumed authority to act on behalf of [FLCA]. . . . This is to notify you that you are not an officer of [FLCA], and that you have no authority to sign contracts for or on its behalf, nor to transact any business in its interest." Wells went so far as to print and distribute a notice to that effect.[27] While it is clear that Wells was upset, it is not clear about Eaton's actual transgression.

Fred V. Owen, acting as FLCA secretary, then wrote second and third letters declaring that FLCA's plans did not call for an outside sales force, so FLCA would not pay commissions to anyone other than its own employees.[28]

Eaton fired off a response to the salvo, announcing that American Security & Fidelity had sent a notice to all purchasers to make payments to AS&F rather than to FLCA. His justification of this was FLCA's assignment of all its contracts to AS&F as security for FLCA debts to AS&F.[29]

Somewhat like a ping pong volley, Wells and Owen, in the fifth and last letter of the day, responded that AS&F's notice to purchasers was a violation of the contract; the assignment of contracts was for security only, and this was "an arbitrary and unwarranted action."[30]

The following day, March 14, Eaton addressed the question of AS&F's refusal to sign deeds by reiterating that the deeds for burial rights were prepared and signed, but he would not release them without payment of what was due AS&F. He also requested a meeting between FLCA trustees and AS&F directors to "map out a plan" that would "be satisfactory and to the best interest of all concerned."[31]

Owen replied that Forest Lawn had not made the payment because "of the failure and neglect of Mrs. K. L. Crowley," the bookkeeper, "to complete the statement . . . for the month of January." However, he now had a figure and was sending American Security & Fidelity not a check, but a note for $3,869 payable in one year.[32]

Eaton sent the note back, refusing to accept it as payment. He said that short-term credit might be accepted, but until an agreement was worked out, American Security & Fidelity "must insist upon the cash." He suggested the parties meet and arrive at an agreement.

Later that day, he sent another letter challenging assertions made by FLCA secretary Fred Owen. Eaton outlined AS&F's position that the FLCA accounts receivable were held as security for the $140,464 owed AS&F. He closed the letter saying that he found Owen's attitude surprising, and once again he expressed a desire to have the parties meet to reach a new agreement.[33]

Perturbed by the ongoing conflict, Owen shot still another letter back to Eaton that day. In it, he said he had believed that during a lunch organized by William Hollingsworth, a gentlemen's agreement had been reached with Eaton had been reached with Eaton that no changes should be made by AS&F or FLCA without notice to the other. The purpose of that understanding was to facilitate reaching an agreement relative to the mausoleum and Little Church of the Flowers. Owen reiterated his criticism of Eaton acting as an officer of FLCA, "usurping the office of the President or Secretary." Owen believed Eaton's actions were intended to force FLCA to act quickly, perhaps to its detriment. He countered that existing contracts were a plan and working arrangement.[34]

> Let me say to you that the way for the Company and the Association to progress peacefully together and with satisfaction and profit to all concerned is to obey the law, live up to our agreements, and let the Association proceed with its work without interference, unwarranted action and illegal methods. . . .

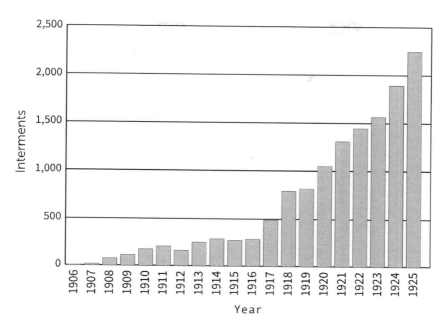

Figure 67. Annual Interments 1906–1926

The writer cannot speak for any other trustee or officer, but for himself says that at the present time, and in the light of the conditions as they exist he has no desire to meet with your Board of Directors in conference "to map out a plan."[35]

Owen failed to acknowledge, or perhaps did not understand, that FLCA could not survive unless things changed—it had continued to go further into debt, and the debt had grown to an amount that it could not repay. William Thomas, an attorney for AS&F, questioned whether the notes issued by FLCA were a violation of the contract restriction on "contracting pecuniary obligations," and even opined that the original contract between TL&I and FLCA was "void for want of mutuality."[36]

Fred Owen wrote his fellow trustees of his disappointment with not having a new agreement between FLCA and AS&F. As he analyzed it, "It appears to me that the procedure during the years

1906 to 1917 was entirely businesslike, and there was no warrant for any other procedure. Methods pursued during 1917 and 1918 were not only contradictory, but were unbusiness-like, and resulted as might be expected in bringing about just the situation that now confronts us." Obviously Owen did not know of the previous turmoil. In what appears to be Hubert Eaton's handwriting, "Bunk" was written in pencil at the top of Owen's letter and underlined it twice.[37] As this letter was to FLCA, this could have been Wells's sentiment, but Eaton would undoubtedly have had the same reaction.

Although everyone was focused on the financial problems, they seemed to overlook a very positive fundamental: interments had increased dramatically. In 1912, the year before the Eaton and Sims sales program began, Forest Lawn had 164 burials. In 1918, Forest Lawn had 800 burials, almost five times the 164 burials in 1912. The financial model needed fixing, but the sales program was producing results that would bring in future business.

A month after the FLCA trustees voted to approve Wells's proposal to stop sales in the mausoleum and the use of the receiving vaults, crematory, and Little Church of the Flowers, Eaton notified FLCA, "We shall take possession of said property [on March 28]. . . . You will, therefore, deliver [the property] free and clear of any encumbrances." Although FLCA earlier had quitclaimed any interest it might have in the property, Eaton wanted to make sure no mechanics liens or other liability had been attached to it since then. In a somewhat conciliatory closing, Eaton offered, "Until such time as there is a definite written agreement between us, we shall be glad to arrange for the exchange of courtesies of the Little Church of the Flowers, and of its conservatory, etc." This was an attempt to try to keep some semblance of cooperation between the parties.[38]

Without any progress in reaching resolution through exchange of letters, the two parties agreed to meet "in joint conference" on April 5 at the Los Angeles Trust & Savings Building to discuss the various issues.[39] That meeting failed to produce a resolution of the conflicts.

Farewell to Wells

Seemingly out of nowhere, Pop Ross wrote William Hollingsworth, one of the directors of AS&F, with a proposal to sell his shares and arrange for Norton Wells's ouster.

> I hold 4,728 shares of the common capital stock of American Security & Fidelity Co., in my name as Trustee. I will deliver said 4,728 shares to you in consideration of the 75¢ per share, and the further consideration that I will procure the resignation of three of the Trustees of Forest Lawn Cemetery Association, one of which will be Norton C. Wells, and cause the election of three other lot owners in whom you have confidence to fill the vacancies on the Board of Trustees of Forest Lawn Cemetery Association caused by above three resignations.[40]

Hollingsworth accepted the proposal with the proviso that everything must be completed before noon on Saturday, April 12.[41] Pop did not indicate what kind of influence he had over Wells or other trustees. However, Pop's certificate for 4,728 shares was duly cancelled in 1920.

When the FLCA board of trustees met on April 16, Norton Wells presented a letter of resignation:

> Since the annual meeting of the Lot owners held January 20th, 1919, when a change in the personnel of the Board of Trustees took place, a state of inharmony has existed, which in my judgment is tending to injure the business of the Cemetery and the interests of the Lot owners.
>
> Therefore, in the hope of promoting harmony, I have decided to resign as President and Trustee of the Forest Lawn

Cemetery Association and hereby tender my resignation to take effect at once.[42]

The trustees passed a resolution thanking Wells for his nine years of service to Forest Lawn, then elected Motley Flint as president. Flint was vice president of the Los Angeles Trust & Savings Bank. Sometime during 1919 he was given 5,000 shares of AS&F common stock "for assistance rendered," creating a potential conflict of interest. Although he had been an officer for only one month, trustee John M. Smalley also presented his resignation, which was accepted.[43]

Eight days after Flint was elected FLCA president, Frank Owens's suggested to him that, as a gesture of thanks, Wells be paid his full salary for the month of April rather than, "paying him off like a discharged employee. . . ." The trustees unanimous agreed with the recommendation at their next meeting.[44]

CHAPTER 19

PROBLEM SOLVED

NORTON WELLS HAD SERVED as president of the Forest Lawn Cemetery Association since January 1910. After Wells resigned in April 1919, the new president, Motley Flint, had to deal with the same conflicts and financial problems that had been plaguing FLCA and AS&F during the terms of Treadwell and Wells.

Turmoil and Tension

The day after Wells's resignation, Motley Flint wrote Hubert Eaton to tell him of the change in president. Despite having voted for a termination of the selling contract with AS&F, Flint told Eaton, "It does seem to me that a vigorous selling campaign should be instituted and that the trustees should keep in close touch with the situation, and everything done to harmonize all interests."[1]

A few days later, after a discussion between Eaton and Flint relative to operations, Flint wrote Eaton that he did not like Eaton's proposal that business should be done under the name of American Security & Fidelity. Flint believed FLCA should have all its business at a single location, closing the city office in downtown Los Angeles. Furthermore, doing business under the name of AS&F would be a mistake, "for the title sounds too much like a cold blooded business proposition." Though banker Flint was generally an Eaton ally, he still had his own opinions and realized his responsibilities as a member of the FLCA board of trustees.[2]

Meanwhile, FLCA was receiving letters from customers who wanted to know whether to make payments to AS&F or FLCA, or who complained about not receiving deeds. In a passive-aggressive move, FLCA secretary Fred Owen began to refer all customer questions and complaints to Motley Flint. So Flint wrote Eaton to say he would not tolerate being bombarded constantly by lot owners—it was unfair, and if it kept up he would resign as trustee, which would also remove him as president. Eaton was at risk of losing a potential ally on the FLCA board of trustees.[3]

Eaton continued to refuse to sign deeds for cemetery property until AS&F received its proper share of the sale proceeds, even though the customer had paid in full. Attempting to adhere to the contracts strictly, AS&F continued to make monthly payments of interest on the loans from the perpetual care fund, while simultaneously protesting that FLCA was not turning over collected funds to it as called for in the agreement.[4]

On the day of the April board of trustees meeting, Motley Flint wrote a letter to the FLCA trustees explaining his view of the situation. He believed that AS&F was "more deeply interested financially in the welfare of the cemetary [sic] than anyone else." Because of this, funds needed for operations would have to come from AS&F. Although he understood that AS&F deserved to be protected financially, Flint declared it would be a great mistake to cede control of everything except the perpetual care fund to AS&F. These disputes had gone on too long, he said, and action was needed now.[5]

From early in Forest Lawn's existence, it had been the practice to make loans from the perpetual care fund to TL&I, with the loans secured by mortgages on TL&I's vacant land. That practice had continued with the merger of TL&I and AS&F. At the next meeting of the FLCA trustees, a motion was made to loan AS&F money from the perpetual care fund in keeping with past practice. Flint, the cautious banker, called to the board's attention a California law that prohibited a cemetery corporation from directly or indirectly loaning money to an officer or director. He told the trustees that he understood that none of the trustees was an officer or stockholder in AS&F. Flint requested that the wording of the statute be included in the minutes of the meeting to show that the trustees were aware of the law.[6]

More meetings between FLCA and AS&F were held in an attempt to reach agreement. Eaton continued to press for control over operations, leaving FLCA responsible only for the perpetual care fund. To put pressure on FLCA, Eaton would not agree to resume issuing deeds or cease collecting funds due to FLCA. The only point the two sides could agree on was that the two vacancies on the FLCA board of trustees should be filled forthwith.[7]

At a special meeting on May 12, 1919, the FLCA trustees discussed an agreement proposed by AS&F to settle matters. The trustees thought so little of it that the minutes recorded, "As fundamental differences of law and of fact appeared in connection with these propositions, no action was possible at the meeting, and [the propositions] were not ordered spread upon the Minutes."[8]

At that same meeting, H. W. Broughton and George H. Storer were elected to fill the trustee vacancies left by the resignations of Wells and Smalley.[9]

Flint urged that the contract dispute between AS&F and FLCA should be settled at once. However, disagreement continued over language that some thought would have made American Security & Fidelity a fiscal agent of FLCA. With no agreement on the contract, AS&F continued to refuse to issue deeds to purchasers of cemetery property unless it received money that it was due. Although the sales program had been stopped, purchasers from previous installment sales completed their payments and expected to be given deeds. To temporarily address this, in May FLCA allowed a representative of AS&F to be on the grounds to make sales.[10]

At the May 14 meeting, the FLCA trustees learned that no progress had been made in resolving the dispute. Trustee Glenn E. Ely, an attorney, reported he had studied AS&F's proposed agreement and believed there were legal objections to it. He told the trustees that he "could not advise the board to enter into any contract which delegated it's [sic] powers and functions to an agency." Therefore, trustees Storer and Broughton were appointed to form a committee to meet with Ely and representatives of AS&F.[11]

After receiving many calls from purchasers of cemetery lots who were complaining of not receiving deeds, Motley Flint asked Owen if FLCA had enough cash to pay AS&F to obtain release of some of the deeds. Owen replied that "there certainly is no money available for [that] purpose." Not only that, but he was concerned about having enough cash to meet the month's expenses.[12]

The back-and-forth sniping continued. Owen pushed for release of burial rights deeds without payment to AS&F. Eaton responded by writing Flint that AS&F had signed every deed presented to it in the first two months of the year, but had yet to receive payment from FLCA for those sales. Fred Owen was told that if he sent the money due AS&F, the deeds would be released. Despite the continued bickering, Eaton believed some of the trustees desired to find a solution. He told Flint his patience was "sorely tried" when he read still another letter from Owen.[13]

Clearly piqued by Owen's correspondence, Eaton wrote him, "It is now 'up to you' to decide whether or not this futile discussion shall continue, or the two corporations enter immediately into an amicable agreement based on constructive principals [sic] for the future untinged by the acrimony of the past few months."[14]

Things had come to a head. If a solution was not found soon, the situation would continue to worsen to the detriment of all. FLCA trustees finally recognized that curtailing sales activity hurt them as much as AS&F. Consequently, FLCA sales of "lots and graves" were resumed in June.

The FLCA trustees closed the month of May with still another meeting to discuss a proposed contract with AS&F. President Flint read the contract aloud, paragraph by paragraph. The most consequential point of contention continued to be language making AS&F an agent for FLCA, thus enabling it to act for and make commitments for FLCA. The trustees thought this would be ceding too much power to AS&F. Owen made a motion to reject the objectionable language. All trustees except M. M. Kauffman, whom Eaton had put on the board of trustees through proxies, voted for the motion to reject the language.[15]

Reality was setting in for FLCA. It was out of money, and revenue was low after stopping the before-need sales program. Eaton told Flint that potential purchasers were still contacting AS&F to buy cemetery property. Because AS&F could still sell mausoleum property, it tried to do that. But when people indicated they wanted earth burial instead of a mausoleum crypt, they had to be referred to the FLCA office, since AS&F could no longer sell ground burial property. Because AS&F had built the mausoleum, it could sell crypts in it, but it did not have the right to sell cemetery ground property that was controlled by FLCA. Eaton told Flint he believed that many of these prospective purchasers never took the trouble to go to the cemetery: "It has been our experience that the purchaser feels that he should be put to the least trouble possible and not required take a trip to the [cemetery] in order that he may sign a contract and pay his money."[16]

Negotiations continued, but FLCA, being virtually insolvent, did not have leverage over AS&F. Glenn Ely believed that FLCA should not continue selling lots unless a fund could be established to pay AS&F its share of sales dollars, thus enabling FLCA to demand that deeds be issued in accordance with the contract.[17]

Resolving the Issues

Four days after the FLCA trustees rejected the language making AS&F the fiscal agent for FLCA, H. W. Broughton, on behalf of the special committee, presented a resolution to the full board to resolve the dispute. Upon a motion by Kauffman and seconded by Broughton, the trustees voted to have AS&F liquidate the indebtedness of FLCA. FLCA was to turn over to AS&F everything it owned, other than the perpetual care fund, in return for AS&F forgiving and cancelling everything owed to it by FLCA. The resolution passed, but Fred Owen voted against it, and Glenn Ely abstained from voting.[18]

Kauffman made a second motion, this one to have AS&F or its nominee take over the maintenance of the cemetery in return for the income from the perpetual care fund. The motion passed, with trustees Ely and Owen abstaining from voting.[19]

Although the FLCA trustees had agreed in principle with AS&F, a formal agreement was necessary to provide the details for implementation. When presented with a memorandum of agreement at the June 23, 1919, meeting, four of the seven trustees approved it. The other three trustees—Ely, Owen, and Storer—voted against it and verbally tendered their resignations.[20] Other motions followed, with the same three trustees being opposed.

After the motions dealing with the FLCA–AS&F issues had been dealt with, Motley Flint called for action on the tendered resignations of Glen Ely, Fred Owen, and George Storer. Each resignation was unanimously accepted.[21]

Eaton was pleased and relieved to have reached an agreement with FLCA, and he certainly could not have achieved this without help from Motley Flint. He wrote Flint a letter of congratulations and sent him a gift of one thousand Marquise cigarettes.

> I have thanked you before for the excellent work you have done in our behalf and we intend to show our thanks in a more befitting way later, but I take this opportunity to compliment you on the ability you possess in handling delicate situations. Affableness, diplomacy, convincing logic, man to man talk, sledgehammerism [sic]—I have seen you use them all and stood by in silent admiration at the directing brain back of these visable [sic] evidences of power to achieve.

I am sorry that I was unable to find the "jug of wine" but Uncle Sam closed the door July 1st, although from the appearance of a bill I have just had the pleasure of approving, I do not believe you are going to suffer.[22]

Forming Forest Lawn Memorial-Park Association

Once the trustees of FLCA approved the formal agreement to turn over management of everything but the perpetual care fund to AS&F, a new nonprofit, mutual benefit corporation of lot owners was formed to operate and develop the cemetery. On June 12, 1919, Forest Lawn Memorial-Park Association (FLMPA) was incorporated and its board of directors held their first meeting. Two days later, at another board meeting, the directors appointed Hubert Eaton as general manager of the new corporation. Eaton was given broad discretion to organize cemetery operations as he saw fit and to do anything legal and within the corporation's bylaws to successfully operate Forest Lawn Memorial-Park. For his efforts as general manager, he was to receive compensation of 2 percent of the gross sales of cemetery property.[23]

In the beginning, FLCA and FLMPA were twins from a corporate structure standpoint. Both were not-for-profit corporations formed to develop and manage cemeteries, membership was automatic for those who owned at least 200 square feet of interment property, and members elected the trustees or directors.

At the August 23, 1919, meeting of the FLMPA board, the directors approved contracts that defined the responsibilities of the three organizations. One new agreement moved the responsibility for cemetery development from FLCA to FLMPA and gave FLMPA responsibility for unsold property maintenance. Perpetual care contributions continued at 33.3 percent of the net price of ground property. FLMPA took charge of all sales activity. Sales dollars—net of amounts for perpetual care—were to be divided on a 50-50 basis for ground property, but AS&F would receive 75 percent of sales of mausoleum crypts and niches. Carefully crafted language about when money was to be paid to the parties took away the contentious issues from the original 1912 contract. AS&F agreed to provide all cemetery maintenance in return for all the income generated by the perpetual care fund. However, it assigned that agreement to FLMPA, making FLMPA responsible for maintenance. Although FLCA would continue to be responsible for the investment of the perpetual care fund, FLMPA would collect the perpetual care funds that were part of the sales price and deposit the money into the perpetual care fund as it was received.[24]

A contract between FLMPA and AS&F put FLMPA in almost the same position that FLCA had been in. FLMPA was to be responsible for "embellishing, improving, and maintaining [Forest Lawn's] lands" and was required to provide all maintenance of the cemetery.[25] AS&F would continue with its construction projects—the Little Church of the Flowers, crematory, and mausoleum.

Looking Ahead

In the fall of 1919, Motley Flint and Hubert Eaton began to lay plans for the future. Flint still believed "that something should be done to expedite and increase sales, thereby making the proposition more attractive from every angle." Eaton concurred, telling Flint somewhat grandly that after studying every successful cemetery in the country, he could not see why the cemetery business should not climb out of its old rut and become energetic and progressive. Although the income from an average cemetery lasted for fifty to seventy-five years, Eaton believed that most of that income could be received in fifteen years—albeit with higher selling costs, which would be offset by getting the money sooner. He told Flint that he had "studied this question and its facts and figures until I know I am correct."[26]

Eaton wrote Flint in early October laying out the challenges faced as FLCA, FLMPA, and AS&F moved forward. No matter how one looked at it, he proclaimed, the problem that overshadowed all issues with the cemetery business was how to sell cemetery lots. The issues of attaining a fair return for investors and accumulating

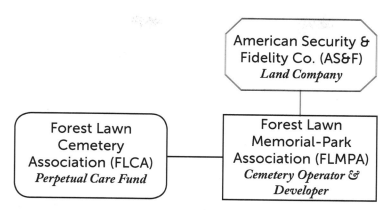

Figure 68. Forest Lawn Memorial-Park Association
In 1919, FLMPA assumed responsibility for operating the cemetery, including all sales and development activity, and FLCA was left with only holding the perpetual care fund.

adequate perpetual care funds would disappear with the sale of cemetery property. The closest thing to selling plots was selling life insurance, but there is "a sacredness, a sentimentality and a disturbing directness attached to the sale of a cemetery lot, which does not pertain to life insurance."[27]

> My eight years experience here and elsewhere has taught me that a cemetery lot . . . is probably the hardest product to sell on the market. . . . Sale of this commodity deals with a subject that is most abhorrent to the average human mind, death. The average individual will discuss almost anything with you except death. He does not even wish to think about it, much less arrange for it at a time when he feel[s] that it is a long way off.[28]

One of the problems Eaton recognized was that it was difficult to recruit salesmen; established and successful salespeople would "rarely ever consider it." So the sales manager would take those who needed the job, and over a long period of careful coaching would find the one in twenty-five who could be successful. The ones who were successful would make a good income, while the others would be unlikely to make a decent living. He explained to Flint that Inglewood Cemetery understood working for the long term when it hired many of Forest Lawn's salesmen after they were terminated and gave them five-year contracts.[29]

Eaton believed that people attending funerals were the greatest advertising Forest Lawn could have. It acquainted them with Forest Lawn and made them think of making plans for burial if they had not. Best of all, it was advertising with no cost.[30]

According to Eaton, the "before need" method had a lot of "lost motion" in it. It would be costly to ramp up and would have scant immediate results. However, those who were contacted but did not buy would be likely to buy lots in Forest Lawn in the future, with little further selling expense. These were the people who had made purchases during the disputes with FLCA and kept American Security & Fidelity from having large bank borrowings.[31]

Because he thought Pasadena was "clannish and hard to change," Eaton told Flint he wanted to maintain an office there with two or three salesmen. The Pasadena market should belong to Forest Lawn, since Mountain View, the only cemetery in that area, was no competitor for the beauty of Forest Lawn. Eaton wanted to "awaken" the people of Pasadena to the fact that within six miles was another cemetery, more beautiful and capable of "every form of burial."[32]

When the annual meeting of lot owners was held in January 1920, the trustees of FLCA reported that although Forest Lawn had continued to improve during 1919, making "rapid strides towards its ultimate goal of becoming the most beautiful Memorial-Park in California," progress had been hampered by "internal dissension." With these issues resolved, "entire harmony" now prevailed, and everyone was now "working towards one end—that of benefitting Forest Lawn." With 964 interments in the prior year, the people of Los

Angeles, Pasadena, and surrounding area were increasingly finding
Forest Lawn to be the proper final resting place for their loved ones.[33]

A New FLMPA

Despite the creation of Forest Lawn Memorial-Park Association,
the corporate structure of Forest Lawn still did not work financially.
By 1925, FLMPA had reached practical insolvency, just as FLCA
had in 1919.

On January 9, 1926, AS&F notified FLMPA of its intent to
cancel the 1919 agreement. A special meeting of the FLMPA board
of directors was called to discuss the matter. E. C. Hauser, John
F. Huber, and John Kemp—the entire board—were present for the
discussion. Huber reported that FLMPA now owed $317,000 to
AS&F, more than its accounts receivable, and was unable to carry
insurance or pay for cemetery improvements and development as
required under the agreement. He recommended that the FLMPA
directors accept AS&F's cancellation. In return, FLMPA would
transfer all its property, real and personal, to AS&F. AS&F would
then cancel the debt owed it and indemnify FLMPA from any
obligations resulting from the 1919 contract. This was a repeat of
the 1919 AS&F cancellation of FLCA debt. FLMPA and AS&F
entered into a formal settlement agreement on February 9, 1926.

That same day, FLMPA was replaced by a new corporation with
a slightly different name: Forest Lawn Memorial Park Association,
Inc. ("FLInc"). John W. Kemp and John F. Huber, who had been
on the board of the Forest Lawn Memorial-Park Association, were
two of the five directors of the new corporation. The intent was to
avoid having a majority of the old directors start the new FLInc to
ensure it qualified legally as a new, separate corporation and had
no responsibility for the old FLMPA. AS&F would now have the
responsibility for development, and FLInc would be responsible for
operations and sales.

Immediately following the organization meeting of FLInc members,
the directors held their first meeting. After they elected officers and

approved the bylaws, director John Huber moved to appoint Hubert Eaton as general manager, with a one-year contract that would renew automatically. In addition to compensation based on sales, Eaton was to be provided with an automobile and chauffeur. The contract recognized that he might "have other interests"—AS&F was not specifically mentioned—so he would not be required to "devote the whole of his time and attention to the business of the corporation."

One month later, one of the directors of the new association, Charles W. Partridge, resigned as director and vice president. E. C. Hauser, who had been on the board of the now defunct FLMPA, was elected to fill the spot.

In April, after the closure of FLMPA, FLInc changed its name to Forest Lawn Memorial-Park Association. FLInc was now the new FLMPA. There was an important difference in the structure of the old and new corporations. While the original FLMPA had automatic membership, the new FLMPA elected its members. This allowed Hubert Eaton to have friends and employees as the overwhelming majority of members, assuring him an element of control.

Solution Found

Although Eaton had first approached Forest Lawn as just a sales project, his understanding of cemeteries grew over the five years from the time he and Sims signed their selling contract. During the various disputes with TL&I and FLCA, Eaton realized that the business model did not work. If the three entities did not cooperate and coordinate their respective roles, chaos and discord would follow. As a practical businessman, he struggled to find the solution and finally found a sustainable financial structure: AS&F would provide the land and develop the cemetery; FLMPA would operate Forest Lawn and make all sales; FLCA would only be responsible for the perpetual care fund. With Eaton achieving effective control of both AS&F and FLMPA, discord between the corporations ended.

More importantly, his Baptist upbringing led him to think differently about cemeteries. As he said in his Builder's Creed, cemeteries should be more than just practical repositories for the deceased—they should be places where those who were gone should be honored, but they should also be places for the living. He now knew what he wanted to accomplish and was committed to making Forest Lawn Memorial-Park a place of beauty and inspiration as well as a sacred repository for the dead.

Forest Lawn was now set for the future, with a clear philosophy about how it would be different from other cemeteries as well as having a sound, sustainable financial structure.

Epilogue

OVER THE COURSE OF his career, T. Paterson (Tom) Ross designed over 250 buildings of many types, including apartment houses, churches, flats, single-family homes, hotels, a mausoleum, and other office and commercial structures. He married his second wife, Belle, in 1921. Tragedy followed in 1922 when, during an inspection at a building site, a load in an elevator shifted and caused bricks to fall on Tom's head. The resulting concussion left Ross partially paralyzed and unable to speak. T. Paterson Ross died on April 26, 1957, in Santa Cruz at the age of eighty-four.[1]

After his resignation as president of FLCA, bitter over the way things had unfolded, Norton Wells left Southern California and had no further contact with Forest Lawn. He moved back to San Francisco with his wife, Florence. He remained there until he died on July 25, 1958, at the age of seventy-eight. His funeral service was held at the Oriental Lodge in San Francisco, followed by cremation at the Woodlawn Cemetery in Colma.[2]

Former FLCA trustee John Llewellyn passed away in New York on April 17, 1919. He is interred in Forest Lawn near the Llewellyn family monument moved from Evergreen Cemetery in 1910. By the time Llewellyn passed away, Eaton had begun to establish uniform

321

size standards for flush memorials, but an exception was made for John Llewellyn. His family was allowed to place a small granite marker with just the initials "J. L." on it, similar to memorials for the six Llewellyn family members who had been moved from Evergreen Cemetery.

After his involvement with Forest Lawn, J. B. Treadwell became involved in the movie industry. He participated in many real estate deals, including a copper mine in Arizona with his brother, George Treadwell. As a resident of Glendale, J. B. continued to harass Forest Lawn for the rest of his life. In a 1932 speech to the Forest Lawn sales force, Eaton told his salesmen that he had "inherited an enemy"— J. B. Treadwell, who "had a "life-long ambition to fight Forest Lawn." He told the salesmen that one day he woke up and found that Treadwell,

> had a parade going up and down Glendale Avenue with caskets on trucks, etc. [Treadwell] was out to get my goat and I had to fight back. Then all of a sudden I began searching our records and decided he was the best friend Forest Lawn had. One day I met him on the street. I smiled the best I knew how. He was surprised that I smiled. I said to him, "Mr. [Treadwell], my directors have decided to pay you a salary. You are the best friend we have." Then I told him why – and it nearly broke his heart.[3]

During the formative years of Forest Lawn Memorial-Park, Eaton refined his vision. He first limited where upright monuments could be placed. Then, he offered discounts for lots without the possibility of a monument. Finally, he banned the monuments altogether. Rather than have legions of large monuments visually competing with each other, Eaton strategically placed high quality art in places so that it would benefit all cemetery property owners. He made this art, largely statuary, into "distinguished memorials" which could be purchased by families. As these memorials sold, they funded additional statuary and art became more prominent throughout the park. Eaton made many trips to Europe seeking works appropriate for Forest Lawn. Hubert Eaton was committed to quality art in classical themes—and, he was willing to pay to get that quality. He was willing to think big. For example, when he acquired Jan Styka's painting of the Crucifixion—an enormous canvas 45 feet by 195 feet—he was willing to build a special auditorium for no purpose other than to display the painting.

During his lifetime, Eaton received multiple honorary doctorates.[4] As a result of these honorary degrees, he preferred to be known as Dr. Hubert Eaton.

Seeing Hubert Eaton's success with his memorial-park plan, cemeteries across the country tried to emulate it. Many just banned upright monuments, allowing only flush memorials. A few tried to add several pieces of statuary. But, capturing the spirit of the memorial-park was more difficult than that. Most saw it as a business or marketing strategy rather than a commitment to be different. Grasping the philosophy of The Builder's Creed and being willing to put it into action proved to be elusive for most.

Hubert Eaton remained general manager of Forest Lawn Memorial-Park Association and president of American Security & Fidelity until his death in 1966. During Eaton's lifetime, he continued to refine his vision of a "memorial-park" as a place that not only performed a practical function, but as a place of beauty and inspiration to the community. Monuments and tombstones were banned, and statuary was strategically placed to enhance the beauty of the memorial-park. In addition, Forest Lawn sponsored many free programs for the community. Eaton's memorial-park plan changed the way cemeteries were viewed throughout the United States and influenced cemetery design in many other countries. When he opened the first funeral home (mortuary) on dedicated cemetery property, he shattered the traditional separation of preparation of the dead, funerals, and burial.

Figure 69. FLCA Merged into FLMPA 1996

In 1996, FLCA merged into FLMPA giving FLMPA the responsibility for all cemetery operations as well as the Perpetual Care Fund, now known as the Endowment Care Fund. AS&F continues to develop all interment property.

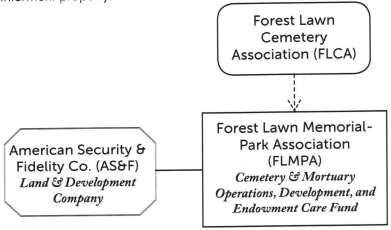

Figure 70. Last One Standing 1999

In 1999, FLMPA acquired all the cemetery and mortuary assets of AS&F. A single, independent board of directors was responsible for all aspects of Forest Lawn.

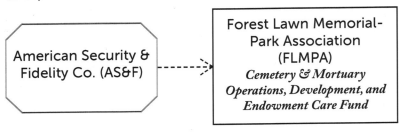

Although it took many decades, the combination of funeral homes with cemeteries has now become quite common, except in states where funeral directors have successfully lobbied to keep them separate.[5]

Upon Eaton's death, he was succeeded by his nephew, Frederick Eaton Llewellyn, who, like Eaton, served as general manager of FLMPA and president of AS&F. Llewellyn, a graduate of the California Institute of Technology and Harvard Business School, instituted progressive management philosophies to the organization. Fred Llewellyn gave up his roles as president and general manager in 1987, and his son, John F. Llewellyn (author of this book) became general manager of FLMPA and president of AS&F on January 1, 1988. He was responsible for the simplification of the corporate structure of Forest Lawn by consolidation of the various corporations. When AS&F ceased to exist in 1999, John became president and CEO of FLMPA. In 2011, John stepped down as president, but remained on the FLMPA board of directors a chairman of the board. At that time, Darin B. Drabing became president of FLMPA.

Eventually it became obvious that there was no reason for the existence of both Forest Lawn Cemetery Association and Forest Lawn Memorial-Park Association. In 1996, FLCA merged into FLMPA. After the merger, FLMPA assumed responsibility for the endowment care fund (previously called the perpetual care fund). At the same time as the merger, FLMPA amended its bylaws to eliminate the members and have the board of directors elect its own membership each year.

The final consolidation occurred in 1999, when Forest Lawn Memorial-Park Association acquired the cemetery and mortuary assets of American Security & Fidelity Corporation and its wholly owned subsidiary, Forest Lawn Company. For the first time since the idea for a cemetery emerged in 1905, there was now a single board of directors responsible for the entire institution—cemetery, cremation, and funeral home (mortuary). Forest Lawn had now achieved a stability of leadership that would serve it well into the future and preserve the ideals, values, and culture that make it unique.

The men meeting in San Francisco in 1905 only hoped for financial success of their little cemetery in Tropico. Although the dream of financial success came true, the organization structure that finally made that possible was very different from the one they started with. Forest Lawn Cemetery evolved into Forest Lawn Memorial-Park, creating a new standard for cemeteries. Although the idea of eliminating tombstones and injecting art was revolutionary, the idea of cemeteries as a place for the living was radical. Forest Lawn became famous not just for its physical appearance, but for the belief espoused in Hubert Eaton's Builder's Creed that cemeteries should be more than a sacred repository for the departed, they should be places for the living that can uplift and educate communities.

Appendix A. Major Events Timeline

1905

August: Tropico Land & Improvement Company (TL&I) incorporated.

September 15: J. B. Treadwell purchases 158 acres from Susan Glassell Mitchell for $52,300.

September 18: J. B. Treadwell sells TL&I 130 acres for $28,000 in cash, a mortgage for $32,000, and 100,000 shares of stock in TL&I with a par value of $1.00.

1906

January 11: Forest Lawn Cemetery Association (FLCA) incorporated; J. B. Treadwell elected president and William J. Blain elected superintendent.

January 22: TL&I sells FLCA 116 acres; title to be conveyed upon FLCA paying for individual lots. Deeds for interment rights must be signed by both FLCA and TL&I.

August 26: First cemetery lot sold to W. I. Foley.

Forest Lawn entry arch and receiving vault constructed.

1907

December 31: Death of Susan Glassell Mitchell.

1908

FLCA completes construction of a receiving vault.

September: J. B. Treadwell complains to T. Paterson Ross (Tom) about William Blain's drinking and J. B. says he wants out.

October: J. J. Lockwood admits using money received due perpetual care fund for operations.

1909

January 25. Lucie Lambourn, as executrix of the Susan Glassell Mitchell (her mother) estate, publishes a notice to creditors.

April: Pop Ross becomes concerned about misuse of money collected for the perpetual care fund.

April: Lockwood resigns from FLCA over mishandling of perpetual care trust funds.

May 1. Charles O. Morgan hired as FLCA secretary and Dr. George Heath hired as salesman.

John Llewellyn of the Llewellyn Iron Works is given stock in TL&I to entice him to become a trustee of FLCA and to move his family interred in Evergreen Cemetery to Forest Lawn for re-interment as well as moving the family monument to Forest Lawn.

Treadwell continues to complain to Tom Ross about Blain's drinking.

1910

January 11: Norton Wells replaces J. B. Treadwell as president and general manager of FLCA.

Charles Morgan elected assistant secretary and assistant treasurer of TL&I.

Citizens protest against Forest Lawn's immense hillside sign.

Suit filed on behalf of Susan Glassell Mitchell's granddaughter to gain an undivided one-half interest in 151 acres sold to J. B. Treadwell (partition suit) and subsequently to TL&I and FLCA. TL&I loses suit against Mitchell estate to clear title.

Blain dies from complications after surgery.

Wells keeps Forest Lawn out of Glendale annexation of Tropico.

Charles Sims writes Wells regarding the promotion and sale of cemetery lots.

1911

January: Charles Morgan fails in attempt to take control of FLCA.

The partition suit continues to be the biggest issue facing TL&I and FLCA.

Tensions mount with Treadwell and Pop Ross considers taking legal action against Treadwell

Hubert Eaton was expected to visit Forest Lawn on behalf of Sims's company, American Securities Co. but fails to arrive before year-end.

1912

Sims writes Wells that he and Eaton are still interested in a selling contract with Forest Lawn. In March, Eaton meets with Tom and Pop Ross in San Francisco to discuss terms.

TL&I and FLCA sign a selling contract with Hubert Eaton and Charles Sims.

Eaton and Sims assign their interest in the selling contract to newly formed American Securities Co., incorporated in Maine.

TL&I loses land litigation resulting in loss of land through court ordered partitioning.

1913

Before need selling program begins.

Settlement with J. B. Treadwell over irregularity with original land sale to TL&I.

Dispute begins regarding distribution of proceeds from sale
of cemetery lots between TL&I, FLCA, and American
Securities.

1916

November: American Security & Fidelity Co.. incorporated

1917

Eaton writes The Builder's Creed.

Merger of TL&I and American Securities Co. into AS&F
is completed.

FLCA stops sales, then allows AS&F on site for selling,
then resumes sales.

FLMPA takes on all selling responsibility as well as all
operations and development.

AS&F purchases land TL&I lost through litigation.

Eaton and Tom Ross make grand tour of US cemeteries.

Building permit for mausoleum.

1918

Crematory opens.

Little Church of the Flowers dedicated.

New contracts between AS&F and FLCA.

Construction begins on mausoleum.

1919

FLCA elects new trustees favorable to Eaton.

FLCA cancels contracts with AS&F.

FLCA stops making before need sales.

AS&F refuses to sign deeds to purchasers unless it is paid
for the property.

Pop Ross persuades Norton Wells to resign as president and
trustee of FLCA.

AS&F agrees to liquidate all debts of FLCA in return for being given all assets except the perpetual care fund.

AS&F agrees to take over maintenance of cemetery in return for income from perpetual care fund. The maintenance responsibility is then assigned to FLMPA.

Forest Lawn Memorial-Park Association (FLMPA) incorporated and steps in to provide maintenance as AS&F's nominee.

New contracts between AS&F, FLCA, and FLMPA.

Mausoleum completed, first entombment April 7.

John Llewellyn passes away.

1920

The FLCA annual report to Forest Lawn lot owners announces that harmony now prevails.

May 1: Azalea Terrace, first unit of Great Mausoleum, dedicated.

1921

Land purchased to expand Forest Lawn.

FLMPA now operates and develops the cemetery as well as being the selling organization.

J. B. Treadwell loses his bid to block dissolution of TL&I.

1926

Forest Lawn Memorial Park Association, Inc. (FLInc). Formed to replace FLMPA which was insolvent. In the new corporation, members are elected rather than automatically becoming members by virtue of cemetery property ownership. AS&F takes over responsibility for development including all land and buildings.

Appendix B. FLCA Certificate of Incorporation

CERTIFICATE OF INCORPORATION

OF THE

FOREST LAWN CEMETERY ASSOCIATION.

- - - - - - - - - - - - -

KNOW ALL MEN BY THESE PRESENTS

That we the undersigned have this day voluntarily associated ourselves together for the purpose of incorporating under the laws of the State of California, and in pursuance of the purpose for which we have been elected, as herein after set forth, a cemetery corporation to be known as FOREST LAWN CEMETERY ASSOCIATION.

And we certify that the objects and purposes for which this corporation is formed are first, to establish and maintain a cemetery in the County of Los Angeles, State of California, and to take by purchase, donation, or devise, lands not exceeding 330 acres in extent, in said County, said lands to be held and occupied exclusively as a cemetery for the burial of the human dead, and to acquire water rights and privileges for use therein, and to survey and subdivide the land so taken into lots and plats, avenues and walks, and to file a map or maps thereof in the Recorder's Office of said County, and to sell and convey the said lots to purchasers and to apply any surplus arising from the sale of said plats an lots and all other sources for the payment for said land and deeds and expenses of the corporation, and for the improvements, embellishments and preservation of said cemetery, and to do all other things requisite and necessary and proper to be done in the establishment, maintenance, embellishment conducting of said cemetery as fully and effectually as such things can be done by a cemetery corporation, organized and incorporated under the laws of the State of California, including as one of the purposes of said corporation the establishment and maintenance in said cemetery of one or more crematories for the cremation of the bodies of the dead, said crematories to be conducted by and under the management and control of said cemetery corporation, and to make reasonable charges for the services in the cremation of said bodies of the dead, and to do all things necessary and proper in the establishment, management and maintenance of first class crematories.

That the principal place of business of said corporation shall be in the City of Los Angeles, County of Los Angeles, State of California.

That the term of the incorporation shall be fifty years.

That the number of trustees who shall have the management of the affairs of this corporation, as aforesaid, shall be seven, and the names and residences of the trustees elected for the first year are:

Names.	Residences.	Name	Residences
J. Schoder,	Los Angeles	C. B. Barnes,	Los Angeles
Jas. H. Dewey,	do	W. B. Scott,	do
W. J. Blain,	do	J. J. Lockwood,	do
J. B. Treadwell,	do		

That this corporation shall have no capital stock.

That the said trustees were duly elected at the meeting of members of said association duly convened and held at No. 615 Chamber of Commerce Bldg., City of Los Angeles, State of California, for the purpose among other things of electing trustees to take charge and management of the business of said association and to form this corporation. That all of said members were then and there present and voted at such election for the above named trustees as is more particularly set forth in the certificate and verification by the officers who conducted the election hereto annexed and made a part of these articles.

In Witness Whereof we have hereunto set our hands and seals this 11th day of January, 1906.

/s/ J. Schoder; /s/ M. B. Scott; /s/ Jas. H. Dewey; /s/ C. B. Barnes; /s/ W. J. Blain; /s/ J. J. Lockwood; /s/ J. B. Treadwell.

Appendix C. 1906 FLCA Rules

Undated changes were made in pencil on the original copy of the cemetery rules. These changes are included as strikeouts for deletions and italics for additions.

Lots, how sold	1. Lots may be bought at the office in Los Angeles or at the Cemetery, but interments will not be allowed in lots not paid for except by special agreement. Lots shall be sold at prices fixed by the Board of Trustees, and in every instance shall thirty-three and one-third per cent be added to the price of lot for the Perpetual Care of the same. No lot shall be sold below the schedule price, nor without Perpetual Care.
What burials permitted.	The Board informs persons who may wish to obtain lots in this Cemetery that they will have the ground they purchase secured to them and their families and heirs for a burial-place forever and for the Burial of such other persons as they may choose to admit, provided such admission is free of charge and without any compensation, and with the consent of the Trustees; but owners
How transferred.	cannot resell or transfer their lots to any other person without the consent of the Board first had and obtained in writing.
Burial permits.	2. The laws of California require a proper death certificate, and no burial will be permitted in the cemetery without a permit from a health officer, coroner or physician.

Interment human beings only.	3. No interment of any body other than that of a human being will be permitted in the Cemetery.
Disinterments.	4. No disinterment will be allowed except by the authority of the person owning the ground in which the interment is made, except by order of court, when a proper receipt for the remains must be given.
Trustees' right.	5. The Trustees desire to leave the improvement of lots, as far as possible, to the taste of the owners; but in justice to all, they reserve the right given them by law to exclude from any lot any headstone, monument or other structure, tree, plant or other object whatever, which may conflict with the regulations, or which may conflict with the regulations, or which they shall consider injurious to the general appearance of the grounds but no trees, plants or flowers growing within any lot shall be removed or trimmed without the consent of the Superintendent.
Trustees' right.	6. The Trustees desire to encourage the planting of trees and shrubbery, but, in order to protect the rights of all and to secure the best general results, they require that such planting shall be done only in accordance with the directions of the Superintendent of the Cemetery.
Iron or wire work.	7. No iron or wire work and no seats will be allowed on lots, excepting by permission of the Trustees, and when any article made of iron begins to rust the same shall be removed from the Cemetery.

Boxes, shells, toys, rusty, unpainted or broken benches, seats and vases, and similar articles in lots and lawns are inconsistent with the proper keeping of the grounds and will be removed.

Floral frames will not be kept over one week from day of interment. Receptacles for cut flowers will be sunk below the lawn level.

Planting

8. Lot owners may have planting or other work done on their lots at their expense upon application to the Superintendent. No workman other than employees of the Cemetery will be admitted to the cemetery, except for the purpose of setting stone work.

No coping or enclosure.

9. No coping nor any kind of enclosure will be permitted. The boundaries of lots will be marked by corner-stones, which will be set by the Cemetery with the centers upon the lines bounding the lot. Corner-stones must not project above the ground and must not be altered nor removed.

Established grade.

10. The grade of all lots is fixed at the time of the preparation of the ground for sale, and no change in the established grade will be allowed.

Mounds over graves.

11. Mounds over graves should be kept low, not exceeding four inches in height; and stone or other enclosures around graves will not be allowed.

Foundations notice given.

12. Foundations for all monuments, headstones, etc., shall be built by the Cemetery at the expense of the lot owner, and fifteen days' notice must be given for the building of foundations. The cost of the same must be paid in advance.

Orders to be left at city office.

Orders for foundations, and bearing the signature of the lost or grave owner, must be left at the office, and be accompanied by a sketch of monument, which must be approved by the Cemetery Management before a permit will be issued for their erection.

Foundation same size as base stone

Every foundation must be at least as wide and as long as the base stone resting upon it, and must not project above the surface of the ground. All foundations must extend as low as the bottom of the grave.

Base stone.

Base stones of monuments, headstones, etc., will not be allowed that have uneven bottoms.

Area of foundation.

The area of the foundation for monument must not exceed 5 per cent of the area, on lot containing 200 square feet or less; not more than 4 per cent of area on larger lot.

Excavation and concrete work.

All excavations for graves, foundations and underground vaults, and all concrete work of any kind underground shall be done by the Association at the expense of lot owner.

Monuments permitted.

13. Only one monument will be permitted on a family burial lot, and that must be in the center of the lot, except on lots of irregular shape, when the Superintendent shall determine.

Where a lot is owned by two parties, and both desire to erect a monument, it is recommended that they unite in erecting a joint memorial.

Any memorial structure exceeding eighteen inches in height shall be considered a monument.

In addition to one monument on a lot, one marker to each grave will be permitted, which shall *be flush with the ground and not more than* ~~not exceed~~ twelve inches in *and be* ~~height,~~ sixteen inches ~~in width, or be more than ten inches or~~ *and* less than four inches in thickness, and must be in one piece, no base being allowed.

No monument will be allowed in single-grave sections and no two monuments of the same design will be permitted within 200 feet of each other.

No monument or headstone will be permitted to be erected on any lot or grave, until the said lot or grave is paid for.

Markers.

14. No headstone shall be erected less than four inches or more than fourteen inches in thickness,

and must not exceed eighteen inches in height or width, including base.

Headstones are permitted on the single-grave sections, but must be in conformity to this rule.

15. No monument, headstone or vase, and no portion of any vault above ground, shall be constructed of other material than cut stone or real bronze. No artificial material will be permitted.

16. All stone and marble work, monuments and headstones must be accepted by the Superintendent as being in conformity with the foregoing rules before being taken into the Cemetery.

All old monumental work removed from other cemeteries must be cleaned thoroughly before being brought into the Cemetery--not after.

17. Any and all indebtedness due this Association must be arranged for before openings will be made in any lot.

18. The Trustees wish, as far as possible, to discourage the building of vaults, believing, with the best landscape gardeners of the day, that they are generally injurious to the appearance of the ground, and unless constructed with great care are apt to leak, and are liable to rapid decay, and in the course of time to become unsightly ruins. Therefore, no vaults will be permitted to be built except on lots sold with that especial privilege.

The designs for the same must be exceptionally good and the construction solid and thorough. The designs must be submitted to the Trustees, and will not be approved unless the structure would, in their judgment, be an architectural ornament to the cemetery.

Exception to rules.

19. The Trustees shall have the right to make exceptions from the foregoing rules in favor of designs which they consider exceptionally artistic and ornamental, and such exceptions shall not be construed as a rescission of any rule.

Material to be removed without delay.

20. Material for stone or marble work will not be allowed to remain in the cemetery longer than shall be strictly necessary, and refuse or unused material must be removed as soon as the work is completed. In case of neglect, such removal will be made by the Cemetery at the expense of the lot owner and contractor, who shall be severally responsible. No material of any kind will be received at the Cemetery on Saturdays, and no work of any kind will be permitted on Sundays or holidays.

Avenues and walks.

21. It shall be the duty and right of the Trustees from time to time to lay out and alter such avenues and walks, and to make such rules and regulations for the government of the grounds, as they may deem requisite and proper and calculated to secure and promote the general object of beauty of the Cemetery.

Drivers of carriages.

22. Funerals on reaching the Cemetery will be under the charge of the Superintendent or his assistants. Drivers must remain on their carriages or stand by their horses during funeral services.

No fast driving.

23. No Vehicle shall be driven in the Cemetery faster than a walk, and no horse shall be left unfastened without a driver.

No firearms or dogs.

24. Persons with firearms or dogs will not be admitted inside the Cemetery.

No soliciting.

25. Soliciting for monumental or any other kind of work will not be allowed on the Cemetery grounds.

Signs and advertisements.

26. Signs and advertisements of every description strictly prohibited in any part of the Cemetery.

Superintendent to enforce rules.

27. The Superintendent is vested with full police power to arrest without warrant any offender in our grounds. He is directed to expel from the Cemetery any person disturbing its sanctity by boisterous or other improper conduct, or who shall violate any of the foregoing rules

Perpetual care.

28. Perpetual Care: --The lawn plan cemetery (with its feature of perpetual care under the immediate direction of the Association, the cost of which is defrayed by the interest received from the investment of an additional amount equal to thirty-three and one-third per cent of the cost of the lot, except where the price is less than one dollar per square foot, then it will be 33 1/3 per cent of one dollar per square foot, paid at the time of the purchase and put into a separate fund managed by seven trustees elected for the purpose) stands as a guardian and care-taker in perpetuity, relieves the lot owner of any further care or expense, and guarantees not only that his plot shall always be kept in good repair, but also that nothing in its surroundings shall be unpleasant or incongruous. When in the fullness of time the Cemetery is entirely occupied, it will form an extensive park, rich in foliage, flowers, mausoleums, statuary, and monuments, with funds ample for its perpetual care- -a handsome memorial gift to posterity without a corresponding burden of tax.

Appendix D. "The Reasons Why"

Forest Lawn Cemetery "among the hills" has all the advantages of other cemeteries in Los Angeles and Pasadena, and in addition possesses superiorities, some of which can never by attained by the other properties.

LOCATION

Forest Lawn is situated at the lower end of the famous San Fernando Valley, near Griffith Park, in the cluster of hills that shelter such beautiful spots as Tropico, Glendale, Eagle Rock and Pasadena. Its exact location is at the junction of San Fernando Road and Glendale Avenue in Tropico.

Forest Lawn is easy of access from all points. It can be reached by Pacific Electric lines (Glendale car) every fifteen minutes. Some of the most beautiful scenic boulevards around Los Angeles and Pasadena lead to Forest Lawn. One is via Vermont Avenue to Los Feliz Road and through Griffith Park to Tropico, or Avenue Twenty to San Fernando Road which passes the gates.

This Park-Cemetery is reached from Pasadena via Colorado Street or Orange Grove Avenue, through Annandale Country Club district, Eagle Rock and Glendale, over a smooth oiled highway, that winds through wooded hills and shaded valleys, giving one a premonition of the beauty centering at Forest Lawn.

TOPOGRAPHY

Forest Lawn is "among the hills," and consequently, the grounds are laid out along rolling contours and verdant slopes. A great mistake has been made in most cemeteries in laying them out on a flat plane, which causes

341

every monument and grave stone to stand out in startling relief. To the intelligent observer or sorrowing relative they seem to shriek "Grave-yard!!" and in time they become veritable stoneyards. The topography of the land in Forest Lawn will always render such an effect an impossibility. The gentle slopes and curing hillside break this dreaded sameness, sheltering many a lovely plot and giving promise of future beauty just beyond. The white stones are seen only as glints of light through the trees, relieving the dark tone of the luxuriant foliage or appear as silent guardians of peace when some straying sunbeam falling on the tall marble shafts lights them into pillars of fire.

The fact that Forest Lawn nestles at the foot of the everlasting mountains is its eternal safeguard against the encroachments of modern city life. Streets may be put through other cemeteries, or when the city had finally grown all around them they may be absolutely closed. Municipal improvements may some day march up to the very gates of Forest Lawn, but further they will never go, for there would be no practical use in delving into the rugged mountains that are banked just behind, like watchful sentries protecting this city of sleeping souls.

NATURAL BEAUTY

The lover of the beautiful immediately recognizes that natural beauty is the highest type of loveliness. Artificiality may at first appeal strongly to the senses, but its charm does not last, and when compared to the intricate delicacy and refinement of nature it soon palls. In Forest Lawn Nature has made an ideal spot for our beloved dead, and the rolling character of the land, gently rising toward the mountains, lends itself readily to the touch of the landscape artist who gives to it the winding driveways, walks, flower beds and vine-covered vaults and buildings that make this park a place of practical use, as well as exquisite picturesqueness.

DRAINAGE

The elevation of Forest Lawn is higher than that of any other cemetery around Pasadena or Los Angeles, and the drainage is perfect. There can be no seepage of water into grave, nor graves that cave. The top soil is a dry sandy loam, which enables the graves to be dug perpendicularly and smooth.

STRATEGIC LEGAL POSITION

Forest Lawn occupies one of the most unique legal positions in the country. It is bounded by the alternate city lines of Los Angeles and Tropico. It is near these cities, and yet not legally in them. It is a province all to itself, and will remain so, as the city cannot incorporate within itself any new sections of land without the consent of those residing therein. Some future time, when municipal life approaches Forest Lawn, this fact may be of immense importance to lot owners.

WATER SUPPLY

This Park-Cemetery owns and controls its own water supply. This supply is inexhaustible, and is pumped from artesian wells to a large reservoir upon one of the high hills in the park, which elevation gives a powerful and constant flow to every part of the cemetery. The sections are covered with a network of water mains beneath the ground, which insures perpetual freshness of all grass and plant life.

Forest Lawn now controls sufficient acreage in connection with its contemplated mausoleum to furnish burial space for hundreds of years, and there is also other ground available, so the cemetery will always be able to add to its holdings if it should ever so desire.

PERPETUAL CARE

The scientific plan of perpetual care is adopted for Forest Lawn Cemetery. This sum in each case equals 33⅓% of the actual cost of the land, and is included in the total price paid by the lot owner. It is put under the control of lot purchasers as a perpetual care fund. There would be little use to put in the time and effort to build up a beautiful cemetery to last for all time unless there was built up at the same time a sufficient fund to care for the property that has been used for burial purposes. The perpetual care plan is a scientific proposition that has been worked out successfully by many cemeteries in the United States, and upon the basis adopted for Forest Lawn, the fund has always been sufficient to keep the property in perfect condition.

Some cemeteries have adopted the perpetual care idea on certain portions or lots, but all lots in Forest Lawn are under perpetual care. This keeps the park a harmonious whole, and there are not unkept [*sic*] or waste places or stone or glaring concrete to break the perfect continuity of the green sward and to distract the mind from the attitude of quiet repose and restful peace.

The perpetual care is included in the original price of the lot, and the purchaser need have no further worry regarding this feature, as the system perpetuates itself, and the laws of California govern, control and absolutely protect this fund. The cemetery laws of California are more advantageous to the lot owner than those of any other state in the Union.

MANAGEMENT

The sales management of Forest Lawn is under the American Securities Company, who act as fiscal agents of cemeteries. The personnel of this Company is composed of cemetery experts, who have made the problem of cemeteries a life study all over the globe, and are giving to Forest Lawn the best of what they have derived from their many sources of information. They are continually adding improvements and permanent benefits, which tend to make this mortuary park more beautiful, and constantly increase the value of lots. Our experts are regularly sent abroad to study and observe mortuary conditions in other countries, and these observations also include mausoleums and crematories.

The American Securities Company and its associated companies, are the only corporations in the world devoting themselves exclusively to the upbuilding [sic] and development of cemeteries. Years ago the men composing these corporations awoke to the fact that the cemetery question was large enough and intricate enough to be a business entirely in itself, and they determined to devote themselves exclusively to its betterment. Through years of experience they have built up a system that is as safe as a bank and scientific as the percentages of a life insurance company, and Forest Lawn is now receiving the benefits of this accumulated knowledge.

PURCHASING PLAN

Through years of trial the American Securities Company has perfected a plan for all purchasers which is beneficial to rich and poor alike. Any desirable person can purchase a lot on small monthly payments, and under a most equitable contract. We also offer other inducements to the man who wishes to purchase for cash.

The thoughtful person recognizes that in the near or distant future they will be confronted with the necessity of making suitable provisions for themselves or their loved ones, who may be called to their eternal rest. The thinking man or woman also knows that when this acute condition does confront them, they will necessarily be obliged to act promptly and without opportunity for intelligent investigation of the many conditions entering into the purchase of a cemetery lot. All the points that we have enumerated heretofore, and that will follow, should be taken into account, and there is no time for these considerations when the dead lie waiting. This choice, if made beforehand, when the mind is free to pay attention to, and weigh these many details, will become a source of satisfaction, and a monument to our thoughtfulness; but if we procrastinate too late, the end will probably be dissatisfaction and the knowledge that our grief has been taken advantage of and we have purchased a lot we did not want and at a price beyond our means.

You have probably never considered a cemetery lot in the light of an investment. Cemetery property, when well located and properly managed, becomes in time exceedingly valuable, and under our purchasing plan a cemetery lot is one of the best investments that can be made. Business men carry our lots upon their books as assets.

We are constantly opening new sections, and these new sections are first offered at introductory prices to desirable people. As these sections progress in development, grading is finished, shrubberies planted and trees start growing, the price logically advances toward the normal price, which is attained when the particular section equals the previous sections in beauty and desirability.

A new cemetery established on sound business principles is more desirable as an investment than an old one with fixed values.

SALESMEN

We have gradually built up a purchasing plan, the scope of which is broad enough to suit the various individuals' needs. The purpose and details of this plan are too numerous to put into this small booklet, and in consequence, we established long ago a corps of experienced salesmen. These salesmen will be glad to call upon you and explain at length all the benefits and advantages of the cemetery proper and our plan of operation. The fact of having our salesmen call upon you, and his subsequent explanations, will put you under no obligation nor embarrassment. If you do not wish to purchase now, we feel at any rate we have done a good work in showing you the danger of procrastination and that you owe it to yourself and your loved ones to attend to this matter without delay.

LOT OWNERS ASSOCIATION

Anyone purchasing a lot in Forest Lawn Cemetery becomes automatically a member of the Forest Lawn Cemetery Association. This Association absolutely governs and controls the Cemetery. The character of men now composing this association is of the highest and best to be found in Los Angeles or Pasadena, and this fact alone speaks most eminently for the stability and permanency of the property.

Inasmuch as the Trustees are elected from the lot owners, it assures that all expenditures of money will be judicially [sic] made; that all improvements will be made with the object of giving the best results; that no unsightly monuments or anything else will be allowed in the cemetery that will mar its beauty, and everything possible will be done for the welfare of those who have an interest in this beautiful park.

Here among the bloom and sweetness of the flowers, nature soothes and softens the grief of the afflicted, and turns one's thought into lighter and brighter channels, and we are brought again to the comforting reflection, that those whom we have laid away "are not dead, but sleeping."

NON-SECTARIAN

Forest Lawn is non-sectarian. "Malice toward none and charity toward all."

INCIDENTALS

Without charge a large tent is erected in stormy weather, and the walks are covered with matting, when neccessary [sic] for the protection of those attending funerals.

All records of burials are kept in duplicate, and all burials are made by actual survey and platted on filing cards, thereby enabling the location of a grave to be exactly found years hence.

Persons wishing to be certain that their remains will never be disturbed by their relatives can reconvey their lot to the Association in trust, at the same time designating who shall be buried in the lot and no other.

Uniformed attendants are always on hand at funerals to give whatever assistance is needed.

Our receiving vault is faced with field stones, and so covered with palms, vines and plants that it seems part of the hillside into which it is recessed.

LETTERS OF COMMENDATION

By permission we take pleasure in publishing some of the letters of commendation from a few of our many satisfied lot owners.

W. K. Cowan, President W. K. Cowan Co., 1140-1141 S. Hope St., Los Angeles, Cal.

The principal reason for my selection of Forest Lawn Cemetery in preference to any other was that it was so situated outside of the city of Los Angeles and other communities that it would be perpetually available for the purposes for which it is intended, while interments in some of the nearer-in cemeteries will be prohibited in a very short time . . . the prices of the lots are not extravagant. . . .

E. D. Unger, Eagle Rock, Los Angeles County, Cal.

The location, rolling ground, beautiful parkways, reasonable prices and terms that you are offering in Forest Lawn Cemetery, with its uniform perpetual care and natural protections for all time, are a few of the reasons for my selection of your property. I wish you every success.

Grayson Merrill, 1004 Los Angeles Investment Bldg., Eighth at Broadway, Los Angeles, Cal.

I wish to add my short expression of deep interest in your plan of development and building of Forest Lawn Cemetery. . . . I consider it just far enough from the center of the city to insure its permanency and yet be readily accessible at all times, together with ... the great care which you are taking in its subdivision and improvements. . . .

Mr. W. A. McIntosh, Pres. Mutual Home Builders' Corporation, 207 Higgins Bldg, Los Angeles, Cal.

I feel I have acted wisely in making this [purchase], as I have not only secured a beautiful spot for the last resting place of my family, one that is assured of perpetual care . . . but I also feel that I have made a wise investment. . . .

C. M. Church, Vice-President Highland Park Bank, Los Angeles, Cal.

We are well satisfied with our lot and think it an ideal location. We came to this determination after a full investigation of other cemeteries in and around Los Angeles, believing that Forest Lawn offered the best inducements in location and accessibility, as well as beauty and permanence. . . .

Mr. John Llewellyn, Vice-President Llewellyn Iron Works, Los Angeles, Cal.

The fact that I was one of the first to purchase a desirable lot in Forest Lawn indicates better than anything I might say that I preferred this cemetery to all others. . . .

The rapid and scientific development which you are constantly carrying on, together with the number of sales you are making to the best class of our citizens, indicates to me that you know your business, which I understand is that of scientific development of cemeteries along the lines of natural parks.

As you probably know, I have taken the trouble to investigate the title and legal phases that enter into the purchase of a lot in Forest Lawn Cemetery, and I have found these items altogether satisfactory. . . .

Under your purchasing plan and system of scientific development, I believe the purchase of a cemetery lot is a very profitable investment . . .

W. A. Roberts, State Senator, Sixty-first Assembly District, Los Angeles, Cal.

Some weeks ago I purchased through your representative a lot in one of your new sections in Forest Lawn Cemetery, which, in view of my knowledge concerning cemetery conditions generally, I believe to be an excellent investment. . . . I think it is an ideal location and with the many improvements that you plan to make, feel that I can see in the future one of the most beautiful properties of its kind in the country. . . .

Mr. C. O. Winters, 105 S. Maryland Ave., Glendale, Cal.

Its natural setting and the development going forward under your guidance make its possibilities as a grand burial park unlimited. . . .

Rev. John L. Maile, Pastor of New Olivet Congregational Church, Corner West Washington Street and Magnolia Ave., Los Angeles, Cal.

In the first place, provision is thus made for "the inevitable" laying down of the earthly tabernacle in which we live, and move, and have our being. This business is much better performed before the necessity for the same arrives.

Then the natural and artificial beauty of "Forest Lawn" is an asset of high sentimental value. . . . Attractive environs are a tribute of love to those who have gone on before; our remembrance of them finds pleasure in that which beautifies and adorns the situation . . . that provision for "perpetual care" is placed on an adequate foundation, that throughout the indefinite future the family resting place will be safely guarded.

A. F. Borden, President Redondo Floral Co., 246 S. Spring St., Los Angeles, Cal.

I believe it to be one of the best investments I have made. . . . As an investment it is one of the best kinds, as well as a provision for the future. I recommend this to our young business and professional men, who will probably not have this opportunity again during their lifetime.

B. McKelvey, of McKelvey & Unger, Real Estate, Insurance, etc., 5001 Monte Vista Ave., Los Angeles, Cal.

I wish to take this opportunity of thanking you for inducing me to buy a lot in Forest Lawn Cemetery. Upon considering the proposition for a short time it appealed to me as the most reasonable and sensible things a man could do for himself and family. Much as we wish it were not so, the fact remains that sooner or later we must all have such a lot, and when necessity demands it, the surviving relatives or friends are usually in no condition to intelligently attend to a matter of this kind. . . .

M. P. Harrison, Vice-President First National Bank, Glendale, Cal.

The fact that I purchased a lot in Forest Lawn indicates my confidence in the Management of your Company and to the future of Forest Lawn. . . .

If it were possible that all to whom you offer this opportunity would avail themselves of it ahead of their absolute need, while their minds are calm and they have plenty of time to make their choice of the spot where they and their loved ones may be laid to rest, they would later congratulate themselves for exercising this foresight rather than to be forced by emergency's demand to hurriedly make a selection. . . .

I think there is no doubt that Forest Lawn will soon be the one most desirable cemetery around Los Angeles. . . .

Mrs. S. E. Sternberg, 451 S. Chicago St., Los Angeles, Cal.

I purchased a lot in Forest Lawn Cemetery in preference to all others . . .

I think it is the most beautiful spot for a cemetery I have ever seen. . . . Its quietness, its beauty, the singing of the birds, the view of the surrounding mountains and valley impressed me more than I can say. Part of the sorrow was taken away in the peace and quietness of the surroundings . . .

I was compelled to purchase a lot at the time of my husband's death. . . . While we received every courtesy and consideration from your company my advice is, "Prepare for such an event (which is sure to come to every family) before you need it." I look back with horror to the ordeal of having to go to cemeteries at such a time to choose a final resting place for my dear one, and therefore advise everyone to attend to these things long before their need.

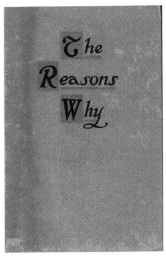

Forest Lawn Archives

Figure 71. Cover of "The Reasons Why"

Appendix E. Little Church Dedication Speech.

THE BIRTH OF A NEW ERA

An Address Delivered by Hubert L. Eaton at the Dedication
of the Little Church of the Flowers in Forest Lawn
Memorial-Park, May 12th, 1918.

Ladies and Gentlemen:

On behalf of the Directors and Trustees of Forest Lawn Memorial-
Park, it gives me pleasure to bid you welcome, and ask you to assist us in
dedicating this Little Church to the memory of our departed loved ones.

It seems as natural for men and women to honor their dead and memo-
rialize important events as it is for them to worship in some manner a
Supreme Power or to hope for immortality. The regard that men and women
of different ages and vocations have shown for their dead, is a reasonable
accurate reflection of their ideals, their civilization and their religion.
Today we believe that America represents the highest and best type of
civilization on the globe. We believe this to be proven and exemplified by
the fact that we tried by every known feasible and honorable method to
keep out of this Great War. Representing then, as we do today, the highest
type of civilization on the globe, it behooves us when memorializing our
dead to leave behind those grim and grewsome signs and symbols that
hitherto have marked grave-yards and cemeteries.

When we scan the pages of sacred and profane writing, we find death
portrayed as a beautiful thing – a transition; a hope of greater life beyond;
a beautiful garden through which the trials and tribulations of this old

351

world can never pass; yet we likewise find that human beings have ever marked the gateway to that beautiful garden with grewsome emblems and depressing ceremonies.

We believe in this respect that Forest Lawn Memorial-Park marks the birth of a new era, for our whole plan is designed to combat and eradicate these depressing influences. This Little Church of the Flowers that we dedicate today is the first step in our general plan. Its erection is based on a poetic theme, because our Architect, Mr. Ross, after a visit to old England, built this Little Church of the Flowers as a replica of that little church wherein Gray wrote his ["Elegy in a Country Churchyard"] . . .

[PAGE MISSING FROM SPEECH]

There isn't time to tell you all that we intend to do in making this Memorial-Park the most beautiful garden in Southern California; a moral uplift to the neighborhood, and a personal pride to our community. The beauty that lies around you today is but a small beginning of our plans for the morrow. If you could close your eyes and see this Park as it will be in the years to come, I believe your vision would show a veritable Garden of Eden. You could see these hills that lie on our right and behind us fashioned into terraces like unto the world-famed hanging gardens of Babylon; the many acres that spread out in a wide expanse on the other side of Mausoleum Hill will be transformed, a park of endless vistas, of placid lakes and splashing fountains, of singing birds and cooing doves, of sunlit slopes, of terraced hillsides that spread tier upon tier, a scene of greensward and beautiful flowers, a spot of warmth and color and life, and over all the solemn hush of still afternoon breathing sanctity and eternal peace. As the art gallery was created for the collection and preservation of pictorial art, so is the Memorial-Park "among the Hills" destined to become the place where works of our great sculptors shall be gathered together, for only in these great and natural amphitheaters can be found the proper setting, the breadth and expanse of space for those noble figures and groups of bronze and marble. Our City Parks and other institutions must have appropriations from year to year, but this great Memorial-Park will be protected by a gigantic Perpetual Care Fund, the principal of which can never be dissipated and the interest upon which will keep forever secure this beauty which we all love.

I wonder how many of you can see this vision, can picture the future as we do; I wonder how many even believe it will come to pass. Listen! I have something in my pocket that I have never seen, and you have never seen, and no one has ever seen. How many of you believe me? Let me see the hands. I am going to take this something out of my pocket and show you that you have never seen it, that I have never seen it and no one has ever seen it. You can go home and tell your friends and your family that you have seen something today that you have never seen before. Now, that thing will disappear; I will never see it again, no one will ever see it again. How many of you believe that?

I hold in here a kernel of a peanut that sees the light of day for the first time; no one has ever seen it before, so I have actually shown you something you have never seen before. Although you may have seen something similar to it, you have never seen this one before. It now disappears. You will never see it again, I will never see it again, and no one will ever see it again.

Now I have a purpose in using this simple little illustration, and that is this: this vision of a greater Memorial-Park shall surely come to pass, and most of you shall see the day when this spot shall be without a rival anywhere in this broad land, a Garden of den, a place to be loved, not abhorred, to be attended, not shunned. Was it not Carlyle who said that the greatest thoughts of his literary life were born during those moments that he spent in silent meditation beside his mother's grave? Can we, you and I, do a tenderer or sweeter act than be dedicating this Little Church to the memory of our departed loved ones.

Then when life shall fade and darken, to the last dim twilight wane,
When our sun's last ray is fading, never here to shine again,
May we hear their voices mingling, with new voices soft and low
Calling to us from the future, from beyond the sunset glow:
And as sinks the sun in splendor, in the glory-tinted West,
May we sink into the future, like the wearied child to rest.

Appendix F. Directors & Officers 1905-1926

Elections of trustees and directors are shown as of annual meeting of lot proprietors or shareholders. Generally, officers were elected at organization meetings of trustees or directors held after the annual meetings of lot proprietors to shareholders. Names and dates taken from corporate minute books.

Abbreviations:

CFO	chief financial officer
Asst-Sec	assistant secretary
Asst-Treas	assistant treasurer
Dir	director
GM	general manager
Pres	president
Sec	secretary
Sup	superintendent
Treas	treasurer
TTE	trustee
VP	vice president

Tropico Land & Improvement Company

August 28, 1905
Albert Burgren, Dir
John J. McLaughlin, Dir
T. Paterson Ross, Dir
Thomas Ross, Dir
J. B. Treadwell, Dir

September 18, 1905
Albert Bergren, Pres
T. Paterson Ross, Treas
Thomas Ross, Sec
J. B. Treadwell — *resigns as Dir, makes proposition to sell land to TL&I; remaining directors agree to purchase the land and after a 20-minute recess Treadwell is re-elected as Dir; Bergren resigns as Pres; Treadwell is elected Pres & Burgren as VP*

October 3, 1905
J. B. Treadwell *resigns as Pres*
T. Paterson Ross, Pres

January 22, 1906
G. Bruce, Dir

November 1, 1906
G. Bruce, Dir
Albert Burgren, Dir
John J. McLaughlin, Dir
T. Paterson Ross, Dir
Thomas Ross, Dir

November 17, 1906
Albert Burgren, VP
T. Paterson Ross, Pres, Treas
Thomas Ross, Sec

November 1, 1907
G. Bruce, Dir
Albert Burgren, Dir
John. J. McLaughlin, Dir
T. Paterson Ross, Dir
Thomas Ross, Dir

November 15, 1907
Albert Burgren, VP
T. Paterson Ross, Pres, Treas
Thomas Ross, Sec

November 2, 1908
Frank W. Dakin, Dir
Albert Burgren, Dir
John. J. McLaughlin, Dir
T. Paterson Ross, Dir
Thomas Ross, Dir

November 16, 1908
Albert Burgren, VP
T. Paterson Ross, Pres, Treas
Thomas Ross, Sec

November 1, 1909
Frank W. Dakin, Dir
Albert Burgren, Dir
John. J. McLaughlin, Dir
T. Paterson Ross, Dir
Thomas Ross, Dir

December 14, 1909
Albert Burgren, VP
T. Paterson Ross, Pres, Treas
Thomas Ross, Sec

January 27, 1910
Charles O. Morgan, Asst-Sec &
    Asst-Treas

October 13, 1910
Frank W. Dakin, Dir
Albert Burgren, Dir
John. J. McLaughlin, Dir
T. Paterson Ross, Dir
Thomas Ross, Dir

November 21, 1910
Albert Burgren, VP
T. Paterson Ross, Pres, Treas
Thomas Ross, Sec

November 1, 1911
Frank W. Dakin, Dir
Albert Burgren, Dir
John. J. McLaughlin, Dir
T. Paterson Ross, Dir
Thomas Ross, Dir

November 6, 1911
Albert Burgren, VP
T. Paterson Ross, Pres, Treas
Thomas Ross, Sec

November 1, 1912
Frank W. Dakin, Dir
Albert Burgren, Dir
John. J. McLaughlin, Dir
T. Paterson Ross, Dir
Thomas Ross, Dir

November 15, 1912
Albert Burgren, VP
T. Paterson Ross, Pres, Treas
Thomas Ross, Sec

October 3, 1913
Albert Bergen, resigns as Dir

November 1, 1913
Frank W. Dakin, Dir
Albert Burgren, Dir
John. J. McLaughlin, Dir
T. Paterson Ross, Dir
Thomas Ross, Dir

November 14, 1913
Albert Burgren, VP
T. Paterson Ross, Pres, Treas
Thomas Ross, Sec

November 2, 1914
G. S. Backman, Dir
Frank W. Dakin, Dir
John. J. McLaughlin, Dir
T. Paterson Ross, Dir
Thomas Ross, Dir

November 27, 1914
G. S. Backman, VP
Frank W. Dakin, Asst-Sec
T. Paterson Ross, Pres, Treas
Thomas Ross, Sec

November 1, 1915
G. S. Backman, Dir
Frank W. Dakin, Dir
John. J. McLaughlin, Dir
T. Paterson Ross, Dir
Thomas Ross, Dir

November 18, 1915
G. S. Backman, VP
Frank W. Dakin, Asst-Sec
T. Paterson Ross, Pres, Treas
Thomas Ross, Sec

November 1, 1916
G. S. Backman, Dir
Frank W. Dakin, Dir
John. J. McLaughlin, Dir
T. Paterson Ross, Dir
Thomas Ross, Dir

November 13, 1916
G. S. Backman, VP
Frank W. Dakin, Asst-Sec
T. Paterson Ross, Pres, Treas
Thomas Ross, Sec

January 17, 1917
*Special meeting of stockholders to
authorize transfer of all assets to
AS&F.*

Forest Lawn Cemetery Association

February 2, 1906
C. B. Barnes, TTE
William J. Blain, TTE & Sup
J. H. Dewey, TTE
J. J. Lockwood, TTE & Sec
J. Schoder, TTE
W. B. Scott, TTE
J. B. Treadwell, TTE, Pres, &
GM

1907
No election of TTEs or officers

January 11, 1908
William J. Blain, TTE (3 yrs) &
Sup
J. H. Dewey, TTE (2 yrs) & VP
J. J. Lockwood, TTE (2 yrs) &
Sec
J. Schoder, TTE (3 yrs)
W. B. Scott, TTE (3 yrs)
J. George W. Walker, TTE (2 yrs)

January 18, 1908
William J. Blain, Sup
J. H. Dewey, VP
J. J. Lockwood, Sec
J. B. Treadwell, Pres & GM *(listed
as TTE at meetings, but not
shown as elected)*
January 12, 1909
William J. Blain, TTE
J. H. Dewey, TTE
John Llewellyn, TTE, VP
J. J. Lockwood, TTE, Sec
(resigned June 14)
Charles O. Morgan, Sec *(from
May 1)*
J. Schoder, TTE
J. B. Treadwell, TTE, Pres, &
GM
George W. Walker, TTE
W. B. Scott *(resigned as TTE Jan.
12; re-elected TTE June 14)*

January 11, 1910
William J. Blain, TTE *(no mention of Sup position at organization meeting, but Wells authorized to hire a new Sup at the June 28 meeting)*
Charles O. Morgan (TTE, 3 years), Sec & Treas
John Llewellyn, VP
J. B. Treadwell *(resigns as TTE at board meeting)*
George W. Walker (TTE, 3 years)
Norton C. Wells, (TTE, 3 years), Pres

January 11, 1911
John Black, TTE & VP *(resigned Jan. 23)*
George H. Heath, TTE *(resigned Jan. 23)*
Charles O. Morgan, Sec & Treas, GM *(resigned Jan. 23)*
George W. Walker *(resigned Jan. 23)*
Hugh S. Wallace, TTE & Pres *(resigned Jan. 23)*

January 23, 1911
Wilbur J. Filley, TTE
John Llewellyn, TTE & VP
Fred V. Owen, TTE
Louis H. Peters, TTE, Sec, & Treas
William Watson, TTE
Norton C. Wells, TTE, Pres, & GM
Charles O. Winters, TTE

January 11, 1912
Wilbur J. Filley, TTE
Fred V. Owen, TTE
John Llewellyn, TTE & VP
Louis H. Peters, TTE (3 yrs), & Sec
William Watson, TTE
Norton C. Wells, TTE, Pres, & GM
Charles O. Winters., TTE

January 20, 1913
Wilbur J. Filley, TTE (3 yrs)
John Llewellyn, TTE & VP
Fred V. Owen, TTE
Louis H. Peters, TTE (3 yrs), & Sec
William Watson, TTE (3 yrs)
Norton C. Wells, TTE (3 yrs), Pres, & manager
Charles O. Winters., TTE (deceased April 4, 1913)
Glenn M. Ely, TTE *(elected Aug. 16)*

January 20, 1914
Glenn M. Ely, TTE (3 yrs)
Wilbur J. Filley, TTE
John Llewellyn, TTE (3 yrs) & VP
Fred V. Owen, TTE (3 yrs)
Louis H. Peters, TTE & Sec
William Watson, TTE
Norton C. Wells, TTE (3 yrs), Pres, & manager

January 20, 1915
Glenn M. Ely, TTE
Wilbur J. Filley, TTE

John Llewellyn, TTE & VP
Fred V. Owen, TTE
Louis H. Peters, TTE (3 yrs), &
    Sec
William Watson, TTE
Norton C. Wells, TTE, Pres, &
    manager

January 20, 1916
Glenn M. Ely, TTE
Wilbur J. Filley, TTE (3 yrs)
John Llewellyn, TTE & VP
Fred V. Owen, TTE
Louis H. Peters, TTE & Sec
William Watson, TTE (3 yrs)
Norton C. Wells, TTE (3 yrs),
    Pres, & manager

January 20, 1917
Glenn M. Ely, TTE (3 yrs)
Wilbur J. Filley, TTE
John Llewellyn, TTE (3 yrs) &
    VP
Fred V. Owen, TTE (3 yrs)
Louis H. Peters, TTE & Sec
William Watson, TTE
Norton C. Wells, TTE, Pres, &
    manager

January 21, 1918
Glenn M. Ely, TTE
Wilbur J. Filley, TTE
John Llewellyn, TTE & VP
Fred V. Owen, TTE
Louis H. Peters, TTE (3 yrs) &
    Sec
William Watson, TTE
Norton C. Wells, TTE, Pres, &
    manager

January 20, 1919
Glenn M. Ely, TTE (resigned
    June 23)
Motley H. Flint, TTE
M. M. Kauffman, TTE
John Llewellyn, TTE & VP
    (resigned Feb. 14)
Fred V. Owen, TTE & Sec
    *(resigned as TTE June 23;
    resigned as Sec July 3)*
John N. Smalley TTE (elected
    Feb. 15, resigned April 16)
William Watson, TTE
Norton C. Wells, TTE, Pres, &
    manager *(resigned April 16)*

April 16, 1919
Motley H. Flint, Pres

May 12, 1919
H. W. Broughton, TTE
George H. Storer, TTE *(resigned
    June 23)*

May 31, 1919
George H. Storer, VP

July 3, 1919
E. S. Field, TTE
M. M. Kauffman, Sec
E. U. Emory, TTE *(elected July 3,
    but election announced as invalid
    at the January 10, 1920 meeting
    of the TTEs as Emory did not
    own the required 200 square feet
    of cemetery property)*

January 10, 1920
William R. Myers, TTE

T. M. Noble, TTE

January 20, 1920
H. W. Broughton, TTE
E. S. Field, TTE
Motley H. Flint, TTE
M. M. Kauffman, TTE
William R. Myers, TTE
M. Noble, TTE
Watson, William, TTE

February 7, 1920
H. W. Broughton, VP
Motley H. Flint, Pres
M. M. Kauffman, Sec

January 20, 1921
H. W. Broughton, TTE
E. S. Field, TTE
Motley H. Flint, TTE
M. M. Kauffman, TTE
William R. Myers, TTE
M. Noble, TTE
William Watson, TTE

> *Minutes do not exist for an organization meeting of the TTEs following the annual meeting of lot proprietors in 1922. However, subsequent minutes refer to Motley Flint as Pres and M. M. Kauffman as Sec*

January 20, 1922
H. W. Broughton, TTE & VP
H. M. Burgwald, TTE
E. S. Field, TTE
Motley H. Flint, TTE & Pres
M. M. Kauffman, TTE, Sec, & Treas

William R. Myers, TTE
William Watson, TTE

January 20, 1923
H. W. Broughton, TTE & VP
H. M. Burgwald, TTE
E. S. Field, TTE
Motley H. Flint, TTE & Pres
M. M. Kauffman, TTE, Sec, & Treas
William R. Myers, TTE
William Watson, TTE

January 21, 1924
H. W. Broughton, TTE & VP
H. M. Burgwald, TTE
E. S. Field, TTE
Motley H. Flint, TTE & Pres
M. M. Kauffman, TTE, Sec, & Treas
William R. Myers, TTE
William Watson, TTE

January 20, 1925
George H. Bentley, TTE
H. W. Broughton, TTE & Pres
H. M. Burgwald, TTE & VP
E. C. Hauser, TTE
John F. Huber, TTE
John W. Kemp, TTE
M. M. Kauffman, TTE & Sec

Forest Lawn Memorial-Park Association

June 12, 1919
Vernon A. Bettin, Dir & Treas
(resigned Dec. 18, 1919)

R. A. Brest, Sec *(resigned July 14, 1919)*

Alex W. Davis, Dir & Pres *(resigned as Pres Dec. 18, 1919)*

Frank E. Smith, Dir & VP *(resigned July 14, 1919)*

July 14, 1919

Hubert Eaton, GM

R. S. Parish, Dir & Sec *(resigned Nov. 24, 1919)*

December 18, 1919

B. E. Bassford, Sec & Treas

E. C. Hauser, Dir & VP

John W. Kemp, Dir & Pres

September 13, 1920

B. E. Bassford, Dir *(signs waiver as a Dir and is referred to as a Dir but no record of election)*

November 9, 1920

B. E. Bassford *does not sign waiver (or future ones) as a Dir but is present*

1921 & 1922

No election of Dirs/Officers

1923

No minutes in files, but new Dir names show up late in 1924

September 29, 1924

Francis Gordon, Sec

Hubert Eaton, *(referred to as manager)*

E. C. Hauser *(referred to as Dir)*

John F. Huber *(referred to as Dir)*

John W. Kemp *(referred to as Dir)*

1925

No election of Dirs/Officers

1926

AS&F assumes liabilities of FLMPA. A new corporation is formed, Forest Lawn Memorial Park Association, Inc. Hyphen added after incorporation. (See Appendix D. Major Events Timeline).

February 13, 1926

M. W. Brown, Dir

Hubert Eaton, GM

Francis Gordon, Dir, Sec & Treas

John F. Huber, Dir

John W. Kemp, Dir & Pres

Charles W. Partridge, Jr., Dir & VP *(resigned April 29, 1926)*

April 29, 1926

E. C. Hauser, Dir & VP

American Security & Fidelity Co.

November 1916

G. F. Allen, Dir *(resigned Dec. 18, 1916)*

E. J. Doyle, Dir *(resigned Dec. 18, 1916)*

H. M. Harrison, Dir & VP *(resigned Dec. 18, 1916)*

I. J. Lipsohn, Dir & Pres *(resigned after the meeting of Dec. 18, 1916)*

M. A. Pickett, Dir, Sec, & Treas *(resigned after the meeting of Dec. 18, 1916)*

December 18, 1916
R. Hildreth, Dir
M. M. Kauffman, Dir
George E. Pratt, Dir

December 22, 1916
A. R. Hildreth, Pres *(resigned as Dir & Pres April 5, 1917)*
M. M. Kauffman, Treas *(resigned as Treas April 5, 1917)*
George E. Pratt, Sec

April 6, 1917
Hubert Eaton, Dir & Pres
Carroll W. Gates, Dir & Treas
W. I. Hollingsworth, Dir & VP
M. M. Kauffman, Dir
George E. Pratt, Dir & Sec *(resigned Sept. 6, 1917)*

September 7, 1917
K. L. Crowley, Dir
M. M. Kauffman, Sec

February 6, 1918
K. L. Crowley, Dir
Hubert Eaton, Dir
Carroll W. Gates, Dir
W. I. Hollingsworth, Dir
M. M. Kauffman, Dir

February 14, 1918
Hubert Eaton, Pres
Carroll W. Gates, Treas
W. I. Hollingsworth, VP
M. M. Kauffman, Sec *(resigned Jan. 15, 1919)*

February 5, 1919
E. G. Carter, Dir
K. L. Crowley, Dir *(resigned Mar. 21, 1919)*
Hubert Eaton, Dir
Carroll W. Gates, Dir
W. I. Hollingsworth, Dir

February 12, 1919
E. G. Carter, Sec
Hubert Eaton, Pres
Carroll W. Gates, Treas
W. I. Hollingsworth, VP

February 4, 1920
E. G. Carter, Dir
Hubert Eaton, Dir
Carroll W. Gates, Dir *(passed away Oct. 15, 1920)*
Frances F. Hager, Dir
W. I. Hollingsworth, Dir

February 6, 1920
E. G. Carter, Sec
Hubert Eaton, Pres
Carroll W. Gates, Treas *(passed away Oct. 15, 1920)*
W. I. Hollingsworth, VP

January 14, 1921
Erasmus Wilson, Dir

February 2, 1921

E. G. Carter, Dir
Hubert Eaton, Dir
Frances F. Hager, Dir
W. I. Hollingsworth, Dir
Erasmus Wilson, Dir

February 10, 1921

E. G. Carter, Sec
Hubert Eaton, Pres
W. I. Hollingsworth, VP
Erasmus Wilson, Treas

February 1, 1922

E. G. Carter, Dir
Hubert Eaton, Dir
France F. Hager, Dir *(resigned June 10, 1922)*
W. I. Hollingsworth, Dir
Erasmus Wilson, Dir

February 10, 1922

E. G. Carter, Sec
Hubert Eaton, Pres
W. I. Hollingsworth, VP
Erasmus Wilson, Treas

August 11, 1922

Catherine E. Schwartz, Dir

February 7, 1923

E. G. Carter, Dir
Hubert Eaton, Dir
W. I. Hollingsworth, Dir
Catherine E. Schwartz, Dir
   (resigned May 1, 1923)

Erasmus Wilson, Dir

February 9, 1923

E. G. Carter, Sec
Hubert Eaton, Pres & GM
W. I. Hollingsworth, VP
Erasmus Wilson, Treas

May 11, 1923

Francis Gordon, Dir

February 6, 1924

E. G. Carter, Dir
Hubert Eaton, Dir
W. I. Hollingsworth, Dir
Roy R. Munger, Dir
Erasmus Wilson, Dir

February 15, 1924

E. G. Carter, Sec
Hubert Eaton, Pres & GM
W. I. Hollingsworth, VP
Erasmus Wilson, Treas

February 4, 1925

E. G. Carter, Dir
Hubert Eaton, Dir
W. I. Hollingsworth, Dir
Roy R. Munger, Dir
Erasmus Wilson, Dir

February 14, 1925

E. G. Carter, Sec
Hubert Eaton, Pres & GM
W. I. Hollingsworth, VP
Erasmus Wilson, Treas

February 3, 1926

E. G. Carter, Dir
Hubert Eaton, Dir
W. I. Hollingsworth, Dir
Roy R. Munger, Dir
Erasmus Wilson, Dir

February 12, 1926

E. G. Carter, Sec
Hubert Eaton, Pres & GM
W. I. Hollingworth, VP
Roy R. Munger, Treas

Notes

Abbreviations

AS&F	American Security & Fidelity Co.
FLCA	Forest Lawn Cemetery Association
FLInc	Forest Lawn Memorial Park Association, Inc.
FLMPA	Forest Lawn Memorial Park Association
Pop Ross	Thomas Ross
TL&I	Tropico Land & Improvement Co.
Tom Ross	T. Paterson Ross

Introduction

1. Kevin Starr, *The Dream Endures: California during the 1940s*, 199.

Principal People and Organizations

1. The dates do not include re-incorporations from one state to another or other forms of change driven by decisions on taxing, corporate law, or regulations.

Chapter 1. Beginnings

1. Los Angeles Tourism & Convention Board, "Historical Timeline of Los Angeles. September 4, 2013, accessed March 13, 2014. http://www.discoverlosangeles.com/blog/historical-timeline-los-angeles."; Benjamin Hale, "The History of the Hollywood Movie Industry," History Cooperative, November 12, 2014, accessed August 4, 2017. http://historycooperative.org/the-history-of-the-hollywood-movie-industry/); Nathan Masters, "A Brief History of Palm Trees in Southern California," *KCET*, December 7, 2011, https://kcet.org/shows/lost-la/a-brief-hirosty-of-palm-trees-in-southern-cali-

fornia. Palm trees are not native to the Los Angeles basin; native palm trees were found many miles to the east in the Palm Springs desert area.

2. Los Angeles Tourism & Convention Board, "Historical Timeline of Los Angeles."

3. Greek for "put to sleep," *koiman*; Greek for "dormitory," *koimētērion*; late Latin coemētērium.

4. David Charles Sloane, *The Last Great Necessity* (Baltimore: Johns Hopkins Press, 1995), 1–2.

5. Jon Brooks, "Why Are There So many Dead People in Colma? And so Few in San Francisco?" KQED, December 15, 2015. https://ww2.kqed.org/news/2015/12/16/why-are-so-many-dead-people-in-colma-and-so-few-in-san-francisco/. Colma was incorporated as a city for cemeteries after San Francisco banned new burials in 1901. Over the next three decades, most of the burials in San Francisco were moved to Colma.

6. Edwin Carpenter, n.d. Southern California Genealogical Society and Family Research Library, accessed September 12, 2012. www.scgsgenealogy.com/LACC-Title.htm. By 1947 all remains had been moved to other cemeteries.

7. "Editorial," *Los Angeles Star*, December 6, 1862, accessed September 14, 2012. http://digarc.usc.edu.

8. Carpenter, "Southern California Genealogical Society."

9. "Historic Cemeteries of Los Angeles," University of Southern California, accessed September 16, 2005. http://www.usc.edu/archives/la/cemeries;. A partial listing; dates retrieved from this source unless otherwise noted; Los Angeles County Cemeteries (lists 87 cemeteries in the Los Angeles area, many of which are inactive); Cecilia Rasmussen, "Curbside L.A. Pioneer Cemeteries: These old resting places have a natural ambiance often missing in modern manicured parks." *Los Angeles Times*, November 21, 1994, B3; Map by A. L. George, c. 1900. Approximate cemetery locations added.

10. Between 1902 and 1910, the remains of all those buried at B'nai B'rith Cemetery were moved to the new Home of Peace Cemetery. B'nai B'rith Cemetery was located in Chavez Ravine and had its first burial in 1858.

11. Sue Silver, "Historic California Cemetery Laws, 1872 Codified Statutes of California, Political Code, Chapter V., Cemeteries and Sepulture." (accessed October 3, 2007). http://www.usgennet.org/usa/ca/county/eldorado/1854_statute.htm.

12. Silver, "Historic California Cemetery Laws."

13. Silver, "Historic California Cemetery Laws."

14. Howard Evarts Weed, *Modern Park Cemeteries* (Chicago: R. J. Haight, 1912) 17–18.

15. "Kinship Fraud Charged," *Los Angeles Times*, June 16, 1931, A18. T. Paterson Ross's first wife was Lillian Bishop Ross, daughter of J. B.

Treadwell. Lillian's sister Florence Treadwell Boynton claimed that Lillian was not J. B. Treadwell's daughter. Eventually Lillian was named executrix, disproving Florence's claim that Treadwell had become infatuated with Lillian and falsely represented Lillian as his daughter.

16. David Parry, "Architects' Profiles: Pacific Heights Architects #24 – T. P. Ross," (n.d.) Accessed August 8, 2005. http://www.classicsfproperties.com/Architecture/TP_Ross.htm

17. "Witness For Railroad In Awkward Fix," San Francisco Call, July 11, 1912:20; "Death Overtakes Celebrated Worker: Treadwell, of Mining Fame, Dies," Los Angeles Times, November 6, 1931, A15; and "Kinship Fraud Charged in Contest of Will," Los Angeles Times, June 16, 1931, A18.

18 "John Treadwell Mining Man, Dead," Arizona Daily Star, November 6, 1931, 1.

19. Tropico Land & Improvement Co. (a Corporation), Appellant, v. Lucie M. Lambourn, Executrix of the Last Will and Testament of Susan Glassell Mitchell, Deceased, Respondent. 1912. 170 Cal. 33, 148 Pac 206 (Transcript on Appeal). Treadwell would later claim that the idea to start a cemetery was entirely his own.

20. Juliet Arroyo, Images of America: Early Glendale (Chicago: Arcadia Publishing, 2005); and Nathan Masters, "The Lost City of Tropico, California" (June 16, 2004) Accessed October 8, 2014. http://www.kcet.org/updaily/socal_focus/history/la-as-subject/the-lost-city-of-tropico.html.

21. Arroyo, 9-10; Kevin Starr, California: A history (New York, NY: Modern Library, 2007) 104; Historic Resources Group, "Historic Resource Survey Report for the Cumberland Heights Neighborhood." (Glendale: City of Glendale Planning Division, Revised December 2004), 8; Tropico Land & Improvement Co. v. Lucie M. Lambourn, 80; and Security Trust & Savings Bank, 16-17.

22. Deed from the Los Angeles County Recorder's Office, page 227, Book of Deeds #76. Typed copy. Deed witnessed by Susan's brother, Hugh, A. Glassell, Jr., and George S. Patton, Sr. (father of general George S. Patton, Jr.).

23. Tropico v. Lambourn, 31, 35, 78-80.

24. "Gambler Loses His Child and Fortune, Custody of Beautiful Lucile Bedford Goes to Aunt," Weekly Arizona Journal-Miner, August 18, 1908, 1, accessed August 25, 2013. http://adnp.azlibrary.gov/cdm/ref/collection/sn85032920/id/1217.

25. "Gambler Loses His Child and Fortune, Custody of Beautiful Lucile Bedford Goes to Aunt."

26 Tropico v. Lambourn, 10–11, 17, 31, 79–80, 82. J. B. Treadwell testified that Hugh Glassell told him in 1905 the "daughters would convey" their interest to their mother. However, the transcript says Lucie M. Lambourn executed the deed to her mother on April 15, 1901, years before the Treadwell

purchase. The Andrew Glassell deed said it "gives and conveys the property
. . . to her for and during her natural life remainder to the issue of her body
living at the time of her decease, forever."

27. Acreage calculated from March 1911 map prepared by Civil Engineer
William C. Wattles, net of railroad right-of-way.

28. Tropico v. Lambourn, 80; Articles of Incorporation of TL&I, filed
August 28, 1905, with the Office of the Territorial Auditor, Territory of
Arizona. Transcribed copy; TL&I, Board of Directors Meeting Minutes,
August 28, 1906, July 1 and 12, 1907; and Treadwell letter to Pop Ross,
June 28, 1906. File copy with March 15, 1919, affidavit of J. B. Treadwell
attached. All the papers and books of TL&I were destroyed in the earthquake and subsequent fire in San Francisco in April 1906. With some help
from Treadwell, Pop Ross could reconstruct the minutes "from memoranda
and from memory" to submit them for approval by the TL&I board of directors. Shareholder records were among the lost papers, so new stock certificates
were printed and the original certificates were transferred or exchanged for
new ones. Shareholder certificates lost in the fire were replaced in accordance
with provisions of California law.

29. TL&I, Board of Directors Meeting Minutes, September 18, 1905;
Notarized, handwritten copy of recorded deed of property from Treadwell
to TL&I dated October 14, 1905. The minutes include a transcription of
Treadwell's proposal which indicates the parcel is 120 acres. A recalcula-
tion of the area from the deed description yielded an area of 131.2 acres;
and Tropico v. Lambourn, 89. Parcel described as 129.3 acres. Today most
common stock has a nominal par value, or even none; if that had been the
case in this transaction, the value of the property would not have been
so inflated.

30. TL&I, Board of Directors Meeting Minutes, September 18, 1905.

31. TL&I, Board of Directors Meeting Minutes, October 2, 1905.

32. Deed dated December 8, 1905, file copy with notation of recording
in "Book 2534 Page 22 of Deeds, Los Angeles CO. Records;" Deed dated
December 15, 1905, file copy with notation of recording February 12, 1906
in "Book 2524 pages 132 Los Angeles Co Records." The land purchased from
Susan Mitchell was referenced as 135 acres, an amount substantially less than
Treadwell's total purchase and slightly more than he sold to TL&I.

33. Forest Lawn Cemetery in Buffalo, New York, was founded in the
mid-1800s and has no relationship to Los Angeles's Forest Lawn. Across the
United States there are more than twenty unrelated cemeteries with "Forest
Lawn" in their names.

Chapter 2. Setting Up Operations

1. Certificate of Articles of Incorporation of the FLCA, January 11, 1906;
March 12, 1907 "certification of being" filed with the Superior Court.

2. FLCA, Board of Trustees Meeting Minutes, February 2, 1906.

3. Agreement between TL&I and FLCA dated January 22, 1906, and February 2, 1906, representing the dates each of the corporation's officers actually signed the agreement.

4. FLCA, Board of Trustees Meeting Minutes, February 2, 1906.

5. FLCA, "Rules of the Forest Lawn Cemetery," February 2, 1906.

6. Silver, Historic California Cemetery Laws.

7. FLCA, Board of Trustees Meeting Minutes, February 2, 1906.

8. California no longer allows the use of "perpetual care fund." In the 1930s, the term "endowment care fund" was adopted.

9. TL&I, Board of Directors Meeting Minutes, January 22, 1906.

10. Mortgage note dated November 17, 1906, signed by Tom Ross, president, and Pop Ross, secretary of TL&I; TL&I Board of Directors Meeting Minutes, November 17, 1906.

11. Copy of Unlimited Certificate No. 127,502, of the Title Guarantee and Trust Company, Los Angeles, Calif., December 4, 1906.

12. "Funeral of W. J. Blain: Body of landscape engineer to be sent east for burial," *Los Angeles Examiner*, July 10, 1910.

13. Treadwell to Tom Ross, December 28, 1907. Handwritten; and Samuel H. Williamson, "Annualized Growth Rate of Various Historical Economic Series.\m" n.d., accessed April 2, 2017. https://www.measuring-worth.com/. Calculated using a contemporary standard of living escalator for the project. Other methods of determining the current value yield results from $48,700 to $1,530,000..

14. Lockwood to "Gentlemen," October 23, 1907. Signed promotional letter.

15. Lockwood to Pop Ross, November 19, 1907; "Statement of Receipts & Disbursements of the FLCA from January 11th, 1906 to April 18, 1907 Inclusive;" Forest Lawn Salesman's Kit, "Cemetery Facts," c. 1932 gives August 26, 1906, as the date of the sale of the first plot; and "Graves Pollute City's Water," *Los Angeles Herald*, February 11, 1906. Reported that "seven or eight bodies have been interred in [Forest Lawn]."

16. C. V. Rowe, Report, October 23, 1906. Rowe's report lists this as a mortgage to J. B. Treadwell, but the November 17, 1906, TL&I Minutes clearly state that the Souden mortgage replaced the Susan Mitchell mortgage; "Statements of Receipts & Disbursements of the Forest Lawn Cemetery Association from January 11th, 1906, to November 5th, 1906 Inclusive."

Chapter 3. Financial Challenges

1. Michael B. Sauter, Douglas A. McIntyre, and Charles B. Stockdale, "The 13 Worst Recessions, Depressions, and Panics In American History," Panic of 1907 (24/7 Wall St., September 9 2010)

Accessed October 1, 2015. http://247wallst.com/investing/2010/09/09/
the-13-worst-recessions-depressions-and-panics-in-american-history/3/

2. Treadwell to T. P. Ross, January 4, 1908. Handwritten.

3. Treadwell to Tom Ross, January 4, 1908. Handwritten; and J. J.
Lockwood to T. Paterson Ross, February 5, 1908.

4. Treadwell to Tom Ross, March 20, 190. Handwritten; and Lockwood
to Pop Ross, March 20, 1908.

5. Treadwell to Tom Ross, undated. Handwritten note on typed schedule
of Inglewood Park Cemetery's incorporation finances; and Treadwell to Tom
Ross, June 30, 1908. Handwritten.

6. Treadwell to Tom Ross, April 24, 1908. Handwritten; Treadwell to
Tom Ross, May 16, 1908. Handwritten. Inglewood apparently had a few
more interments than Forest Lawn, but these were from outside the City of
Los Angeles.

7. "An Agreement to Discontinue Burials and Cremations Sunday."
Undated printed document; Gnerre. Inglewood Cemetery did not become a
part of the City of Inglewood until 1959.

8. Lockwood to Pop Ross, May 25, 1908.

9. Treadwell to Tom Ross, May 16, 1908. Handwritten.

10. Treadwell to Pop Ross, June 30, 1908. Handwritten.

11. Lockwood to Pop Ross, July 25, 1908.

12. Paige & Thorburn to Lockwood, May 7, 1908. Handwritten on Paige
& Thorburn letterhead; Treadwell to Paige & Thorburn, May 13, 1908.
Carbon copy; and Silver, Historic California Cemetery Laws. It is not clear
where Treadwell's 50 percent for development came from. California's 1859
Rural Cemetery Act called for 60 percent of sales proceeds to be used for
repayment of bonds issued to buy cemetery property. The balance was to be
used for operations and development.

13. Lockwood to Treadwell, August 31, 1908; Pop Ross to J. J. Lanigan,
September 2, 1908. Handwritten; and Lockwood to Pop Ross, September 3,
1908. Carbon copy

14. Lockwood to Pop Ross, September 3, 1908. Carbon copy

15. Treadwell to Tom Ross, February 12, 1908. Handwritten.

16. Lockwood to Pop Ross, December 8, 1908.

17. Lockwood to Pop Ross, October 7, 1908.

18. Treadwell to Lockwood October 8, 1908. Handwritten on Ruth
Pierce Mining Company letterhead.

19. Lockwood to Pop Ross, November 3, 1908.

20. Lockwood to Pop Ross, November 9, 1908.

21. Lockwood to Pop Ross, November 9, 1908.

22. Lockwood to Pop Ross, November 11, 1908.

23. Lockwood to Pop Ross, October 2, 1907. Carbon copy,
initialed "J.J.L."

24. Pop Ross to Treadwell, October 8, 1907. Handwritten.

25. Blain to Tom Ross, July 30, 1908. Handwritten. Most states now prohibit kickbacks, finder's fees, and commissions to funeral homes for referring business to cemeteries.

26. Lockwood to Pop Ross, December 31, 1908.

27. Lockwood to Pop Ross, February 3, 1909; and Pop Ross to Lockwood, January 27, 1909.

28. Pop Ross to Lockwood, March 12, 1909. Carbon copy.

29. Lockwood to Pop Ross, March 17, 1909. Signed copy.

30. Pop Ross letter to Lockwood, April 3, 1909. Signed carbon copy.

31. J. B. Treadwell v. AS&F, Reporter's Transcript on Appeal, 132–133.

32. Pop Ross to Treadwell, April 27, 1909. Signed file copy; pencil note on letter says, "Tropico will pay Rowe's bill"; and Treadwell to Pop Ross, telegram, undated.

33. FLCA, Board of Trustees Meeting Minutes, June 14, 1909.

34. Oscar T. Shuck, History of the Bench and Bar of California, 900–901; "Supervisors Reappoint City Justices of Peace," Los Angeles Herald, March 19, 1901, 6; "The Herald on Morrison," Los Angeles Times, November 3, 1898, 8; "C. O. Morgan For City Justice," Los Angeles Herald, October 29, 1898, 6; and "Convention of Republicans: Prohibitionists Convene," Los Angeles Times, August 14, 1914, 12.

35. Rowe to Morgan, May 11, 1909.

36. Rowe to Morgan, May 15, 1909; Morgan to Rowe, May 21, 1909. Carbon copy; Morgan to Row, May 22, 1909. Carbon copy; and Rowe to Morgan, May 24, 1909.

37. Morgan to TL&I, June 2, 1909; Pop Ross on behalf of Tom Ross to Treadwell, June 3, 1909.

38. FLCA, Board of Trustees Meeting Minutes, June 14, 1909.

39. Pop Ross to Morgan, July 27, 1909; Morgan, to T. Rodd, July 29, 1909.

40. FLCA, Board of Trustees Meeting Minutes, November 30, 1909.

41. FLCA, Board of Trustees Meeting Minutes, November 30, 1909; and William B. Thomas to AS&F, March 24, 1919.

42. Wells to Pop Ross, August 15, 1910. Handwritten.

43. FLCA (probably Morgan) to Mrs. Bessie A. Hannon, October 19, 1910. Carbon copy.

44. Heath to Tom Ross, April 2, 1909. Handwritten.

45. Heath to Tom Ross, April 7, 1909. Handwritten.

46. Heath to Tom Ross, May 6, 1909. Handwritten.

47. Heath to Tom Ross, June 9, 1909. Handwritten.

48. Heath to Tom Ross, May 6, 1909. Handwritten.

49. Morgan to Tom Ross, September 14, 1909.

50. Tom Ross to Heath, September 15, 1909. Initialed carbon copy.

51. E. W. Kelly to Tom Ross, September 27, 1909.

52. Heath to Tom Ross, September 27, 1909.

53. Tom Ross to Morgan, October 4, 1909.

54. Pop Ross to Heath, October 13, 1909. Signed carbon copy.

55. Heath to Tom Ross, August 5, 1909. Handwritten.

56. Blain to Tom Ross, August 28, 1909. Handwritten.

57. Michael Hannon, "McNamara Bombing Case (1911)," University of Minnesota Law Library, n.d. accessed September 29, 2015 darrow.law.umn.edu/trialpdfs/McNamara_LA_Times_Bombing.pdf 10–11.

58. Michael Hannon, "McNamara Bombing Case 1911," University of Minnesota Law Library. n.d.) Accessed September 29, 2015.; and Leon F. Scully, Jr., *Bombers, Bolsheviks and Bootleggers: A Study in Constitutional Subversion*, Publius Books, June 2001.

59. Treadwell to Tom Ross, October 21, 1908. Handwritten on Union Hardware & Metal Co. (Los Angeles) letterhead.

60. Treadwell to Pop Ross, November 5, 1908. Handwritten; and Treadwell to Reese Llewellyn, November 5, 1908.

61. Treadwell to Pop Ross, November 5, 1908. Handwritten; and Treadwell to Reese Llewellyn, November 5, 1908.

62. R. G. Dun & Co. report on Rosedale Cemetery Association, October 27, 1908. R. G. Dun reporting was a predecessor of Dun & Bradstreet reporting. During the years FLCA was involved with TL&I or its successors, the reports frequently failed to correctly explain that relationship and made the same mistake of confusing the two independent organizations; and Treadwell to Reese Llewellyn, November 5, 1908.

63. Treadwell to Tom Ross, October 21, 1908. Handwritten on Union Hardware & Metal Co. (Los Angeles) letterhead.

64. Treadwell to Tom Ross, October 21, 1908. Handwritten on Union Hardware & Metal Co. (Los Angeles) letterhead.

65 *Press Reference Library* (Los Angeles: Los Angeles Examiner, 1912), 475.

66. "Memorandum of Agreement," unsigned file copy. The draft called for John Llewellyn to receive 5,750 shares over a nine-month period—penciled amounts next to crossed out larger typewritten amounts. The penciled notation also suggests that John Llewellyn would be given an additional 1,000 shares after one year of service as vice president of FLCA

67. Blain to Pop Ross, February 17, 1909. Handwritten.

68. Treadwell to Tom Ross, October 21, 1908. Handwritten on Union Hardware & Metal Co. (Los Angeles) letterhead.

69. Pop Ross to John Llewellyn, April 28, 1909. Carbon copy.

70. Blain to Tom Ross, August 28, 1909. Handwritten.

71. FLCA, Bylaws, 1906; and Wells to Pop Ross, April 11, 1910. Handwritten. Articles related to John Llewellyn's death, funeral, and estate do not mention a wife, living or deceased.

Chapter 4. Trouble for Treadwell

1. "Summerland Oil Men Up in Arms," *San Francisco Call*, August 12, 1898; and Neal Graffy, "Neal Summerland Oil Fields in the Sea," May 21, 1911, accessed April 10, 2017. https://www.edhat.com/site/tidbit.cfm?nid=55984.

2. "Witness for Railroad in Awkward Fix," *San Francisco Call*, July 11, 1912, 20.

3. "New Richmond in Cemetery Field," *San Bernardiino Daily Sun*, March 9, 1906, 3; "Cemetery Fight May Be Bitter," *Los Angeles Times (San Bernardino)*, March 10, 1906; and "To Start Cemetery," *Los Angeles Times*, March 16, 1906, 44.

4. Lockwood to Pop Ross, October 2, 1907. Carbon copy, initialed "J.J.L."

5. Treadwell to Tom Ross, December 28, 1907. Handwritten.

6. Ross v. American Security & Fidelity Co, 123 Cal. App. 175 (1932); E. G. Carter to Eaton, December 31, 1928, as quoted in court record; and Whitney, Glenn E., "Memorandum on Conversation with TR 8:10 P M to 8:50 P M Tuesday January 3, 1929."

7. J. B. Treadwell v. AS&F, 85–87; Ross v. American Security; and E. G. Carter to J. B. Treadwell, January 7, 1929. As quoted in court record; and Belle Ross telegram to Eaton, October 28, 1929. The expert could tell the word "dollars" was added because ink flowed along the fold.

8. Ross v. American Security & Fidelity Company, 123 Cal. App. 175 (3rd Dist. 1932); and "Death Overtakes Celebrated Worker," *Los Angeles Times*, 1931.

9. Treadwell to Pop Ross, February 16, 1907. Handwritten.

10. Treadwell to Tom Ross, September 28, 1908. Handwritten.

11. Treadwell to Tom Ross, September 26, 1908. Handwritten.

12. Treadwell to Tom Ross, September 30, 1908. Handwritten.

13. Treadwell to Lockwood, September 6, 1908. Handwritten on Magnet Gold Mining & Milling Co. letterhead, but according to an October 7, 1908, letter from Lockwood to Treadwell, the letter was misdated and the correct month was October. Lockwood commented "Yours of Oct.5th (dated Sept, we always knew you were slow but did not think you were amonth [*sic*] behind . . .)"

14. Lockwood to Treadwell (in San Francisco), October 7, 1908. Carbon copy.

15. Treadwell to Lockwood October 8, 1908. Handwritten on Ruth Pierce Mining Company letterhead.

16. Lockwood to Treadwell (in San Francisco), November 21, 1908.

17. Treadwell to Tom Ross, November 24, 1908.

18. Treadwell to Tom Ross, November 28, 1908. Handwritten.

19. Blain to Tom Ross, November 28, 1908. Handwritten.

20. Treadwell to Pop Ross, May 4, 1909. Handwritten.

21. Treadwell to Pop Ross, May 7, 1909. Handwritten.

22. Heath to Tom Ross, June 9, 1909. Handwritten.

23. Tom Ross to J. Llewellyn, June 12, 1909. Carbon copy, initialed "R."

24. Treadwell to Pop Ross, May 13, 1909. Handwritten.

25. Heath to Tom Ross, May 17, 1909. Handwritten.

26. Heath to Tom Ross, May 19, 1909. Handwritten

27. Heath to Tom Ross, May 20, 1909. Handwritten.

28. US Federal Census, 1920; US WWI Draft Registration; and Wells's Death Certificate.

29. Blain to Tom Ross, August 28, 1909. Handwritten.

30. Morgan to Pop Ross, September 7, 1909.

31. Treadwell to Pop Ross, October 13, 1909. Handwritten.

32. Treadwell to Pop Ross, December 13, 1909. Handwritten; and Pop Ross to Treadwell, December 14, 1909. Carbon copy.

33. Treadwell to R. Ross, December 14, 1909. Handwritten

34. Treadwell to R. Ross, December 14, 1909. Handwritten

35. Pop Ross to Blain, December 14, 1909. Signed carbon copy.

36. Blain to Pop Ross, December 14, 1909. Handwritten. Posted on December18 per Pop Ross. Treadwell apparently discussed it with Blain on December 17.

37. Tom Ross to W. J. Blain, December 21, 1909. Carbon copy, not signed or author noted, but reference to "myself and my father" indicates Tom Ross was be the author; and Treadwell to Pop Ross, December 17, 1909. Handwritten.

38. Tom Ross to Blain, December 21, 1909. Carbon copy.

39. FLCA, Lot Proprietors Meeting Minutes, January 11, 1910.

40. FLCA, Board of Trustees Meeting Minutes, January 11, 1910.

41. Pop Ross to W. J. Blain, December 14, 1909. Signed file copy;

Chapter 5. Billy Takes the Cure

1. FLCA, Board of Trustees Meeting Minutes, June 27, 1910. Adjourned to June 28, 1910, for lack of a quorum.

2. Wells to Pop Ross, June 29, 1910. Handwritten on Palace Hotel & Apartments letterhead.

3. Wells to Pop Ross, July 6, 1910. Handwritten·

4. Wells telegram to Rosses, July 7, 1910.

5. Wells to Tom Ross, July 7, 1910. Handwritten.

6. Wells to Los Angeles News, July 13, 1910. Carbon copy, included obituary of W. J. Blain.

7. Wells to Pop Ross, July 10, 1910. Handwritten.

8. Wells to Pop Ross, July 10, 1910. Handwritten.

9. Pop Ross to Wells, July 11, 1910. Signed carbon copy.

10. Pop Ross to Wells, August 9, 1910. Signed carbon copy; Mrs. Eva M. Blain to Wells, July 31, 1910. Handwritten; and Wells to Pop Ross, August 6, 1910.

11. Wells to Mrs. Eva M. Blain August 15, 1910. Carbon copy initialed by Wells.

12. Mrs. Eva M. Blain to Norton Wells, August 19, 1910. Handwritten; Wells to Pop Ross, August 24, 1910. Handwritten; and Pop Ross to Wells, August 27, 1910. Signed carbon copy.

13. "W. J. Blain Estate in Court," *Los Angeles Herald*, September 20, 1910; and File note headed "BLAIN MATTER" that is apparently a quote from the actual court filing.

14. "W. J. Blain Estate in Court," *Los Angeles Herald;* File note headed "BLAIN MATTER"; and Treadwell to Pop Ross, September 25, 1910. Handwritten.

15. Wells to Pop Ross, November 30, 1910. Handwritten; and Pop Ross to Wells, December 3, 1910. Signed carbon copy.

16. Treadwell to Pop Ross, December 20, 1910. Handwritten; and Wells to Pop Ross, December 22, 1910. Handwritten.

17. Thornton to Wells, March 2, 1914.

18. Pop Ross to Thomas C. Thornton, March 9, 1914. Carbon copy

Chapter 6. Attempted Coup

1. Pop Ross to Morgan, February 4, 1910. Signed carbon copy; Morgan to TL&I February 7, 1910; and Pop Ross to Morgan, undated, but from Morgan's reply is February 10, 1910. Carbon copy.

2. Pop Ross to Morgan, undated, but from Morgan's reply is February 10, 1910. Carbon copy.

3. Charles O. Morgan to TL&I, December 5, 1910; Pop Ross to Morgan, December 7, 1910. Signed carbon copy; and Wells to Pop Ross, December 30, 1910. Handwritten.

4. Wells to Pop Ross, December 30, 1910. Handwritten.

5. Pop Ross to Morgan, December 19, 1910. Signed carbon copy.

6 Charles O. Morgan to TL&I, January 5, 1911. Carbon copy; and Samuel H. Williamson, "Annualized Growth Rate of Various Historical Economic Series." The present day value is based upon the consumer price index. Other measures of current value range from $249,000 to $6,980,000

7. Pop Ross to Morgan, January 7, 1911.

8. FLCA, Lot Proprietors Meeting Minutes, January 11, 1911.

9. FLCA, Lot Proprietors Meeting Minutes, January 11, 1911.

10. FLCA, Lot Proprietors Meeting Minutes, January 11, 1911.

11. FLCA, Lot Proprietors Meeting Minutes, January 11, 1911.

12. FLCA, Lot Proprietors Meeting Minutes, January 11, 1911.

13. FLCA, Lot Proprietors Meeting Minutes, January 11, 1911.

14. Charles O. Morgan, to M. Glora, January 11, 1911. Carbon copy.

15. Charles O. Morgan to TL&I, January 14, 1911. Carbon copy; and Charles O. Morgan to Los Angeles Chamber of Commerce, January 18, 1911. Carbon copy.

16. FLCA, Board of Trustees Meeting Minutes, January 23, 1911.

17. FLCA, Board of Trustees Meeting Minutes, January 23, 1911.

18. Wells to United States National Bank, January 24, 1911. Carbon copy; and Wells to Los Angeles Chamber of Commerce, January 25, 1911. Carbon copy.

19. Pop Ross to Morgan, January 28, 1911. Carbon copy on Forest Lawn letterhead initialed "TR" in pencil.

20. Peters to Heath, January 28, 1911. Carbon copy.

21. Wells to Morgan, April 8, 1912. Initialed carbon copy; and Wells to Morgan, April 24, 1912. Initialed carbon copy.

22. Wells to Morgan, April 24, 1912. Initialed carbon copy.

Chapter 7. The Partition Suit

1. Tropico v. Lambourn, 11-12, 31, 35, 78–80. Treadwell later testified that he was told by Leslie Brand and Hugh Glassell that the two daughters were the only heirs. The court record disclosed that Lucie Lambourn and Eileen Mitchell had actually deeded their interests to their mother in 1901, not at the time of Treadwell's 1905 land purchase.

2. "Gambler Loses His Child," *Weekly Arizona Journal–Miner*; "Eileen Mitchell Bedford (1882–1907)," *Weekly Arizona Journal–Miner*, n.d. accessed August 30, 2012; and Tropico v. Lambourn, 65.

3. Tropico v. Lambourn, 5, 17, 31; and Estate of Susan Glassell Mitchell, Deceased, 12,308 (Supreme Court of California, 160 Cal. 618; 117 P. 774 August 30, 1911).

4. "Eileen Mitchell Bedford," *Weekly Arizona Journal–Miner*; "Long Fight for Child of Suicide Is Won by Aunt," *Los Angeles Herald*, August 15, 1908; "Father Fights Aunt For Guardianship," *Los Angeles Herald*, July 17, 1908; and "Cut Off By Will, Girl Gets Riches," *Los Angeles Herald* August 30, 1911, 13.

5. Tropico v. Lambourn, 17, 79–80, 82.

6. TL&I, Board of Directors Meeting Minutes, July 12, 1910; Los Angeles Trust & Savings Bank v. J. B. Treadwell, et al 1910; and Tropico v. Lambourn, 17, 18, 129.

7. Tropico v. Lambourn, 19, 25; and Minutes of TL&I board of directors meeting July 12, 1910.

8. Tropico v. Lambourn, 18.

9. Wells to Pop Ross, August 24, 1910. Handwritten; Wells to Pop Ross, August 29, 1910. Handwritten; and Pop Ross to Wells, August 27, 1910. Signed carbon copy.

10. Tropico v. Lambourn, 20.

11. Tropico v. Lambourn, 62.

12. Pop Ross to Wells, February 4, 1911.

13. Pop Ross to Wells, February 4, 1911.

14. FLCA, Board of Trustees Meeting Minutes, March 13, 1911. Thornton represented Eva Blain in her conflict with FLCA and TL&I.

15. Wells to Pop Ross, February 27, 1911.

16. Wells to Pop Ross, March 2, 1911.

17. Pop Ross to Thornton, March 18, 1911.

18. Wells to Pop Ross, February 1, 1911; and Tropico v. Lambourn, 49-51.

19. Wells to Pop Ross, February 1, 1911.

20. Wells to Pop Ross, March 18, 1911.

21. Pop Ross to Wells, March 21, 1911.

22. Pop Ross to Wells, March 21, 1911.

23. Thornton to TL&I, March 30, 1911.

24. Pop Ross to Thornton, March 31, 1911.

25. Pop Ross to Thornton, April 22, 1911.

26. Wells to Pop Ross, March 14, 1911.

27. Thornton to Tom Ross, April 3, 1911.

28. Wells to Pop Ross, March 23, 1911; Pop Ross to Thornton, March 31, 1911.

29. Pop Ross to Wells, March 27, 1911.

30. Thornton to Tom Ross, April 3, 1911.

31. Pop Ross to Thornton, April 22, 1911.

32. Thornton to Tom Ross, April 24, 1911.

33. Thornton to Tom Ross, April 24, 1911.

34. Thornton to Pop Ross, May 20, 1911.

35. Thornton to Pop Ross, May 20, 1911.

36. Thornton to Pop Ross, December 27, 1911.

37. Pop Ross to Thornton, June 2, 1911.

38. Thornton to Pop Ross, December 27, 1911, and January 3, 1912.

39. Thornton to Pop Ross, January 3, 1912.

40. Pop Ross to Thornton, January 5, 1912. Signed file copy.

41. Thornton to Tom Ross, January 24, 1912.

42. Pop Ross to Max Loewenthal, March 20, 1912. Signed carbon copy. Some documents spell the attorney's name as "Lowenthal," but the printed documents related to the California Supreme Court Appeal spell it as "Loewenthal, Max"," for consistency all references use the latter spelling; and Wells to Pop Ross, March 22, 1912.

43. Pop Ross to Thornton, January 22, 1912. Signed carbon copy; Thornton to Tom Ross, January 24, 1912; and Wells to Pop Ross, March 22, 1912.

44. Pop Ross to Wells, March 18, 1912. Signed carbon copy; and Wells to Pop Ross, March 22, 1912.

45. TL&I v. Lambourn, 68; Wells to Pop Ross, March 27, 1912; TL&I Board of Directors Meeting Minutes, April 8, 1912; and Wells to Pop Ross, April 23, 1912.

46. Pop Ross to Eaton, October 3, 1917. The property northeast of the railroad tracks was a combination of land given outright to Susan Glassell Mitchell and land subject to life estate rights. The division did not affect land southwest of the tracks owned by TL&I or Treadwell.

47. Wells telegram to Sims, September 27, 1912; and Wells to Sims, October 3, 1912.

48. Wells telegram to Sims, October 1912.

49. TL&I Board of Directors Meeting Minutes, May 12, 1913)

50. Wells telegram to Eaton, February 19, 1913.

51. Wells to Pop Ross, May 4, 1915; and Pop Ross to Wells, May 6, 1915.

52. Pop Ross to Wells, May 6, 1915. Signed carbon copy; and Pop Ross to Wells, May 24, 1915. Signed carbon copy.

53. Wells to Pop Ross, May 22, 1915; Wells refers to him as "Mr. Griffin" in letters of July 31, 1915, and August 11, 1915, but finally gets it right in letter to Pop Ross on August 21, 1915; Wells to Pop Ross, August 21, 1915; and Pop Ross to Wells August 18, 1915. Carbon copy.

54. Wells to Pop Ross, October 1, 1915, relating Griffith's comments.

Chapter 8. Wells Makes His Mark

1. Wells to Pop Ross, February 13, 1910. Handwritten; and Wells to Pop Ross, March 16, 1910. Handwritten.

2. Wells to C. Weston Clark, Chairman Fraternal Committee, Rotary Club, September 21, 1910. Initialed carbon copy; and LA5 Rotary.

3. "See City's Needs From Many Angles," *Los Angeles Examiner*, February 10, 1910; and "Association Seeks Many Improvements," *Los Angeles Herald*, February 19, 1910.

4. "Frown On Call To The Grave: Immense cemetery sign stirs northern section," *Los Angeles Times*, February 18, 1910.

5. E. Forbes, "Letter to the Editor." *Los Angles Express*, February 21, 1910.

6. Wells to Pop Ross, January 20, 1910. Handwritten on stationary from The Woodward Hotel in Los Angeles; Wells to Tom Ross, February 12, 1910. Handwritten; and Wells to Pop Ross, February 14, 1920. Handwritten.

7. "Supervisors Powerless to Remove Billboards," *Los Angeles Herald*, March 1, 1910.

8. Wells to Pop Ross, March 1, 1910. Handwritten on Palace Hotel & Apartments, Los Angeles letterhead.

9. Wells to Pop Ross, March 1, 1910. Handwritten.

10. Wells to Pop Ross, April 11, 1910. Handwritten.

11. Pop Ross to Wells, August 6, 1910. Carbon copy; and Wells to Pop Ross, August 10, 1910. Handwritten.

12. Wells to W. R. Light, Country Road Overseer, June 23, 1910. Initialed carbon copy.

13. Wells to N. C. Burch, May 6, 1912. Initialed carbon copy.

14. Wells to Pop Ross, June 15, 1910. Signed carbon copy.

15. Pop Ross to Wells, June 18, 1910. Carbon copy.

16 Wells to Tom Ross, May 12, 1914.

17. Pop Ross to Treadwell, November 4, 1909. Signed carbon copy.

18. Wells to Pop Ross, February 13, 1910. Handwritten; and Wells to Pop Ross, February 15, 1910.

19. Deed dated February 15, 1910. Signed by Reese Llewellyn and William Llewellyn, witnessed by George Heath and notarized by Charles O. Morgan.

20. Wells to Pop Ross, April 15, 1910. Handwritten.

21. Wells to Pop Ross, March 10, 1910. Handwritten.

22. Wells to Pop Ross, April 25, 1910. Handwritten.

23. Wells to Pop Ross, February 13, 1910. Handwritten.

24. Pop Ross to Wells, February 28, 1910. Signed carbon copy.

25. Wells to Pop Ross, March 1, 1910. Handwritten on Palace Hotel & Apartments letterhead.

26. Wells to Pop Ross, April 11, 1910. Handwritten; and Wells to Pop Ross, June 29, 1910. Handwritten on Palace Hotel & Apartments letterhead.

27. Wells to Tri State Automobile & Supply Co., March 14, 1911.

28. Wells to Pop Ross, February 11, 1911.

29. "Glendale Plans for a Big Consolidation," *Los Angeles Examiner*, March 13, 1910; and Norton C. Wells (chmn), Frank L. Huhleman, and I. H. Russell, Report of the Special Committee on Annexation. (Glendale: Glendale Valley Improvement Association, 1910).

30. Wells to Pop Ross, August 29, 1910. Handwritten.

31. Wells to Pop Ross, March 2, 1911.

32. Nathan Masters, "The Lost City of Tropico, California."

33. Wells to Pop Ross, February 11, 1911. Carbon copy; and Nathan Masters, "The Lost City of Tropico, California."

34. The re-alignment never took place. Years later, Forest Lawn Company, a wholly owned subsidiary of AS&F, acquired property on the corner of Brand Blvd. and Depot Street which had been re-named as Forest Avenue. In 2002, Forest Lawn Mortuary, as the successor to Forest Lawn Company for that land, agreed to closure of the street to enable expansion of school play-

ground area. In return, it received a planting easement along the school and park department along Glendale Ave., across from Forest Lawn-Glendale.

35. Frank Primrose, secretary–treasurer, Loudon Park Cemetery Company, to FLCA, March 17, 1910.

36. Charles Sims purchased the Lorraine Park Cemetery after it had gone bankrupt. Although the location of Mount Olivet Cemetery was referred to as San Francisco, it is undoubtedly Colma.

37. Wells to Pop Ross, April 4, 1910. Handwritten.

38. Pop Ross to Wells, April 6, 1910. Signed carbon copy.

39. Seward Cole, "Should the City Discriminate in Favor of the Hollywood Cemetary? [*sic*]" Los Angeles Record, July 27, 1910; Holly Leaves, "Death of Mrs. Cole." August 24, 1918, 11, accessed May 28, 2016. https://books.google.com/books?id=MtRRAAAAYAAJ; and "Decision No. 4549," Vol. XIII, in Decisions of the Railroad Commission of the State of California, 709-710. (Sacramento, California State Printing Office, 1917).

40. Seward Cole, "Should the City Discriminate in Favor of the Hollywood Cemetary? [*sic*]" Los Angeles Record, July 27, 1910; Holly Leaves, "Death of Mrs. Cole." August 24, 1918, 11, accessed May 28, 2016. https://books.google.com/books?id=MtRRAAAAYAAJ; and "Decision No. 4549," Vol. XIII, in Decisions of the Railroad Commission of the State of California, 709-710. (Sacramento, California State Printing Office, 1917).

41. Stephen L. Richards for law firm of Richards, Hart & Van Dam to FLCA, August 28, 1912. The cemetery was developed in 1912 and for many years was run by one of Stephen's relatives, Lynn Richards—a Utah state senator and the first president of the Western Cemetery Alliance, a trade association representing cemeteries in the eleven Western states, including Hawaii.

42. Wells to Stephen L. Richards, September 14, 1912. Carbon copy.

43. Wells to Stephen L. Richards, September 14, 1912. Carbon copy.

Chapter 9. Settlement with Treadwell

1. Wells to Treadwell, October 30, 1911. Initialed carbon copy.

2. J. B. Treadwell v. FLCA, 1913.

3. Release signed by Oscar M. Souden, December 23, 1912; Carroll Allen of Flint, Gray & Barker to FLCA, December 26, 1912; and Wells to Pop Ross, December 30, 1912.

4. Pop Ross to J. B. Treadwell, January 4, 1913. Carbon copy with handwritten changes.

5. Carroll Allen to Pop Ross, January 7, 1913. File copy; and Wells to Carroll Allen, January 10, 1913. File copy.

6. Wells to Pop Ross, January 24, 1913. Treadwell had assigned the notes to Clyde E. Cate, who now was the one seeking payment.

7. Pop Ross to Wells, January 26, 1913. California law still provides that it is illegal for a regulated cemetery to make loans to officers or directors from operating or endowment care funds (CA H&S §8360).

8. Pop Ross to Wells, January 26, 1913. Carbon copy; and Pop Ross to Wells, January 30, 1913. Signed carbon copy.

9. Wells to Pop Ross, February 20, 1913; and Pop Ross to Wells, January 30, 1913. Signed carbon copy; Wells to Pop Ross, February 20, 1913.

10. Pop Ross note in reply to telegram from Eaton, undated. In the interrogatories in J. B. Treadwell v. AS&F it states that Treadwell retained 26 acres.

11. Pop Ross to Wells, March 13, 1913. Signed carbon copy. Treadwell's notes were now ostensibly owned by Cate.

12. Wells to Pop Ross, March 15, 1913; Pop Ross to Wells, March 18, 1913. Carbon copy; and "List of STOCKHOLDERS in TROPICO LAND and IMPROVEMENT CO, San Francisco. Cal." With Pop Ross's signature as secretary and handwritten notations "Certified correct," "As per Stock Ledger, October 16, 1909," and "Please return (proxies retained by Mr. Akers Nov 1—1909." Akers was the corporation's agent in Arizona. Generally, proxies were sent to Akers in Arizona to hold stockholders meetings without the principals being physically present.

13. Pop Ross to Wells, March 21, 1913. Signed carbon copy. The list of stockholders then showed H. E. Huntington, presumably the railroad tycoon, owning 5,000 shares; and TL&I Board of Directors meeting minutes, May 12, 1913.

14. Wells to Pop Ross, March 24, 1913; and Pop Ross to Wells, March 25, 1913. Signed carbon copy

15. TL&I Board of Directors Meeting Minutes, March 13, 1913; Wells to Pop Ross, March 24, 1913

Chapter 10. Eaton and Sims Arrive

1. Wells to Charles B. Sims, July 2, 1910.

2. Valhalla Cemetery Co., "Modern Cemeteries," Valhalla News, January 1925, 3–4.

3. "Cemetery Development Service," Park and Cemetery, February 1924, 307; and Valhalla Cemetery Co., 3–4.

4. Valhalla Cemetery Co., 3–4.

5. Valhalla Cemetery Co., 3–4.

6. Valhalla Cemetery Co., 3–4; Park and Cemetery, "Cemetery Development Service," February 1924, 306-307; and Paul Elvig, president Evergreen–Washelli Cemetery, email to author, August 25, 2005. The Washelli Cemetery is now known as Evergreen-Washelli Cemetery.

7. Valhalla Cemetery Co., 3–4.

8. Sims to Wells, August 29, 1910. Carbon copy.

9. Wells to Sims, September 24, 1910. Signed. There are inconsistencies between various documents about land acreages.

10. Sims to Wells, October 1, 1910.

11. Wells to Sims, September 24, 1910 and Sims to Wells, October 1, 1910.

12. Sims to Wells, October 1, 1910.

13. Sims to FLCA, October 27, 1910. Carbon copy.

14. Wells to Sims, March 21, 1911; and Wells's letters to Union Bank & Trust Co., The Bank of Mobile, and City Bank & Trust Co., March 21, 1911.

15. Hancock, *The Forest Lawn Story*, 26, 32-36, 54; and Eaton, "Family History of Hubert (Lewright) Eaton." Harold William Eaton, born April 13, 1878, died August 31, 1882, from tonsillitis in Liberty, MO; Lee Boardman Eaton, born August 4, 1876, died March 10, 1877, from pneumonia and measles in Liberty, MO; Moriarty F.S.A., G. Andrews, "Family of John Eaton of Wales," 1943. Family tree by Moriarty refers to Lee as Lewright and traces the Eaton family from about 1685 in Wales, through the American Revolution, and to April 1943.

16. Eaton, "Personal History," 2; and St. Johns, 58, 62, 66.

17. Eaton, "Personal History," 2; and St. Johns, 58, 62, 66.

18. Eaton, "Personal History," 2; and St. Johns, 66–78. Eaton, "Personal History," 2; and St. Johns, 58, 62, 66–68

19. Ralph Hancock, *The Forest Lawn Story*, 50-53 and Sims to Wells, February 23, 1912. Officers of National Securities Company shown on letterhead; and St. Johns, 82–85. The books by Hancock and St. Johns say that Marsh referred Eaton to Forest Lawn, but correspondence indicates Sims made the first contact with Forest Lawn and Eaton arrived there because of his relationship with Sims.

20. Eaton to Wells, July 13, 1911. Eaton's letter does not mention Sims.

21. Eaton to Wells, July 13, 1911. Signed carbon copy.

22. Sims to Wells, February 23, 1912. Carbon copy on Valhalla Cemetery (St. Louis) letterhead.

23. Pop Ross to Wells, March 18, 1912. Signed carbon copy.

24. Wells to Motley H. Flint, April 10, 1912. Initialed carbon copy.

25. Eaton to Wells, May 2, 1912. On Adaven Mining and Smelting Co. letterhead, from Reno. "Adaven" is "Nevada" spelled backward. The letterhead shows W. O. Van Arsdale as president, F. G. Crowell as vice president, J. H. Eaton as Secretary, E. D. Fisher as treasurer, and H. L. Eaton as manager; suggesting that Eaton's claim of ownership might be a bit of exaggeration.

26. Eaton to Wells, June 21, 1912. On Adaven Mining and Smelting Co. letterhead, from Reno.

27. FLCA, Board of Trustees Meeting Minutes, July 11, 1912.

28. Wells telegram to Sims, July 12, 1912.

29. Wells to Sims, July 12, 1912. Initialed carbon copy.

30. Agreement dated July 11, 1912, between TL&I and FLCA, as the "first parties" and "second parties," Charles B. Sims, and H. L. Eaton.

31. Agreement dated July 11, 1912, between TL&I and FLCA.

32. Agreement dated July 11, 1912, between TL&I and FLCA.

33. Agreement dated July 11, 1912, between TL&I and FLCA.

34. Agreement dated July 11, 1912, between TL&I and FLCA.

35. TL&I Board of Directors Meeting Minutes, September 18, 1912.

36. "Certificate of Organization of a Corporation Under the General Law: State of Maine," September 9, 1912; and Agreement between Sims, Charles Marsh, and Eaton, September 27, 1912; Handwritten assignment by Sims and Eaton on first page of contract between TL&I, Forest Lawn, Sims, and Eaton. Although the agreement between Sims, Marsh, and Eaton called for Sims to transfer the Forest Lawn contract, Eaton and Sims made the actual assignment as provided in the contract with TL&I and Forest Lawn because the contract was with both men; Memorandum signed by Eaton, Marsh, and Sims, October 29, 1912.

37. American Securities Company, "Special Meeting of the Board of Directors," October 29, 1912.

38. Xenophon P. Wilfley to Sims, September 23, 1912.

39. American Securities Company Certificate of Organization of a Corporation Under the General Law State of Maine, September 9, 1912.

40. Sims to B. F. Edwards, September 25, 1912.

41. Letter to Wells, most likely from Sims, October 7, 1912, carbon copy; Wells telegram to Sims, October 11, 1912; and Tropico v. Lambourn, 115. The stock had a par value of $1, so in his letter Sims was offering the Rosses two shares for the price of one.

42. Eaton to Wells, July 16, 1912. Carbon copy. Although no signature block is shown on the letter, it is from Reno and refers to the photos Wells sent Eaton, so it appears it is from Eaton.

43. Eaton to Wells, July 16, 1912; Wells to Sims, August 17, 1912; Sims to Wells, August 23, 1912. Carbon copy; and Wells to Sims, August 30, 1912.

44. Wells to Eaton, September 13, 1912.

45. Wells telegram to Sims, September 27, 1912; and Wells to Sims, October 3, 1912.

46. Wells telegram to Sims, October 11, 1912; and Tropico v. Lambourn, 115.

47. TL&I Board of Directors Meeting Minutes, May 12, 1913)

48. Wells telegram to Sims, October 29, 1912.

49. Sims telegram to Wells, October 30, 1912. Signed file copy; and Wells to Eaton, November 14, 1912.

50. Wells to Sims, November 18, 1912; and Wells telegram to Sims, November 29, 1912.

51. Sims telegram to Wells, November 30, 1912. File copy of text.

52. Wells to Pop Ross, January 10, 1913; Pop Ross to Wells, January 13, 1913.

53. Lyons & Beavis to Getzendanner, March 19, 1913.

54. Eaton to Tom Ross, January 17, 1913; and Wells to Pop Ross, April 7, 1913.

55. Sims to Wells, July 22, 1912. Carbon copy.

56. Wells to Sims, July 30, 1912; and Sims to Wells, August 8, 1912.

57. Wells to Sims, August 10, 1912; and Sims to Wells, August 14, 1912. Carbon copy.

58. Sims to Wadham, August 14, 1912. Carbon copy.

59. Wells to Pop Ross, April 7, 1913.

60. Eaton to Sims, April 8, 1913. Carbon copy.

61. Eaton to Sims, April 8, 1913. Carbon copy.

62. Eaton to Sims, April 10, 1913. Carbon copy.

63. Eaton to Sims, April 8, 1913. Carbon copy; Cosgrove to Eaton, May 5, 1913; Hazlett to Cosgrove, May 16, 1913. Carbon copy; and Bates, *History of the Bench and Bar of California*, 484.

64. Cosgrove to Hazlett, May 23, 1913. File copy.

65. Hazlett to Eaton, May 24, 1913.

66. Sims to B. F. Edwards, September 25, 1912.

67. Pop Ross to Sims, February 7, 1913. Signed carbon copy.

68. Eaton to George Law, February 5, 1914. File copy.

69. George Law to Eaton, February 18, 1914.

Chapter 11. Property Management Challenges

1. Peter L. Ferry to Wells, March 21, 1912.

2. Peter L. Ferry to Wells, March 21, 1912.

3. Pop Ross to Wells, May 2, 1913

4. Wells to Pop Ross, May 1, 1913.

5. Wells to Pop Ross, May 1, 1913.

6. Wells to Pop Ross, May 1, 1913.

7. Wells to Pop Ross, May 31, 1913.

8. Wells to Pop Ross, May 1, 1913.

9. Wells to Pop Ross, May 31, 1913; and "The Trustees Meeting," *Tropico Sentinel*, May 28, 1913.

10. Wells to Pop Ross, May 31, 1913.

11. Wells to Pop Ross, May 9, 1914.

12. Wells to Pop Ross, May 9, 1914.

13. Wells to Pop Ross, May 9, 1914.

14. Pop Ross to Wells, July 29, 1914. Signed carbon copy.

15. Henry P. Goodwin to FLCA, July 24, 1914.

16. Wells to Pop Ross, April 6, 1915.

17 Goodwin to Wells, May 17, 1915.

18. Henry P. Goodwin to Wells, May 19, 1915.

19. Wells to Pop Ross, June 2, 1915; and Pop Ross to Wells, June 12, 1915.

20. Wells to Pop Ross, April 6, 1915; and Pop Ross to Wells, April 7, 1915.

21. Wells to Pop Ross, April 20, 1920.

22. Wells to J. C. Coleman, June 1, 1915. Carbon copy.

23. Wells to J. C. Coleman, June 1, 1915. Carbon copy; J. C. Coleman to Wells, June 3, 1915; Pop Ross to Wells, June 12, 1915; Wells to Kress House Moving Company, June 21, 1915. Initialed carbon copy.

24. "A 38-Ft. Cobblestone Arch Raised and Moved." *Field and Office, Engineering News*, December 16, 1915, 1178–1179; Eva B. Cole to Pop Ross, July 10, 1915; Eva B. Cole to Pop Ross, July 17, 1915; and Tom Ross to Kress House Moving Company, November 8, 1915.

25. Diana Sherman, "A River for Los Angeles: The Story of the Los Angeles River Greenway," May 17, 2004, Accessed September 30, 2014. http://ocw.mit.edu/courses/history/21h-234j-downtown-spring-2005/assignments/; and Tim Black, Arroyo Seco Flood Timeline., n.d., accessed March 23, 2006. http://www.arroyoseco.org/History/ArroyoSecoFloodTimeline.pdf. Three years later, the first bond issue would be approved, providing funds for flood control. This would lead to the creation of the Los Angeles County Flood Control District in 1915, and to the construction of a vast network of concrete washes and dams to control the flow of storm and wastewaters.

26. Wells to Pop Ross, January 26, 1914.

27. Wells to Pop Ross, January 26, 1914; and Pop Ross to Wells, February 24, 1914. Signed carbon copy.

28. Wells to Pop Ross, February 25, 1914; Black, Arroyo Seco Flood Timeline.

29. Wells to Pop Ross March 18, 1914; Wells telegram to Pop Ross, March 17, 1914; and Pop Ross telegram to Wells, March 17, 1914. File copy of text.

30. Wells to Pop Ross, March 21, 1914.

31. Wells to Pop Ross, May 9, 1914; and Wells to Pop Ross May 23, 1914.

32. Eaton to FLCA, May 19, 1915. Carbon copy.

33. Eaton to FLCA, August 30, 1915.

34. Wells to Eaton, September 1, 1915.

35. Wells to Pop Ross, December 8, 1915.

36. "Banker Shot to Death," *Los Angeles Herald*, December 23, 1915, 1; and *Los Angeles Evening Herald*, "Tropico Banker Slain," December 23, 1915.

37. "Nephew of Slain Main Tells Possible Motive," *Los Angeles Evening Herald*, December 23, 1915.

38. "Tropico Millionaire is Killed," *Los Angeles Evening Herald*, December 23, 1915; "Prominent Citizen of Tropico Foully Murdered," *Tropico Sentinel*, December 23, 1915; and Wells to Pop Ross, December 24, 1915. There are some timing inconsistencies between the accounts of Wells and the two newspapers.

39. "Tropico Millionaire is Killed," *Los Angeles Evening Herald*.

40. "Tropico Millionaire is Killed," *Los Angeles Evening Herald*. It is interesting that according to Hubert Eaton's personal history, Eaton was sworn in as a Deputy Sheriff at the Los Angeles Hall of Justice on September 13, 1938

41. "Tropico Millionaire is Killed," *Los Angeles Evening Herald*; "Prominent Citizen of Tropico Foully Murdered," *Tropico Sentinel*; and Wells to Pop Ross, December 24, 1915. There are some timing inconsistencies between the accounts of Wells and the two newspapers.

42. "Slayer Silent at Inquest," *Los Angeles Herald*, December 24, 1915.

Chapter 12. Startup Tensions

1. Wells to Pop Ross, February 20, 1913.

2. Pop Ross to Wells, April 28, 1913. Carbon copy; and Pop Ross to Wells, May 9, 1913. Signed carbon copy.

3. Since the amount due the perpetual care fund would come from the final payments on a contract, these examples ignore the amount eventually due the fund.

4. Wells to Pop Ross, May 15, 1913.

5. Wells to Pop Ross, May 23, 1913.

6. Pop Ross to Wells, May 26, 1913. Signed carbon copy.

7. Wells to Pop Ross, June 2, 1913.

8. Pop Ross to Wells, June 3, 1913. Signed carbon copy.

9. Eaton to Wells, June 3, 1913. A handwritten notation says, "Same letter sent to TL&I same date."

10. Eaton to TL&I and FLCA, September 1, 1913.

11. Eaton to TL&I and FLCA, September 1, 1913.

12. Eaton to Wells, June 3, 1913. A handwritten notation says, "Same letter sent to TL&I same date."

13. Wells to Pop Ross, June 6, 1913. Handwritten.

14. TL&I, Board of Directors Meeting Minutes, June 5, 1913.

15. Wells to Pop Ross, June 6, 1913. Handwritten.

16. Wells to Pop Ross, June 6, 1913. Handwritten.

17. T. Ross Pop to Wells, June 30, 1913. Signed carbon copy.

18. Wells to Pop Ross, July 31, 1913. Handwritten postscript.

19. Pop Ross to Eaton, September 24, 1913. Carbon copy

20. A. W. Burgren to Pop Ross, October 3, 1913.

21. Pop Ross to Wells, October 6, 1913. Signed carbon copy.

22. Wells to Pop Ross, October 6, 1913. Handwritten.

23. Sims to Williams, Goudge & Chandler, October 7, 1913. Carbon copy

24. Herbert J. Goudge to American Securities Company, October 7, 1913.

25. Pop Ross to Wells, October 6, 1913. Signed carbon copy.

26. Wells to Pop Ross, October 8, 1913.

27. Pop Ross to Wells, October 8, 1913. Signed carbon copy.

28. Pop Ross to Wells, October 8, 1913. Signed carbon copy; and Wells to Pop Ross, October 9, 1913.

29. Pop Ross to Wells, October 10, 1913. Signed carbon copy.

30. Eaton to TL&I and FLCA, October 10, 1913. On American Securities Company letterhead.

31. Pop Ross to Wells, October 14, 1913. Signed carbon copy. Someone, probably Thomas Ross, put a handwritten notation opposite this: "all bluff"; and Pop Ross to Wells, October 14, 1913. Signed carbon copy.

32. Pop Ross to Wells, October 19, 1913. Signed carbon copy; and Samuuel H. Williamson, "Annualized Growth Rate of Various Historical Economic Series." The present day value is based upon the consumer price index. Other measures of current value range from $53,600 to $1,500,000.

33. Pop Ross to Wells, October 19, 1913. Signed carbon copy.

34. Pop Ross to Wells, October 19, 1913. Signed carbon copy.

35. Pop Ross to Wells, October 19, 1913. Signed carbon copy.

36. Wells to Pop Ross, October 22, 1913.

37. Hazlett to Eaton, October 20, 1913.

38. Hawkins to Eaton, c/o F. W. Llewellyn, Mexico, MO, October 27, 1913.

39. Eaton to Pop Ross and Tom Ross, November 3, 1913. Handwritten on American Securities letterhead. Pop Ross has added the notations "mailed Nov 2," "Received 230 pm Nov 6th," and "no answer" to the letter. Frederick William Llewellyn was married to Eaton's sister, Mable, and was the father of Frederick Eaton Llewellyn, who, in 1966, succeeded Eaton as general manager of Forest Lawn Memorial-Park Association and president of American Security & Fidelity Corporation.

40. Eaton Western Union Night Letter to Pop Ross, November 3, 1913.

41. Pop Ross telegram to Eaton, November 4, 1913. Signed file copy of text; and Pop Ross to Wells, November 4, 1913. Signed carbon copy.

42. Wells to Pop Ross, November 8, 1913.

43. Eaton to Pop Ross, November 5, 1913. On Planters Hotel letter-head; Eaton to Pop Ross, November 10, 1913. Handwritten telegram text on Western Union form

44. Wells to Pop Ross, November 17, 1913.

45. Eaton telegram to Pop Ross, November 10, 1913.

46. Pop Ross to Eaton, November 10, 1913; and Pop Ross to Wells, November 11, 1913. Carbon copy

47. Agreement "To H. L. Eaton, Esq., and His Associates" dated St. Louis, MO, November 18, 1913. Signed by Sims, Marsh, and others on behalf of the St. Louis group and by Eaton and others on behalf of the California group.

48. Contract dated November 18, 1913,

49. Eaton to Wells, November 17, 1913. Carbon copy

50. Wells to N. P. Dodge & Co., January 24, 1916. Initialed carbon copy.

51. Charles F. Werner to Wells, January 31, 1917; and Wells to Charles F. Werner, February 16, 1917. Carbon copy.

Chapter 13. Trying to Cooperate

1. Pop Ross to Wells, November 22, 1913. Signed carbon copy.

2. Wells to Pop Ross, November 26, 1913.

3. Pop Ross to Wells, December 8, 1913. Signed carbon copy.

4. Eaton to Pop Ross, December 30, 1913.

5. Pop Ross to Eaton, January 2, 1914. Signed carbon copy; and Pop Ross to Wells, January 7, 1914. Signed carbon copy.

6. Eaton to Pop Ross, February 11, 1914

7. Pop Ross to Wells, February 3, 1914. Signed carbon copy.

8. Pop Ross to Wells, January 23, 1914. Signed carbon copy; and Eaton to TL&I and FLCA, February 11, 1914.

9. Wells to Pop Ross, February 23, 1914; and Pop Ross to Wells, February 24, 1914. Signed carbon copy.

10. Pop Ross to Wells, February 26, 1914. Signed carbon copy; and G. A. Brock to Eaton, April 2, 1915; Los Angeles Chamber of Commerce, Industrial Bureau, c. 1915.

11. Eaton to TL&I and FLCA, March 3, 1914.

12. Pop Ross to Eaton, March 12, 1914. Signed carbon copy; and Wells to Pop Ross, March 18, 1914.

13. Eaton to TL&I and FLCA, May 7, 1914.

14. Eaton to Pop Ross, March 23, 1914.

15. Eaton to Pop Ross and Tom Ross, August 10, 1914; and Eaton to Tom Ross, August 11, 1914.

16. Eaton to Pop Ross and Tom Ross, August 10, 1914; and Eaton to Tom Ross, August 11, 1914.

17. Eaton to Pop Ross and Tom Ross, August 10, 1914; and Eaton to Tom Ross, August 11, 1914.

18. Eaton to Tom Ross, August 11, 1914.

19. T.P. Ross telegram to Eaton, August 12, 1914. Handwritten file copy of text; Eaton to Pop Ross and T.P. Ross, August 13, 1914.

20. Wells to Pop Ross, August 24, 1914.

21. Eaton to Pop Ross, August 25, 1914.

22. T. Ross to Eaton, August 21, 1914. Signed carbon copy; and Pop Ross to Wells, August 26, 1914.

23. Eaton to Pop Ross and Tom Ross, September 19, 1914.

24. Eaton to Pop Ross, October 27, 1914.

25. Pop Ross to Eaton, November 2, 1914. Typed copy.

26. Pop Ross to Eaton, November 2, 1914. Typed copy.

27. Eaton to Pop Ross, December 23, 1914.

28. FLCA, "Statement of Income and Expenditure for the Twelve Months Ended December 31, 1914."

29. Jo J. De Haven to Wells, February 10, 1915. The Interment Association of California, formed in 1931, was the first statewide trade association for cemeteries and is now called the Cemetery and Mortuary Association of California.

30. Wells to Jo J. De Haven, February 13, 1915. Carbon copy; Wells to Eckley, February 13, 1915; Wells to Harry W. Watson, February 13, 1915; Wells to Pop Ross, February 17, 1915; Los Angeles Investment Company; American Globe, "City of the Departed." October 21, 1922; and American Globe, "Los Angeles Investment Company Piles Up Corporation History." August 1915, 7-8.

31. Wells to Jo J. De Haven, February 19, 1915. Carbon copy; Wells to William Cleaver, February 19, 1915. Carbon copy; Wells to W. H. Eckley, February 19, 1915. Carbon copy; Wells to Harry W. Watson, February 19, 1915; and Wells to Right Rev. Thomas J. Conaty, February 20, 1915. Carbon copy.

32. Jo J. De Haven to Wells, February 27, 1915.

33. Jo J. De Haven to Wells, March 17, 1915.

34. Pop Ross to Wells, March 11, 1915. Carbon copy; Wells to Pop Ross, March 16, 1915; and Pop Ross to Wells, March 17, 1915. Signed carbon copy

35. Eaton to TL&I and FLCA, April 6, 1915.

36. Eaton to TL&I and FLCA, June 25, 1915.

37. TL&I board of directors meeting minutes, July 8, 1915; Pop Ross to Wells, July 8, 1915. Carbon copy; and Agreement between TL&I, FLCA, and American Securities, July 8, 1915.

38. Eaton to TL&I and FLCA, October 29, 1915. Carbon copy.

39. Eaton to TL&I and FLCA, October 29, 1915. Carbon copy.

40. Eaton to TL&I, November 30, 1915.

41. Wells to Tom Ross, December 6, 1915

42. Ben S. Hunter to Hazlett, November 29, 1915.

43. Eaton to Hawkins, December 2, 1915. Carbon copy.

44. Hawkins to American Sureties [sic] Co., December 30, 1915.

45. Hawkins to American Sureties [sic] Co., December 30, 1915.

46. Eaton to TL&I and FLCA, December 14, 1915.

47. Eaton to TL&I and FLCA, December 14, 1915.

48. Tom Ross and Pop Ross to Eaton, January 29, 1916; and Contract modification addressed to Eaton, January 29, 1916. Signed by Tom Ross and Pop Ross for TL&I; and by Wells and Peters for FLCA.

49. Pop Ross to Eaton, October 22, 1915.

50. Pop Ross to Eaton, October 22, 1915. Second letter of same date.

51. TL&I audit statement, October 15, 1915. Copy; and Estimated Value of Tropico Land & Improvement Co. on October 15, 1915, ". . . estimated from various data held by Hubert L. Eaton and is approximately correct within $3,000.0."

52. Wells to Pop Ross, November 19, 1915.

53. Wells to Jewel City Undertaking Co., December 8, 1915. Initialed carbon copy.

54. Eaton to Pop Ross, February 1, 1916.

Chapter 14. Expanding Sales Efforts

1. Eaton to Wells, May 26, 1914.

2. Eaton to Forest Lawn lot owners, May 26, 1914. Draft.

3. Eaton to Getzendanner, May 26, 1914. Carbon copy

4. Wells to Pop Ross, June 27, 1913.

5. Pop Ross to Wells, June 30, 1913. Signed carbon copy; and Wells to Pop Ross, July 2, 1913.

6. Pop Ross to Wells, July 16, 1913. Signed carbon copy.

7. Pop Ross to Wells, July 16, 1913. Signed carbon copy.

8. Wells to Pop Ross, July 30, 1913.

9. Pop Ross to Wells, July 31, 1913. Signed carbon copy.

10. Letterhead used in March 20, 1914 letter from Wells to Eaton. The letterhead also listed cemeteries American Securities Company and Associated Companies claimed to have established: Pine Crest (Mobile), Greenwood (Montgomery, AL), Lincoln (Montgomery, AL), Valhalla (St. Louis), Mount Hope (St. Louis), and Peach Tree Hills (Atlanta). It also identified that it was "operating" Forest Lawn; Letterhead used on May 7, 1914 letter from Eaton to TL&I and FLCA; Letterhead used on May 9, 1914 letter from Wells to Pop Ross.

11. Eaton to Pop Ross, March 4, 1914.

12. Eaton to Pop Ross, March 4, 1914.

13. Eaton to A. S. Theberge, Superintendent, Industrial Department, Pacific Coast Territory, Metropolitan Life Insurance Co., March 25, 1914.

14. Forbes Lindsay, Associate Manager Pacific Mutual Life Insurance Company, to Eaton, March 30, 1914; and A. S. Theberge to Eaton April 15, 1914. In the early 1940s Eaton began formation of the Forest Lawn Life Insurance Company as a wholly owned subsidiary of Forest Lawn Company, which was a successor to TL&I

15. Wells to Pop Ross, March 31, 1914. Handwritten postscript to letter; and Calvary Cemetery was moved from San Francisco in 1937. Nuala Sawyer "The Old Calvary Cemetery Grounds Are Right Under Your Feet, Hoodline, May 19, 2014 http://hoodline.com/2014/05/calvary-cemetery-grounds-are-right-under-your-feet Accessed November 30, 2017."

16. Eaton to Woodlawn Cemetery, August 30, 1915.

17. The public generally uses the term "ashes" to refer to the material left after a body is cremated. Although ashes blown by the wind is a romantic visual, it does not reflect the actual by-product of cremation. When a body is cremated, the residual is largely calcium from bones. The remaining bone fragments are then "processed" to the consistency of course sand.

18. Wells to Tom Ross, January 13, 1914.

19. National Retail Monument Dealers Assn. Inc., form letter, undated. Many states, including California, no longer allow the use of "perpetual care" for cemeteries. "Endowment Care" is now more commonly required

20. Eaton to National Retail Monument Dealers Ass'n, Inc., August 31, 1914.

21. Eaton to Carol Price, secretary, Ohio Retail Monument Dealers Association, February 23, 1915. Carbon copy

22. Eaton to Mike Glora, March 6, 1915. Carbon copy

23. Weed, *Modern Park Cemeteries*, 50

24. Frank Church to American Securities Co., December 8, 1914.

25. Eaton to FLCA, September 13, 1915. Carbon copy.

26. Eaton to Jay D. Brunner, Pacific Coast Concrete Co., August 29, 1914. Carbon copy. It has become common practice for cemeteries to require some sort of vault or outer burial container to help prevent subsidence of graves.

27. Eaton to FLCA, August 20, 1915; and Getzendanner handwritten proposed reference letter; Eaton to "To whom it may concern," August 23, 1915. Carbon copy.

28. Eaton to Getzendanner, June 6, 1916. Carbon copy; and "Cemeteries in the County of Los Angeles."

29. Eaton to Getzendanner, June 6, 1916. Carbon copy; Eaton to Getzendanner, July 6, 1916. Eaton refers to the blueprint as being of Myrtle Heights Cemetery. Carbon copy; and Eaton to Getzendanner, July 6, 1916. Carbon copy, second letter of same date. I catch your point that it is not good landscape gardening . . . but, of course, the common herd does not always know these fine points and ordinary things many times look very beautiful to this class of people."

30. Paul Sacks, secretary, Eagle Development Corporation to Forest Lawn Cemetery Co., August 12, 1915.

31. Pop Ross to Wells, August 18, 1915. Carbon copy; and Wells to Eagle Development Corporation, August 21, 1915. Initialed carbon copy.

32. Paul Sacks to Wells, August 25, 1915.

33. Wells to Eagle Development Corporation, September 18, 1915. Initialed carbon copy.

34. Ralph Hancock, *The Forest Lawn Story*, 53..

35. Eaton to Times-Mirror Co., October 2, 1915. Carbon copy.

36. Emery, Sales School Programs, November 17, 1917, November 27, 1917, and December 8, 1917. Carbon copies.

37. Charles O. Harding to William H. Stephens, October 15, 1917. Copy.

38. Charles O. Harding to William H. Stephens, October 15, 1917. Copy.

39. Charles O. Harding to William H. Stephens, October 15, 1917. Copy.

40. Letter to Rt. Rev. H. J. Johnson, St. Paul's Guild Hall. File copy undated.

41. Letter to Rt. Rev. H. J. Johnson, St. Paul's Guild Hall. File copy undated.

42. Letter to Rt. Rev. H. J. Johnson, St. Paul's Guild Hall. File copy undated; Letter to Rt. Rev. H. J. Johnson, St. Paul's Guild Hall. File copy undated; and Cypress Lawn.

43. Eaton to W. M. Holden, September 9, 1915. Carbon copy; and Eaton to H. N. Bradbury, December 9, 1915. Carbon copy.

44. H. N Bradbury to Eaton, December 11, 1915; and Eaton to H. N. Bradbury, December 28, 1915.

45. Eaton to A. E. Campbell, Esq., February 4, 1915. Carbon copy.

46. Eaton to Getzendanner, June 15, 1915. Carbon copy.

47. Eaton to William D. Pierce, March 2, 1915. Carbon copy.

Chapter 15. Eaton the Entrepreneur

1. Eaton to Huntington Beach Co., December 31, 1914; Eaton to O. E. Darling, February 10, 1915. Carbon copy; O. E. Darling to Eaton, March 3, 1915. Handwritten; O. E. Darling to Eaton, March 18, 1915; *Los Angeles Times*, "The Huntington Beach Co.," April 23, 1990. The company went extensively into petroleum drilling after oil was discovered in the 1920s and is currently owned by Chevron Oil Company; and City of Huntington Beach. n.d. "HB History." City of Huntington Beach, accessed September 29, 2016. http://www.huntingtonbeachca.gov/about/history/.

2. Eaton to Huntington Beach Co., December 31, 1914; Eaton to O. E. Darling, February 10, 1915. Carbon copy; O. E. Darling to Eaton, March 3, 1915. Handwritten; and O. E. Darling to Eaton, March 18, 1915. The "Bullard Lands" may have been in El Dorado County, California.

3. Getzendanner to Eaton, April 22, 1915. Carbon copy.

4. Pop Ross to Wells, April 22, 1915. Signed carbon copy; and Eaton to O. E. Darling, April 6, 1915. Carbon copy.

5. O. E. Darling to Frank G. Schumacher, April 25, 1915. Carbon copy; and F. G. Schumacher to O. E. Darling, April 27, 1915. Handwritten on Schumacher Investment & Realty Co. letterhead.

6. F. E. Hose to O. E. Darling, April 28, 1915. Handwritten; O. E. Darling to F. E. Hose, April 29, 1915. Carbon copy; and F. E. Hose reply to Darling May 4, 1915.

7. Eaton to G. M. Smith, July 14, 1915. Carbon copy. Copies of identical letters to other shareholders also are in the files.

8. Eaton to G. M. Smith, July 14, 1915. Carbon copy.

9. Eaton telegram to American Securities office, July 20, 1915; Eaton telegram to Estelle McDonald, July 17, 1915; Estelle McDonald telegram to Eaton, July 27, 1915; and Jas. O. Lawshe to American Securities, March 10, 1915. Names are from letterhead.

10. R. Merritt Llewellyn to Eaton, August 27, 1915.

11. Eaton to R. Merritt Llewellyn, September 22, 1915. Carbon copy.

12. Eaton to R. Merritt Llewellyn, September 22, 1915. Carbon copy.

13. Wells to Pop Ross, October 9, 1915. Handwritten postscript to letter.

14. Memorandum dated February 26, 1916. No attribution but has pencil notation in Eaton's handwriting, "Never used."

15. Memorandum dated February 26, 1916. No attribution but has pencil notation in Eaton's handwriting, "Never used."

16. Memorandum of agreement signed by C. W. Gates, Eaton, and W. I. Hollingsworth, dated April 10, 1916.

17. Eaton, "Personal History," 3; Memorandum dated May 19, 1916. Signed by C. W. Gates, W. I. Hollingsworth, and Hubert L. Eaton. It bears a note written by Eaton: "6/24/17 This agreement never carried into effect because we dropped the purchase of Eagle Rock land"; Eaton letter to G. S. Backman, November 20, 1917. Carbon copy.

18. "Frank D. Hamilton, Liberty Banker, Buried Saturday," *Lathrop Optimist*, Lathrop Missouri, October 6, 1956, 1.

19. Eaton, "Personal History," 3; Memorandum dated May 19, 1916. Signed by C. W. Gates, W. I. Hollingsworth, and Hubert L. Eaton. It bears a note written by Eaton: "6/24/17 This agreement never carried into effect because we dropped the purchase of Eagle Rock land"; Eaton letter to G. S. Backman, November 20, 1917. Carbon copy.

20. Eaton to R. Merritt Llewellyn, June 7, 1916. Carbon copy.

21. Eaton to R. Merritt Llewellyn, June 7, 1916. Carbon copy.

22. Herbert Goudge to George E. Pratt and Associates, July 3, 1916.

23. Wells to Pop Ross, July 12, 1916.

24. Wells to Pop Ross, July 12, 1916.

25. Pop Ross to George E. Pratt, July 28, 1916.

26. C. W. Gates and W. I. Hollingsworth to Pop Ross, August 7, 1916. Acceptance signed by R. Ross.

27. Pop Ross to TL&I Stockholders, August 21, 1916. Carbon copy.

28. R. Merritt Llewellyn to Eaton, August 30, 1916; and Eaton to R. Merritt Llewellyn September 6, 1916. Carbon copy.

29. Pop Ross to Wells, September 12, 1916. Signed carbon copy.

30. Archer to Pop Ross, September 12, 1916.

31. Pop Ross to Archer, September 14, 1916. Signed carbon copy.

32. Pop Ross to Archer, September 14, 1916. Signed carbon copy.

33. W. E. Pearson to Eaton, September 11, 1916; and Eaton to W. E. Pearson, October 11, 1916. Carbon copy.

34. Eaton to Herbert J. Goudge, October 5, 1916. Carbon copy.

35. Henry J. Goudge to Eaton, October 16, 1916.

36. AS&F, Board of Directors Meeting Minutes, November 23, 1916. Over the years AS&F changed state of incorporation and became a holding company with all operations placed in wholly owned subsidiary Forest Lawn Company. At the time of AS&F's acquisition by FLMPA, AS&F was a Nevada corporation and was named American Security & Fidelity Coporation rather than the original American Security & Fidelity Co.

37. Hamilton to AS&F, November 25, 1916.

38. Hamilton to AS&F, November 25, 1916.

39. Hamilton to AS&F, November 25, 1916.

40. Hamilton to AS&F, November 25, 1916.

41. Hamilton to AS&F, November 25, 1916.

42. Hamilton to AS&F, November 25, 1916.

43. Hamilton to AS&F, November 25, 1916.

44. Eaton telegram to L. E. Wynn, November 29, 1916.

45. Tom Ross and Pop Ross to George E. Pratt and Associates, December 11, 1916.

46. K. L. Crowley to TL&I, December 21, 1916.

47. AS&F note to Citizens Trust & Savings Bank, December 18, 1916. File copy; Memo regarding borrowing, December 15, 1916. Unsigned carbon copy; Frank D. Hamilton by William Hazlett, his attorney-in-fact, "Appointment of Trustee," December 23, 1916. Accepted by Citizens Trust on December 27, 1916; and Pop Ross to Barnett E. Marks, December 26, 1916. Carbon copy.

48. AS&F Board of Directors meeting minutes, December 18, 1916, TL&I Board of Directors meeting minutes, December 26, 1916.

49. R. Merritt Llewellyn to AS&F, December 30, 1916; and R. Merritt Llewellyn to Eaton, December 30, 1916. The new preferred stock was to have a coupon rate of 6 percent.

50. Eaton to R. Merritt Llewellyn, January 6, 1917. Carbon copy.

51. Eaton to R. Merritt Llewellyn, January 6, 1917. Carbon copy.

Chapter 16. Building for the Future

1. Hubert Eaton approved this version of "The Builder's Creed" in 1955. The original version used "Perpetual Care Fund," which was later changed to "Endowment Care Fund." In a November 7, 1949, memo from Hubert Eaton to Mr. Donley, Eaton asked for the cost to make the change from "perpetual care fund" to "care fund"—a change executed sometime in 1950. A February 1, 1955, "Authorized Version of The Builder's Creed" with a note signed by Margaret Gillis, Frederick E. Llewellyn's secretary, showed the change to "Endowment Care Fund." Sometime in the early 1950s, the change to "Endowment Care Fund" was made in the stone inscription of the Creed outside the Great Mausoleum in Forest Lawn Glendale. At times prior to that, various minor changes had appeared in printed versions of the Creed. Among those was a version that read "a Christ who smiles" rather than the original "a Christ that smiles."

2. Eaton to Dr. William Watson, January 8, 1917. Carbon copy.

3. George Pratt to Mr. McCallister at Young & McCallister, February 16, 1917. Carbon copy of letter and attachment.

4. Wells to Frank B. Gibson, March 17, 1914. Initialed carbon copy; and Frank B. Gibson to J. C. Bratten, March 20, 1914. Handwritten letter; Wells to Eaton, March 20, 1914

5. Wells to Frank B. Gibson, March 17, 1914. Initialed carbon copy; and Wells to Eaton, March 20, 1914, on American Securities Co. letterhead; and Eaton telegram to American Securities Co., March 21, 1914.

6 Pop Ross to Eaton, November 2, 1914. Typed copy and Eaton to R. Merritt Llewellyn, January 6, 1917. Carbon copy.

7. George E. Pratt to TL&I shareholders March 19, 1917. Carbon copies.

8. George E. Pratt to TL&I shareholders March 19, 1917. Carbon copies.

9. George E. Pratt to FLCA, March 1, 1917. Carbon copy.

10. George E. Pratt to FLCA, March 1, 1917. Carbon copy.

11. George E. Pratt to FLCA, March 1, 1917. Carbon copy.

12. George E. Pratt to FLCA, March 1, 1917. Carbon copy. Apparently, Emery had not actually been hired yet. Emery applied for the job in a March 28, 1917 letter to AS&F.

13. Frank B. Gibson to Wells, February 3, 1917; and Harry Watson to Frank Gibson, November 25, 1914..

14. Wells to Frank B. Gibson, February 20, 1917. Initialed carbon copy.

15. Frank B. Gibson to Wells, February 24, 1917.

16. Jo J. De Haven to Wells, February 27, 1917. Addressed to "Martin C. Wells."

17. Lawrence F. Moore to Eaton, March 7, 1917; Lawrence F. Moore to Wells, March 7, 1917; and Wells to Lawrence F. Moore, March 8, 1917.

18. Lawrence F. Moore to Wells, March 14, 1917.

19. Lawrence F. Moore to Wells, March 14, 1917.

20. E. H. Neuhrenberg to Wells, March 23, 1917.

21. Henry E. Brett to FLCA, April 22, 1917.

22. Lawrence F. Moore to Eaton, May 10, 1917.

23. Wells to Tom Ross, July 5, 1917. Initialed carbon copy.

24. Eaton to Getzendanner, March 13, 1917. Carbon copy.

25. Getzendanner to Eaton, March 14, 1017.

26. George F. Emery to AS&F, March 28, 1917. File copy.

27. George F. Emery to Eaton, September 17, 1917. File copy with November 9 pencil notation from Wells that a $50 payment would be made that day but in the future commissions would be paid on the fifteenth based on sales and receipts in the prior month.

28. AS&F, Board of Directors Meeting Minutes, February 9, 1917.

29. Pop Ross for Tom Ross to Wells, March 13, 1917; Wells letter to Tom Ross, March 15, 1917. Carbon copy; and Wells letter to Ray S. Malburg, November 23, 1917. Carbon copy.

30. Wells to Tom Ross, April 19, 1917. Carbon copy.

31. Tom Ross to Wells. Handwritten, undated.

32. Wells to Tom Ross, April 19, 1917. Initialed carbon copy; and Charles Bovensiep, proprietor Detroit Mausoleum Equipment Works, to S. A. Bruner Tile Co., June 18, 1917. Illustration from promotional material included with letter..

33 Eaton telegram to Wells, July 2, 1917. Sent from Creston, Iowa. Punctuation added as penciled on original document; and Wells to Tom Ross, May 9, 1917. Initialed carbon copy

34. Eaton telegram to Wells, July 2, 1917.

35. Eaton letter to Wells, July 3, 1917. One of three letters of same date, all on Hotel Blackstone letterhead.

36. Eaton letter to Wells, July 3, 1917.

37. Eaton to Wells, July 3, 1917.

38. Eaton to Wells, July 3, 1917.

39. Eaton to Wells, July 3, 1917. Second of three letters of same date; and "The Story of Graceland."

40. Eaton to Wells, July 3, 1917. Second of three letters of same date.

41. Eaton to Wells, July 3, 1917. Second of three letters of same date.

42. Eaton telegram to FLCA, July 16, 1917.

43. Pop Ross letter to Wells, July 24, 1917.

44. Wells to Tom Ross, July 8, 1917. Initialed carbon copy.

45. Tom Ross telegram to FLCA, July 13, 1917.

46. Eaton to Wells, July 3, 1917. Third of three letters of same date.

47. Jo J. De Haven to Wells, July 26, 1917.

48. Wells to H. Neuhrenberg, August 20, 1917. Initialed carbon copy; and Silver, "1931 Statutes of California, Chapter 1148."

49. "Tropico Annexation Loses by 215 Votes," *Los Angeles Herald*, August 30, 1917, 13.

50. Wells to Pop Ross, March 12, 1917. Initialed carbon copy.

51. Wells letter to Tom Ross, September 17, 1917. Carbon copy; and Tom Ross to Wells, September 19, 1917

52. Wells to Tom Ross, September 17, 1917. Carbon copy; and Pop Ross to Wells, September 19, 1917.

53. Eaton to Murray M. Harris, March 20, 1918. Carbon copy.

54. Wells, "COPY OF Letter to Undertakers," January 17, 1918.

55. George Emery to Ernest Layrock, June 5, 1917. Carbon copy. Current California law prohibits cremation of animals with human remains as well as interment of anything other than human remains in licensed cemeteries.

56. Dr. Frank Crane, "Community Mausoleums," Chicago, 1917; Eaton to Cecil E. Bryan, February 8, 1918 and February 27, 1918. Carbon copies; and Cecil E. Bryan; "Long Beach California Sunnyside Mausoleum." Forest Lawn acquired Sunnyside Memorial Gardens, now known as Forest Lawn-Long Beach, in 1978.

57. Wells to C. R. Vesper, December 15, 1917. Initialed carbon copy.

58. Tom Ross to Wells, November 6, 1917. Handwritten; Wells to Tom Ross, December 8, 1917. Initialed carbon copy; and Wells to Tom Ross, December 10, 1917. Initialed carbon copy.

59. Wells to L. M. Barker, October 8, 1917. Carbon copy; Wells to Tom Ross, November 15, 1917. Carbon copy; and Wells letter to Tom Ross, December 8, 1917. Carbon copy.

60. Eaton telegram to AS&F, January 12, 1918.

61. Eaton telegram to AS&F, 11:26 a.m., January 12, 1918; and Wells telegram to Eaton, 12:54 p.m., January 12, 1918; Eaton telegram to AS&F, January 13, 1918.

62. Wells to Eaton, June 20, 1918;

63. "Church of Flowers to be Dedicated Today," *Los Angeles Times*, May 12,1918.

64. "Church of Flowers to be Dedicated Today," *Los Angeles Times*, May 12,1918.

65. Eaton, "The Birth of a New Era," speech at dedication of the Little Church of the Flowers, May 12, 1918; No record has been found that contradicts Eaton's statement that "The Builder's Creed" was written on January 1, 1917, but it is possible that the "final" version was written later, as

a more eloquent expression of the vision expressed at the Little Church of the Flowers dedication.

Chapter 17. Consolidation and New Roles

1. American Securities Company telegram to William, Burleigh & McLean. File copy.
2. TL&I, Special Meeting of Shareholders Minutes, January 17, 1917. Typed transcription.
3. Bill of Sale signed by Tom Ross and Pop Ross, February 10, 1917. Transcribed carbon copy.
4. Hamilton, February 6, 1917, notarized transfer to Eaton.
5. AS&F (signed by Pratt & A. R. Hildreth) to TL&I, February 9, 1917. Copy of letter certified by Pratt as secretary of AS&F.
6. George E. Pratt to FLCA, March 1, 1917. Carbon copy.
7. Tom Ross and Pop Ross to FLCA March 2, 1917. As copied in FLCA, Board of Trustees Meeting Minutes, June 7, 1917.
8. Eaton to Dr. William C. Watson, March 9, 1917. Carbon copy.
9. Eaton to William Hazlett, January 9, 1918, carbon copy; Eaton to Frank D. Hamilton, undated carbon copy of draft; and Hamilton, February 6, 1917, notarized transfer to Eaton.
10. Eaton to Hazlett, January 9, 1918. Carbon copy.
11 Hazlett to Eaton, February 14, 1918. Multiple letters.
12. AS&F records of annual meetings of stockholders, 1920-1928.
13. AS&F Board of Directors Meeting Minutes, October 26, 1918; November 1, 1918; and February 20, 1919.
14. American Securities Company telegram to William, Burleigh & McLean. File copy.
15. Eaton to Williamson of Burleigh & McLain, January 19, 1917. Carbon copy.
16. Eaton to F. G. Crowell, C. F. Burton, W. O. Van Arsdale, and G. E. Ricker, April 15, 1917. Carbon copy; K. L. Crowley v. American Securities Company, Supreme Judicial Court of the State of Main, petition dated April 21, 1917; and Eaton to F. G. Crowell, C. F. Burton, W. C. Van Arsdale, and G. E. Ricker, April 25, 1917.
17. TL&I, Special Meeting of Shareholders Minutes, January 17, 1917. Typed transcription.
18. George E. Pratt to FLCA, March 1, 1917. Carbon copy.
19. George E. Pratt to FLCA, March 1, 1917. Carbon copy.
20. George E. Pratt to FLCA, March 1, 1917. Carbon copy.
21. FLCA, Board of Trustees Meeting Minutes, June 7, 1917.
22. Eaton to Wells, June 13, 1917. Initialed carbon copy.
23. Eaton to Wells, June 13, 1917. Initialed carbon copy.

24. Eaton to Wells, June 13, 1917. Initialed carbon copy.

25. Eaton to Wells, June 13, 1917. Initialed carbon copy.

26. FLCA, Board of Trustees Meeting Minutes, June 19, 1917; AS&F to FLCA, June 22, 1917; and AS&F to FLCA, June 23, 1917.

27. AS&F to FLCA, June 22, 1917. Eaton & Pratt signed as corporate officers; Eaton, Hollingsworth, & Gates signed as personally guarantors.

28. California Health & Safety Code, section 8360.

29. FLCA, Board of Trustees Meeting Minutes, June 7, 1917.

30. Eaton to Max Loewenthal, May 22, 1917. Carbon copy; Max Loewenthal to Eaton, May 25, 1917; and "Notice of Guardian's Sale of Real Estate At Private Sale," California Independent, June 14, 1917.

31. "Deed of Guardian Private Sale," August 22, 1917. File copy; AS&F to "Los Angeles Trust & Savings Bank, as guardian of the estate of Lucile R. Bedford, a Minor." File copy; Bruce Grigsby, Trust Officer, Los Angeles Trust & Savings Bank to AS&F, July 5, 1917; and AS&F board of directors meeting minutes, June 26, 1917. The directors authorized the purchase without a mention of purchase price in the resolution.

32. FLCA Board of Trustees Meeting Minutes, October 1, 1917. Years later, the IRS would take the opposite position, holding that a percentage sales contract was private inurement that could lead to revocation of a nonprofit cemetery's tax exemption.

33. Eaton to Loewenthal, February 14, 1918. According a letter to John Llewellyn the following day, the meeting was delayed from February 15 to February 19.

34. Eaton to Wells, February 13, 1918.

35. FLCA Board of Trustees Meeting Minutes, October 25, 1918

36. FLCA, Board of Trustees Meeting Minutes, October 15, 1918.

37. AS&F agreement with FLCA, October 31, 1918;

38. FLCA, Board of Trustees Meeting Minutes, October 25, 1918.

39. FLCA, Board of Trustees Meeting Minutes, October 25, 1918.

40. FLCA, Board of Trustees Meeting Minutes, October 25, 1918.

41. FLCA, Board of Trustees Meeting Minutes, October 25, 1918.

42. TL&I Board of Directors Meeting Minutes, May 3, 1917.

43. Treadwell to Pop Ross, May 8, 1917. Copy in TL&I Board of Directors Meeting Minutes, May 22, 1917.

44. Pop Ross to Treadwell, May 17, 1917. Copy in TL&I Board of Directors Meeting Minutes, May 22, 1917.

45. "Answer to Citation and Protest Against Dissolution in the Matter of the Voluntary Dissolution of Tropico Land & Improvement Company, a corporation." Superior Court of the State of Arizona in and for the County of Maricopa, verified by J. B. Treadwell on June 7, 1917.

46. Barnett E. Marks telegram to Eaton, June 9, 1917.

47. Eaton telegram to Wells, June 27, 1917.

48. Eaton to Wells, July 3, 1917; and Wells to Eaton, June 18, 1917.

49. "Citation of Authorities in the Matter of the Voluntary Dissolution of Tropico Land & Improvement Company, a corporation." Superior Court of the State of Arizona in and for the County of Maricopa, submitted by Barnett E. Marks, Attorney for petitioner.

50. Barnett E. Marks to Eaton, August 28, 1917.

51. AS&F telegram to Barnett E. Marks, October 31, 1917; Barnett E. Marks to AS&F, October 31, 1917; and "List of Shareholders of the TROPICO LAND & IMPROVEMENT CO, October 2–1917," AS&F held 139,823 shares, Treadwell held only 500 shares, 25 shares were held as "qualifying shares" by directors, and shareholders who could not be found accounted for the balance of the 141,623 shares.

52. Eaton to Barnett E. Marks, November 3, 1917. Carbon copy; and Marks to Eaton, November 15, 1917.

53. Superior Court of the State of Arizona in and for the County of Maricopa, No. 9974, Final Decree of Dissolution. File copy.

54. Eaton to Park and Cemetery magazine, October 5, 1918; O. H. Sample to Eaton, October 10, 1918; and Forest Lawn Archives.

55 Chas. L. Dingley to FLCA, November 2, 1918.

Chapter 18. Eaton Versus Wells

1. Owen, undated document signed as secretary. Owen served as secretary of FLCA from January 21, 1919, until July 3, 1919.

2. Owen, signed as secretary, undated. Owen was secretary of FLCA from January 21, 1919, to July 3, 1919.

3. St. Johns, 121-122; and Eaton Personal History, "Eaton Family Tree."

4. Eaton Family History, unpublished. Leroy, "Roy," Henderson was born on July 2, 1907. Hubert Eaton formally adopted Roy on August 12, 1926, and he was known as Roy Eaton after that date.

5. AS&F Board of Directors to FLCA Lot Proprietors, January 8, 1919. Signed by Eaton.

6. Flint, Walker, E. U. Emery, Ogg, and Kauffman to Lot Owners, January 14, 1919. When Emery was nominated for election to the FLMPA board of directors in 1919, it was discovered that he did no own enough property to qualify.

7. Wells to Salesmen, January 15, 1919. Initialed file copy.

8. FLCA to Lot Proprietors, January 16, 1919.

9. FLCA, Lot Proprietors Meeting Minutes, January 20, 1919.

10. FLCA, Board of Trustees Meeting Minutes, February 15, 1918.

11. FLCA Lot Proprietors Meeting Minutes, January 20, 1919.

12. FLCA Lot Proprietors Meeting Minutes, January 20, 1919.

13. FLCA Lot Proprietors Meeting Minutes, January 20, 1919.

14. FLCA Lot Proprietors Adjourned Meeting Minutes, January 21, 1919.

15. FLCA, Board of Trustees Meeting Minutes, January 21, 1919.

16. FLCA Board of Trustees Minutes, February 15, 1919.

17. FLCA Board of Trustees Minutes, February 15, 1919.

18. FLCA Board of Trustees Minutes, February 15, 1919.

19. FLCA Board of Trustees Minutes, February 15, 1919.

20. FLCA Board of Trustees Minutes, February 15, 1919.

21. FLCA, Board of Trustees Meeting Minutes, February 15, 1919; and "Statement of Facts," c. early 1919, 2-3. Typed on Kemp, Mitchell & Silberberg letterhead with pencil notation at top: "Read by Kemp to Trustees of F. L. C. Assn. in Directors room of L. A. T. & Sav Bank."

22. "Statement of Facts," 3.

23. FLCA, Board of Trustees Meeting Minutes, February 27, 1919.

24. Owen to AS&F, February 28, 1919; and Eaton to FLCA, February 28, 1919.

25. Wells, unsigned and undated but content establishes creation as early 1919.

26. A G. Carter (AS&F secretary) to FLCA, March 6, 1919; and Carter and Eaton to FLCA, March 8, 1919.

27. Owen and Wells to Eaton, March 13, 1919.

28. Owen to AS&F, March 13, 1919.

29. Eaton to FLCA, March 13, 1919.

30. Owen and Wells to AS&F, March 13, 1919.

31. Eaton to FLCA, March 14, 1919.

32. Eaton to FLCA, March 14, 1919.

33. Eaton to FLCA, March 14, 1919.

34. Owen to AS&F, March 15, 1919.

35. Owen to AS&F, March 15, 1919.

36. William B. Thomas to AS&F, March 24, 1919.

37. Owen to FLCA Trustees. Signed but undated.

38. Eaton to FLCA, March 28, 1919. Carbon copy.

39. FLCA Board of Trustees Meeting Minutes, March 29, 1919; and Eaton to Wells, March 29, 1919.

40. Pop Ross to W. I. Hollingsworth, April 9, 1919.

41. Pop Ross to W. I. Hollingsworth, April 9, 1919.

42. Wells to FLCA Trustees, April 16, 1919. Quoted in FLCA Board of Trustees Meeting Minutes, April 16, 1919.

43. FLCA Board of Trustees Meeting Minutes, April 16, 1919; and "Personal Memoranda," March 1, 1924. Handwritten notations of

"Confidential!," "Destroy at my death," and initialed "HLE" — Hubert Lewright Eaton.

44. Owen to Flint, April 24, 1919 and FLCA Board fof Trustees Meeting Minutes, April 30, 1919.

Chapter 19. Problem Solved

1. Flint to Eaton, April 17, 1919. Motely Flint, like those who followed him as president of FLCA, was not a full-time employeee. After Eaton's formation of FLMPA the position of FLCA president was more akin to chair of a volunteer board than president and chief executive officer.

2. Flint to Eaton, April 21, 1919.

3. Flint to Eaton, April 26, 1919.

4. Eaton to Flint, April 18, 1919. Carbon copy; and Eaton to Flint April 30, 1919.

5. Flint to FLCA Trustees, April 30, 1919. File copy with "Flint, Motley" in penciled block letters above the title of president.

6. FLCA Board of Trustees Meeting Minutes, April 30, 1919. The minutes show that the quoted Section 573 was from the California Penal Code Chap. 173.

7. Owen to Flint, May 8, 1919. Carbon copy.

8. FLCA, Board of Trustees Meeting Minutes, May 12, 1919.

9. FLCA, Board of Trustees Meeting Minutes, May 12, 1919.

10. FLCA, Board of Trustees Meeting Minutes, April 30, 1919, May 14, 1919, and May 31, 1919.

11. FLCA Board of Trustees Meeting Minutes, May 14, 1919; and file copy of opinion by Ely.

12. Owen to Flint, May 22, 1919. Carbon copy.

13. Eaton to Flint, May 26, 1919. Carbon copy.

14. Eaton to Owen, May 27, 1919. Carbon copy.

15. FLCA, Board of Trustees Meeting Minutes, May 31, 1919.

16. Eaton to Flint May 22, 1919. Carbon copy.

17. Ely to Owen, May 29, 1919.

18. FLCA Board of Trustees Meeting Minutes, June 4, 1919.

19. FLCA Board of Trustees Meeting Minutes, June 4, 1919.

20. FLCA Board of Trustees Meeting Minutes, June 23, 1919.

21. FLCA Board of Trustees Meeting Minutes, June 23, 1919.

22. Eaton to Flint, July 17, 1919. Carbon copy. Eaton's mention of Uncle Sam is a reference to President Woodrow Wilson's curtailment of liquor sales to save grain for food production for the US war effort. The Eighteenth Amendment to the US Constitution had been ratified in January 1919, to be effective one year later, beginning the Prohibition era in the United States. In October 1919, Congress passed the Volstead Act providing the methods

of enforcing prohibition. History Channel, Prohibition, A&E Television Networks, LLC. n.d. accessed June 29, 2015. http://www.history.com/topics/prohibition.

23. FLCA Board of Trustees Meeting Minutes, June 14, 1919. The president was legally the chief executive officer of the corporation. Hubert Eaton was general manager of FLMPA during his lifetime—never president. This was to avoid the conflict resulting from being president and chief executive officer of AS&F and its various subsidiaries. However, for many years the bylaws essentially gave the general manager the powers of the board of directors when it was not meeting—much more power than a present-day CEO gets..

24. Agreements between FLCA and FLMPA dated August 23 1919, from FLCA Board of Trustees Meeting Minutes, January 10, 1919; and Agreement between FLMPA and AS&F, dated August 23, 1919, from FLMPA Board of Directors Meeting Minutes, August 23, 1919. Signed copy in minutes.

25. Agreement between FLMPA and AS&F, dated August 23, 1919.

26. Flint to Eaton, September 30, 1919; and Eaton to Flint, October 1, 1919. Carbon copy.

27. Eaton to Flint, October 2, 1919. Carbon copy.

28. Eaton to Flint, October 2, 1919. Carbon copy.

29. Eaton to Flint, October 2, 1919. Carbon copy.

30. Eaton to Flint, October 2, 1919. Carbon copy.

31. Eaton to Flint, October 2, 1919. Carbon copy.

32. Eaton to Flint, October 2, 1919. Carbon copy.

33. "REPORT OF THE BOARD OF TRUSTEES of the FOREST LAWN CEMETERY ASSOCIATION to the LOT OWNERS AT THEIR ANNUAL MEETING, JANUARY 20, 1920." The transfer of the responsibility for development work from FLMPA to AS&F did not happen until the following year.

Epilogue

1. Parry, "Architects' Profiles."

2. Wells's death certificate.

3. Eaton, "Speech Given By Mr. Hubert Eaton At Sales Meeting May 26, 1932, 8:00 A.M." Penciled note "Steno Notes. Not in Speech book."

4. Hancock, *The Forest Lawn Story*, 117 and Eaton Personal History. Doctor of Human Letters (L.H.D.) William Jewell College, Novbember 10, 1950. Doctor of Laws (LL.D.), Pepperdine College, June 1, 1952. Doctor of Science (Sci.D.), University of Redlands, August 30, 1963.

5. About 40 states allow common ownership of funeral homes and cemeteries. Other states prohibit combinations as a competitive threat

to stand-alone funeral homes. By 2017, Forest Lawn Memorial-Park Association operated cemeteries in Glendale, Hollywood Hills (Los Angeles), Cathedreal City, Covina, Cypress, and Long Beach. Under its trade-style, Forest Lawn Memorial-Parks & Mortuaries, its wholly owned subsidiary, Forest Lawn Mortuary operated mortuaries (funeral homes) in Arcadia (FD 2186), Cathedral City (FD 1847), Coachella (FD 640), Covina Hills (FD 1150),Cypress (FD 1051), Glendale (FD 656), Hollywood Hills (FD 904), Indio (FD 967), Long Beach (FD 1151). Sales offices licensed as funeral establishments were in City of Industry (FD 2121) and Whittier (FD 2302).

Bibliography

"About Los Angeles Herald. (Los Angles [Calif.]) 1900—1911." n.d. (accessed July 14, 2015). http://chroniclingamerica.loc.gov/lccn/sn85042462/.

Adams Hill Homeowners Associaiton. "A Brief History of the Neighborhood: Adams Hill and Adams Square." n.d. (accessed July 8, 2005). www.adamshill.org/history/history.html.

"Adobes of Rancho San Rafael," n.d. Historic Adobes of Los Angeles County. (accessed October 7, 2005). http://laokay.com.

"After the Cemetery Sign." 1910. Los Angeles Times. March 1: 14.

"After the Grand Jury." 1914. Los Angeles Times. Feburary 27: II2.

American Securities Company. The Reasons Why. Glendale, CA.: American Securities Company, c. 1915.

"Andrew Glassell Has Passed to the Beyond." 1901. Los Angeles Herald. January 29: 16.

"Application for Membership of Charles Blackburn Sims," Wisconsin Society of the Sons of the American Revolution, February 28, 1926.

Arroyo, Juliet M. Images of America: Early Glendale. Chicago: Arcadia Publishing, 2005.

AS&F Foundation. n.d. "History." (accessed Septemaber 1, 2012). http://asf-foundation.org/history.html.

"Asks Accounting of Eileen Bedford Estate: Los Angeles Trust and Savings Bank Suies Mrs. Lambourn on Account of Child." 1910. Los Angeles Herald. March 8: 1.

"Association Seeks Many Improvements." 1910. Los Angeles Herald. February 18: 5.

"Backyard Tourists Exploring Home." n.d. (accessed April 1, 2013). http://www.backyardtouristsla.com/2012/11/home-of-peace-cemetery-provides-final-rest-to-rabbis-moguls-and-stooges.html.

"Banker Shot To Death: Tropico Millionaire is killed in quarrel over tombstone; Slayer cuaght." 1915. Los Angeles Evening Herald. December 23: 1.

Barry, James H. "Franklin Hichborn Praises Reform Governor Hiram W. Johnson, 1911," in *Major Problems in California History*, edited by Secheng, Chan and Spencer C. Olin. Boston, MA: Cengage Learning, 1997.

Bates, J. C., ed. *History of the Bench and Bar of California*. San Francisco, CA: Bench and Bar Publishing Co., 1912. https://books.google.com/books?id=ax0LAQAAIAAJ.

"Battle Is On for $100,000 Property." 1912. *Los Angeles Herald*. January 18. 1.

Beecher Mausoleum Guardian Angel Assoc. "Cecil E. Bryan." n.d. (accessed December 10, 2014). http://beechermausoleum.org/cecil-e-bryan.

"Berkeley Square." n.d. (accessed March 31, 2016). http://www.berkeleysquarelosangeles.com/2011/05/7-llewellyn-milner-house.html.

"Billboard Protest Is Presented." 1910. *Los Angeles Express*. February 28: 9.

Billiter, Bill. 1990. "The Huntington Beach Co.: City's Benefactor or Boss?" *Los Angeles Times*, April 23: 106.

Black, Tim. "Arroyo Seco Flood Timeline." (accessed March 23, 2006). http://www.arroyoseco.org/History/ArroyoSecoFloodTimeline.pdf.

Boynton, Charles C. n.d. Ancestry.com. http://search.ancestry.com. (accessed August 13, 2017).

"Bringing Up the Dead," 2006. *The Standard*, March 25. (accessed September 12, 2012). http://thestandard.com.

Brooks, Jon. 2015. "Why are there so many deal people in Colma?" December 15. https://ww2.kqed.org/news/2015/12/16/why-are-so-many-dead-people-in-colma-and-so-few-in-san-francisco/.

Bryan, Cecil E. 1929. "AACS Proceedings of the 43rd Annual Convention." International Cemetery, Cremation, and Funeral Association (ICCFA). September. (accessed June 13, 2017). https://www.iccfa.com/reading/1920-1939/mausoleums. The "AACS" was the American Association of Cemetery Superintendents, a predecessor to the ICCFA.

Bryan, Cecil E. *Community Mausoleums*. Chicago, Il: Cecil E. Bryan, Inc., 1917.

Carpenter, Edwin H. n.d. Southern California Genealogical Society and Family Research Library. (accessed September 12, 2012). www.scgsgenealogy.com/LACC-Title.htm.

Casey, Thomas H. n.d. "The Law Offices of Thomas H. Casey: Law Firm Cases." (accessed Janaury 12, 2016). http://www.tomcaseylaw.com/cases.php.

Caughey, John and Caughey LaRee, ed. *Los Angeles: Biography of a City*, Berkeley and Los Angeles: University of California Press, 1977.

"Cemeteries in the County of Los Angeles." n.d. The Church of Jesus Christ of Latter-day Saints. n.d. (accessed 13 2016). July. https://familysearch.org/wiki/en/Cemeteries_in_the_County_of_Los_Angeles#Whittier_Heights_Cemetery.

"Cemetery Advertising Protested By Citizens." *Los Angeles Herald*. February 14: 3.

"Cemetery Development Service." 1924. *Park and Cemetery*. February: 306-307.

"Cemetery Fight May Be Bitter." 1906. *Los Angeles Times*. March 10: II.12.

"Charles O. Morgan For Justice." 1910. *Los Angeles Daily Times*. August 12: II8.

"Church of Flowers to be Dedicated Today." 1918. *Los Angeles Times*. May 12: 6.

"Citizens of Hollywood Ask Burial Restriction." 1910. *Los Angeles Herald*. October 14: 4.

"City Justices: Court holds they are elected for two years." 1896. *Los Angeles Times*, October 19: 9.

City of Huntington Beach. n.d. "HB History." City of Huntington Beach. (accessed September 29, 2016). http://www.huntingtonbeachca.gov/about/history/.

City of Los Angeles v. City of San Fernando, et al. 1975. L.A. No. 30199, (14 Cal.3d 199) (May 12).

"City of the Departed." 1922. *American Globe: Investors Magazine*. October 21.

Cole, Seward. 1910. "Should the City Discriminate in Favor of the Hollywood Cemetery?" *Los Angeles Record*, July 27.

"C. O. Morgan For City Justice" 1896. *Los Angeles Herald*. October 28: 6.

"Continuance." 1916. *Los Angeles Times*. February 19: 20.

"Convention of Republicans: Prohibitionists convene." 1914. *Los Angeles Times*. August 14: II2.

"Coroner Rides Luxuriously," 1908. *Los Angeles Daily Times*, December 22: 15.

County of Los Angeles, Department of Public Works. n.d. "San Gabriel River and Montebello Forebay Water Conservation System." (accessed March 23, 2006). http://ladpw.org/wrd/publication/system/background.cfm.

County of Santa Barbara, Planning and Development, Energy Division. n.d. "Summerland Oil & Gas Production." (accessed August 14, 2017). http://www.sbcountyplanning.org/energy/information/summerland.asp.

"Court Gives Child $5 From $215,000 Estate." 1910. *Los Angeles Herald*. October 22: 8.

Cowan, Robert G. *A Backward Glance: Los Angeles 1901-1915*. Los Angeles: Torrez Press, 1969.

"Crushable: Union Terrace." n.d. (accessed November 17, 2015). http://tenderfab.com/tag/t-patterson-ross/.

"Cut Off By Will, Girl Gets Riches." 1911. *Los Angeles Herald*. August 30:13..

Cypress Lawn Heritage Foundation. 2002. "Hamden Noble's Dream and Cypress Lawn's Beginning." *Heritage Newsletter*. July: 1.

Cypress Lawn Memorial Park. n.d. "About Us." (accessed October 31, 2012). http://www.cypresslawn.com/_mgxroot/page_10941.php,.

"Death Overtakes Celebrated Worker: Treadwell, of Mining Fame, Dies." 1931. *Los Angeles Times.* November 6: A15.

Dodd, Penny. n.d. "Olive Grove Cemetery." U. S. Gen Web Archives. (accessed May 3, 2014). http://files.usgwarchives.net/ca/losangeles/cemeteries/olive.txt.

Disney, Charles Elias. n.d. "Dr. Hubert L. Eaton ~ 'My Tribute to My Friend.'" (accessed November 12, 2014). http://huberteaton.com/index.html.

"Donald L. Bryant." n.d. (accessed December 5, 2015). http://search.ancestry.com/cgi-bin/sse.dll?viewrecord=1&r=an&db=FindAGraveUS&indiv=try&h=124698411.

"Do Not Indorse. Prohibitionists Convene." 1914. *Los Angeles Times.* August 14: 12.

Eaton, Hubert. *The Commemoral: The cemetery of the future.* Los Angeles: Interment Association of California, 1954. Republished by Forest Lawn Memorial-Park Association 1994.

Eaton. n.d. "Personal History." [unpublished].

"Earl and Harriman Scotched Together: Latter intimates tha he will contest the nomination of Rose." 1913. *Los Angeles Times.* May 9: III1.

"Editorial." 1862. *Los Angeles Star.* December 6.

"Eileen Mitchell Bedford (1882–1907)." n.d. (accessed August 30, 2012). http://www.findagrave.com.

"Eleven Ex-Officials Indicted, Arrested." 1913. *Los Angeles Times.* November 15: III1.

"Espee System Absorbs Oil: J. B. Treadwell makes known the companyy's intention." 1903. *Los Angeles Times.* October 5, 1903: 3.

Estate of Susan Glassell Mitchell, Deceased. 1911. 12,308 (Supreme Court of California, 160 Cal. 618; 117 P. 774 August 30).

"Evergreen Cemetery." (accessed September 10, 2005). http://www.usc.edu/isd/archives/la/cemeteries/la_cemeteries_evergreen.html.

"Father Fights Aunt For Guardianship." 1908. *Los Angeles Herald.* July 17: 5.

Fields, Robin. 1999. "Grim Time for Funeral Firms." *Los Angles Times,* October 24: C1.

"File Petition for Probate." 1908. *Los Angeles Herald.* July 15: 3.

"Final Resting Place Where the Beauties of Nature Reign Supreme: Forest Lawn Cemetery Is a Little City of the Dead." 1916. *American Globe: Investors Magazine.* November: 15.

"Find Banker's Slayer Guilty: Jurymen bring in verdict of second-degree murder." *Los Angeles Times.* April 23: 8.

Fogelson, Robert M., *The Fragmented Metropolis: Los Angeles, 1850-1930*, Berkeley and Los Angeles: University of California Press, 1993.

Forbes, E. 1910. "Letter to the Editor." *Los Angles Express*, February 21.

Forest Lawn Memorial-Park Association. c. 1932. "Cemetery Facts." *Forest Lawn Salesman's Kit.*

Forest Lawn Memorial-Park Association. 1963. *Forest Lawn Art Guide.* Forest Lawn Memorial-Park Association.

"Frank D. Hamilton, Liberty Banker, Buried Saturday," *Lathorp Optimist*, Lathrop, Missouri, October 11, 1956, 1.

"Fred Eaton Back From Owens River," *Los Angeles Express*, August 4, 1908.

"Frown On Call To The Grave: Immense cemetery sign stirs northern section." 1910. *Los Angeles Times.* February 18: 17.

"Funeral of W. J. Blain: Body of landscape engineer to be sent east for burial." 1910. *Los Angeles Examiner.* July 10.

"Gambler Loses His Child and Fortune, Custody of Beautiful Lucile Bedford Goes to Aunt." 1908. *Weekly Arizona Journal-Miner.* August 18: 1.

George, A. L., C. E. 1900. "Sectional & Road Map for Los Angeles County, including part of Orange & Ventura Counties." Library of Congress. Stoll & Thayer Co. (Los Angeles). http://hdl.loc.gov/loc.gmd/g4361.la000025.

"Glendale, California." (accessed July 8, 2005). http://en.wikipedia.org/wiki/Glendale,_California.html.

"Glendale, California Biographies: Richardson, William C. B." n.d. (accessed July 19, 2017). http://theusgenweb.org/ca/losangeles/GlendaleBios/Richardson_William_C_B.htm.

"Glendale History - A Brief Look." Glendale Historical Society. (accessed September 13, 2012). http://www.glendalehistorical.org/history.html.

"Glendale Plans for a Big Consolidation." 1910. *Los Angeles Examiner.* March 13.

Gnerre, Sam. 2014. "The Inglewood Park Cemetery predates the city's incorporation." July 26. http://blogs.dailybreeze.com/history/2014/07/26/the-inglewood-park-cemetery-predates-the-citys-incorporation/.

Graceland Cemetery. n.d. "Story of Graceland." (accessed October 18, 2015). http://www.gracelandcemetery.org/the-story-of-graceland/.

Graceland Fairlawn - Funeral Home. n.d. "History & Staff." FuneralOne. (accessed January 22, 2017). http://www.gracelandfairlawn.com/who-we-are/history-and-staff.

Graffy, Neal. 2011. "Summerland Oil Fields in the Sea." May 21. (accessed April 10, 2017). https://www.edhat.com/site/tidbit.cfm?nid=55984.

"Greater Glendale Meeting's Subject: Improvement Association Gathering Favors Consolidation of Valley Towns." 1910. *Los Angeles Express.* August 25.

Green Lawn Memorial Park. n.d. "About Greenlawn Memorial Park." (accessed July 3, 2016). http://www.greenlawnmemorialpark.com/history.

Hale, Benjamin. 2014. "The History of the Hollywood Movie Industry." History Cooperative. November 12. (accessed August 4, 2017). http://historycooperative.org/the-history-of-the-hollywood-movie-industry/

Hancock, Ralph. *The Forest Lawn Story*. Los Angeles: Academy Publishers, 1955. Also, Angelus Press. Los Angeles, 1964.

Hannon, Michael. n.d. "McNamara Bombing Case (1911)." University of Minnesota Law Library. (accessed September 29, 2015). darrow.law.umn.edu/trialpdfs/McNamara_LA_Times_Bombing.pdf.

"Hartwell Is Elected Coroner: Office vacated by Lanterman is filled." 1908. *Los Angeles Herald*. January 28: 10.

"HB History." n.d. City of Huntington Beach. (accessed September 29, 2016). http://www.huntingtonbeachca.gov.

Henderson, G. C., Robert A. Oliver, and Edward Weston. n.d. *Tropico: The City Beautiful*. Tropico (Glendale), California.

"Herald Examiner–Filming Location." n.d. (accessed July 14, 2015). http://www.herald-examiner-los-angeles-filming-location.com/about/.

"Herald Examiner Will Halt Publishing Today." 1989. *Los Angeles Times* (San Diego). November 2: 1.

"Herald on Morrison." 1898. *Los Angeles Times*. November 3: 8.

"Historical Resident Population." n.d. Given Place Media. (accessed February 10, 2017). http://www.laalmanac.com/population/po02.htm.

"Historic Cemeteries of Los Angeles." n.d. (accessed September 16, 2005). http://www.usc.educ.isd/archives/la/cemeteries/.

Historic Resources Group. 2004. "Historic Resource Survey Report for the Cumberland Heights Neighborhood." Glendale: City of Glendale Planning Division, September 30 (revised December 2004).

Historic Resources Group. 2014. "South Glendale Historic Context Statement." August 14.

"Historical Timeline of Los Angeles," 2012. Discover Los Angeles, September 10, (updated September 4, 2013, and September 1 2016). (accessed November 28, 2016). http://www.discoverlosangeles.com.

History Channel. n.d. "Prohibition." A&E Television Networks, LLC. (accessed June 29, 2015). http://www.history.com/topics/prohibition.

History of California and an Extended History of Los Angeles and Environs. Biographical. Vols. II & III. Los Angeles: Historic Record Company, 1915.

"History of the [Los Angeles City] Cemetery," n.d. Southern California Genealogical Society and Family Research Library, http://www.scgsgenealogy.com.

"History of the Town of Colma," n.d. (accessed March 29, 2006).History Guild, http://www.colma.ca.gov.

"History of ULARA Adjudication," n.d. Upper Los Angeles River Area Watermaster. (accessed Janury 17, 2016). http://ularawatermaster.com.

Holly Leaves. 1918. "Death of Mrs. Cole." August 24: 11. https://books.google.com/books?id=MtRRAAAAYAAJ.

"Huntington Beach Co.: City's Benefactor or boss?" 1990. *Los Angeles Times.* April 23: A1, A27.

Ingram Construction. n.d. "Community Mausoleums Construction Since 1978." (accessed June 13, 2017). https://www.mausoleum.com/.

"Inquest is Held Over Slain Banker." 1915. *Los Angeles Evening Herald.* December 24: 3.

Jeanette. 2012. "Home of Peace Cemetery Provides Final Rest to Rabbis, Moguls and 'Stooges'." November 10. (accessed August 24, 2015). http://www.backyardtouristsla.com/2012/11/home-of-peace-cemetery-provides-final-rest-to-rabbis-moguls-and-stooges.html.

Jenkins, W. C. 1914. "Post Cineres Gloriam Venit." *National Magazine,* April-September: 637-647.

"John B. Treadwell Mining Man, Dead." 1931. *Arizona Daily Star.* November 6: 1.

"John Llewellyn To Be Buried Tomorrow." 1919. *Los Angeles Herald.* April 28: 1.

Kath, Laura. *Forest Lawn: The first 100 years.* Glendale, CA: Tropico Press 2006.

Keister, Douglas. n.d. "A Brief History of the Community Mausoleum." (accessed June 13, 2017). http://www.daddezio.com/cemetery/articles/mausoleum.html.

Kenny, Robert W., "Reviewed Work: A History of the Los Angeles Labor Movement, 1911-1941 by Louis B. Perry and Richard S. Perry," *Southern California Quarterly,* (Berkeley: University of California Press, June 1964). (accessed October 1, 2015). http://www.jstor.org.

"Kern County Fields: A vast inland sea." 1900. *Los Angeles Times* (Exclusive Petroleum-Oil Number). April 28: 9.

"Keystone vs. South Spring Hill: Action dismissed for want of prosecution." 1901. Jackson (California): *Amador Ledger.* February 1: 3.

Kielbasa, John R. *Historic Adobes of Los Angeles County.* Pittsburg: Dorrance Publishing, 1998.

"Killing Over 'Tombstones' Is Claim." 1915. *Los Angeles Evening Herald.* December 23: 1.

"Kills Banker; Taken By Posse." 1915. *Los Angeles Evening Herald.* December 23: 1.

"Kinship Fraud Charged in Contest of Will." 1931. *Los Angeles Times*. June 16: II-18.

Klein, Norman M., *The History of Forgetting: Los Angeles and the Erasure of Memory*. (New York, NY: Verso., 1997).

Lasher, George W. *George W. Eaton, D.D. LL.D.: A memorial*. Hamilton, N.Y.: Colgate University, 1913.

Laurel Hill Cemetery v. The City and County of San Francisco, etal. 1907. S.F. 3855 (California Supreme Court, December 4).

Lillian Bishop Ross, as Executrix, etc., Appellant, v.American security fidelity company (a Corporation) et al., Respondents. 123 Cal.App. 175 (Cal. Ct. App. 1932)

"Llewellyn Funeral Arranged for Monday." 1919. April 25. *Los Angeles Herald*. April 25: 5.

Llewellyn Iron Works. 1926. "Elevators, Catalog 36A." Internet Archive. (accessed March 31, 2016). https://ia802703.us.archive.org/26/items/Elevators_46/ElevatorsLlewellynIronWorks.pdf.

"Llewellyn Will Filed for Probate." 1919. *Los Angeles Herald*. June 25.

Locke, Michael. 2015. "W. C. B. Richardson House c. 1873." December 15. Flickr. (accessed August 5, 2017). https://www.flickr.com/photos/michael_locke/23756267635.

"Looks on Murder as Scene for Screen" 1915. *Sacramento Union*. December 24: 9.

"Long Beach, California Sunnyside Mausloleum now kno [*sic*] as Forest Lawn." n.d. (accessed May 21, 2015). http://www.cecilebryan.com/Home/CA_Long_Beach.html.

"Long Fight for Child of Suicide is Won by Aunt." 1908. *Los Angeles Herald*. August 15: 12.

Lorraine Park Cemetery. n.d. "Welcome." (accessed October 27, 2005). http://www.lorrianepark.com/welcome.php.

Los Angeles Chamber of Commerce, Industrial Bureau. c. 1915. "More Smoke Stacks, More Payrolls and More Prosperity for Los Angeles and Southern California."

"Los Angeles City Cemetery." 2006. Southern California Genealogical Society and Family Research Library. June 16. (accessed September 12, 2012). http://www.scfsgenearlogy.com/LAXCC-Title.htm.

"Los Angeles County Cemeteries." n.d. (accessed June 8, 2015). http://www.epodunk.com/cgi-bin/localList.php?local=10443&locTGroup=Cemeteries&direction=down.

Los Angeles County, Department of Public Works. n.d. "History of the Los Angeles River." (accessed March 23, 2006). http://ladpw.org/wmd/watershed/LA/history.cfm.

LA5 Rotary Club of Los Angeles. n.d. "Our History." (accessed January 8, 2017). http://www.rotaryla5.org/about-us/our-history.

"L.A.'s Evergreen Cemetery a Monument to a Rich Past." 1983. *Los Angeles Times*. January 23: F1.

"Los Angeles Investment Company." n.d. (accessed April 1, 2016). http://www.antiquehomestyle.com/plans/la-investment/index.htm.

"Los Angeles Investment Company Piles Up Corporation History." 1915. *American Globe: Investors Magazine*. August: 7-8.

"Los Angeles Investment Copmany's Heads Named." 1914. *Los Angeles Times*. January 21: II2.

Los Angeles Tourism & Convention Board. 2013. Historical Timeline of Los Angeles. September 4. (accessed March 13, 2014). http://www.discoverlosangeles.com/blog/historical-timeline-los-angeles.

Los Angeles Trust & Savings Bank v. J. B. Treadwell, et al. 1910. 74065 (Superior Court of California, Los Angeles, April 9).

"Lucile Richmond Bryant." n.d. (accessed December 21, 2015). http://search.ancestry.com/cgi-bin/sse.dll?viewrecord=1&r=an&db=FindAGraveUS&indiv=try&h=124698613.

"Lucile Toland Bedford Lambourn." n.d. (accessed December 5, 2015). http://familyrecord.net/getperson.php?personID=I62028&tree=CorlissOrdway.

Masters, Nathan. 2011. "A Brief History of Palm Trees in Southern California." KCET. KCET. December 7. https://www.kcet.org/shows/lost-la/a-brief-history-of-palm-trees-in-southern-california.

Masters, 2014. "The Lost City of Tropico, California." *KCET*. KCET. June 16. (accessed October 10, 2014). http://www.kcet.org/updaily/socal_focus/history/la-as-subject/the-lost-city-of-tropico.html.

"Mayor Harper Resigns." 1909. *Los Angeles Herald*. March 12: 1.

"Mayor Harper Resigns His Office Under Threats." 1909. *Los Angeles Examiner*. March 12.

"Mayor Harpter Resigns While Under Hot Fire." 1909. *San Francisco Call*. March 12: 1.

McLane, Charles R. 1907. "Coroner's Certificate of Death: Eileen Bedford." Prescott, Arizona: Yavapai County, 355-359. http://interactive.ancestry.com/60874/45300_541673-00357.

Missouri Department of Health and Senior Services. "Missouri Death Certificates, 1910 - 1965." n.d. (accessed August 4, 2015). http://health.mo.gov.

"Modern Cemeteries." 1925. *Valhalla News*, January. Valhalla Cemetery Co.: 3-4.

Morris, Ann. "Mount Hope Cemetery." 2003. National Register of Historic Places Registration Form. United States Department of the Interior, National Park Service. March 12.

Morris. "Sacred Green Space: A Survey of Cemeteries in St. Louis County." St. Louis. Missouri State Historic Preservation Office. 2000. https://dnr. mo.gov/shpo/survey/SLAS032-R.pdf

"Motely H. Flint Slayer, Now Sane, Placed in Death Row." 1940. *Los Angeles Times*. March 29: 5.

"New Richmond In Cemetery Field: What he wants and what he proposes to do." 1906. *San Bernardino Daily Sun*. March 9: 3.

Newmark, Harris. 1916. *Sixty Years in Southern California: 1853—1913.* Edited by Maurice H. Newmark and Marco R. Newmark. New York, New York: The Knickerbocker Press. (accessed July 14, 2015). https:// archive.org/details/sixtyyearsinsout00newmrich.

Newmark, Maurice H. and Newmark Margo (eds), *Sixty Years in Southern California 1955-1913*. New York: The Knickerbocker Press, 1916.

"Nephew of Slain Main Tells Possible Motive." 1915. *Los Angeles Evening Herald*. December 23: 1.

"Notable Improvements Now Going Ahead in Forest Lawn Memorial Park." 1917. *Los Angeles Times*. March 11: 1.

"Noted Mining Man Is Dead." 1931. *Madera Tribune*.November 6: 4.

"Notice of Guardian's Sale of Real Estate At Private Sale." 1917. *California Independent*. June 14.

"Old Nevadan Dies on Coast." 1931. *Reno Gazettte-Journal*. November 6: 16.

"Olive Grove Cemetery." Acessed April 1, 2013. http://www.findagrave.com/ cgi-bin/fg.cgi?page=cr&CRid=8236.

Olivet Memorial Park. n.d. "About Olivet Memorial Park." (accessed July 3, 2016). http://www.burialplanning.com/cemeteries/olivet-memorial-park/ cemetery-about/.

"Owens River Project Indorsed." 1907. *Los Angeles Examiner*. June 13.

"Pacific Crest Cemetery." n.d. (accessed October 13, 2014). https://www. facebook.com/pages/Pacific-Crest-Cemetery/100882023289482.

Parry, David. n.d. "Architects' Profiles: Pacific Heights Architects #24 – T. P. Ross." (accessed August 8, 2005). http://www.classicsfproperties.com/Architecture/TP_ Ross.htm.

"Petition to Annex Tropico to City." 1915. *Los Angeles Evening Herald*. June 11: 15.

"Pioneer Steel Man Dead." 1919. *Architect and Engineer of California*. May: 124.

"Piratical Raid: Attempt to confiscate Summerland's water front." 1898. *Los Angeles Times*. October 26: 10.

Press Reference Library: Notables of the Southwest. Los Angeles: Los Angeles Examiner 1912.: 475.

"Prominent Citizen of Tropico Foully Murdered Last Thursday." 1915. *Tropico Sentinel*. December 29.

"Prominent Mining Man Dies at L. A." 1931. *Salt Lake Telegram*. November 6: 22.

Publicity Department of the Glendale Branch of Security Trust & Savings Bank. 1924. *First of the Ranchos: The Story of Glendale*. Glendale, California: Securuity Trust & Savings Bank.

"Raging River Razes Bridges, Rips Banks," *Los Angeles Times*, February 11, 1914: I1.

Railroad Commission of the State of California. "Decision No. 4549." Vol. XIII, in Decisions of the Railroad Commission of the State of California, 709-710. Sacramento, California: California State Printing Office., 1917

Rasmussen, Cecilia. 1994. "Curbside L.A. Pioneer Cemeteries: These old resting places have a natural ambiance often missing in modern manicured parks." *Los Angeles Times*. November 21: B3.

"Recall Originated in Examiner Interview." 1909. *Los Angeles Examiner*. March 27.

"Reese James Llewellyn, (1862-1935)," n.d. http://www.findagrave.com, accessed April 4, 2016. "Relatives Fight for Custody of Child." 1908. *Los Angeles Herald*. July 10: 4.

"Rips to Rages Own Defence: Mizar calmly admits killing banker Richardson." *Los Angeles Times*. April 22: 11.

"Rites Arranged for Treadwell. 1931. *Arizona Republic*. December 29: 2.

"Rites Conducted for Treadwell." 1931. *Los Angeles Times*. November 8: 14.

Roman, James. *Chronicles of Old Los Angeles*. New York, New York: Museyon Inc., 2015.

Ross v. American Sec. & Fidelity Co., et al. 1932. (District Court of Appeal, Third District, CA, 1932 Cal. App. LEXIS 855 (Cal. App. 1932) April 29).

Rubin, Barbara, Robert Carolton, and Arnold Rubin. *L.A. In Installments: Forest Lawn*. Santa Monica, CA: Westside Publications, 1979.

San Gabriel Cemetery Association. n.d. "About--History." (accessed Ocober 29, 2013). http://sangabrielcemetery.com/history.

"San Gabriel River and Montebello Forebay Water Conservation System." n.d. Department of Public Works, County of Los Angeles, http://ladpw.org.

"San Francisco Architect Injured," *Architect and Engneer*, vol 71 np. 2, 11/1922, p. 109.

Sauter, Michael B., Douglas A. McIntyre, and Charles B. Stockdale. 2010. "The 13 Worst Recessions, Depressions, and Panics In American History." September 9. (accessed

October 1, 2015). http://247wallst.com/investing/2010/09/09/
the-13-worst-recessions-depressions-and-panics-in-american-history/3/.

Sawyer, Nuala. 2014. "The Old Calvary Cemetery Grounds Are Right Under
Your Feet." Hoodline, May 19. http://hoodline.com/2014/05/calvary-
cemetery-grounds-are-right-under-your-feet Accessed November 30,
2017."

"Say Unappy Mowan [*sic*] Tried Suicide at Beach." 1907. *Los Angeles Herald*.
April 10: 1.

Scully, Leon F., Jr. *Bombers, Bolsheviks and Bootlegers: A Study in Constitutional
Subversion*. Houston: Publius Books, 2001.

"See City's Needs From Many Angels: Northern Improvement Bodies Talk of
Sewers, Streets, and Sidewalks." 1910. *Los Angeles Examiner*. February 10.

"Seek Accomplice in Tropico Slaying." 1915. *Los Angeles Evening Herald*.
December 25:12.

"SF Panama-Pacific Exhibition 1915." n.d. (accessed April 6, 2006). http://
www.askart.com/AskArt/interest/panama_pacific_exposition_1515.html.

Sherman, Diana. 2004. n.d. "A River for Los Angeles: The Story of the
Los Angeles River Greenway." May 17. (accessed September 30, 2014).
http://ocw.mit.edu/courses/history/21h-234j-downtown-spring-2005/
assignments/.

"Short History of the Los Angeles River," n.d. The River Project. (accessed
March 23, 2006). http://www.theriverproject.org/history.html.

Shuck, Oscar T. (ed). *History of the Bench and Bar of California*. Los Angeles:
California Printing House, 1901.

"Shuler Plans Radio Appeal." 1931. *Los Angeles Times*. November 1931: 2.

Silver, Sue. n.d. "Historic California Cemetery Laws, 1872 Codified Statutes
of California, Political Code, Chapter V., Cemeteries and Sepulture."
(accessed October 3, 2007). http://www.usgennet.org/usa/ca/county/
eldorado/1854_statute.htm.

Simpson, Kelly. 2012. "Legacy of Early Developers Still Remains."
KCET. March 8. https://www.kcet.org/departures-columns/
legacy-of-early-la-developers-still-remains.

Simross, Lynn. 1983. "L.A.'s Evergreen Cemetery a Monument to a Rich
Past." *Los Angeles Times*. January 23: F1.

Sims, Annie Noble. 1918. "Three Early Landowners of the County of Isle of
Wight, Virginia: Jeremiah Exum, Michael MacKquinney, and William
Pope, With Notes on Some of Their Descendants." Edited by Lyon G.
Tyler and William Clayton Torrence. *William and Mary College Quarterly
Historical Magazine* (William and Mary College) XXVII (1): 111-112.

Sims, Charles Blackburn. 2011. "The Wisconson Society of the Sons of
the American Revolution: Application for membership." February 26.

Ancestry.com. U.S., Sons of the American Revolution Membership Applications, 1889-1970 [database on-line]. Provo, Utah.

"Slayer Silent at Coroner's Inquest." 1915. *Los Angeles Herald*. December 24: 3.

Sloan, David Charles. *The Last Great Necessity: Cemeteries in American History*. Baltimore: Johns Hopkins Press, 1995.

"Some Recent Works of T. Paterson Ross, Architect and A. W. Burgren, Engineer." 1912. *Architect and Engineer of California*. November: 46-65.

Southern California Genealogical Society. n.d. "Los Angeles City Cemetery: History of the Cemetery." (accessed July 30, 2015). http://www. scgsgenealogy.com/free/LACC-History.html.

Southern Pacific Company. 1905. "Transportation of Corpses and Funeral Parties." Circular No. E 126. San francisco: Southern Pacific Company, July 15.

"Spreckles Not to Buy Stock." 1902. *Oakland Tribune*. February 4: 7.

Stamats & McClure. *Glendale California: The Jewel City*. Tropico (Glendale), California: Stamats & McClure, 1912.

St. Johns, Adela Rogers. *First Step Up Toward Heaven*. Englewoods Cliffs, NJ: Prentice Hall, Inc. 1959.

Starr, Kevin. *The Dream Endures: California entering the 1940s*. New York, NY: Oxford University Press, 1977.

Star. *California: A history*. New York, NY: Modern Library, 2007.

"State Demands Death Penalty for Mizar." 1916. *Los Angeles Herald*. April 22: 3.

Stimson, Grace Heilman, "The Crime of the Century," in *Los Angeles: Biography of a City*, ed. John Caughey and LaRee Caughy, 260-265, Berkeley and Los Angeles: University of Califorinia Press, 1977.

Stop Oil Seeps California. n.d. "Summerland History ... and Mystery?" (accessed August 14, 2017). http://www.soscalifornia.org/summerland-history/.

"Straange Woman Figures In Oil Lands Inquiry: S. P. Counsel Charges Federal Witness With Using Her to Bribe; Sensation Blows up and T. J. Griffin Gives Damaging Testimony Against Company." 1912. *The San Francisco Call*. July 10: 20.

"Suicide." 1907. *Prescott Morning Courier*. April 9. 2

"Summerland Oil Men Up In Arms." 1898. San Francisco Call. August 12: 3.

"Summerland Steal: Treadwell merely a Southern Pacific tool." 1898. *Los Angeles Herald*. July 16: 9.

"Supervisors Powerless to Remove Billboards." 1910. *Los Angeles Herald*. March 1: 5.

"Supervisors Reappoint City Justices of Peace." 1901. *Los Angeles Herald*. March 19: 6.

"38-Ft. Cobblestone Arch Raised and Moved." 1915. *Engineering News*. December 16: 1178-9.

"Thousands of Acres Inundated by Storm," *Los Angeles Times*, February 19, 1914, I12, ProQuest Historical Newspapers.

"To Start Cemetery." 1906. *Los Angeles Times*. March 18: 46.

"Treadwell, Dean of State Mining Engineers, Dies: Pioneer Californian and associate of 'Lucky' Baldwin passes away at L. A." 1931. *Modesto News-Herald* (Modesto, California). November 6: 8.

Treadwell v. American Security & Fidelity Company, et al. *See:* Lillian Bishop Ross as Executrix v. Americcan Security & Fidelity. Treadwell's daughter was substituted for him upon his death.

Treadwell v. Forest Lawn Cemetery Association. 1913. Stipulation signed by attorneys for each party (January 24).

"Trip Back in Time to Tropico." Glendale Historical Society. (accessed March 20, 2012). http://www.glendalehistorical.org/tropico.html.

"Tropico." Califorinia: Tropico Improvement Association, c.1903.

"Tropico-Glendale Merger Boosted." 1917. *Los Angeles Herald*. September 17: 9.

"Tropico Annexation Loses by 215 Votes." 1911. *Los Angeles Evening Herald*. August 30: 13.

"Tropico Banker Shot and Killed on Street." 1915. *Los Angeles Times*. December 24: 15.

"Tropico Banker Slain." 1915. *Los Angeles Evening Herald*. December 23: 1..

"Tropico Beauty." California: Tropico Improvement Assocaition, c.1903.

"Tropico-Glendale Merger Boosted." 1917. *Los Angeles Herald*. September 17: 9.

Tropico Land & Improvement Co. (a Corporation), Appellant, v. Lucie M. Lambourn, Executrix of the Last Will and Testament of Susan Glassell Mitchell, Deceased, Respondent. 1912. 170 Cal. 33, 148 Pac 206 (Transcript on Appeal).

Tropico: Los Angeles County California." Tropico, California: Tropico Improvement Assocaition, 1903.

'Tropico Polls Heavy Vote Favoring Incorporation." 1911. *Los Angeles Herald*. March 8.

"Tropico: The Beautiful Link City." 1916. *American Globe Investor's Magazine*. November: 3.

'Trustees Meeting: Reports of Committees Made and Considered." 1913. *Tropico Sentinal*. May 28.

"Undue Influence Is Basis for Contest: Suit to break Mrs. Mitchell's will is filed." 1908. *Los Angeles Herald*. November 15: 1.

U.S. Department of the Interior, National Park Service, "Mount Hope
    Cemetery," National Register of Historic Places Registration Form,
    November 7, 2005.
U.S. Selective Service System. World War I Selective Service System Draft
    Registration Cards, 1917-1918. Washington, D.C.: National Archives and
    Records Administration. M1509, 4,582 rolls.
Upper Los Angeles River Area Watermaster. "History of ULARA
    Adjudication." (accessed January 16, 2016). http://ularawatermaster.com/
    index.html?page_id=911.
U.S. Census Bureau. 1920. "U.S. Federal Census."
U.S. Departement of Veterans Affairs, Office of Public Affairs. "Memorial
    Day History." (accessed September 24, 2015). http://www.va.gov/opa/
    speceven/memday/history.asp.
Wattles, William J. "Map of Forest Lawn Cemetery." 1906. Forest Lawn
    Cemetery Association. January 10.
"W. J. Blain Estate in Court." *Los Angeles Herald*. September 20: 8. California
    Digital Newspaper Collection: http://cdnc.ucr.edu.
Weed, Howard Evarts. *Modern Park Cemeteries*. Chicago: R. J. Haight, 1912.
Wells (chmn), Norton C., Frank L. Huhleman, and I. H. Russell. 1910.
    "Report of the Special Committee on Annexation." Glendale: Glendale
    Valley Improvement Association.
"Widow Is In Charge: Relict [*sic*] of man shot at Tropico becomes
    Administratrix of his estate, valued at more than a quarter of a million
    dollars." 1916. *Los Angeles Times*. January 27: 11.
Wiley, H. I., Surveyor-General of the State of California. 1886. "Corrected
    Report of Spanish and Mexican Grants in California, Complete to
    February 25, 1886." Sacramento: State of California Printing.
Williamson, Samuel H. "Annualized Growth Rate of Various Historical
    Economic Series." (accessed November 27, 2017). https://www.
    measuringworth.com/.
"Witness For Railroad In Awkward Fix: J. B. Treadwell Likely to Find
    Himself Called On to Explain Testimony; Oil Operator Is Directly
    Contradicted by Statement of T. J. Griffin." 1912. *The San Francisco Call*.
    July11: 20.
"Worst in Years Over Foothills," 1914 *Los Angeles Times*, February 19: I13.
Zimmerman, Tom. *Paradise Promoted: The Booster Campaign that Created Los
    Angeles*. Los Angeles: Angel City Press, 2008.

Index

Illustration page numbers shown as italics *108*
Notes in footnotes page numbers shown as bold **109**

A

Act to authorize the Incorporation
of Rural Cemetery
Associations (1859) 8
Act to protect the bodies of Deceased
Persons (1854) 8
Adaven Mining & Smelting
Company 138, 144
startup of 136–137
Adler, performs burial service for Blaine,
William 63
Aire Libre (Pueblo, Mexico) 136
Allen, Carroll 126–127
Allen, G. F.
director of AS&F 361
formation of AS&F 236
Altadena Country Club 224
American Necropolis Company, Sims,
Charles, president 132
American Securities Company (Georgia)
134, 137, 141
American Securities Company
(Maine) xxv, 150
absorbed into AS&F 273–274, 297,
330
assignment of Sims and Eaton
contract 142
cemetery contract with San Diego
149–150
cemetery lot sales 167–171, 329
contract disputes with TL&I 167–184,
330
dissolution 276
future of 225–228
incorporation 141–144
letterhead 205–206
merger with TL&I 330
perpetual care fund 143
prospect card c. 1916 *214*
recruiting and training salesmen
216–220
resignation of Getzendanner, E. D.,
sales manager 212
special meeting of shareholders to
authorize dissolution 276–277
American Security & Fidelity
Corporation (AS&F) xxv
acquisition by FLMPA *324*, 325
acquisition of TL&I 283, 293
agreements with FLCA 284–285, 291
assumes responsibility for development 317
automobile ownership 282
buying more land 247
choice of crematory manufacturer
248–251
city office 145
conflict with FLCA 299–304,
307–312

crematory operation turned over to FLCA 285
directors and officers 361–364
Eaton, Hubert president, AS&F 323
Emery, George 248
FLMPA's acquisition of *324*, 325
formation 235–236, *236*
future policy 246–247
Hamilton, Frank 236–239
Little Church of the Flowers 247, 285
Llewellyn, Merritt 240–241
loans to FLCA 291–292, 311
perpetual care fund 278–281, 284
Pratt's ideas 277–278
refuses to sign deeds without payment 330
resistance to making fiscal agent for FLCA 309
revenue split between FLCA and AS&F *285*
Selling System use 284
American Trust & Security Company 235
Annandale Country Club 341
Appellate Court of California, Second District 102
Appellate Court of California, Third District 61
Archer, Tobias R.
   appeal in TL&I lawsuit 100, 102
   as lawyer for Blain, Eva 233–234
Arizona
   corporate law 15
   Superior Court 288
   Supreme Court 288
attorney-in-fact **239**
automobile expenses and ownership
   AS&F, TL&I, and FLCA 281
   Heath, George 47–49, 115
   Norton Wells 115–116
Azalea Terrace, Great Mausoleum *263–264*, 264, 268
   dedication of 265–268, 331

B

Backman, G. S. 356–357

Baldwin, Elias "Lucky" 11
Bancroft, C. A. 155
Bankers Trust Company 136
Bank of Mobile 135
Barnes, C. B. 20, 333, 357
Barron, Sam 136
Bassford, B. E. 361
Bedford, Charles 14
Bedford, Eileen Glassell xxv, *14*
   marriage 14
   Mitchell, Susan's will 14–15
   property ownership rights 13–15, 87–88
   suicide xxii, 88
Bedford, Lucile Richmond xxv
   adoption by Lambourn, Lucie 97
   Lambourn, Lucie as executrix of estate 99
   Los Angeles Trust & Savings Bank as guardian 282
   property rights 87–89
   settlement of partition suite and, 100, *101*, 102, 144
before need 131. *See also* preneed
Bennett, as Sims' partner 183
Bentley, George H. 360
Berean Hall 295
Berkeley, CA 146
Bettin, Vernon A. 360
"Birth of a New Era" (speech) 270, 351
Black, John 81–83, 358
Blain, Eva M. xxix
   court petition of, following death of husband 76–78
   death and funeral of husband 74–76
   TL&I stock 78, 233
Blain, Merrill W. 75
Blain, William J. (Billy) xxv, 333
   compensation for Wells 69–71
   death and funeral 74–75, 105, 328
   drunken behavior 61–65, 73, 77, 328
   financial problems of FLCA and 35, 38, 40–41
   Heath, George, concerns about 50
   hillside sign controversy 108
   hiring of new salesman 46

Lanigan, J. J., salesman 38–40, 64
life insurance policy 75
perpetual care fund 44
promised shares in TL&I 77–78
salary not paid 30, 33, 60, 77
selling cemetery lots 33
superintendent 20, 27, 327
Treadwell, J. B. 61–65
treatment for alcoholism 74–75
trustee, FLCA 20, 81, 358
visit to undertakers 67
Blochman, L. A. 147–148
Bonney-Watson Co. (Seattle) 248
Borden, A. F. 349
Bordwell, Judge Walter 102
Boston & Montana Copper 135
Boynton, C. C. xxv
    representing Treadwell, J. B. 89–91,
        93–98
Bradbury, H. N. 220
Brand, Leslie 15, 87–88
Bratten, J. C. 246
Bresee Brothers & Todd Undertaking
        Company 114
Brest, R. A. 361
Brett-Benton Type D-2 retorts 250
Brett, Henry E. 250–251
Bridge and Structural Iron
        Workers Union 51
Brougher, J. Whitcomb 270
Broughton, H. W.
    FLCA indebtedness 311
    trustee, FLCA 309–312, 360
Brown, M. W. 361
Bruce, G., director, TL&I 355
Brunner, Jay D. 211, *212*
Bryan, Cecil E. 262
The Builder's Creed 241, *242*, 243–244,
        271, *272*, 318, 323, 330
Bullard Lands 224
Burch, N. C. 109
Burgren, Albert W. 1
    business partner of Ross, Tom 9–10
    director, TL&I 16, 355–356
    president, TL&I 16
Burgwald, Hugo M. 360

burials, discontinuing on Sundays 35

C

California. *See also* Los Angeles;
        Southern California
    1854 Statute 8
    1859 Statute 8
    Assembly Bill 646 193
    cemetery lot sales 134
    corporate law 16
    land purchases 13–14
    ownership of cemetery property 259
    perpetual care funds 22, 36, 281
    statehood 13
California Club 46, 53
California Crematorium 249
California Institute of Technology 325
California Mausoleum Company 251
California Supreme Court xxix, 102
Calvary Cemetery (Los Angeles) 6
    discontinuing Sunday burials 35
Calvary Cemetery (San Francisco) 208
Campbell, A. E. 220
"car landing" improvements 28
Carre, Wilton E.
    superintendent 73
    support payments to ex-wife 220
Carter, E. G. 363–365
Carter, Kathy xix
Casa Verdugo 116
cemeteries
    churchyard 3
    early, in Los Angeles 4–6
    evolution of 2–4
    frontier 3
    lawn-park 3–4
    location of 9
    memorial-park 4
    Potter's fields 3
    rural 3
    town or city 3
    types of 2–4
Cemeteries Improvement
        Corporation 251
cemetery associations 8–9
cemetery lot sales

at Forest Lawn 30, 33–36, 140–141, 167, 215–220
by American Securities Co. 134, 167–171, 329
by FLCA 278, 299
cash distribution of proceeds *168*
Eaton, Hubert xvii, 102, 138–141, 145–146, 167, 172–181, 203–221, 234–235, 299
installment payments 168–170
cemetery on the hill 4
A Cemetery Should Be Forever (Llewellyn) 444
Chapman, Alfred B. 12–13
Chase, P. B. 295–296
Chicago, Ross and Eaton visit cemeteries, crematories, and mausoleums 255–256
Christianity and evolution of cemeteries 2
Church, C. M. 348
Church, Frank 211
churchyard cemeteries 3
Cienaga Schoolhouse 52
Citizens Trust and Savings Bank
collateral for loan to AS&F 276
shares held in trust at, for Eaton, Hubert 274
shares held in trust at, for Hamilton, Frank 239
City Bank & Trust Co. 135
city cemeteries 3
Civic Association of Los Angeles, hillside sign controversy 108
Cleaver, William 194
close-to-the-ground markers 4
Cole, Cornelius 121
Cole, Eva B. 160
Coleman, J. C. 160
Cole, Seward, ad protesting Hollywood Cemetery 121–122
Colma, California 4, 9, 120, 193, 220
columbarium 209
at Forest Lawn 232, 240, 245, 252, 293
construction of 249

Columbia Realty Co., Eaton's interest in expanding 224
"Community Mausoleums" (booklet) 262
Comstock Mine 11
Conaty, Bishop Thomas J. 194
concrete burial vaults 211, *212*
Connell, James E. 149
Conrad, Grant 193
contract between FLCA and TL&I for cemetery lot sales 144
copings, prohibition of 22
corporate organization charts *23, 139, 236, 279, 315, 324,* 325
Cosgrove, Terence B. 149
Cowan, W. K. 347
cremation 245
charges for 20
collapsed graves 212
Cypress Lawn 250
discontinuation on Sundays 35
equipment 245, 250
Honolulu 249
opposition to 249
pet 262
Sacramento 249
sales of services 283
witnessing 250
Cremation Society of Southern California, discontinuation of Sunday burials and 35
crematory(ies) xxvi, xxvii, 209
at Mount Olivet Cemetery (Colma) 249
choosing a manufacturer 248–251
construction of 252, 257–258, 283, 293, 298, 314, 330
equipment for 245–246
fuel 256
maintenance of 20
pitch by Moore, Lawrence for building 249–251
plans for 232, 240, 247, 291, 293
under AS&F 285
under FLCA 245, 298
Crematory Supply Company (Piedmont, CA) 249

Crowley, K. L.
  bookkeeper 302
  cashier, AS&F 239
  director, AS&F 362
cumulative voting 296
Cypress Lawn Cemetery (Colma, CA)
  18, *31*, 221
  Blain, William J. (Billy) employment
    27
  Carre, Wilton 73
  cremation 250
  mausoleum crypt owners 259
  Nobel Chapel 219, 257
  receiving vault 260, *261*

D

D. W. Newcomer's Sons Undertakers 248
Dakin, Frank W. 355–357
Darling, O. E.
  as sales manager at Columbia Realty
    224–226
  door-to-door prospecting for
    Huntington Beach sales 224
Davidson, Sandy, retorts of 250
Davidson, Suzanne xix
Davies, J. Mills 106
Davis, Alex W. 361
Decoration Day 108, 159, 204
defamation suit against Scott and
    Treadwell 127
De Haven, Jo J.
  bidding on crematory 249
  sharing information 193–194,
    258–259
demurrer **92**, 125, 288
Dennis & Loewenthal 100
Denver Crematory 248
Depot Street 18, 118, 120, 154, 164
Dewey, Jas. H. 20, 333, 357
Dingley, Charles 289
Directors & Officers 354
  American Security & Fidelity
    (AS&F) (1916-1916) 361–364
  Forest Lawn Cemetery Association
    (1906-1925) 357–360

Forest Lawn Memorial-Park Associa-
    tion (1919-1926) 360–361
  Tropico Land & Improvement
    Company (1905-1917) 355–357
dividing cash receipts 167–170, *168–169*,
    177–181, 185–187, 194–199, *285*
Dodge & Company. *See* N. P.
  Dodge & Company
domestic cemeteries 3
Doyle, E. J.
  director, AS&F 361
  formation of AS&F 236
Drabing, Darin B. 325

E

Eagle Development Corporation 213, 215
Eagle Rock District 116
  Eaton starting new cemetery 223–225,
    228–230, 237
  ordinance prohibiting sale of cemetery
    property 230
Eaton, Ann Munger
  death of xvii
  loan to Eaton, Hubert 276
  marriage 292
Eaton, Hubert L. xxvi, *136*, 218
  acting on behalf of FLCA *300*, 301
  Adaven Mining and Smelting
    Company and 136
  agreement with TL&I and FLCA 138
  American Securities Company
    (Maine) 143
  analysis of land value 278–279, *280*
  art and xxii, 4, 268, 322–323, 352
  assignment of interest in selling
    contract to American Securities
    142, 329
  background 135
  "before need" sales 316
  The Builder's Creed 241–244, *242*,
    272, 318, 330
  cemetery sales program xvii, 203–221
    beginning 145–146
    contract for 140–141
    disputes over cash 167, 172–181
    protecting system 234–235

coming to Los Angeles and Forest Lawn Cemetery 137–138
conflict with Wells, Norton 292–294
contract with TL&I 138–139
contract with TL&I and FLCA 329
cultivating esprit de corps among cemetery lot owners 203
death of xvii, 323
dedication of Little Church of the Flowers 268–273, 351–353
director, AS&F 362–364
dispute between American Securities, TL&I, and FLCA 167–183, 168–169
early life and education 135
exchanging promotional material with other cemeteries 220–221
first research chemist 135
FLCA elects new trustees favorable to Eaton 330
Flint, Motely 312
flush memorial standards 321–322
on Forest Lawn (Omaha) 255
forming new company 225, 227
as founder of Forest Lawn Memorial-Park 4
general manager, FLMPA 313, 323, 361
gentlemen's agreement between AS&F and FLCA 302
grand tour of U.S. cemeteries 254–258
instructions for special meeting of the American Securities shareholders to authorize dissolution 276–277
insurance plan 205–206, 208
interest in buying TL&I 189–192
Llewellyn, Merritt correspondence with 226–227, 232–233
lot repurchase offer 204–205
marriage to Henderson, Ann Munger 292
mausoleums 209–212, 255–257
memorial-park concept xxvi, 4, 245–247, 293, 322–323
mining career 135–136
monuments, banning 322

negotiations to acquire TL&I 231–233
new cemetery 224–232
new cemetery in Eagle Rock Valley 228–230
obvious support for by Flint and Kauffman 295
partition suit settlement 144–145
personal guarantee against liens 281
Pierce, William, Eaton's reply to inquiry, saying his sales system "brings in the bacon" 221
planning for the future 225–228, 246–248, 314–316
president of AS&F 276, 323, 362–364
proxy votes 292–293
"The Reasons Why" booklet and 203, 221, 244, 341–351, 350
reference letter for Getzendanner, E. D. 212–213
refining his vision 322
Ross, Pop, and plans to start a new cemetery 231–232
San Diego Cemetery 148–149
scouting for a new cemetery location 224–225
selling residential lots 223
Sims, Charles 136–143, 179–186, 329
tension with Glora, Mike 230–231
transforming Forest Lawn Cemetery 252
upright monuments 322–323
visit to Forest Lawn 137–138
Eaton, James Rodolphus 135
Eaton, Joseph 136
Eaton, Mabel 135. See also Llewellyn, Mabel
Eaton, Martha Lewright 135
Eaton, Roy Munger 292
Eckley, W. H. 193, 194
Edmonds, Rev. W. E., dedication of the Little Church of the Flowers 268
Edwards, B. F. 143, 149
El Campo Santo Cemetery (Los Angeles) 6
Elder, Charles A. 193

electric lighting 256, 265
electric mud 135
"Elegy Written in a Country
    Churchyard" (Gray) 247, 270
Elliott, J. M. 227–229
El Monte Cemetery (a.k.a. Savannah
    Cemetery) 6
Ely, Glenn M. xxvi
    law governing power of trustees 283
    trustee, FLCA 295–299, 309–312,
        358–359
Emery, E. U.
    failed election as FLCA trustee 359
    lot owner 294
Emery, George F.
    pet cremation 262
    sales manager 216, 248, 251–252
endowment care fund. See perpet-
    ual care fund
Episcopal Church, Los Angeles 219
Estey organ 260
Evergreen Cemetery (Los Angeles) 5,
    6, 113, 328
    boundaries 122
    discontinuation of Sunday burials and
        cremations 35
    Los Angeles Cemetery Association
        194
    moving Llewellyn family from 55,
        111–114, 321
executrix, Lambourn, Lucie 88–91,
    99, 103, 328

F

Fairfield, E. C. 164
Fairlawn Cemetery (Decatur, IL),
    opening 132
Fairmont Cemetery (Denver) 221
Ferndale Park Cemetery (San
    Bernardino, CA), Treadwell's
    efforts in starting 58
Ferry, Peter L. 153
Field, E. S. 359–360
Filley, Wilbur J. 295, 358–359
First National Bank
    Richardson, Burt, vice president 154

Richardson, W. C. B., vice president
    18
First Step Up Toward Heaven (St.
    Johns) xvii
FLCA. See Forest Lawn Cemetery
    Association (1906-1996) (FLCA)
Fletcher, George 208
FLInc. See Forest Lawn Memorial Park
    Association (FLInc)
Flint, Motley H. (1864-1930) xxvi
    as lot owner 294–296
    Eaton, Hubert and 312
    FLCA trustee 295–296, 298–299,
        359–360
    plans for the future and 314–317
    president of FLCA 306–313
    vice president, Los Angeles Trust &
        Savings Bank 138, 306
flood in Cajon Pass 161
flush memorials 323
Foley, W. I. 30, 327
Forbes, E. 107
Ford auto 189, 282
foreign corporation 98
Forest Avenue right-of-way 24
Forest Hill Cemetery (Kansas
    City, MO) 150
Forest Lawn Cemetery Association
    (1906-1996) (FLCA) xxvi
    accounting issues 40–41
    advertising 110, 293
    agreements with
        American Securities 141, 299
        AS&F 291, 330
        TL&I 20
    annual meeting of lot owners 176,
        293–296, 316
    articles of incorporation 58, 245, 332
    auto issues 47–51, 281
    Blaine, William J. (Billy) as superin-
        tendent 20, 327
    borrowing from AS&F 284
    bylaws 55, 81–82
    cash flow problems 43–45
    cemetery lot sales 20–22, 30, 33–35,
        278, 299

contract with Eaton, Hubert and
  Sims, Charles 138–140
Lanigan, J. J. as salesman 46–47
new agreement for 310–311
city office 145, 297–298, 298, 307
collections on accounts 45, 45–46
conflict with AS&F 298–304,
  307–311
contract dispute 167–181
contract with AS&F 330
contract with Sims and Eaton 138,
  139
contract with TL&I 20, 22, 23, 24,
  139
copings prohibited 22
crematory
  opening 261–262, 330
  operation 285
cumulative voting 295–296
development of interment property
  211
directors and officers 20, 81–84,
  357–360
efforts to reign in Eaton 300, 301
election of trustees favorable to Eaton
  295–296
enticing John Llewellyn to be trustee
  52–55
financial and organizational problems
  33–55, 192, 291–292, 297–298,
  311–312
Flint, Motely, as president 307–312
Forest Avenue right-of-way 24
Glora, Mike, as superintendent 210
Heath, George, as salesman 46–50
hillside sign 108
incorporation 20, 327, 332–333
interments 303
land litigation 328–329. See also partition suit
letterhead 27, 110–111, 140
liquidation of indebtedness 311–312
loan from TL&I 36
Lockwood, J. J., as secretary 34–42
Los Angeles Chamber of Commerce
  membership 83–84

lot owners meetings 70, 81–83,
  293–296
lot repurchase offer 204–205
members 313
merged into FLMPA 324, 325
Morgan, Charles O. 42
  attempted coup 79–83
  FLCA secretary 42–44, 55, 328–329
mortgage
  chattel 68
notice about Hubert Eaton 300
perpetual care fund 143
  amounts for 140
  loan to AS&F 281, 284
  misuse 39, 40–41, 43–45
Pratt, George, analysis of corporate
  structure 277
property tax exemption 289
purpose of 20
rejecting proposal for AS&F to be
  fiscal agent 311
relations with other cemeteries
  119–121
resignations
  Lockwood, J. J. 41, 42
  Treadwell, J. B. 62, 64
  Wells, Norton C. 305–306, 321
revenue division 285
rules (1906) 22, 334–340
selling contract with Eaton and Sims
  134–139, 329
settlement with Treadwell, J. B.
  125–130
sources of income 283
special committee of trustees 298–299
special trustees meeting 296–298
termination of sales 298, 307, 330
TL&I sale of land to FLCA 20–22,
  21
Treadwell, J. B. elected president 20
Wells, Norton C., elected trustee and
  president 70
Wells's report to special meeting of
  trustees 296–299
Forest Lawn Cemetery (Glendale/
  Tropico, CA) 6

annexation 116–118, *117*, 259, 329
artists conception, c. 1914 207
"car landing" improvements *30*
cemetery plan
    1906 *29*
    c. 1911 *119*
    1914 *207*
    c. 1918 *266*
changing name to Forest Lawn
    Memorial-Park *246*
collections on accounts 45–46
crematory 232, 240, 245–246
damage to adjacent railroad right-of-
    way 160
damage to railroad right-of-way adja-
    cent to 161
Decoration Day at 204
discontinuation of Sunday burials 35
entry arch *26, 27,* 155–160, *156, 157,*
    158, 327
gopher infestation 162
growth and increased visibility 153
hillside sign controversy 106–109
improving financial condition
    203–204
interments 34, **289**
    1906-1926 *303*
land purchase for 11–16
Llewellyn family
    monument, moving to Forest Lawn
        55, 111–114, *112,* 328
    support for 50–55
location *6, 24*
lot sales 167
mausoleum *208,* 209–212
naming 18
park leading to cemetery *25*
plans 9–10
protests over expansion 106
receiving vault 27–28, *28,* 30
sale of first lot 30, 327
Sims, Charles, claims establishment
    of 132
street improvements and 153–156
undertaker referrals and 36–39
well casing collapse 162

Forest Lawn Cemetery (Omaha) 255
Forest Lawn Company 325
Forest Lawn entry arch 61, 140,
    155–161, 327
Forest Lawn Memorial-Park
    as new name 246
    centennial xvii
    cremation of pets 262
    Eaton's plans for improvements
        246–247
    Great Mausoleum 262–266, *265*
        Azalea Terrace *263, 264*
    Little Church of the Flowers *253,*
        267–270, 268–273
    Los Angeles building requirements
        259
    mausoleum
        construction 264–266
        location *266*
    publicity for crematory 262
    Ross, Tom as architect 252
Forest Lawn Memorial-Park Association
    (FLMPA) (1917-) xxvi
    acquisition of AS&F *324,* 325
    assumes responsibility for sales 330
    bylaws 313
    contract with AS&F 313
    directors and officers 1919-1926 360
    directors & officers 361
    Eaton, Hubert, general manager 313,
        323
    endowment care fund 325
    FLCA merges into FLMPA *324,* 325
    formation of 313–314, 317
    incorporation 313
    insolvency 317, 331
    maintenance, responsibility for 314,
        331
    replacement of, with Forest Lawn
        Memorial Park Association, Inc.
        317–318
Forest Lawn Memorial Park Association,
    Inc. (FLInc) 317–318, 361
    Eaton, Hubert as general manager 318
    formation 331
    name change 318

Forest Lawn Mortuary 323
  California license numbers (FD #s)
    404
The Forest Lawn Story
    (Hancock) xviii–xix
Fort Moore Hill Cemetery (Los
    Angeles) 4
Founders Memorial Cemetery 6
frontier cemeteries 3
funeral home xviii, xxii, 323. *See*
    also mortuary and undertakers

G

gas pump 163
Gates, Carroll W. xxvi
  formation of new company with
    Eaton, Elliott, and Hollingsworth
    225–226, 227–228
  land purchase 230–231
  personal guarantee against liens 281
  trustee, FLCA 362
Geiger, J. H., at 1919 FLCA lot owners
    meeting 295
general manager xxvi, 20, 82, 83, 313,
    318, 323, 328, 387, 403
gentlemen's agreement between AS&F
    and FLCA 302
Getzendanner, E. D.
  Cemeteries Improvement Corpora-
    tion 251
  noncompetition agreement 213
  resignation 212
  sales manager xxvi, 146, 204, 221
  scouting for new cemetery 224
  Whittier Heights Cemetery 212–213
Gibson, Frank B., supplier of crematory
    equipment 245–246, 248–249
Glassell, Andrew (1827-1901) 12–13
  descendents *14*
  gift of land to daughter 13, 87
Glassell, Hugh (1859-1938) xxvii
  land bequest and 13–14
  land purchase from Mitchell, Susan,
    by Treadwell 95
Glassell, Susan. *See* Mitchell, Susan
    Glassell (1856-1907)

Glendale
  annexation 116–118, *117*
  merger of Tropico an Glendale 259
  possible names for 12
Glendale Avenue 12
  access 24
  improvements 153, 156, 158
Glendale Improvement Association 116
Glora, Mike
  cemetery superintendent 82–84, 159,
    164
  deputy sheriff and murder of Rich-
    ardson, Burt 163–165
  Eaton's tensions with 230–231
  mausoleum flyer 210
Gooch, Doug xix
Goodman & Martinoni Undertaking 114
Goodwin, Henry P., movement of
    arch 158–159
gophers and gopher guns 162
Gordon, Francis
  as director AS&F 363
  as secretary FLMPA 361
Goudge, Herbert J. xxvii
  contract between American Securities,
    FLCA, and TL&I 175–178
  opinion on Eagle Rock statute 230
  protecting Eaton's sales system 235
Graceland Cemetery (Chicago), Eaton
    and Tom Ross visit 256
Granath, Clint xix
Grand Avenue 5
Grand Avenue School 8
Granger, Ralph 148
grant deed 94
Gray & Co. *See* N. Gray & Co
    Undertaking
Gray, Thomas 247, 270
Great Falls, Montana 135
Great Mausoleum *265*, 268. *See*
    also mausoleum
  dedication 331
  Memorial Terrace entrance and
    Builder's Creed *242*
Great Partition lawsuit 13

Greenwood Cemetery
(Montgomery, AL) 138
Greenwood Cemetery (San
Diego) 147, 148
Griffin, G. J., relationship with
Treadwell 58
Griffith, D. W. 2
Griffith, E. C., Loewenthal's petition for
rehearing 103
ground squirrels 163
guardian of Lucile Bedford
Lambourn, Lucie 88
Los Angeles Trust & Savings Bank
88, 96, 144–145, 282

H

Hager, Frances F. 362–363
Hamilton, Frank D. xxvii
Blain, Eva's, TL&I stock holdings 233
exchange of stock holdings 274–276
land in Eagle Rock 229–230
proposal for AS&F financing 236–239
Hancock, Ralph xviii
Harbor View Cemetery (a.k.a. San Pedro
Cemetery) 6
Harding, Charles 217–218
Harris, Murray, organ for Little Church
of the Flowers 260–261
Harrison, H. M.
director of AS&F 361
formation of AS&F 236
Harrison, M. P. 349
Harvard Business School, 325
Hauser, E. C.
director and vice president of FLMPA
317–318, 361
director, FLInc 318
trustee of FLCA 360
Hawkins, Prince A. (1871-1939) xxvii,
178–179, 186, 198
Hazlett, William B. (1869-1952) xxvii
agreement to protect TL&I and
FLCA 162
alleged illegal loans 127–128
AS&F stock 275
AS& stock 239

distribution of cash receipts 171, 173,
177–178, 197
opinion on San Diego Cemetery
purchase 149
TL&I dissolution 287
Hearst, William Randolph 2
Heath, Dr. George H. xxvii
as medical doctor 85–86
automobile expenses 46–50, 115
Blain's drunkenness 50, 64–67
concern about Treadwell, J. B. 66
FLCA lot owners meeting 1911 81
Llewellyn monument 55
overpayment 85–86
salesman for FLCA 121, 249, 328
trustee of FLCA 81, 83, 358
visit to undertakers 66–67
Henderson, Ann Munger. See Eaton,
Ann Munger
Henderson, Leroy ("Roy") 292
Hildreth, R., trustee, FLCA 362
hillside sign controversy 106–109, 328
Holden, W. M. 219
Hollingsworth, William I. (1862-
1937) xxvii
Blain, Eva, shares in TL&I 233
FLCA lot owners meeting 1919 296
formation of new company with
Eaton, Elliott, and Gates 225,
227–232
gentlemen's agreement with Eaton 302
ouster of Wells, Norton C. 305–306
personal guarantee against liens 281
trustee, FLCA 362–364
Hollywood, CA 2, 5
Hollywood Cemetery (Los Angeles) 6
discontinuing Sunday burials 35
efforts to close 121–122
legislation 193
Home of Peace Cemetery (Los
Angeles) 6
homestead cemeteries 3
horse
for TL&I stock 54
hitching 22, 123
horse-drawn buggies 1

Huber, John F.
  creation of FLInc 317–318
  director FLMPA 361
  trustee, FLCA 360
Huntington Beach Company 223–227
  Darling, O. E. 224–225
  Eaton selling residential lots 223–224
  Gates, Carroll 226
Huntington, Henry E. 223

I

Illinois College of Law and Sims,
    Charles 131
Incorporation of Rural Cemetery
    Associations (1859) 8
Inglewood Cemetery (Inglewood,
    CA) 6, 316
  as competition 34
  legislation 193
Interurban Sentinel, advertising 109, 110
Iona section 162, 219

J

James, Dr. C. S. 106
J.B.-Executrix suit 90
Johnson, Right Reverend H. J. 219
Jonathan Club 53, 284

K

Kauffman, M. M.
  director of FLMPA 362
  FLCA annual meeting 1919, proxy
    voting 296
  proxy solicitation for FLCA annual
    meeting of lot owners 294
  support for Eaton 295
  trustee of FLCA 295–296, 359–360
    appointed to special committee 299
    qualifications questioned 299, 300
Kavannah, Mr. 148
Kelly, E. C., automobile expenses for
    FLCA 48–49
Kemp, John W.
  as ally of Eaton, Hubert 295
  creation of FLInc 317–319
  director of FLMPA 361

  trustee of FLCA 360
King, L. C. 142
Kinsey, E. R. 138
Knickerbocker Trust Company, failure 33
Knights of Pythias 194
Kress House Moving 157, 158, 159–161

L

labor unions, Llewellyn Iron Works
    family opposition to 51
Lambourn, Lucie Mitchell (1880–
    1930) xxviii
  Bedford, Lucile and 95
  adoption of 97
  legal guardian 88
  executrix of Mitchell, Susan's estate
    88, 99, 328
  J.B.-Executrix suit (Treadwell
    lawsuit against Lambourn)
    90–91
  TL&I-Executrix suit 89–90, 98,
    102, 102–103
  land, interest in 14–16, 87–90
  partition lawsuit 96–97. See
    also J.B.-Executrix suit and TL&I-
    Executrix suit
  TL&I appeal 102
Lanigan, J. J.
  Blain's drunkenness 62
  easing out of FLCA 64
  financial problems of FLCA 35
  salesman for FLCA 33, 38–40, 46
Lankershim, California 189
Larabee, C. T., at FLCA lot owners
    meeting in 1919 295
The Last Great Necessity: Cemeteries in
    American History (Sloane) 2–3
Law, George, secretary of Forest Hill
    Cemetery 150
lawn-park cemeteries 3
Lawrence B. Burck Co. 109
Layrock, Ernest 262
lead management 216
Liberty Bank (Liberty, Missouri),
    Hamilton, Frank's affilia-
    tion with 229

life estate 87
Lipsohn, I. J.
    director of AS&F 362
    formation of AS&F 236
Little Acre of God Cemetery 6
Little Church of the Flowers
    construction 254, 258, 260–261
    dedication 268–271, 270, *271*, *272*.
        See also Appendix E. Little Church
        Dedication Speech
    design decisions 252–253
    FLCA use of 285, 304
    indemnification from liens resulting
        from construction 281
    organ recitals 270
    pipe organ 260–261
    plans for 245, 247–248
    publicity 270
    toilet location *253*
Llewellyn, David 49, 55
Llewellyn family 50–52, 209, 321
    moving family monument to Forest
        Lawn 55, 111–114, *112*, 328
    support for Forest Lawn Cemetery 55
Llewellyn, Frederick Eaton (1917-
    1999) **50**, 325
Llewellyn, Frederick William 226–227
Llewellyn Iron Works xxviii, 50–51, *51*,
    53, 268, 328, 348
Llewellyn, John (1871-1919) xxviii, *53*
    approval of 1912 contract 138
    business borrowing 51–52
    death and burial 321, 331
    moving Llewellyn monument to
        Forest Lawn 111, 113–114
    outing of Blain 65–66
    ownership of TL&I shares 127
    partition lawsuit 90
    replacing Treadwell with Wells 70–71
    resignation as FLCA trustee 296
    Treadwell recruiting to FLCA board
        of trustees 50–55, 111, 328
    trustee of FLCA 55, 81, 83, 295–296,
        357–359
    vice president Llewellyn Iron Works
        348

    vice president of FLCA 55, 83, 296
Llewellyn, John F. 325
Llewellyn, Mabel 179, 226. *See
    also* Eaton, Mabel
Llewellyn, Reese
    movement of family monument to
        Forest Lawn 113–114
    president of Llewellyn Iron works 53
    Treadwell's efforts to recruit 50–53
Llewellyn, R. Merritt
    American Securities shareholder
        226–227
    AS&F preferred stock 246
    AS&F shareholder 240–241
    correspondence with Eaton, Hubert
        229, 232
Llewellyn, William, signing deed to
    Evergreen Cemetery lot 114
loans
    allegations of illegal 127
    AS&F bank borrowings 316
    borrowing against stock held in trust
        276
    by the perpetual care fund 24
    from TL&I to FLCA 22, 36
    Llewellyn family bank loans 52
    perpetual care fund to AS&F 278,
        284, 300, 308
    perpetual care fund to TL&I 44–45
    prohibited 309
    Souden, Oscar to TL&I 26, 93, 97,
        100
Lockwood, J. J.
    Blain as superintendent 63
    financial concerns 36–38, 40–41
    perpetual care fund shortage 37–42,
        44, 328
    resignation 41–42
    salary 30
    secretary, FLCA xxviii, 34, 36, 59,
        328, 333–334
    trustee, FLCA 20, 357
lodge **114**
Lodi Mines Company 136
Loewenthal, Max (1858-1927)
    xxviii, 174–175

deal with TL&I and American Secu-
    rities 233
opinion on plans for Forest Lawn
    283–284
partition lawsuit 99–100, 102–103
purchase of Bedford property 282
Long Beach cemetery 224
Lorraine Cemetery (Baltimore, MD) 120
Los Angeles. See also California
early cemeteries 4–6, 6–7, 8–9
elevators 53
formation of Rotary International.
    club number 5 105
in the early 1900s 1–2
Los Angeles and Glendale Railway
    Company a.k.a. Los Angeles and
    Salt Lake Railroad 26
Los Angeles and Pacific Railroad 52
Los Angeles and Salt Lake Railroad
    a.k.a. Los Angeles and Glendale
    Railway. See Los Angles and
    Glendale Railway Company
Los Angeles Athletic Club 53
Los Angeles Catholic Diocese 194
Los Angeles Chamber of Commerce
    Building 20, 47
    FLCA member of 83–84
    formation of Industrial Bureau 188
Los Angeles City Cemetery 4–6
Los Angeles City Council 5, 121
Los Angeles Country Club 53
Los Angeles Examiner, founding of 2
Los Angeles Hall of Records 53
Los Angeles Investment Company,
    failure 193
Los Angeles Times plant bombing 51
Los Angeles Trust & Savings Bank
    Flint, Motely, as vice president 138,
        306
    guardian of Bedford, Lucile 88, 96
    loan to AS&F 276
    partition suit settlement 144
    purchase of Bedford property 282
lot vs. plot, use of words 8
Loudon Park Cemetery
    (Baltimore) 119–120

Lyman, Judge 288
Lyons & Beavis 146

M

Maile, Rev. John L. 348
Marks, Barnett E.
    AS&F's agent in Phoenix, AZ 239,
        277
    dissolution of TL&I 287–288
Marsh, Charles S. 136, 138, 141, 143
Martinoni. See Goodman & Martoni
    Undertaking
Martin, Wendy xviii
Masonic Building Association, establish-
    ment of Ferndale Park Cemetery 58
Masonic Cemetery Association of San
    Francisco 219
mausoleum. See also Great Mausoleum
    at Forest Lawn 208, 209–212, 265,
        268
    building permit 265–267, 330
    community 209–211, 245
    construction 212, 291, 293, 330
    crypt rosette 254
    first entombment 331
    pros and cons 209–211
mausoleum patents 142
McCabe, Henry D., hillside sign
    controversy 108
McDonald, Estelle 226
McIntosh, W. A. 295, 347
McKelvey, B. 349
McLaughlin, John J. 16, 355–357
McLean. See Williamson, Burleigh &
    McLean, dissolution of American
    Securities
McManigal, Ortie, Los Angeles Times
    plan bombing 51
McNamara, Jim, Los Angeles Times
    plant bombing 51
McNutt, Judge Cyrus F. 97
memorialization 3, 243
memorial-park xxvi, 3, 4, 245–247, 293,
    322–323. See also Forest Lawn
    Memorial-Park and Forest Lawn
    Memorial-Park Association

Merchants National Bank 149

Merrill, Grayson 347

Metropolitan Life Insurance Company, Theberge, A. S., superintendent, Los Angeles office 206, 208

Mills College 292

Mitchell, Susan Glassell (1856-1907) xxvii, xxviii
  death 88, 98, 327
  disapproval of Eileen's marriage 14
  distribution of estate 90
  gift of land from father 13
  Lambourn, Lucie, executrix of estate 88–91, 328
  land sale 12–16, *17*, 117
  life estate 87, 89
  partition suit 88–103, *101*
  Treadwell purchase of land 12–16, *17*, 87–88
  will 14, 88, 97

Mizar, Thomas *164*
  monument sales yard 163–164
  murder of Richardson, Burt 163–165

Modjeski, Ralph 264

Moore, Lawrence F.
  crematory equipment sales 249–251
  president, Crematory Supply Company 249

Morgan, Charles O. xxviii, *42*
  accounting responsibility 43
  assistant secretary-treasurer, TL&I 79–80, 328, 356
  attempted coup 81–85
  background 42
  collections on accounts 45–46
  perpetual care fund shortage 44
  representing Heath, Dr. George 85
  resignation 83
  secretary, FLCA 42, 55, 67, 82, 328, 358–359
  sending FLCA reports to TL&I 81
  wants more money 80

Morningside Cemetery (a.k.a. Sylmar Cemetery and Founders Memorial Cemetery) *6*

mortgage 24, 30, 199, 327

AS&F borrowing from perpetual care fund 278–279, 281, 284

chattel 68

loan from Mitchell, Susan 16

loan from Souden, Oscar 26, 93, 97, 102, 126, 144

loan to TL&I 44

mortuary 227, 323–325. *See also* funeral home and undertaker

mortuary securities 206

Mountain View Cemetery (Altadena, CA) 316

Mountain View Cemetery (Oakland, CA) 289–290

Mountain View Cemetery (Prescott, AZ) 120

Mount Auburn Cemetery (Cambridge, MA) 3

Mount Greenwood Cemetery (Chicago, IL 120

Mount Hope Cemetery (St. Louis, MO) 142, 182

Mount Olivet Cemetery (Colma, CA)
  crematory 249
  legislation warning 193
  operations 120, 258
  Rowe, C. V., accountant for 42

Mt. Scott Park Cemetery (Portland, OR), Eaton's sales system 234

Mueller, Oscar, settlement of TL&I-Executrix lawsuit 98

Munger, Roy R., director, AS&F 363–364

murder of Richardson, Burt 164–165

mutual benefit corporations 19

Myers, William R., trustee, FLCA 359–360

N

National Bank of Commerce (St. Louis, MO) 143

National Cemetery Association of San Francisco, Treadwell, president 58

National Erectors Association, labor dispute with Bridge and Structural Iron Workers Union 50–51

National Retail Monument Dealers
Association, opposition to commu-
nity mausoleums 209–210, 264
National Securities Company 137–138
Neuhrenberg, E. H.
crematory equipment 250
operation of Cypress Lawn (Colma,
CA) 259
Newcomb, Helen, dedication of LIttle
Church of the Flowers 268
Newcomer's Sons Undertakers. *See* D.
W. Newcomer's Sons Undertakers
Newhall, California 189
newsletters 204
N. Gray & Co. Undertaking, insurance
product offered by 208
Noble Chapel in Cypress Lawn, design
by Ross, Tom 9–10, *11*, 219, 257
Noble, Hamden, design of Cypress Lawn
(Colma, CA) 209, 219
Noble, T. M., trustee, FLCA 360–361
N. P. Dodge & Company, inquiry about
Sims, Charles 183

O

Oak Hill Cemetery (Bloomington,
IL), Sims, Charles B. establish-
ment of 132
Oak Lake Cemetery (Seattle) a.k.a.
Washelli Cemetery 132
Oakland, CA, possible new cemetery
146, 150, 189, 190, 192
Oakwood Cemetery (Sharon, PA) 121
Odd Fellows Cemetery (San Francisco),
Fletcher, George, superin-
tendent 208
Ogg, Thomas, Forest Lawn Cemetery
lot owner 294
Ohio Retail Monument Association 210
Olive Grove Cemetery (Los Angeles) *6*
opposition to Forest Lawn expansion 106
Orange County, California, selling resi-
dential lots 223–224
Oriental Lodge (San Francisco) 321
outer burial containers 212
Overholtzers Undertaking 114

Owen, Fred V.
liquidation of FLCA indebtedness
311–312
secretary, FLCA 299, 301–304, 308
trustee, FLCA 83, 295–296, 310–312,
358–359

P

Pacific Coast Concrete Company,
concrete burial vaults 211
Pacific Crest Cemetery (Los Angeles) *6*
Pacific Electric "Rec Car" lines 12, 118
Pacific Mutual Life Insurance
Company 206
Paige & Thorburn Investments 35
Parish, R. S. 361
partition suit xxv, 88–103, 105, 247
aftermath 103
anticipating loss of property 98
appeals and reconsideration 99–100,
102
background 87
court ruling 99
division of property 100–102, *101*
foreign corporation argument 98
settlement 95–97, 144–145
suits and countersuits 88
Thornton, Tom C., joins TL&I legal
team 91
warranty deed discovery 94
Partridge, Jr., Charles W. 318, 361
Pasadena market area 316
Peach Tree Hills Cemetery
(Atlanta, GA) 138
Pearson, W. E., inquiry about Eaton's
sales system 234–235
Pendleton, L. B. 138
Père Lachaise Cemetery (Paris) 3
perpetual care fund 331
American Securities 143
AS&F borrowing from 278–281, 284,
308
collections for 140–141
FLCA trustees 281, 308, 309, 313
income 283, 284, 312, 331
investments 23, 43–44

legislation proposed to increase
liability for investment 193
loan to AS&F 281
rules and regulations 23
shortage 40–44, 80, 125, 328
allocation to Blain, Lockwood, and
Treadwell 44
pet cremation 262
Peters, Louis H.
secretary and treasurer, FLCA 83, 85,
116
trustee, FLCA 83, 295, 358–359
Pickett, M. A.
director, AS&F 362
formation of AS&F 236
Pierce Brothers Undertaking 37, 114
Pierce, William, inquiry about Eaton's
sales methods 221
Pine Crest Cemetery (Mobile,
AL) 132, 138
plot vs. lot, use of 8
Portland Gas & Coke Company 246
potters' fields 3
Pratt, George E. (1881-1973) xxviii
director, AS&F 230, 362
ideas for FLCA and AS&F working
together 277–278
letter to AS&F shareholders
explaining planned improvements
at Forest Lawn 247–248
mausoleum 268
option to purchase of TL&I stock 231
philosophy of AS&F 246–247
secretary, AS&F 230, 238, 246–248,
251–252, 274, 362
Premier automobile, exchange for
TL&I shares 54
preneed 131–132, 132
Price, Carl 210
prospect card c. 1916 214
Protestant Cemetery (Los Angeles) 4
proxies 81, 84, 293–296, 311, 381
public graveyards 8
Public Land Commission 13
pueblo land grant 147

Q

quitclaim deed 130, 285

R

Ramon C. Cortines School 4
Rancho San Rafael 13
"The Reasons Why" 203, 221, 244,
341–351, 350
receiving vault 30, 327
Blain's funeral rites 75
construction 27–28, 285
Forest Lawn improvements 240
income to AS&F 239
replacement of original 260
Red Car line 12, 118
resignation
Black, John, trustee, FLCA 83
Burgren, Albert, president, TL&I 18
Eaton, Hubert from Teziutlan Copper
Company 136
Ely, Glenn M., trustee, FLCA 312
FLCA trustees 305
Getzendanner, E. D., sales manager,
American Securities 212
Heath, George, trustee, FLCA 83
Llewellyn, John, trustee, FLCA 296
Lockwood, J. J., secretary, FLCA
41–42
Marsh, Charles, secretary, American
Securities 143
Morgan, Charles O., trustee, secre-
tary, treasurer, and general
manager, FLCA 83
Owen, Fred, trustee, FLCA 312
Smalley, John M., trustee, FLCA 306
Storer, George, trustee, FLCA 312
Treadwell, J. B.
president and director, TL&I 16–17
president and trustee, FLCA 64
Walker, George W., trustee, FLCA
83
Wallace, Hugh W., trustee, FLCA 83
Wells, Norton 305
R. G. Dun & Co. 52

Richardson, Burt W. (1859-
  1915) xxix, *163*
  attempt to close Depot Street 154
  murder of xxii, 163–165
  opposition to monument sales 163
  paying for road improvements
    153–154, 156–157
  vice president, First National Bank
    154
Richardson, E. W. 164
Richardson, William Carr Belding (W.
  C. B.) (1815-1908) xxix, 12, 153
  Depot Street land 18
Richards, Stephen L. 122–123
Rivers, Howard L., nomination as FLCA
  trustee 295–296
Riverside Cemetery (Denver) 221
Riverside Mausoleum 251
Roberts, W. A. 348
Rosedale Cemetery (Los Angeles) *6*
  discontinuing Sunday burials 35
  land purchase 52
  Los Angeles ordinance and bound-
    aries 122
  R. G. Dun & Co. report 52
  sales over life of cemetery 52
Rosehill Cemetery (Chicago), Eaton and
  Tom Ross visit 256–257
Rose Hills Memorial Park (Whittier,
  CA) 212. *See* Whittier
  Heights Cemetery
Ross, Belle 321
  ownership of TL&I stock 61
Ross & Burgren 10
Ross, Lillian 10, 93
Ross, Thomas (Pop) (1852-1930)
  xxix, 1, 9
  administrative details 10
  appeal of court ruling 99
  automobile expenses 49, 115–116
  Blain, Eva 75–78, 233–234
  Blain, William J. (Billy), drunken-
    ness 73
  break between Eaton and Sims 179
  Burgren, Albert wants to sell shares in
    TL&I 174

buy-back proposal 204–205
claim from Mitchell, Susan estate 88
collections on accounts 45
compensation for Wells 69–70
compromising with American Securities 177–179
contract with Eaton and Sims 138
director, TL&I 16, 355–357
dispute between American Securities,
  FLCA, and TL&I 167–184
dissolution of TL&I 286
division of cash 167–169, 172–181
Eaton, Hubert 224, 228–233, 246
entry arch 158–159
financial problems 35, 37–38
foreign corporation argument 98
Heath, Dr. George, hiring of 46
hiring Allen, Carroll 126
meeting with Eaton 137
Morgan, Charles O. 79–84
ouster of Wells, Norton 305
partition suit 90, 93, 97, 99, 102
perpetual care fund shortage 40–42,
  44, 328
persuading Wells, Norton to resign
  330
protest letters 185, 187, 190–191, 195
Scott, W. B., threat of complaint to
  state 127
secretary, TL&I 16, 355–357
Treadwell, J. B., settlement negotiations 128
Ross, T. Paterson (Tom) (1873-
  1957) xxix, *10*
  appeal of court ruling 99
  architect xxi, 1, 9–10, 252–253, 258,
    321
  automobile expenses 48–49
  Blain's drunkenness 63–64, 328
  comments on Wells's proposed letter-
    head design 110–111
  community mausoleum 245
  concussion 321
  crematory equipment 249
  death 321
  director, TL&I xxix, 16, 355–357

dispute between American Securities,
    TL&I, and FLCA 167–184
entry arch 160
FLCA sales challenges 33–34
grand tour of cemeteries with Eaton
    254–257, 330
lack of follow-through 258
Little Church of the Flowers 252–253,
    253, 260
marriage to Belle 321
marriage to Lillian xxix
Morgan requests more pay 80
Noble Chapel in Cypress Lawn 9, *11*,
    219, 257
partition suit 93
president, TL&I 18, 355–357
sale of TL&I stock holdings 231–232,
    239
TL&I contract with Eaton and Sims
    138
Treadwell, J. B. 59–60, 92
    assignment of notes 130
treasurer, TL&I 16
visits to Cypress Lawn Cemetery 257
visit to Forest Lawn 36
Rotary International, formation
    of club 105
Rowe, C. V.
    FLCA audit report 43
    Mount Olivet Cemetery (Colma) 42
    TL&I audit report 30, 200
rules and regulations 22, 259, 262, 334
rural cemeteries 3, 8

S

Sacks, Paul, of Eagle Development
    Corporation 213, 215
St. Johns, Adela Rogers xvii–xviii, 292
St. Philip's Cemetery (Charleston, SC) 3
sales, division of receipts. *See* dividing
    cash receipts
sales manager 315
    Darling, O. E. 224–225
    Emery, George 216, 251
    Getzendanner, E. D. 146, 204, 212,
    220

Heath, George xxvii
Sample, O. H. 289
San Diego Cemetery Commission 147
San Diego Cemetery Corporation 193
San Diego City Cemetery 147–149
San Fernando, CA 189
San Fernando Mission Cemetery (Los
    Angeles) 4, *6*
San Fernando Road 116–117,
    133, 154, 156
San Francisco 1–2, 4, 9–10, 150,
    193, 219, 234
    earthquake and fire 10, 53
San Gabriel Cemetery (San
    Gabriel, CA) *6*
San Pedro Cemetery 6
Santa Eulalia Ranch xxix, 12
#Saying Goodbye Your Way
    (Llewellyn) 444
Schoder, J., trustee, FLCA 20,
    81, 333, 357
Schroeder, Sandi xix
Schumacher, Frank G., ownership of
    land in Eagle Rock 225
Schwaebe-Atkinson Motor
    Company 48–49
Schwartz, Catherine E., direc-
    tor, AS&F 363
Scott, W. B.
    allegation of illegal loans 127–128,
    130
    trustee, FLCA 20, 333, 357
Sharp Undertaking 114
Shrine Temple, design by Ross, Tom 10
Sierra Club 53
Silver Mining & Smelting Company 135
Sims, Charles B. (1868-1945)
    xxv, xxix, *133*
    agreement with TL&I and FLCA
    138–141, 329
    American Securities Company
    (Maine) 141–143
    assignment to American Securities
    Co. (Maine)
    142, 329
    background 131

cemeteries established by 132
cemetery sales program 131–133,
    140–141, 167, 170–181
city attorney of Urbana, Illinois 132
death of wife 138
dispute between American Securities,
    FLCA, and TL&I 167–184
division of cash receipts *168*, 168–170
Eaton, Hubert 135–137, 179–186
interest in other cemeteries 150
marriage 171
mausoleum *208*, 209, 245
opening Pine Crest Cemetery 132
preneed sales 131
president, American Necropolis
    Company 132
president, Southern Investment
    Company 138
references 135, 138
sales programs 132
San Diego cemeteries 148
scientific sales campaign 131, 133
Wells, Norton 131, 133–135
Sims, Sara Jane 131
Sims, William B. 131
Sloane, David Charles 2–4
Smalley, John N.
    member of special committee of
        FLCA trustees 299
    trustee, FLCA 306, 309, 359
Smith, Frank E. 361
Souden, Oscar M.
    mortgage 26, 93, 97, 102
    partition suit 100
Southern California. *See also* California
    life in xviii
    Spanish land grants 13
Southern Investment Company, Sims as
    president 138
Southern Pacific Railroad xxix, 10–11, 58
    funeral cars *31*
Spanish land grants 13
Spring Grove Cemetery
    (Cincinnati) 4, 120
Starr, Kevin xxiii
Sternberg, S. E. 350

Stevens, William 217
Stocks, Harry, contractor who built origi-
    nal entry arch 157
Storer, George H., trustee, FLCA
    309–310, 312, 359
    chairing 1919 FLCA lot owners
        annual meeting 295
    opposition to agreement with AS&F
        312
Sublett, Andrew 5
Sunday burials and cremations 35, 114
Sunnyside Mausoleum (Long
    Beach, CA) 264
Sunnyside Memorial Gardens (Long
    Beach, CA) 264
superintendent 3, 20–22, 68, 71
    Blaine, Wiliam J. (Billy) as FLCA
        superintendent 27, 30, 33, 61–63,
        73
Superior Court
    Arizona 288
    Los Angeles 99, 282
Supreme Court
    Arizona 288
    California xxix, 102
Sutch Undertaking Company, W. H. 114
Sylmar Cemetery (Los Angeles) 6
System of Cemetery Sales 227

T

Taft, William Howard 38
Tally, W. E. 138
tax exemption 9, 118, 289–290
tenth assistant chemist 135
Teziutlan Copper Company 136
Theberge, A. S., superintendent of
    Metropolitan Life's Los Angeles
    Office 206, 208
Thomas, William B., attorney for
    AS&F xxix, 303
Thornton, Tom C. xxix
    Blain, Eva's lawsuit 77–78
    foreign corporation argument 98
    Lambourn, Lucy, settlement of parti-
        tion suit 96–97

member of TL&I's legal team 91–94, 96, 102

partition suit 91–102

possible suit against Title Guarantee & Trust Company 99

warranty deed discovery 94

Thorpe, Dr., administered "liquor cure" to Blain, William J. (Billy) 74

Title Guarantee & Trust Company 15, 26, 87, 91, 103

TL&I. *See* Tropico Land & Improvement Company (TL&I) (1905-1921)

TL&I-Executrix suit 89–90, 94, 98

tombstones xxi, xxii, xxix, 4, 163, 256, 323

town or city cemeteries 3

Treadwell, George, real estate sales 322

Treadwell, John B. (J. B.) (1846-1931)) xxi, xxx, 10

    area quitclaimed to 129, 130

    Boynton, C. C., attorney 90–91, 93–94, 96

    car landing improvements 28, *30*

    claims against Mitchell, Susan's estate 88–89

    concern about finances 33, 35–37, 66–67

    deception in land sale to TL&I 16, 117, 127–128

    director and president, TL&I 16–17, 355

    dissolution of TL&I 286–288, 331

    drunken behavior of Blain, William J. (Billy) 61–65, 73, 328

    entry arch layout 157

    founding Forest Lawn Cemetery 57

    Glassell, Hugh

        involvement in land purchase 13–14

        partition suit settlement negotiations 95

    intent to resign 62–68, 70

    land interests near Forest Lawn 118

    Llewellyn family 50–55

    Lockwood shares in TL&I 60–61

movie industry 322

oil wharf 57–58, *59*

partition suit 88–90, 97

perpetual care fund shortage 41–42

potential for lawsuits by FLCA or TL&I 92–94

president, FLCA 20, 327

president, National Cemetery Association of San Francisco 58

president, TL&I 18, 57

promissory notes from FLCA 126–130

purchase of land from Mitchell, Susan 12–15, *17*, 87–89, 103, 327

questionable ethics 57–58, 60–61

real estate deals 322

sale of land to TL&I 16, 327

search for land for cemetery 12

settlement with FLCA and TL&I 125–130, *129*

Southern Pacific Railroad 10, 58

starting Ferndale Park Cemetery (San Bernardino) 58

suit against Lambourn, Lucy as executrix of Mitchell, Susan's estate 91

temporary water connection to Forest Lawn 162

trustee, FLCA 20, 333, 357–358

warranty deed from Mitchell, Susan 94

Wells, Norton becomes president, FLCA 67–68, 70–71

Treadwell, Lillian 10, 93

Trinity Cemetery (New York) 3

Tropico Bank 105

Tropico becomes independent municipality 118

Tropico, City of 12

    annexation of land to Glendale 116–118, *117*, 259

    FLCA agreement to move arch 158

    Glendale Avenue road improvements 154–155

    incorporating as independent municipality 118

Richardson, W. C. B. and creation of town 18
Wells's success in keeping Forest Lawn out of annexation 329
Tropico Depot 12
Tropico Land & Improvement Company (TL&I) (1905-1921)
appointment of Morgan, Charles as assistant secretary-treasurer, TL&I 79
Burgren, Albert, president 16
cemetery lot sales begin 30
chattel mortgage on FLCA's personal property 68
contract disputes with American Securities 167–184, 330
contract with FLCA 20, 22, 23
court rules against TL&I in partition suit 99–100
creating Forest Avenue right-of-way 24
Depot Street 18
directors and officers 355–357
dispute over shares issued to Lockwood, J. J. 60–61
dissolution 286–288
dividends, beginning payment of 69
division of property after loss of partition suit 100, 101
Eaton's interest in gaining control of TL&I 189–192, 231–233
first mortgage bought by perpetual care fund 44
for-profit land company 19
grant deed from Treadwell 94–95
incorporation of 15, 327
land sale to FLCA 21
loan to FLCA 36
merged into AS&F 273–274, 283, 297
merger with AS&F 330
Morgan, Charles O., appointed assistant secretary-treasurer 328
mortgage, refinancing 26
partition suit 88–103, 328–329
loss of 99–100
Ross, Pop, secretary 16
Ross, Tom, president 18
sale of land to FLCA 20–22, 21, 327
sales contract with FLCA, Eaton, and Sims 138–141, 329
settlement with Treadwell, J. B. over deception in original sale of land 128–130, 129, 330
special meeting of stockholders (1917) 273, 357
stock certificate 15
stock given to Llewellyn, John, as enticement to join FLCA board of trustees 54–55, 328
Treadwell, J. B., president, TL&I 57, 355
types of cemeteries 3

U

undertakers 34–35. See also funeral home; mortuary
commissions to 40
insurance 208
referrals 36–37, 46–47, 67, 114, 265
TL&I stock 130
Unger, E. D. 347
Union Bank & Trust Co. 135
University of Illinois 131
U.S. National Bank 26
Utica Cemetery (Utica, NY) 121

V

Valhalla Cemetery Association, Eaton establishing 228
Valhalla Cemetery (Milwaukee, WI) 132
Valhalla Cemetery (St. Louis, MO) 132, 237
Valhalla Mausoleum 208
Van Nuys 189
Vesper, C. R. 265

W

Wadham, Cosgrove & Titus 149
Wadham, James E. 147–148
Walker, George W. 81–83, 294–295, 357–358
Wallace, Hugh S. 81–83, 358

warranty deed
　　in partition suit 94
　　protection for buyer 15
Wasatch Land & Improvement
　　Company 122–123
Washelli Cemetery (Seattle) a.k.a. Oak
　　Lake Cemetery 132
Watson, Harry, Bonney-Watson Co.
　　(Seattle) 248
Watson, Harry W., Hollywood
　　Cemetery 193
Watson, William
　　comments for "The Reasons Why" 244
　　trustee, FLCA 83, 295–296, 358–360
Webber, Herbert, applying to manage
　　mausoleum sales 251
Weed, Howard, on locating cemeteries 9
Wells, Florence 321
Wells, Norton C. (1874-1958) xxx,
　　67, 358–359
　　advice on cemetery development 123
　　attempted coup by Morgan, Charles
　　　81–84
　　automobile expenses 115–116
　　Blain, Eva's request for money 75–76
　　Blain, William (Billy) 73–75
　　break between Eaton and Sims
　　　180–184
　　building relationships with under-
　　　takers 114
　　chairman, Glendale Special
　　　Committee on Annexation
　　　116–118
　　choice of crematory manufacturer
　　　248–251
　　clash with Richardson, Burt over
　　　street improvements 153–154
　　compensation for 69–70
　　concern with FLCA finances 292,
　　　297–299
　　conflicts with Eaton, Hubert 292–294
　　contacts with other cemeteries
　　　119–123, 258–259
　　contract with Eaton and Sims
　　　137–141, *139*, 145–146

correspondence with De Haven, Jo J.
　　249
correspondence with Sims, Charles,
　　on cemetery lot sales 131, 133–135,
　　137
damage to railroad right-of-way adja-
　　cent to Forest Lawn 160–161
death and funeral 321
design decisions 252–254, 257–258
designing letterhead for FLCA
　　110–111
director, Tropico Bank 105
dispute with American Securities,
　　FLCA, and TL&I 167–184
Eagle Development as possible
　　replacement for American Securi-
　　ties 213, 215
FLCA lot owners meeting, 1919
　　294–296
flood in Cajon Pass 161
gopher infestation 162
Greenwood Cemetery (San Diego)
　　147–148
hillside sign controversy 106–109
hiring Allen, Carroll, to collect on
　　notes due Treadwell 126
investigating San Diego cemeteries
　　147–148
mausoleum, support for 245
member, Rotary Club number 5, Los
　　Angeles 105
Moore, Lawrence, on crematory and
　　columbarium construction 249
moving entry arch *155*, 155–160, *156*,
　　157, *158*
moving Llewellyn monument to
　　Forest Lawn 111–114, *112*
newspaper advertising 109–110, *110*
ouster by Ross, Pop 305
partition suit 90–93, 99, 144–145
president, FLCA 68, 70, 83, 296, 328
resignation 305–306, 330
sign for Lawrence B. Burck Co. 109
stopping sales in mausoleum 304
street improvements 153–154
thwarting annexation to Glendale 329

Treadwell, J. B. 92, 125–130
trustee, FLCA 70, 295–296, 358–359
Werner, Charles 183
West Lawn Cemetery (Omaha), Eaton,
        Hubert's, comments on 255
Westminster Cemetery
        (Philadelphia) 121
Whiskey Row gambler 14
Whittier Heights Cemetery
        212–213, 251
William Jewell College 135, 229
Williams, Goudge & Chandler, legal
        opinion for Sims, Charles 175
Williamson, Burleigh & McLean, disso-
        lution of American Securities 276
Wilmington Cemetery (Los Angeles) 6
Wilson, Erasmus, director,
        AS&F 362–364
Wilson, Horace S., attorney for Mitchell
        Estate in TL&I-Executrix
        lawsuit 98
Winters, Charles O.
    comments in "The Reasons Why" 348
    trustee, FLCA 83, 358
Woodlawn Cemetery (Chicago), buyer
        protection bond 209
Woodlawn Cemetery (Colma, CA),
        cremation of Wells, Norton 321
Workman Cemetery a.k.a. El Campo
        Santo or Little Acre of God
        Cemetery (Los Angeles) 6
World War I
    impact on U.S. economy 190
    restrictions on construction materials
        267
Wright & Callender building 47
Wright, Frank Lloyd 264

Y

Young & McCallister 244

About the Author

John Llewellyn is a third generation Californian and is uniquely positioned to tell the story of Forest Lawn Memorial-Park's early history. During forty-five years with Forest Lawn—including twenty-three as its chief executive officer and being the third and last generation of the family to lead the organization—he has seen the organization evolve from domination by Hubert Eaton to an enduring institution. He is currently chairman of the board of directors.

Llewellyn's first book, *A Cemetery Should Be Forever*, was a primer for new cemetery managers and boards of directors members on the complexity of running cemeteries. His second book, *Saying Goodbye Your Way*, was a guide to help consumers be in control when making decisions about buying funeral, cremation, or cemetery services.

He has chaired industry trade associations as well as other non-profit organizations. Llewellyn as served as a director or trustee of more than two dozen organizations, including business, foundation, hospital, museum, and social service organizations as well as being a director of several for-profit companies.

A graduate of the University of Redlands with a major in economics, Llewellyn also earned an MBA from the University of Southern California. John and his wife, Carol, live in Pasadena, California, with their dog, Spotless.

Made in the USA
San Bernardino, CA
29 September 2018